Ex Post Evaluation of Competition Cases

Ex Post Evaluation of Competition Cases

Edited by

Assimakis Komninos
Nicolas Petit

Wolters Kluwer

Published by:
Kluwer Law International B.V.
PO Box 316
2400 AH Alphen aan den Rijn
The Netherlands
E-mail: international-sales@wolterskluwer.com
Website: lrus.wolterskluwer.com

Sold and distributed by:
Wolters Kluwer Legal & Regulatory U.S.
7201 McKinney Circle
Frederick, MD 21704
United States of America
E-mail: customer.service@wolterskluwer.com

ISBN 978-94-035-3730-6

e-Book: ISBN 978-94-035-3750-4
web-PDF: ISBN 978-94-035-3771-9

About the Global Competition Law Centre

Brugge | College of Europe
Collège d'Europe | Natolin

GCLC | Global Competition Law | Centre

The Global Competition Law Centre (GCLC) forms part of the College of Europe and aims at promoting cutting-edge research in competition law and economics. It disseminates ideas and promotes research and benefits from a large network of competition professionals, built through the organisation of regular activities in Europe and elsewhere. Since its inception in January 2004, the GCLC has gained credentials as a high-level discussion forum for academics, practitioners, and enforcement officers in the competition field across the world. The GCLC regularly organises conferences, lunch talk seminars and evening policy talks, publishes books, and hosts a working papers series. In addition, the GCLC awards a yearly prize for the best dissertation in competition law and policy written at the College of Europe.

Editors

Assimakis Komninos is a Partner at White & Case LLP, a visiting research fellow at University College London and a Member of the Executive Committee of the Global Competition Law Centre (GCLC) of the College of Europe. Previously, he was a Commissioner at the Hellenic Competition Commission.

Nicolas Petit is Professor of Competition Law at the European University Institute, Invited Professor at the College of Europe, and member of the Executive Committee of the Global Competition Law Centre (GCLC) of the College of Europe.

Contributors

Christian Ahlborn is the Global Head of Linklaters' Antitrust & Foreign Investment Group and also co-heads the firm's Technology sector team.

Jan Blockx is a tenure-track assistant professor at the University of Antwerp. Before entering academia in 2016, he was a private practice competition lawyer in Brussels for ten years.

Xavier Boutin is a founding partner at Positive Competition. Prior to joining consulting and founding Positive Competition, Xavier was a member Chief Economist Team of the European Commission's DG Competition, and before that a research fellow at INSEE in France. A graduate from the Ecole Polytechnique, he also holds a degree from ENSAE and a PhD in Economics from EHESS (Paris School of Economics). He is also a founding and board member of l'Entente, the association of French-speaking practitioners in Brussels.

Paolo Buccirossi is the Director and founder of Lear. He is adjunct professor of Economics at the University of Rome Tor Vergata and visiting professor at the College of Europe. Previously, he was an economic advisor at the Italian Competition Authority.

Maurice de Valois Turk is a partner at Oxera Consulting. He holds a Master's from the University of Maastricht and the University of East Anglia (Centre for Competition Policy) as well as a diploma in Strategy & Innovation from Said Business School at the University of Oxford.

Benoît Durand is a Partner at RBB Economics, a faculty member at the Brussels School of Competition, a visiting professor at Barcelona Graduate School of Economics and an associate editor of the Antitrust Law Journal.

Verity Egerton-Doyle is a Managing Associate in the Antitrust and Foreign Investment Group at Linklaters LLP.

Daniel Gore is a partner at RBB Economics. He is co-author of *The Economic Assessment of Mergers under European Competition Law* (Cambridge University Press, 2013).

Ignacio Herrera Anchustegui is Associate Professor at the Faculty of Law of the University of Bergen, and a member of the Bergen Center for Competition Law and Economics (BECCLE). His PhD thesis 'Buyer Power in EU Competition Law' was awarded the 2017 Concurrences PhD award.

Scott McInnes is a Partner at Bird & Bird LLP. He is an expert in the payments sector, advising on payments (more generally financial services) regulations, as well as competition law. Prior to joining Bird & Bird, Scott worked for four years in-house at Mastercard, and before that for more than seven years at Jones Day.

Nayantara Ravichandran is an Associate in the Antitrust and Foreign Investment Group at Linklaters LLP.

Ashwin van Rooijen is a Partner in the antitrust practice of Clifford Chance LLP. He holds an LLM degree from the Free University of Amsterdam and from the University of California Berkeley, and a PhD on the interrelationship between competition and intellectual property laws from the University of Amsterdam.

Alen Veljan is Head of Corporate Strategic Sales – Europe at Elavon and Visiting Professor at Hamburg University of Applied Sciences. He holds a PhD in Economics from the Universidad Rey Juan Carlos in Madrid.

Summary of Contents

Table of Contents

Preface

Competition experts like to discuss decisional errors. Academic conferences and journals abound with anecdotal examples of erroneous anticompetitive intervention or non-intervention. However, when asked to formulate how they establish decisional error, competition experts usually struggle to formulate a test. Subjectivity, sometimes ideology, comes in handy in rescue. Competition experts also tend to discuss decisional errors more than successes. In the literature, the study of procompetitive intervention appears to be a less popular exercise. Competition agencies are often the main suppliers of evidence of success. While self-assessment is good administrative practice, it hardly however provides convincing evidence due to the inherent conflict of interest of agencies judging their own competition cases. In the end, the evaluation of competition cases echoes the famous 'I know it when I see it' saying by Justice Potter.

This book seeks to improve our understanding of evaluation of competition cases. To that end, we asked groups of competition experts to report on past European Union (EU) competition cases with a simple question in mind: has competition intervention delivered?

The cases studied have two common features. First, they are all relatively old cases. The idea was to allow experts to operate in a free intellectual environment as remote as possible from ongoing cases and policy debates. Second, the selected cases are mostly intervention cases. Decisions to reject antitrust complaints or phase I approvals in merger proceedings supply less data points about theories of harm, market evidence, and possible remedies. The result is a set of reports focused on five distinct issues, industries or practices: the *Microsoft* decisions, cases involving payment card systems, the treatment of buyer power mergers, cases about parallel trade of pharmaceutical products, and the analysis of dominant firms' rebates and price reductions.

The reports published in this book illuminate the wealth of hard methodological issues, purposive questions, and operational challenges involved in any *ex post* evaluation of a competition case. Evaluating the benefits and costs of previous interventions in retrospective cases raises very concrete questions: what was the agency trying to achieve in the relevant market(s) under consideration? If the enforcement goals have not been achieved, is this due to an analytical problem, a remedial one, or both? How to confidently diagnose enforcement failure or success when a counterfactual case of a market bereft of suspected conduct is missing?

The book is timely. At a time when claims of weak competition enforcement are increasingly loud, and competition agencies are under heavy pressure to be more interventionist, it is important to look back and ask how decision makers have delivered so far. As readers will notice, the reality is complex, nuanced, and to some extent messy. The learnings require time and effort to unpack and do not lend themselves to clear, unequivocal, policy prescriptions. If one thing is sure, however, it is that sweeping claims that we have enforced too little or that we have enforced too much belong more to rhetoric than to empirics.

This book is the result of a research project that the GCLC ran in the past two years on *ex post* assessment of competition enforcement in Europe. For the time and resources invested in the project, we wish to thank all authors of the reports, who acted as our 'hubs', and also the members of each study group, who acted as our 'spokes'.

Finally, we sincerely thank the participants at the 2021 GCLC annual conference – where the draft reports were presented. We also express our gratitude to the GCLC executive committee for its patience and support during our time travel into competition law history.

Assimakis Komninos
Nicolas Petit

CHAPTER 1

Methods for the *Ex Post* Assessment of Competition Law Decisions: A Concise Guide

Paolo Buccirossi

§1.01 INTRODUCTION

The purpose of this chapter is to provide a non-technical introduction to the methodological choices that can be made to conduct the *ex post* assessment of one or more enforcement decisions adopted by a competition authority. The reader may find it useful to understand the approaches that have been employed in the studies collected in this book or as a guide to her own work. Although the retrospective analysis of policy interventions implies several technical choices that are frequently forced or constrained by the availability of information, it is useful to describe the logic that supports it.

I first clarify the questions that can be addressed in an *ex post* assessment. This is normally a crucial step as any research should always make clear on which issues it intends to shed light on. I will try to be comprehensive. However, on one side novel questions might arise in the specific examination of a case, and on the other side, not all the questions are necessarily answered in a single study.

Then I will present the different approaches that can help in answering the various questions. Their description will be necessarily limited to their fundamental logical basis. The technical issues are left out of the chapter.

To simplify the exposition, I use loosely some terms and assign a conventional meaning to others. In particular when I talk of competition law enforcement, I refer to decisions made by a competition authority (mainly the European Commission) concerning the application of some rules in relation to mergers (Merger Regulation),[1] agreements (Article 101 TFEU) and abuse of dominance (Article 102 TFEU). Hence, I do not consider other competition policy activities, such as the enforcement of State Aid rules or non-enforcement initiatives, such as advocacy, market inquiries and the like.

Following a classification conventionally adopted by the European Commission, I refer to agreements and abuse of dominance as 'antitrust', although the expression typically has a broader meaning.

Finally, I use the expressions 'infringement' and 'conduct' loosely as they will be employed also to discuss merger cases in which, strictly speaking, the subject of the decision is not a conduct but rather a structural change that occurs through the modification of the undertakings' control and in which even a prohibition decision does not imply that the merging parties infringed the law.

A final caveat is that I do not enter the never-ending (and maybe futile) discussion about the choice of the welfare standard that should guide competition law and its enforcement, mostly because any researcher may freely decide whether she wants to appreciate the effects of an enforcement decision on consumer or social welfare. Therefore, I do not need to say anything about this.

§1.02 THE RELEVANT QUESTIONS

Competition law enforcement decisions serve two general purposes. The first and most immediate is to stop a conduct or prevent a merger that is likely to alter competition in a way that is detrimental for consumer and/or social welfare. The most immediate aim of an enforcement action is to remedy a market failure caused by anticompetitive conduct or merger, possibly recreating the competitive conditions that would have existed but for the illegal conduct. The second aim is to deter similar conducts in the future, not only in the market interested by the decision.

The general aim of an *ex post* evaluation of an enforcement decision is to assess whether the decision was 'appropriate' with respect to these purposes and, to the extent it was not, to understand the reasons why it did not accomplish its intended goals.[2]

This general objective can be spelt out by asking some more specific questions that lead to different types of assessment.

1. The merger cases examined in this book were decided under Council Regulation (EEC) No 4064/89 of 21 December 1989. However, anything I write applies also to the current merger control, i.e., Council Regulation (EC) No 139/2004 of 20 January 2004.
2. These are actually some of the objectives that competition authorities pursue when the engage in this type of analysis, as pointed out by Kovacic William. E., *Using Ex Post Evaluations to Improve the Performance of Competition Policy Authorities*, 31 J. Corp. L., 503–547 (2006); *see also* Fabienne Ilzkovitz & Adriaan Dierx, *EU Competition Policy and Ex Post Evaluation: Key Concepts*, in *Ex Post Economic Evaluation of Competition Policy: The EU Experience* (Fabienne Ilzkovitz & Adriaan Dierx, eds, Kluwer 2020).

First, we are interested in knowing the effects of the decision on the market variables that were likely to be affected by the investigated conduct. The hypothesis we make and that we want to test is that the illegal behaviour has/would have determined a less competitive market and that the decision was able to reverse/prevent this outcome.[3] Hence, we may refer to this evaluation as the 'assessment of the outcome'. In practice we focus on a limited number of economic variables that are the ones that are most likely affected by the conduct or the most relevant ones from a welfare perspective. For instance, we may investigate whether the decision had been capable of impeding a price increase or of inducing a price reduction.

This brief description of this type of analysis already highlights a potential issue that is particularly relevant for antitrust decisions. The market outcome is (or may be) affected by two events: the infringement and the decision. This poses some challenges that will be discussed in section §1.03[B] As a preliminary observation we just note that the assessment of the outcome requires disentangling the effects of the former event from that of the latter, as our interest is to evaluate the appropriateness of the decision. However, the decision cannot exist without the infringement and the effects of the two events are clearly intertwined. In merger cases the problem is less severe (or does not exist) as the decision is adopted before the merger takes place and the actual merger (if any) we observe in the market is itself the result of the decision.

The second type of assessment we may want to perform concerns the analysis that motivates the decision. Hence, we refer to this as the 'assessment of the analysis'. Any competition law decision contains (sometimes implicitly) a description of *how* the conduct under investigation is capable of distorting competition. This description is called the 'theory of harm' (ToH). It spells out the channels through which a certain behaviour alters the decisions made by other market participants so that, eventually, the market shifts toward an equilibrium in which consumers (and others) are worse off. Therefore, this ToH contains a number of factual assertions and inference links that identify a causal relationship between the conduct and the development of the market. In an *ex post* assessment of the analysis, we exploit the observation of actual market dynamics in the aftermath of the decision to check the ToH. In particular, the aim is to establish if the factual assertions are true/false and if the inference links are valid/invalid. In addition, the assessment may aim at understanding if other theories of harm could have been used to support the decision or an alternative decision. The same type of assessment regards the possible efficiency justifications of the investigated conduct. Indeed, an efficiency justification has the same components of a ToH with the only (crucial) difference that it predicts a welfare improvement.

The *ex post* assessment of the analysis differs from a legal review of the decision, although the two have much in common. The main difference is that the *ex post* assessment uses (also) information that was not available at the time of the decision. So, it may well be that a decision was sound and flawless from a legal viewpoint when it was adopted and given the information that was then available and, yet, it is based

3. Or conversely, for negative decisions, that the investigated behaviour was not illegal and was unable to distort competition so that an infringement decision would not have led to a more favourable outcome.

on a ToH that, with the benefit of hindsight, we can judge wrong. Indeed, novel information may reveal that a factual assertion was not true as it seemed during the proceeding, or that the economic theory underpinning the causal links was inappropriate for that specific case or completely meritless. However, this information was not available when the Commission had to decide the case and therefore, we cannot use it to maintain that the decision was illegitimate.

The third type of assessment looks at the broader consequences of an enforcement decision. Indeed, a decision engenders effects that go beyond the specific market and the undertakings involved. It clarifies the scope of the applied rule and guides the decision-making of other actors. It also makes tangible the negative consequences of infringing competition law through the imposition of a sanction and/or by triggering civil suits for damages compensation. The relevance of these goals of any enforcement activity cannot and should not be understated. One may argue that in fact the real purpose of a prohibition is to deter the prohibited conduct so that the social harm it causes does not occur. Therefore, in the *ex post* evaluation we want to comprehend to what extend the decision was effective in deterring future anticompetitive behaviour and we may refer to this analysis as the 'assessment of deterrence'. Of course, deterrence depends on many other features of a competition policy regime and of the institutional setting in which competition law enforcement takes place, such as the sanctioning policy, the strength of the judiciary and the effectiveness of the rule of law, just to name a few. However, individual decisions may play an important role as they are indispensable to define the concrete content of a general prohibition, more so when, as in the case of competition law, the formal rules do not precisely set the boundaries between legal and illegal behaviour.

In summary, we have three different types of assessment that address the questions asked below:

(1) Assessment of the outcome
Did the decision have an impact on the affected market? Did it improve consumer or social welfare?

(2) Assessment of the analysis
Was the decision based on a valid ToH? With the benefit of hindsight, were the factual assertions underpinning it true? Were the inference links valid? Were all the relevant theories of harm (and efficiency justifications) properly investigated by the Commission?

(3) Assessment of deterrence
Was the decision able to deter similar anticompetitive behaviour? Did the decision provide clear guidance on which conducts should be deemed illegal?

§1.03 AN OVERVIEW OF THE AVAILABLE APPROACHES

Having stated the questions we want to address in an *ex post* assessment of a competition law enforcement decision, we can discuss the approaches we can adopt to answer them. In what follows I will only illustrate the logic that one may (or should) follow to perform this evaluation without entering into technical issues that are clearly outside the scope of this chapter.

It is important to warn that a method that works for all cases does not exist. We have to adapt it to the specific infringement and the specific circumstances of the case. Therefore, it is of paramount importance to understand the logic of the exercise.

[A] A Preliminary Step: The ToH of the Decision and the Outcome Variables

The first step is a concise but clear description of the ToH underpinning the decision. As I already said a ToH is a nexus of propositions. Some of them concern facts and the evidence used to prove them. Others draw causal links between facts. Altogether they build a story (i.e., a chain of events) that explains why a certain conduct results in a consumer (or social) harm. The validity of ToH (and its completeness) is the subject of a specific *ex post* assessment that, in the sequence I am proposing, comes after the assessment of the outcome. So, one may wonder why we should start from something that will be assessed later on. The main reason is that the ToH of the case helps identify the economic variables that are likely to be affected by the decision, as they are those that were allegedly influenced by the prohibited (or investigated) conduct. Hence, the ToH of the case reveals the outcome variables (OVs) that we will look at in the assessment of the outcome.

There are several variables that we may consider. First, the variables that directly enter the consumer welfare function are likely relevant. They are price, quantity, quality, variety, etc. From the ToH we understand what the Commission's concern was. Did it fear that the investigated conduct would have permitted one or several undertakings to raise their price, to reduce output, to delay innovation, to limit the portfolio of available products? These effects directly impair consumer welfare. Hence, the description of the ToH guides the selection of the OVs we will focus on in the *ex post* assessment.

Sometimes, the selected OVs are difficult to observe or to measure (or reliable data to do so is not available). If so, we may move one step back in the chain of events and consider other variables that are likely to influence those we are interested in. For instance, the ToH may argue that a certain conduct was able to impede the entry of new firms in the market and that this, in turn, would have affected the market equilibrium. Although the rate of entry does not enter the consumer welfare function, we can infer the impact of the decision on the market outcome from the examination of its impact on entry.

Some factors have a dual role: they are arguments of the consumer welfare function and, at the same time, able to shape the competitive dynamics. For instance, search or switching costs are costs that consumers bear and, as such, have a direct (negative) impact on consumer surplus; at the same time, they influence the intensity of competition and therefore can alter the value of other variables (e.g., price) so that consumers are furtherly harmed.

At the end of this preliminary step, we have a (limited) number of OVs that will be examined in the assessment. This might include:

- price;
- volume of trade;
- elements of product differentiation (including 'vertical' differentiation, i.e., quality, and horizontal differentiation, i.e., variety/choice);
- innovation;
- expansion or entry;
- search or switching costs.

In European competition law cases 'market integration' may be considered a legitimate OV to the extent that it is one of the goals of competition law. For instance, this is clearly a relevant OV to assess the impact of the decisions in the pharmaceutical parallel trade cases.

Although one may be tempted to select several OVs, numerous constraints will limit the selection. The most relevant constraints are the availability of information, and the time it takes to perform the analysis. As a consequence, most research focuses on a single OV, sometimes, but rarely, it investigates two OVs. In any case, it is a good practice to justify the choice made in light of existing limitations.

[B] Assessment of the Outcome

The purpose of the assessment of the outcome is to establish the effects produced by the decision on the selected OVs.[4] The questions we want to answer are: Did the decision have an effect on the OVs? Did it determine a different value of these OVs so as to improve consumer or social welfare?

These questions indicate that we are looking for a causal link between the decision and the OVs. This calls for the appraisal of a counterfactual situation: the decision causes the observed value of the OVs if in its absence the value of the OVs would have been different. For the sake of exposition, in the following I will often exemplify this part of the exercise assuming that the price is the variable of interest. So, we can say that the decision had an effect on price if we can establish that without the decision the value of the price would have been different from the observed one. This will answer the first question. If the answer is positive, we can move on and establish

4. A very comprehensive survey of the available methodologies for the *ex post* assessment of merger decision is Ormosi, Peter et al., *A Review of Merger Decisions in the EU: What Can We Learn from Ex-post Evaluations?* Eur. C. (2016); the interested reader may consult it to have information about the several studies performed in various jurisdictions and references to the relevant literature. The *ex post* assessment of abuse of dominance cases is much less developed: the only contributions I am aware of are: Böckers Veit et al., *Alleged Abuse by E.ON of Its Dominant Position in the German Wholesale Electricity Market* (Fabienne *Ilzkovitz* & Adriaan *Dierx* eds, Wolters Kluwer 2020), and Marrazzo Alessia et al., *The Telekomunikacja Polska Anituts Case* (Fabienne Ilzkovitz & Adriaan Dierx eds, Wolters Kluwer 2020).

whether in the counterfactual the price would have been higher or lower. In the former case we can say that the decision was effective in improving consumer welfare.[5]

This notion of causality is not restricted to direct effects, nor is it limited to a situation where the decision is the only cause of the OV.

A counterfactual, by definition, is a purely hypothetical situation. Therefore, we cannot observe it. It has to be built. The material we use to make this construction is the information about observable variables. Most of the time the information concerns the same OV but in a different context, which might be (a) a different period of time (time-series data), (b) a different product or geographic market (cross-section data) or (c) a combination of the two (panel data). Sometimes the information is about: (d) several different variables that do not depend on the OV but can influence it. Other times the information is just: (e) the opinion of market participants or industry experts. Depending on the information we use, we have different approaches that have been named (in the order of appearance): (a) before (during) and after; (b) yardstick; (c) difference-in-differences (diff-in-diff; (d) simulation; (e) survey.

The information itself does not suffice to build the counterfactual. To use it we need a model. A model is like the technical drawing that identifies the pieces of information that we need to use and describes how to assemble them. Finally, we have to employ some statistical or computational techniques which are the tools used to work on the input according to the chosen model.[6]

Although this is a simplistic description of the process of building a counterfactual, it contains, in a nutshell, the necessary elements. The result of this process is a counterfactual value (or a counterfactual time series) of the OVs of interest.

The main question is how much can we trust this construction? This question concerns each of the elements described above: how much can we trust the information we use? How much can we trust the model? And about the techniques? Another way to ask these questions is: what are the assumptions we make in constructing the counterfactual? Are they sound? What kind of evidence can we use to test their validity or reliability?

I do not intend to answer all these questions in this short article. The more limited purpose is to explain the logic we can follow. To do so, I will first refer to the approaches I previously referred to as 'before and after', 'yardstick' and 'diff-in-diff' also because they are the most frequently used. Then I will make some cursory remarks on simulations and surveys.

In the simplest formulation of the before-and-after approach the counterfactual value of the OV is the one we observe in the period before the decision.[7] The

---

5. In this discussion I am knowingly avoiding all the complexities that may arise when the decision causes effects on the price *and* other variables, so that it may improve consumer surplus through its price effects and reduce it through the other effects or vice versa.
6. We have to avoid a possible confusion between counterfactual and benchmark. A benchmark might be the same market in the past or another market (or more). The benchmark is observable. The counterfactual is never observable. It is a purely hypothetical construction, and we use one (or several) benchmarks (and other ingredients) to build it.
7. Using the terminology defined above the information we use is the time series of the price; the model we adopt is one in which the counterfactual price is the before price and the statistic

assumption we make is that, absent the decision, the OV would have taken the value it took before the decision was adopted, or analogously that the decision is the only factor that directly or indirectly triggered all the events that determined a change, if any, in the OV. Very often this assumption is not really sound and the level of trust we can have on the counterfactual we build in this way is low. In particular so, if we know that there are other factors that are independent of the decision, that influence the OV and that varied over time. For instance, suppose we observe that the price of product X before the decision is higher than the price observed after it. We can argue that the decision *caused* a price reduction if we take the before price as its counterfactual value. However, if we know that the cost of some X's inputs changed in the two periods – and we posit that input costs affect the price and are independent of the decision – our trust in this counterfactual is obviously low. This does not imply that the before-and-after approach has to be put aside but rather that we have to use a different model which requires enriching the information set we use and adapt the computational technique. For instance, we can use a model in which the price depends also on the input cost. As a consequence, we have to collect information about these costs in the before and after periods and postulate a relationship between these 'control' variables and the OV. The counterfactual built through this process is based on the assumption that we consider in a proper manner all the variables that are independent of the decision and that affect the OV. We have to explain why (or to what extent) we think this assumption is reliable and acknowledge the limitations that it might entail.

A simple version of the before-and-after approach applied through a regression analysis is described by equation (1).

$$OV_t = \alpha + \beta * D_t + \mu * Z_t + \varepsilon_t, \qquad (1)$$

where:
OV_t is the OV in the market affected by the decision at time t;
D_t is a dummy variable representing the decision that takes the value of 1 in the post-decision period and 0 elsewhere;
Z_t is a vector of other demand and supply-side factors that vary over time and that may affect the OV but are not influenced by the decision; and
ε_t is the error term.

The coefficient of interest is β which provides an estimate of the average change in the OV caused by the decision.

The logic of the yardstick approach is similar. The counterfactual value of the OV is the one we observe in the period after the decision in a different product or geographic market (or another benchmark, e.g., a different firm). The underlying assumption is that the only factor that may cause different values that the OV takes in the market interested by the decision and in the benchmark is the decision itself. Again, we may have evidence that shows that this assumption is inappropriate. Therefore, we

---

technique might be a simple average computed in the before period. Even in this naïve formulation the model and the technique may be different. For instance, we can eliminate from the computation some outliers because they impair the trust we can have on the calculation of the average.

can enrich the model, the information set and adapt the technique to take into account other factors that can influence the OV in the two settings.

Again, a simple formalisation can illustrate the applicable approaches. Equation (2) describes a version of a yardstick regression model.

$$OV_{it} = \alpha + \gamma * D_i + \mu * Z_{it} + \varepsilon_t, \quad (2)$$

where:

OV_{it} is the OV in market i at time t;

D_i is a dummy variable representing the decision that takes the value of 1 in the market interested by the decision and 0 elsewhere;

Z_{it} is a vector of other demand and supply-side factors that vary across markets and over time and that may affect the OV but are not influenced by the decision; and

ε_i is the error term.

The coefficient of interest is γ which estimates the average change in the OV caused by the decision.

The diff-in-diff approach combines the two previous approaches.[8] Its logic can be better explained by introducing some new terminology. We refer to the decision as the *treatment*; the market interested by it is called the *treated market* and the observations of the variables of interests in this market form the *treated group*; the observations of the variables of interest in the benchmark market (i.e., not influenced by the decision) form the *control group*; finally, the OV is observed in both groups in the *treated period* and in the *untreated period* (e.g., before the decision). The effect caused by the decision (i.e., the difference between the actual value of the OV and its counterfactual value) is obtained through a double differentiation: first, for each group, we compute the difference between the value of the OV in the treated period and its value in the untreated period; then, we compute the difference between the first difference computed in the treated group and the one computed in the control group.[9] The advantage of this approach is that we do not have to assume that the decision is the only cause of a time variation, as long as the other factors that vary over time are the same (and have the same type of influence) in the treated and in the control group. Similarly, we do not have to assume that the decision is the only difference between the treated market and the untreated market, as long as any other difference does not change over time. Therefore, we do not need to say if we trust these assumptions as they are no longer relevant. However, as the previous statement clarifies, the approach still relies on some assumptions. More specifically, it assumes that any time-variant factor affects both markets in the same way and that market-specific factors are time-variant. Needless to

---

8. A technical yet accessible description of this approach is described by Joshua D. Angrist & Jörn-Steffen Pischke, *The Credibility Revolution in Empirical Economics: How Better Research Design Is Taking the Con Out of Econometrics*, 24 J. Econ. Persps, 3–30 (2010).

9. Formally, let the OV take four values OV_{ij} with $i = T,U$ and $j = t,u$, where T is the treated group, U is the control (untreated) group, t is the treated period and u is the untreated period. The effect of the treatment is it > $E = (OV_{Tt} - OV_{Tu}) - (OV_{Ut} - OV_{Uu})$. This implies that the counterfactual value of OV is $OV_c = OV_{Tu} + (OV_{Ut} - OV_{Uu})$, that is the 'before' value of the OV in the treated market plus its time variation in the control group. The formal description makes clear that the double differentiation can follow a different order which is perfectly equivalent, i.e., $E = (OV_{Tt} - OV_{Ut}) - (OV_{Tu} - OV_{Uu})$.

say, these assumptions are less strict if we enrich the model and control for time-variant factors that may have a different impact on the two groups.

The simplest equation for the implementation of this approach is (3):

$$OV_{it} = \alpha + \beta * D_t + \gamma * D_i + \delta D_t * D_i + \mu * Z_{it} + \varepsilon_{it}, \qquad (3)$$

where:
OV_{it} is the OV in market i at time t;
D_i is a dummy variable that takes the value of 1 in the market interested by the decision and 0 in the control group;
0 is a dummy variable that takes the value of 1 in the post-decision period and 0 in the other periods;
D_t is a dummy variable representing the decision that takes the value of 1 only in the post-decision period *and* in the market interested by the decision and 0 elsewhere;
$D_t * D_t = DiD$ is a vector of other demand and supply-side factors that vary across markets and over time and that may affect the OV but are not influenced by the decision; and
ε_{it} is the error term.

This time the coefficient of interest is δ which provides an estimate of the average change in the OV caused by the decision. Indeed, this coefficient estimates the difference between the average behaviour of the OV in the affected market, before and after the decision, *minus* the difference between the average behaviour of the OV in the comparator market, before and after the decision.

The formal presentation of these approaches serves only the purpose of explaining their logical foundations. Although a well-executed regression analysis contributes to a more reliable identification of a causal relationship, some important insights can also be gained through an informal analysis that does not need equations.

A formal approach is inevitable if the assessment is based on a simulation. Indeed, a simulation predicts the counterfactual values of the OVs by using a model in which the variables of interest are linked to other observable variables, that may be referred to as the determinants, through some equations. Hence, we can reconstruct their counterfactual values by using these equations and the counterfactual value of the determinants. Sometimes the determinants but-for value is implied by the decision. For instance, if the competition authority blocked a merger, we can determine the counterfactual equilibrium price by using a market model in which the parties to the merger combine their assets and operate a single firm, as this would be the fundamental change in the market in the absence of the decision. If the decision is insufficient to establish the counterfactual scenario, we have to use one of the methods described above to define the but-for value of the determinants.

The main drawback of a simulation model is that its results are quite sensitive to the modelling assumptions and that most of the time it is very difficult or even impossible to test them. Hence, the selection of the model is often the result of an a priori choice that is based only on theoretical considerations.

Finally, a survey relies on the opinion of some 'experts' to gauge the effects of a decision. Although this may seem a totally different approach, its main ingredients are not really dissimilar. In expressing their view, the experts will implicitly or explicitly compare the actual market outcome with that that would have prevailed if the decision had not been adopted. This is just an information and we have to decide if it can be relied upon. To do so, we will consider the number of experts that share the same view, their qualifications, etc.

A survey is the most flexible research tool that can be employed to conduct the *ex post* analysis of an enforcement decision. It involves the collection of information and views from a sample of market participants (such as customers and competitors), through a written questionnaire or a set of interviews. Given their flexibility, surveys can be employed for any type of decision, and it is the only available approach to assess the impact of a decision on aspects that are difficult to measure or for which there is no data. A survey may also be carried out to add insights and help the interpretation of the results obtained through other approaches.

All the described approaches can be combined and indeed this is a common and a good practice. Using several methods is a way to test the robustness of the results. Sometimes the result obtained with one of them will be the input for the application of another method. For instance, we can use a before-and-after approach to estimate the counterfactual value of an intermediate OV (e.g., entry) and use this in a simulation model to get some indication about another OV (e.g., price or output).

[C] Some Additional Remarks on the Notion of 'Counterfactual'

I have defined the counterfactual as the 'absence' of *the* decision. Yet, this statement may have very different meanings depending on the competition law infringement and on specific circumstances of the case.

In merger cases the adopted decision might be: (1) unconditional clearance; (2) conditional clearance; (3) prohibition. The counterfactual scenario depends on the alternative course of action by the competition authority we postulate. This choice is restricted by several considerations. First, it depends on the powers given to the competition authority. The European Commission can only impose conditions that were proposed by the merging parties; moreover, it can only accept the proposed remedies if the notified merger was incompatible with the internal market. Therefore, the only reasonable counterfactual if the merger has been approved without remedies is a prohibition decision. If the merger has been approved subject to some remedies, we may have two counterfactuals: a prohibition or an unconditional clearance (a clearance subject to a different set of remedies that the parties did not propose is legally impossible). If the merger was prohibited, an unconditional approval is a relevant counterfactual, whereas a conditional clearance only makes sense if the parties offered some remedies that were rejected by the Commission.

The second consideration that may drive this choice is the feasibility of a complete analysis given the time constraint and availability of information. This frequently leads to the selection of just one counterfactual: a prohibition for mergers that were cleared (with or without remedies) an unconditional approval for prohibited mergers. Of course, if the research question is about the effectiveness of the specific remedies this will be an unsatisfactory choice.

A similar problem exists in antitrust cases whenever they imply some remedial actions. Cartel decisions only order the involved undertakings to cease the illegal behaviour. Therefore, the counterfactual is one in which the cartelists keep colluding explicitly. In all other antitrust cases, an infringement decision (or a commitment decision) forces the addresses to adopt a different behaviour that is not univocally determined. Therefore, these decisions (directly or indirectly) impose remedies that are not straightforward and obvious. Whatever we observe in the market *after* the decision might be an effect (if any) of the decision *and* of the specific remedies that were consequently adopted. Therefore, at least in principle we might consider many counterfactuals that differ from the actual world in terms of the corrective measures implemented by the concerned undertakings. The usual consideration about the feasibility of this analysis (due to the constraints a researcher faces) applies here as well.

In antitrust cases a different issue exists. While merger control is *ex ante*, the enforcement of Article 101 takes place *ex post*. Therefore, the scenario we observe *after* the decision is affected by *both* the allegedly illegal behaviour (let's call it the infringement) *and* the decision. Using the terminology introduced before, we might say that the actual world might have been affected by two treatments: the infringement and the decision.[10] Since the decision is the treatment whose effects we want to understand, the ideal control group would be a similar market in which the same infringement occurred but where the competition authority did not intervene; this market was affected by the infringement but not by the decision, i.e., the treatment. Finding such a benchmark is impossible most of the times.

Hence, if we want to disentangle the effects of these two treatments and isolate those that should be attributed to the decision, we should build two counterfactuals: one without the infringement (and without the decision); one with the infringement but without the decision. The first counterfactual allows to estimate the effect of the infringement on the OVs; the second the effects of the infringement on the OV that the decision was able to fix. The methodological considerations offered before are still valid. However, they will apply to a two-stage process. In the first stage one has to build the first counterfactual using information before the infringement, or from a different market during the infringement of both sources of data. Once the effects of the infringement have been established, one can move to the second stage and assess to what extent the decision was able to restore competition in the market.

Sometimes this two-stage process is not feasible because we lack a proper benchmark to assess the effects of the infringement. For instance, a proper 'before' period might not exist because an abuse is the reaction by the dominant firm to a new threat. Therefore, the period before the abuse is one in which there was neither the abuse nor the threat and there is no way to use the before period to estimate the effects of the abuse. If so, we can answer our research question only partially. To exemplify, we can find that the decision had the effects of determining a price reduction, but we cannot say to what extent it was able to cure the negative consequences of the

10. This issue is discussed in Marrazzo Alessia et al., cited at *supra* n. 4.

anticompetitive behaviour. For instance, in a cartel case, we can establish that the decision caused the price to fall, but we cannot say if it was completely effective unless we have an estimate of the overcharge caused by the cartel. More importantly, if we find that the decision had no effects, we are not in the position to establish whether this is so because it did not restore normal competition in the market (i.e., the decision was ineffective) or because the alleged infringement did not cause any effect in the first place. A third possibility is that the anticompetitive conduct was ended before it was able to harm consumers (one may think about a predatory strategy that is stopped at the beginning of the predation phase). In this case we cannot say that there was not an abuse nor that the decision was ineffective (quite the opposite). In conclusion a finding of 'no effects' has three potential explanations: (1) the decision was so timely that the infringement did not produce any effect; (2) the decision was completely ineffective; (3) there was no infringement (or it did not produce any effect).

[D] Assessment of the Analysis

A decision on certain conduct contains a number of factual statements and logical propositions, which are used by the Commission to predict the likely consequences of the conduct on the market. These represent the arguments on which a decision is based.

The assessment of the analysis[11] does not need to cover all these statements. Only a subset of them plays a critical role, in the sense that if one of them turned out to be wrong or invalid the decision may have been inappropriate. We can refer to them as the 'key arguments'. The *ex post* evaluation of the analysis should focus on these key arguments.

A statement of fact consists of the description of an observable phenomenon. In general, it does not involve any judgment as it consists of the pure observation of a characteristic of the market. Therefore, assessing their validity means verifying whether each of them was true or false at the time the decision was made and whether its status has changed since then.

---

11. Most of the existing literature only focuses on the assessment of the outcome. This reflects the desire of the various actors (competition authorities, economists, and so on) to answer a sharp question: was the decision 'right'? I have always thought that the most interesting questions are those that investigate the analysis and try to understand 'why' it was right or wrong. Indeed, in a somehow pioneering (for Europe) exercise we did for the European Commission almost fifteen years ago we insisted on this part of the assessment and also devised a methodology to perform it (*see* Buccirossi Paolo et al., *Ex Post Review of Merger Control Decisions: A Study for the European Commission*, 2006, available at https://www.learlab.com/publication/ex-post-review-of-merger-control-decisions/). After the publication of that study several competition authorities engaged us to carry out an *ex post* assessment of some merger decisions, but they explicitly asked us not to evaluate the analysis underpinning them. The only notable exception is the UK CMA for which we conducted a retrospective analysis of some mergers in digital markets, *see* Argentesi Elena et al., *Ex-post Assessment of Merger Control Decisions in Digital Markets*, 2019, available at https://www.learlab.com/wp-content/uploads/2019/06/CMA_past_digital_mergers_GOV.UK_version-1.pdf.

Sometimes these characteristics cannot be described in a precise manner. For example, the decision may contain propositions such as 'entry barriers are high' or 'consumers have a tendency to multi-home'. In the *ex post* assessment, one has to consider if, on the basis of the available information, these statements are true in the sense that they provide a sound foundation for the implications that are drawn from them in the decision.

A logical proposition, instead, consists of a reasoning that, on the basis of a set of factual premises, draw some conclusions. Because of its complex structure, there are two notions of validity that apply to a logical proposition. One refers to the internal coherence of reasoning: a logical proposition is valid if, when the premises are true, the conclusions are also true. If the conclusions do not logically follow the premises, then the proposition is inconsistent and unreliable.

The second notion of validity, which is the main test one wants to perform, concerns the economic theory underlying the reasoning: a logical proposition is valid if the conclusions are linked to the premises through a valid economic theory.

The validity of a logical proposition, in the two senses just discussed, is different from its truthfulness and this difference must be understood and kept in mind when assessing the analysis of a decision. If one or more of the premises of a logical proposition, which are statements of fact, are false, then the conclusion is also false. However, the logical proposition may still be valid if the reasoning behind it is correct because it is consistent and based on a valid economic theory.

A further evaluation entails assessing whether the competition authority has exhaustively addressed all the meaningful ways a conduct might have altered competition or enhanced welfare. In other words, we may want to establish if the analysis performed by the enforcer was complete or if there were alternative theories of harm or efficiency justifications that would have deserved some attention and that in fact were neglected.

[E] Assessment of Deterrence

Law enforcement does not have only the goal of stopping harmful behaviour but also to prevent it. A competition authority has several means to pursue this general objective, including soft law instruments (e.g., guidelines) or the dissemination of information about its enforcement priorities or assessment criteria. Individual decisions may contribute to this purpose. They may have three deterrent effects. First, they can discourage the addressees of the decision to undertake the same (or similar) anticompetitive conduct in the future. This may be called 'specific deterrence' or 'desistance' and aims at avoiding recidivism. Second, the decision may discourage firms that are active in the same market or industry from engaging in anticompetitive conducts (not necessarily the same ascertained in the decision). This may be referred to as 'sector-specific deterrence'. Third, the decision may extend its effects beyond the investigated industry by discouraging firms active in a different sector from undertaking the same anticompetitive conduct. This third effect may be called 'general deterrence'.

In all three deterrence effects the hypothesis is that a decision affects the cost-benefit analysis that drives the decision of a rational firm to undertake a possible action that may be deemed illegal. This analysis includes, on the cost side, the expected negative consequences of infringing competition law. This expectation may be affected by the knowledge that the firm is 'monitored' by a competition authority (specific deterrence), that a certain sector is under the radar because its competitive conditions are unsatisfactory or can be altered (sector-specific deterrence) or that a certain conduct is considered an infringement (general deterrence).

The *ex post* assessment may concern all the three notions of deterrence just defined. However, I think that the most interesting question is the one concerning general deterrence. This stems from a combination of factors: (1) a clear (i.e., predictable) partition between legal and illegal conducts; (2) the probability that illegal conducts are uncovered and successfully prosecuted; (3) the overall sanction imposed on infringers (which include damages, reputation, etc.). Individual decisions affect mostly (1), as the other factors depend on some general features of a competition policy regime.[12] Indeed, the existing literature addresses mostly the deterrence properties of competition law enforcement in general or of the enforcement efforts carried out with respect to one type of infringement (e.g., cartels or mergers).[13]

Hence, the assessment of the deterrence properties of the decisions should address mostly the question whether they were able to set the boundaries of the prohibition and the applicability of the ToH on which they were based.[14]

Some insights can be gained by observing whether there has been a certain pattern: an increase in the number of antitrust decisions concerning the same practice (or the same ToH) and a steadily decline afterwards. This pattern signals that the decision clarified the illegality of a conduct which determined the intervention of other competition authorities; subsequently, firms refrained from undertaking the same conduct (were effectively deterred) as they were aware of its illegality.

Another way to assess deterrence is by soliciting the expert opinion of legal (and to a limited extent, economic) counsels; they can reveal the frequency with which they advised their clients against a certain practice; this analysis can be carried out through a survey.[15]

---

12. For a general discussion of the role of accuracy and predictability in law enforcement *see* Kaplow Louis, *The Value of Accuracy in Adjudication: An Economic Analysis*, 23(1) J. Legal Stud. 307–401, 1994. Broulık Jan, *Preventing Anticompetitive Conduct Directly and Indirectly: Accuracy Versus Predictability*, 64(1) Antitrust Bull. 115–127 (2019) discusses the role of predictability and accuracy in competition law.
13. *See* Buccirossi Paolo et al., *Measuring the Deterrence Properties of Competition Policy: The Competition Policy Indexes*, 7(1) J. Competition L. & Economics 165–204 (2011) and Buccirossi Paolo et al., *Competition Policy and Productivity Growth: An Empirical Assessment* 95(4) Rev. Econ. & Statistics 1324–1336 (2013); Dierx Adriaan et al., The Deterrent Effects of Competition Policy (Fabienne Ilzkovitz & Adriaan Dierx eds, 2020).
14. Of course, this evaluation does not concern hard core cartels (e.g., price-fixing, bid-rigging) for which the theory of harm is straightforward.
15. The latter approach may underestimate the deterrence effect of a decision if firms change their behaviour without seeking the advice of an antitrust expert.

Finding that a decision or a group of decisions had general deterrence effects is normally good news. But this should not be taken for granted. Much depends on the answers we give to the previous questions concerning the assessment of outcome and of the analysis. Indeed, if we conclude that certain decisions were inappropriate, as they were based on an inaccurate ToH (or missed relevant efficiency justifications) so that they eventually engendered a lower welfare, their impact is even more negative if we find that they prevented welfare-enhancing conducts beyond the investigated market and the specific firms involved in the case.

§1.04 CONCLUSION

Retrospective analyses of policy decisions provide information that is essential to improve them. Both appropriate and inappropriate past decisions contain lessons for future action. Hence, the purpose of carrying out this exercise is not to detect mistakes but rather to understand the positive and negative effects of individual decisions on the interested markets - and more broadly on the economy - and the mechanisms that produced these effects.

One of the main challenges of an *ex post* analysis is to identify causal relationships. This requires intelligent interpretation of the available data which, in turn, calls for the knowledge of the institutional features of the affected industry, an appropriate economic theory and the use of adequate empirical techniques. The methods concisely described in this chapter are simple tools that can be used to perform this task.

Another relevant challenge is to understand whether any conclusion reached through the evaluation of individual cases can be extended to address broader policy issues. Probably the best way to achieve this is to accumulate evidence from individual cases that gradually improves our ability to grasp the connections between policy choices and the outcomes they lead to and to submit this evidence to an open and unbiased debate involving academics, practitioners, and policymakers. The chapters in this book are an excellent example of this approach.

CHAPTER 2

Ex Post Assessment of European Competition Policy: The *Microsoft* Cases[*]

Daniel Gore & Ashwin van Rooijen[**]

§2.01 INTRODUCTION

This chapter assesses the effectiveness of remedies implemented in two landmark cases that the European Commission (hereafter 'Commission') brought against Microsoft Corporation (hereafter 'Microsoft'), namely the Microsoft workgroup server and Windows Media Player (WMP) case (hereafter 'Microsoft I')[1] and the Microsoft Internet Explorer case (hereafter 'Microsoft II').[2]

These cases arguably formed the basis and intellectual framework for the European Commission's modern day scrutiny of digital platforms.[3] In various respects, these cases presented the first opportunity for the European Commission and the General Court to assess concepts such as dynamic competition, network effects, interoperability, platforms, and multihoming under the European Union (EU) competition law framework in an in-depth manner. As such, these cases are also likely to

* This report also benefitted from helpful comments and directions by P, Bucciroci, A. Boutin, N. Petit, A. Komninos, W. Page, H. First, and C. Argenton.

** The authors would like to thank Jasmine Peng for invaluable research assistance. The views expressed in this chapter are the authors' own.

1. *See* Commission Decision 2007/53/EC of 24 March 2004 [2007] OJ L32/23 (hereinafter 'the Decision'), available at https://ec.europa.eu/competition/antitrust/cases/dec_docs/37792/37792_4177_3.pdf and Case T-201/04 *Microsoft v. Commission* [2007] ECR II-3601 (hereinafter 'the CFI Judgment').
2. *See* Statement of Objections: European Commission, MEMO 09/15, 17 January 2009, available at https://ec.europa.eu/commission/presscorner/detail/en/MEMO_09_15 and Commitment decision: European Commission, https://ec.europa.eu/competition/antitrust/cases/dec_docs/39530/39530_2550_8.pdf.
3. Lewis Crofts, *Microsoft Showdown Opened the 'Floodgates' for EU's Big Tech Cases, Madero Says*, *MLex* (14 December 2020).

prove important precedents for finalisation and application of the European Commission's 2020 legislative proposals: Digital Services Act and Digital Markets Act.

However, while frequently cited for their substantive analysis, much less has been said about the effectiveness of remedies imposed in these cases: Assuming that the Commission identified valid antitrust concerns, did it succeed in addressing those concerns through effective remedies? How does one measure effectiveness in these cases, and to what extent did effectiveness of the remedies hinge on the legal choice of theory of harm? If the remedies were not effective, what, if anything, could these cases teach us for future antitrust enforcement?

The purpose of this paper is to offer a preliminary assessment of some of these questions.

The focus of our analysis will be on the direct impact of remedies on the affected markets in terms of addressing the Theories of Harm (ToH) identified by the Commission. In particular, our analysis focuses on the behavioural remedies imposed by the Commission rather than on the imposition of fines.

Of course, as already alluded to above, the Microsoft cases may well have had a deterrence impact beyond the behavioural remedies imposed in these cases. For example, the substantial fines imposed by the European Commission in Microsoft I may well have sent a strong signal underscoring the importance of EU antitrust compliance more generally, and specifically for large platforms. Irrespective of their actual effectiveness, the mere prospect of being required to change one's business conduct following the imposition of behavioural remedies may also deter companies from engaging in anticompetitive conduct. Further, irrespective of fines or behavioural remedies, the legal and economic analysis supporting the Commission's cases may help other firms avoid an infringement.

Nevertheless, these indirect deterrence effects on others are more difficult to assess and quantify than the direct effects of the remedies and fall outside the scope of this paper.

We have structured our analysis around the legal and economic concepts at issue in Microsoft I and II. For this reason, we assess the interoperability element of Microsoft I separately (section §2.02) and the tying element of Microsoft I and II jointly (section §2.03).

§2.02 ToH1: INTEROPERABILITY

[A] Legal and Economic Concerns

The Microsoft I case concerned competition in workgroup server operating systems (OSs) – computer programs that run server computers at the backbone of organisations' computer networks. In order to function properly, workgroup server OS must communicate – or interoperate – with the client PC OS run on individual PCs in the organisation's network.[4] The concerns raised by complainant Sun Microsystems (hereafter 'Sun') were, in essence, that Microsoft used its Windows PC OS dominance to foreclose the separate market for workgroup server OSs by refusing to supply Sun and others with critical information on the protocols that Windows used to communicate with workgroup server OSs - thus enabling Microsoft to reserve this market to itself.

In particular, Sun alleged, and the Commission agreed, that Microsoft had thus successfully eliminated virtually all of its competitors in workgroup server OSs, leaving only marginal, ineffective competitive constraints in place.

In its 2004 Decision, the Commission found that Microsoft was dominant in client PC OSs, where its Windows OS ran on more than 90% of PCs. Crucially, the Commission dismissed Microsoft's Schumpeterian defence, according to which Windows' success was only temporary and its position constrained by the constant threat of entry by rivals.[5]

The Commission's concern with respect to Microsoft's conduct was one of leveraging i.e., Microsoft seeking to transfer market power in the market for PC OSs to the market for workgroup server OSs by limiting the ability of rivals in the latter market to supply products compatible with Microsoft's products in the former market.[6] The Commission found that Microsoft's interoperability information constituted an essential facility, and that Microsoft's refusal to provide rivals access to that information amounted to an unlawful refusal to deal, contrary to Article 102 TFEU.

Essential facility-type claims face a high standard of proof, and the Commission's decision set out in detail why Microsoft's interoperability information was not merely important but indeed indispensable for rivals' viability to compete in workgroup server OSs, providing a detailed assessment of foreclosure in the market.[7] Essential facilities arguments also raise questions about the impact on innovation incentives and intellectual property rights, which we discuss below.

Incentives to innovate. A common concern underlying essential facility cases is that forcing a dominant firm to share facilities with rivals can undermine incentives to invest, both on the part of dominant firms - who are faced with the prospect of having to share the fruits of their innovation investments - and also of rivals, who, instead of innovating themselves, can rely on the efforts undertaken by the dominant firm. The Commission thus assessed Microsoft's defence according to which imposing a duty to deal on Microsoft would diminish its incentives to innovate.[8]

---

4. For more information about the technological background, *see* Colin Jackson, *The Basic Technology Issues at Stake, in Microsoft on Trial,* Chapter 1, 5-11 (Luca Rubini ed. Edward Elgar Publishing 2011) and Ian S. Forrester QC, *Victa Placet Mihi Causa: The Compulsory Licencing Part of the Microsoft Case,* in *Microsoft on Trial,* Chapter 3, 83-85 (Luca Rubini ed. Edward Elgar Publishing 2011).
5. Decision, paras 769-771.
6. Decision, paras 772 and 784.
7. *See* Decision, paras 666-687 and CFI Judgment, para. 337.
8. *See* Decision, paras 709 et seq.

The Commission expressed the view that Microsoft's incentives to innovate would not materially be undermined by imposing a duty to license.[9] The key finding underlying this conclusion was that Microsoft was not being required to license any of its software code, but only information *about* that software - conversely, rivals could not use the interoperability information to clone Microsoft code but needed the information to develop their own workgroup server OSs. An analogy could be drawn to cases involving access to network infrastructure, such as rail networks: while mandated access to the rail network for new network operators would undermine incentives to innovate in competing rail networks upstream, it does enable rivals to offer new and innovative rail services downstream, for example, by using new rolling stock or offering rail services at more convenient times.

Essential facility cases - Microsoft I included - thus involve a trade-off not only between protecting incentives to innovate on the part of rivals and incentives to innovate on the part of the dominant firm, but also balancing incentives to innovate in related markets: in this case the markets for workgroup server OSs and PC OSs.[10] The Commission's assessment was that the need to protect Microsoft's incentives to innovate in the PC OSs market was outweighed by the need to protect third parties' incentives to innovate in workgroup server OSs.

That finding does raise the risk of encouraging free riding behaviour and a deleterious impact on dynamic innovation incentives. Granting interoperability access to Microsoft's rivals lessened the incentive for those rivals to make investments in establishing their own forms of interoperability. Where the alternative to innovation is access via an interoperability remedy, rather than no interoperability, the incremental benefit to innovation may be significantly reduced, lessening the incentive to invest in such innovation. This may prevent alternative and innovative products from emerging, and instead encourage a more limited market equilibrium whereby firms compete on the basis of common mandated access solutions.[11] This may harm dynamic competition that encourages the development of new products even if it achieves a short-term benefit in terms of increased static competition amongst firms supplying similar products.

This trade-off between short- and long-term effects from a regulator's point of view will depend in part upon the extent to which innovation and market dynamics could be expected to address interoperability barriers. If those barriers are sufficiently high that there is no realistic prospect of them being circumvented by rivals then a regulator might reasonably opt to capture the static benefits of promoting competition on the basis of common interoperability standards in the expectation that dynamic competition is unlikely to arise spontaneously. Conversely, if there is evidence that

9. *See* Decision, para. 729.

10. *See* Nicholas Economides and Ioannes Lianos, *The Quest for Appropriate Remedies in the EC Microsoft Cases: A Comparative Appraisal*, in *Microsoft on Trial*, Chapter 13, 403 (Luca Rubini ed. Edward Elgar Publishing 2011) and Ian S. Forrester QC, *Victa Placet Mihi Causa: The Compulsory Licencing Part of the Microsoft Case*, in *Microsoft on Trial*, Chapter 3, 100 (Luca Rubini ed. Edward Elgar Publishing 2011).

11. *See* Ian S. Forrester QC, *Victa Placet Mihi Causa: The Compulsory Licencing Part of the Microsoft Case*, in *Microsoft on Trial*, Chapter 3, 92 (Luca Rubini ed. Edward Elgar Publishing 2011).

rivals might be able to overcome interoperability obstacles then it may be better not to mandate access but to allow firms to compete to find the best means of achieving interoperability. In this regard, while cloud-based solutions these days are increasingly replacing workgroup server-based solutions for tasks such as document hosting and sharing, those cloud-based solutions were not yet available at or even near the time the Commission issued its decision in Microsoft I – thus suggesting that barriers to competition may indeed have been very high at the time the Commission issued that decision.

In terms of rivals' attempts to establish interoperability with Microsoft Windows without Microsoft's help, the Commission and complainants cited evidence showing that rivals had failed, after costly reverse engineering efforts, to replicate Microsoft's interoperability information; the Commission also found that successful reverse engineering attempts could in any case be undermined if Microsoft chose to change its interoperability protocols.

During the Commission investigation, Microsoft sought, unsuccessfully, to cite Samba as evidence that it was unnecessary to provide any interoperability documentation to competitors for them to develop competing products.[12] Several leading industry participants, including IBM, HP, SGI and Quantum had already begun to embrace Samba solutions.[13]

Free-riding behaviour promoted by an interoperability remedy could also be expected to reduce innovation incentives on Microsoft itself. Where absent the remedy, Microsoft could expect to capture for itself the benefits of improvements in Windows OS and/or interoperability with workgroup OS, the Commission remedy would require those benefits to be shared with rivals. This reduces the scope for a competitive advantage to be gained through investment in product development, reducing the incentive to pursue such investments.

This point was recognised by the Commission, which took into account the impact of the remedy on innovation incentives. The Commission sought to balance the potential harmful effect on Microsoft's innovation incentives with potential benefits in respect of rivals' innovation, ultimately emphasising the importance of the latter.[14]

Intellectual property rights v. competition rules. The Microsoft I case also raised important, and related, questions about the extent to which competition rules could be used to override intellectual property rights.[15] Microsoft claimed that it was entitled to refuse access to its interoperability information, as that information was protected by various different intellectual property rights.[16] The Commission acknowledged that

---

12. *See* Andrew Tridgell, *Freeing Up the Windows Workgroup Protocols*, Samba (20 December 2007), https://www.samba.org/samba/PFIF/PFIF_history.html and Decision, paras 683 et seq.
13. *See* Stephen Shankland, *Microsoft Steps on Samba's Toes*, ZDNet (9 May 2002), https://www.zdnet.com/article/microsoft-steps-on-sambas-toes-5000122696/.
14. *See* section F, Assimakis P. Komninos and Katarzyna A. Czapracka, *IP Rights in the EU Microsoft Saga, in Competition Law and the Enforcement of Article 102* (Federico Etro and Ioannis Kokkoris eds, Oxford University Press 2010).
15. *See* Ian S. Forrester QC, *Victa Placet Mihi Causa: The Compulsory Licencing Part of the Microsoft Case, in Microsoft on Trial*, Chapter 3, 102–103 (Luca Rubini ed. Edward Elgar Publishing 2011).
16. *See* Decision, paras 743 and 1050.

competition rules should not normally be used to override the exclusivity created by intellectual property rights, as that would undermine the incentives to innovate those intellectual property rights aimed to create – an objective shared by both intellectual property rights and competition rules. However, citing the *Magill* case, it noted that, in exceptional circumstances, competition rules could be relied upon to mandate access to intellectual property rights. Pursuant to that case law, the Commission was required to show not only that the facility is indispensable and that a refusal to provide rivals access to that facility would eliminate them from the market, but also that the rivals needed access to the intellectual property-protected facility in order to develop new products or services for which there was potential consumer demand.[17] The Commission sought to meet this burden by demonstrating that the workgroup servers Sun aimed to introduce were novel.

Overall, the Commission's 'refusal to deal' theory of harm seems reasonably closely aligned with the actual concerns held by Sun and other rivals, insofar as they had asked for – but had been refused – access to this information. Sun and others did not claim that there were other forms of abusive conduct that had enabled Microsoft to leverage its Windows client PC dominance into workgroup server OSs.

[B] Remedy

The remedy imposed by the European Commission was the mirror image of the conduct found to be abusive. Having found that competition in the workgroup server OS market was limited due to the difficulties that competitors faced developing products which would be able to successfully interoperate with the near universal Microsoft Windows OS, the Commission's remedy sought to ease that interoperability. As such, it could be expected to remove the identified barrier to rivals' ability to compete effectively.

However, like other 'access remedies', imposing a duty to deal on Microsoft required the Commission to address several specificities of access, including the beneficiaries, scope, timing, and price of the interoperability information to be provided.

As regards the beneficiaries of access, the decision sought to force Microsoft to provide the interoperability information to any firm having an interest in developing workgroup server OSs. Although the case rested on the notion that Microsoft's refusal to supply prevented the emergence of new products – in the form of innovative workgroup server products – the remedy was not limited to firms seeking to introduce such new products.

With respect to the scope of the interoperability information to be provided, the decision required Microsoft to provide 'complete and accurate' specifications for all interoperability protocols relied upon by Microsoft's own workgroup server OSs.[18]

17. *See Ibid.*, section E.
18. *See* Decision, paras 999 and 1003.

Determining the price of the interoperability information gave rise to further questions. Interoperability access can provide a basis for rivals to compete only insofar as that access is on economically viable terms. As well as the level of charges set for interoperability access, the ability of rivals to compete will also be affected by the structure of charges. Economic theory states that firms paying fixed access terms will not pass the costs of access on to their own customers, but that access terms that vary with volumes (such as percentage royalties) will affect pricing, and hence firms' ability to compete.

The determination of pricing for products and services that would not ordinarily be supplied via market mechanisms is a difficult area for regulators. This is particularly true in cases involving the supply of services, such as interoperability terms, with effectively zero marginal costs. This is demonstrated in the difficulties faced in setting fair, reasonable and non-discriminatory prices in other regulatory contexts, such as standard essential patents.

The Commission avoided this difficulty in its Microsoft I interoperability remedy by requiring Microsoft to provide interoperability information, but not specifying the terms for such access beyond requiring that they be 'reasonable and non-discriminatory'. Microsoft set terms for that access, which then, perhaps unsurprisingly, became the subject of further dispute between the parties. In 2008, the Commission imposed a fine of EUR 899 million for non-compliance with the remedy, on the grounds that the access fees set by Microsoft were not reasonable, a position substantively confirmed by the General Court in 2012.[19]

The fact that the question of whether the access terms set by Microsoft were indeed reasonable and therefore compliant with the interoperability remedy was not ultimately resolved until eight years after the original infringement decision, via an appeal to the General Court, might be regarded as a negative reflection on the remedy as originally designed.

In order to oversee the effectiveness of the – technically complex – remedy, the Commission required Microsoft to appoint a monitoring trustee, who was given far-reaching powers to assist the Commission in verifying Microsoft's compliance with the remedies.[20] Having found that the trustee's powers went too far, the General Court annulled the trustee appointment – the silver lining in Microsoft's otherwise unsuccessful appeal against the Commission's Decision.[21]

[C] Effectiveness of the Remedy

The intended purpose of the interoperability remedy was to promote the development of competition in the market for workgroup server OS. This can be considered both directly, in terms of the development of the market structure; and indirectly, by investigating the extent to which third parties sought to take up the interoperability

19. *See* Decision C(2008)764, n. 126.
20. *See* Decision, paras 1043–1048.
21. *See* CFI Judgment, para. 1278.

opportunities provided by the remedy. We review the evidence on these two points in turn.

[1] Development of the Workgroup Server OS Market

There is no clear evidence that the remedy was successful in promoting workgroup server market competition that challenged Microsoft's position. Far from declining, Microsoft's share in the workgroup server market increased after the implementation of the remedy.

As illustrated below, in the mid-1990s, Novell's NetWare was the leading workgroup server OS for file and print sharing, whilst Unix was used for other applications such as databases and email.[22] However, throughout the late 1990s, both NetWare and Unix lost significant market share to Microsoft and later to Linux. In particular, Microsoft's Active Directory was one of Microsoft's most distinctive and innovative server technologies, and was the focus of Sun Microsystems' original demand for what the Commission later termed 'Interoperability Information'.

Figure 2.1 The Growth of Microsoft's Share in the Workgroup Server OS Market 1996Q1–2001Q3

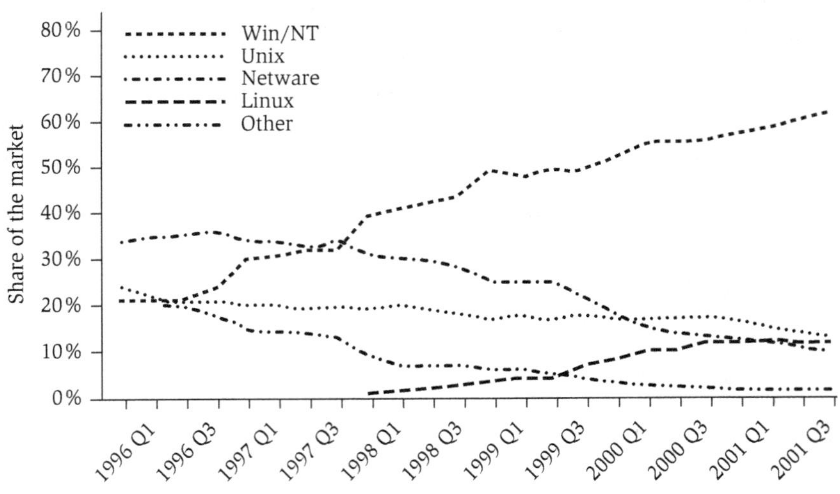

Source: Figure 1 in Christos Genakos, Kai UweKühn and John Van Reenen, *The European Commission Versus Microsoft: Competition Policy in High-Tech Industries*, CentrePiece (2007), http://eprints

22. *See* William H. Page and Seldon J. Childers, *Bargaining in the Shadow of the European Microsoft Decision: The Microsoft-Samba Protocol License*, 102 NW. U. L. Rev. Colloquy 332 (2008), https://scholarlycommons.law.northwestern.edu/cgi/viewcontent.cgi?referer=https://www.google.com/&httpsredir=1&article=1114&context=nulr_online.

.lse.ac.uk/4600/1/The_European_Commission_versus_Microsoft_Competition_Policy_in_High-Tech_Industries.pdf.

Subsequently, Microsoft continued to expand its share in the workgroup server OS market. In comments to the European Parliament in March 2007, Commissioner Neelie Kroes noted that when the Commission began its antitrust investigation in 1999, Microsoft held a share of between 35% and 40%, rising to around 60% by 2004, and standing at between 70% and 75% in 2007.[23] Similarly, the Commission's 2005 and 2008 Decisions noted that Microsoft's market share continued to grow following the 2004 infringement Decision.

In the 2004 Decision, one of the market data sources considered by the Commission was the International Data Corporation (IDC) Worldwide Quarterly Server Tracker data for a server type segment termed 'volume servers' (or 'low-end servers' in earlier IDC publications).[24] As shown in Figure 2.2, as of 2002, Windows had a revenue share of 60%; by 2009, this had risen to 68%. During this period, various Linux vendors almost doubled their combined share, capturing over a fifth of the market by 2008, whereas Unix and NetWare continued their decline. Novell removed NetWare from its product list in 2011.

23. *See* Paul Meller, *EU Official: Microsoft's Behavior 'Unacceptable'*, IDG News Service (22 March 2007), https://www.computerworld.com/article/2544050/eu-official--microsoft-s-behavior--unacceptable-.html.

24. IDC's server class taxonomy segments the server market into three server classes: the 'volume server' segment (consisting of all systems with an average selling value (ASV) below USD 25,000), the 'midrange enterprise server' segment (consisting of all systems with an ASV from USD 25,000 to USD 249,999), and the 'high-end enterprise server' segment (consisting of all systems with an ASV of USD 250,000 and above). The Commission decision also noted that a limitation of the IDC data is that there are volume servers that are not workgroup servers.

Figure 2.2 Worldwide Market Share by Server Customer Revenue, Volume Servers Only

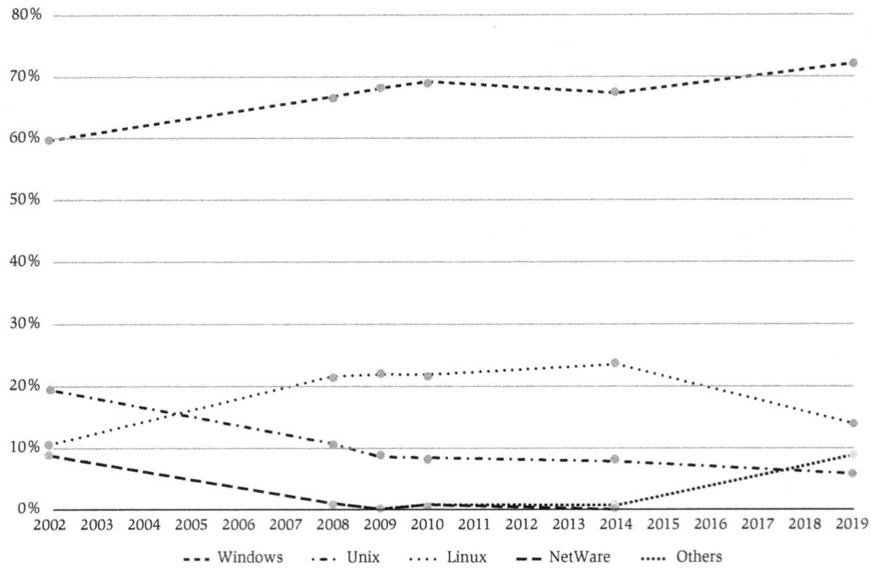

Source: 2002 data taken from footnote 606 of the *2004 European Commission Decision*; 2008–2014 data taken from Table 25 of IDC, *Market Analysis: Worldwide and Regional Server 2010–2014 Forecast*, Vol. 1 (April 2010), *https://www.novell.com/docrep/documents/ie6so4xkex/Worldwide_and_Regional_Server_2010-2014_Forecast.pdf;* 2019 data taken from Statista, *Global server share by operating system 2018–2019*, Statista (13 May 2020), *https://www.statista.com/statistics/915085/global-server-share-by-os/#: ~ :text = In%202019%2C%20the%20Windows%20operating,to%20their%20overall%20market%20share.*

Note: 2010 and 2014 data are contemporaneous forecasts.

Microsoft's position has not changed materially in subsequent years, its share remaining above 70% as of 2019.

In the absence of a counterfactual to these developments, it is difficult to draw strong conclusions on the impact of the remedy on market structure. It may be the case that Microsoft's position in the workgroup server OS market would have grown more rapidly absent the remedy. However, the continued expansion of Microsoft in this market, and the modest expansion of rivals would suggest prima facie that the remedy did not have a significant impact in opening the market to competition.

[2] Third Parties Requesting and Obtaining Interoperability Access

Initially, few third parties pursued interoperability access via the Commission remedy. In 2008, the Commission noted that no firm seeking to develop a competing OS for workgroup servers had yet taken a license under the program; the only licences taken had been for products that didn't directly compete with Microsoft's server OS.[25]

A month after the Court decision in 2007, Microsoft agreed to comply and make workgroup server Interoperability Information available to third parties at a price deemed reasonable. The most tangible, and perhaps the only, outcome was the Workgroup Server Protocol Programme (WSPP) agreement between Microsoft and Samba, brokered by a non-profit organisation called Protocol Freedom Information Foundation (PFIF).[26] In December 2007, PFIF signed an agreement with Microsoft to receive protocol documentation required for full interoperability with Windows workgroup server products and to make it available to Free Software projects such as Samba under non-disclosure terms.[27,28] PFIF paid a one-off fee of EUR 10,000 to Microsoft. Although the documentation itself was to be held in confidence by PFIF and Free Software engineers, the agreement permits (i) publication of source code of the implementation of Windows workgroup server protocols, as well as (ii) discussion of the protocol information among implementers which would aid technical cooperation among engineers. The agreement, however, does not fully address the concerns that Samba and the wider open source community had over Microsoft's patent claims for these protocols.

In February 2008, Microsoft announced new Interoperability Protocols, which made available all access protocols for high-volume products used by any other Microsoft product. These protocols were made freely available without requiring developers to take a licence. This approach was formalised in a 2009 interoperability undertaking provided to the Commission.

This final step does then appear to have produced greater user of interoperability access by rival developers. As of 2012, Heiner reports that around fifty firms had chosen to enter into license agreements with Microsoft, and Microsoft was aware of about ninety commercial products, from firms including Cisco Systems, Symantec, EMC and McAfee, that implemented Microsoft's protocols.[29]

Consistent with Microsoft's change in attitude toward Samba and more generally interoperability with Linux, Microsoft also entered into technical collaboration and licensing agreements with leading vendors who offer or support Linux, including Attachmate (which recently acquired Novell's Linux business), Red Hat and Citrix. Microsoft's increased compliance with industry standards and standardisation effort can also be seen in its participation in hundreds of standards groups and consortia via

25. *See* Chapter 7, Andrew I. Gavil and Harry First, *The Microsoft Antitrust Cases: Competition Policy for the Twenty-First Century* (MIT Press 2014).
26. *See* Nicholas Economides and Ioannes Lianos, *The Quest for Appropriate Remedies in the EC Microsoft Cases: A Comparative Appraisal, in Microsoft on Trial,* Chapter 13, 424 (Luca Rubini ed. Edward Elgar Publishing 2011).
27. *See* The Samba Team, *Samba and the PFIF*, Samba (20 December 2007), https://www.samba.org/samba/PFIF/.
28. *See* Andrew Tridgell, *Freeing Up the Windows Workgroup Protocols*, Samba (20 December 2007), https://www.samba.org/samba/PFIF/PFIF_history.html.
29. David A. Heiner, *Microsoft: Remedial Success*, 78(2) Antitrust L. J. 329–362 (2012).

an internal Corporate Standards Group comprising engineers, standards specialists and lawyers.[30]

In December 2012, Samba announced the release of Samba 4.0, the first compatible Free Software implementation of Microsoft's Active Directory protocols, acknowledging 'help from the official protocol documentation published by Microsoft Corporation' and even 'interoperability testing by Microsoft engineers that made [Samba's] implementation interoperable'.[31] The release also won praise from Microsoft.[32]

The picture is therefore mixed on the success of the interoperability remedy. Initially its impact was limited, but there was ultimately some usage of the access remedy once Microsoft relaxed access conditions. The tortuous process towards the implementation of the remedy, which only appears to have reached a form that had the desired impact on the market in 2008, underscores the practical difficulties in designing interoperability and access remedies.

Moreover, even if rivals were eventually granted interoperability access, this has not resulted in any material change in server OS marker structure; Microsoft continues to hold a leading position. Care should be taken in interpreting this as necessarily indicating a failure of the remedy; however, if the interoperability access identified as an issue by the Commission is considered to have been addressed by the remedy, then Microsoft's continued success cannot be presumed to indicate some further failure of competition, but may simply reflect competition on the merits within the server OS market.

§2.03 ToH2: TYING

In this section, we discuss concerns in respect of tying of Microsoft products raised by the Commission in Microsoft I – in respect of WMP – and Microsoft II – in respect of Internet Explorer (IE).

[A] Legal and Economic Concerns

More so than in the interoperability case, the two Microsoft tying cases – WMP (Microsoft I) and IE (Microsoft II) – demonstrate that economic and legal concerns are not always identical, and that the choice of the legal theory of harm can affect (and limit) the range of available remedies.

30. *Ibid.*
31. *See* The Samba Team, *Samba Team Releases Samba 4.0*, Samba (11 December 2012), https://www.samba.org/samba/news/releases/4.0.0.html.
32. *Ibid.* Thomas Pfenning, director of development for Windows Server, remarked that, 'Active Directory is a mainstay of enterprise IT environments, and Microsoft is committed to support for interoperability across platforms. We are pleased that the documentation and interoperability labs that Microsoft has provided have been key in the development of the Samba 4.0 Active Directory functionality.'

The concern in both tying cases related to the potential anticompetitive effect of leveraging market power from the Windows OS into related markets.[33] In Microsoft I, this concern related to tying WMP to Windows OS; in Microsoft II, the theory of harm related to tying IE to Windows OS.[34] The potential anticompetitive effect of such bundling arises from exclusion of single-product rival firms that are not able to compete effectively with the bundle. This situation derives from the low implicit incremental price of the tied good when combined with the tying good for customers that would purchase the latter in any case. By offering WMP and IE at zero marginal cost to customers of its Windows client PC OS, Microsoft undermined demand for rival media players and browsers, respectively, which - unlike WMP and IE - were generally not pre-installed on Windows PCs.

Closely related was the fact that both WMP and IE, by virtue of this pre-installation, were prominently placed on and readily accessible from the user's Windows desktop.[35] This rendered users - already equipped with a media player and browser - less likely to seek out competing media players or browsers, given that finding and downloading such alternative products required efforts from the user. This theory of harm was informed by behavioural economics, which suggests that end user inertia and other biases that prevent consumers from making optimal decisions may facilitate leveraging of market power.[36]

In both cases, the foreclosure effects realised by Microsoft's pre-installation of WMP and IE were exacerbated by network effects and incompatibility.[37] Because content producers knew that WMP was installed on every single Windows PC, whereas rival media players had a far smaller installed base, they had an incentive to provide their content in WMP's proprietary format in order to reach the largest audience. This, in turn, encouraged more use of WMP by consumers, which led to even more content creators providing WMP-compatible content, thus creating a feedback loop benefiting WMP but undermining rival media players. A similar effect arose with IE, which relied on a version of the web's HTML language that was not fully compatible with that used in most rival browsers.

While the WMP investigation was pursued as a relatively straightforward case of leveraging dominance in one market (Client PC OSs) into another (media players), the concerns expressed in IE involved not only leveraging but also monopoly maintenance. In particular, the Commission - mirroring concerns expressed earlier by the United States (US) Department of Justice - was concerned that, by foreclosing rival web browsers, Microsoft not only came to dominate the browser market but could also

33. *See* Decision, para. 772.
34. *Ibid.*
35. *See* Decision, para. 845 and CFI Judgment, para. 1041.
36. Nicolas Petit and Norman Neyrinck, *Back to Microsoft I and II: Tying and the Art of Secret Magic*, 2(2) J. Eur. Competition L. & Practice, 117–121 (2011).
37. *See* Decision, para. 533 and Maria J. Gil-Moltó, *Economic Aspects of the Microsoft Case: Networks, Interoperability and Competition*, in *Microsoft on Trial*, Chapter 11, 349 (Luca Rubini ed. Edward Elgar Publishing 2011) and Nicholas Economides and Ioannes Lianos, *The Quest for Appropriate Remedies in the EC Microsoft Cases: A Comparative Appraisal*, in *Microsoft on Trial*, Chapter 13, 402 and 403–404 (Luca Rubini ed. Edward Elgar Publishing 2011).

prevent web browsers from replacing the client PC OS as the main platform through which users engaged with applications. Indeed, applications were increasingly being made available through web pages that could, in theory, be run in web browsers on any platform, not just Microsoft's Windows. However, as a result of the tie between Windows and IE, web creators tended to optimise their web pages for IE rather than competing web browsers, thus keeping users dependant on Microsoft solutions.

The development of the browser market provides some prima facie support for the Commission's concerns. IE expanded rapidly following the mid-1998 introduction of the Windows 98 OS into which it was incorporated. At the start of 1998, two and a half years after its introduction, IE's user share was around 40% (*see* Figure 2.3). The market leader at this point was Netscape Navigator, which held a circa 60% share. By the end of 1998, within months of being pre-installed with Windows OS, IE had overtaken Netscape Navigator, to reach a market share of around 65%.

Figure 2.3 Internet Browser Shares

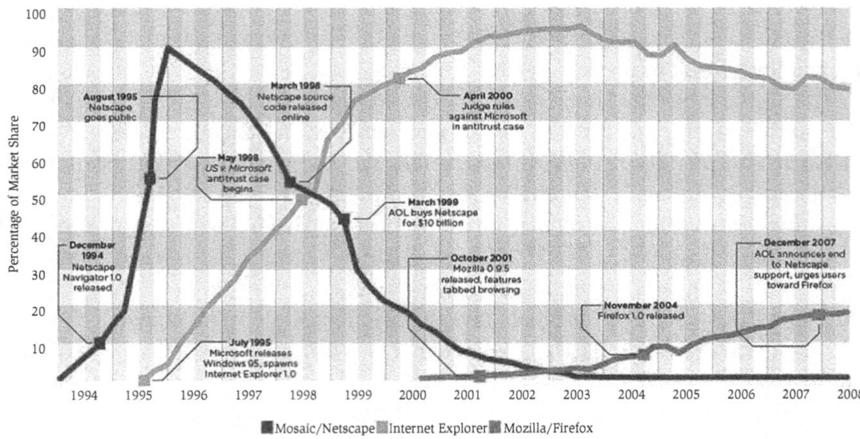

Source: Wired.com https://hsto.org/getpro/habr/post_images/dbe/3a1/8aa/dbe3a18aad1a92aebdb3c423714e8966.jpg.

In short, therefore, the economic concern in both the WMP and IE cases was that Microsoft, by pre-installing WMP and IE, removed users' incentive to use media players and browsers competing with WMP and IE, exacerbated by a positive feedback loop as content and web creators adhered to the WMP and IE formats through which they could expect to reach users on the entire Windows installed base.

The legal case may not perfectly have captured these economic concerns. In both cases, the Commission alleged abusive-tying by Microsoft. Under established case law, the key elements of a tying case – and thus the key elements on which the WMP and IE cases were based – are (i) the separate nature of the tying and tied products, and, crucially, (ii) the fact that consumers of the (dominant) tying product are given no choice but to obtain that product together with the tied product.

Microsoft argued that consumers benefited from being provided with an OS equipped with a media player and a browser, and that nothing prevented consumers from downloading additional media players or browsers. In the WMP case, the Commission, upheld by the General Court, rejected these arguments, noting that even if consumers might prefer having a media player, they might well prefer to use a different media player than the one pre-installed by Microsoft. They were however unlikely to do so as downloading and installing another media player required a certain degree of technical competence, with users having little incentive to pursue such alternatives due to the ready availability of WMP. In the IE case, Microsoft relied on similar arguments and faced a similar response.

It is debatable whether the Commission's choice for a tying theory of harm in the WMP and IE cases aligned with the actual (economic) concerns in both cases. As noted above, the actual concerns were that, as a result of Microsoft's conduct, consumers were incentivised to use Microsoft's media player and browser rather than competing products. However, under the legal theory of harm pursued, the focus was not so much on consumers being incentivised to use Microsoft's products in preference to rivals', but rather that they had no choice but to obtain Windows together with WMP and IE. As discussed below, the mere re-introduction of that choice (namely, the ability to obtain Windows without WMP or IE if preferred) would remove this legal concern, even if consumers might have no incentive to obtain a version of Windows without WMP or IE.

[B] Potential Alternative Remedies

The preceding discussion raises the question of how the Commission might alternatively have sought to remedy its tying ToH. Insofar as the tying ToH fundamentally relate to WMP/IE being provided to customers purchasing Windows OS at no additional cost, the Commission could have considered breaking this tie entirely.[38] This could be achieved by requiring Microsoft to only supply WMP/IE as separate products to Windows; or even, taking a step further, by mandating a divestment of the WMP/IE businesses. This would allow rival media players and browsers supplied by non-OS suppliers to compete on an equal footing with WMP and IE.

However, this approach would potentially create its own consumer detriment, by requiring users to choose and source a media player/browser in order to access media content. At the time of Microsoft I, when online delivery of software was less widespread than today, this could have been a non-trivial barrier to using media content for at least some Windows users. In the case of Microsoft II, separation of OS and web browser would have been an even greater impediment to users, as without a

38. *See also* Derek Ridyard and Markus Baldauf, *Microsoft v. Commission: A Pricing Perspective on Non-price Abuses*, in *Microsoft on Trial*, Chapter 12, 390-391 (Luca Rubini ed, Edward Elgar Publishing 2011).

pre-installed browser, consumers would be unable to access the internet in order to find and download a browser.[39]

While separation would be problematic from a user perspective, one might expect Original Equipment Manufacturers (OEMs) to respond to such a remedy by pre-installing media players/browsers on their machines prior to sale to consumers. It would appear reasonable to consider OEMs sophisticated and informed customers, well placed to make decisions between media players, and therefore not susceptible to default bias of the sort that might lead to consumers not considering alternatives to WMP/IE when already bundled with Windows OS. Moreover, OEMs, unlike consumers, would be able to spread fixed search and installation costs associated with deciding amongst media players and browsers across many machines.

This logic would however then call into question the necessity for intervention against bundling. If media player and browser decisions are made not only by consumers but also by OEMs then arguments about consumer default bias and inertia appear less relevant. In practice, as discussed in the following section, there is evidence in respect of media players that OEMs did indeed circumvent tying of WMP by installing other media players in parallel with WMP.

As an alternative approach, the Commission could have sought to make its media player remedy more effective by mandating a price difference between Windows XP and Windows XP Edition N. This would have addressed a concern that WMP was supplied at too low a price to allow rivals to compete effectively by creating an implicit non-zero price for WMP. (It is not clear that there would be a realistic equivalent approach for Microsoft II due to the necessity in practice of a browser to access alternative browsers. In this context, customers wishing to use a browser would be forced to purchase an IE enabled version of Windows and so any issues of default bias and inertia would remain.)

This would have been an unattractive prospect for any regulator however, requiring a determination of the 'correct' incremental price to be charged for WMP. Mandating prices is an area that competition enforcers sensibly prefer to avoid, given the variety of factors influencing price, the complexity of defining pricing schemes to avoid circumvention, and the ongoing costs of monitoring compliance. Pricing is a particularly complex issue in the context of software products, for which the marginal cost of supply is effectively zero, and in which zero pricing can be considered an efficient, though not sustainable, market outcome. As noted above in section §2.02[B], neither the Commission nor the Courts sought to define a specific price for workgroup server interoperability in Microsoft I.

Moreover, a remedy that mandated non-zero pricing for WMP would lessen competitive pressure on suppliers of competing media players, potentially leading to an increase in their prices and/or lessening in their quality. In the short term, this regulator-mandated lessening of competitive constraints could thus be expected to create a consumer detriment. Rival media player manufacturers might seek to argue

39. Nicolas Petit and Norman Neyrinck, *Back to Microsoft I and II: Tying and the Art of Secret Magic*, 2(2) J. Eur. Competition L. & Practice, 117–121 (2011).

that a move away from an implicit zero price for WMP would provide incentives for greater innovation. However, it is notable that many technology markets characterised by network effects and zero marginal costs, such as online search and social media platforms, have gravitated towards zero (monetary) price/advertising funded business models. Of course, the costs and benefits of these business models have themselves become the focus of extensive debate amongst competition practitioners in recent years.

In summary, there are clear drawbacks to obvious alternative remedies that might have more directly addressed the economic basis for tying ToH.

We now turn to an assessment of the performance of the two remedies that the Commission pursued in the Microsoft I and II cases.

[C] Effectiveness of the Remedy

[1] Windows XP Edition N Remedy

Windows XP Edition N (hereafter 'XP N') has become notorious for its lack of commercial impact.[40] According to a Microsoft fact sheet, as of April 2006, there had been negligible demand for XP N from PC manufacturers, retailers and consumers.[41] Microsoft reported that no PC manufacturers had ordered or pre-installed XP N on PCs, and that only 1,787 copies of XP N had been sold to retailers and distributors in Europe.[42] In contrast, 35.5 million copies of the bundled Windows XP product were sold in Europe over the same period. While there were no data systematically tracking the number of copies purchased by end users, the French retailer FNAC, which had ordered the largest proportion (46%) of XP N copies, stated that there was no consumer demand for the product.

Nonetheless, WMP's market position did decline over time. Figure 2.4 shows use of streaming media players in the period preceding and following the introduction of Windows XP Edition N. Nielsen data show that WMP's streaming share of unique users rose from 45% in January 2004 to 48% in January 2005, before declining steadily to 37% by January 2009. The beneficiary of this decline was Apple iTunes, which grew from 1% to 20% of streaming over the same period.

40. *See* Jean-François Bellis and Tim Kasten, *The Microsoft Windows Media Player Tying Case*, in *Microsoft on Trial*, Chapter 4, 133 (Luca Rubini ed. Edward Elgar Publishing 2011).
41. Microsoft, *Fact Sheet: Windows XP N Sales*, Regmedia (April 2006), https://regmedia.co.uk/2009/06/12/microsoft_windows_xp_n_fact_sheet.pdf.
42. *See* Nicholas Economides and Ioannes Lianos, *The Quest for Appropriate Remedies in the EC Microsoft Cases: A Comparative Appraisal*, in *Microsoft on Trial*, Chapter 13, 430 (Luca Rubini ed. Edward Elgar Publishing 2011).

Figure 2.4 Streaming Media Player Shares

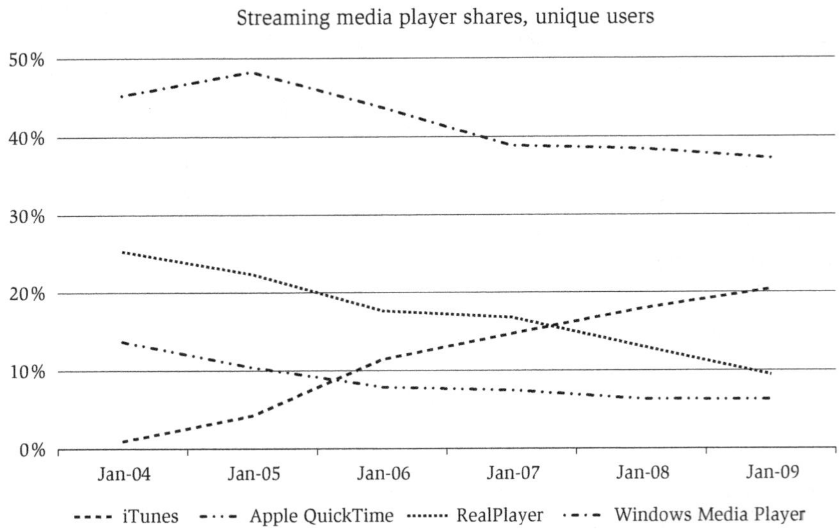

Source: Nielsen data (13 March 2009), accessed at http://www.websiteoptimization.com/bw/0903/#: ~ :text = Summary%3A%20The%20popularity%20of%20Apple's,remained%20unchanged%20at%2050.7%25%20share.

Over time, Microsoft did steadily improve WMP, with format support and Media Transfer Protocol improved with the release of Windows Vista in January 2007.[43]

Given the lack of take up of Windows XP Edition N, it is difficult to attribute this decline in share and improvements in quality to the Commission remedy. Instead, WMP's market share decline, and potentially also its quality improvements, appear to reflect competition from iTunes, combined with OEMs' choice to install a greater range of media players. PC manufacturers had responded to demand for enhanced multimedia functionality by pre-installing an increasing number of non-WMPs on PCs. PC manufacturers pre-installed an average of 1.4 non-WMPs on PCs sold in Europe in 2004; by 2006 this had more than doubled to an average of 3.2.[44]

If one takes the view that the minimal sales of Windows XP Edition N imply that the remedy effectively failed to have the intended impact, then the actual market outcomes observed could be considered to represent the counterfactual to that remedy. That is, the above decline of WMP at the expense of iTunes, improvements in WMP, and increased range of OEM media player installations might be considered likely to have arisen absent any intervention against tying in Microsoft I. On this basis the merits

43. Sergey Tkachenko, *Microsoft Is ditching Windows Media Player*, Winaero (4 March 2018), https://winaero.com/microsoft-ditching-windows-media-player/.
44. Microsoft, *Fact Sheet: Windows XP N Sales*, Regmedia (April 2006), https://regmedia.co.uk/2009/06/12/microsoft_windows_xp_n_fact_sheet.pdf.

of the Commission's tying theory of harm with respect to WMP could perhaps be questioned. While it is difficult to make forecasts in markets as dynamic as the technology and software industry, if rivals were within a relatively short period of time able to find means of competing against WMP notwithstanding the minimal penetration of the unbundled Windows XP Edition N, then the tying conduct would seem not to have in fact represented a significant impediment to rivals' ability to compete effectively. On this basis, the need for intervention against Microsoft's tying strategy may be questioned.

[D] Remedy

The Commission's choice of remedy in the WMP case appears to have been driven by the legal nature of the case. WMP was a prohibition decision under Article 7 of Regulation 1/2003 in which the Commission conclusively established an infringement and unilaterally imposed a remedy on Microsoft. This required the Commission to impose a remedy that addressed the legal concern identified by it and was proportionate in relation to those concerns. As noted above, the key legal concern was that Microsoft did not offer customers the choice to obtain its dominant client PC OS, Windows, without WMP.[45] Thus, the core of the WMP remedy was an obligation on Microsoft to restore customer choice as to obtaining Windows with or without WMP. To that end, the Commission required Microsoft to '*offer a full-functioning version of the Windows Client PC Operating System which does not incorporate Windows Media Player*' adding that '*Microsoft Corporation retains the right to offer a bundle of the Windows Client PC Operating System and Windows Media Player*'.[46]

Because the legal concerns did not extend to pricing concerns, Microsoft remained free to charge identical prices for both Windows with WMP and Windows XP Edition N. Similarly, because the prominent placement of WMP was not a core element of the legal case, the Commission did not require Microsoft to change the prominent placement of WMP in the Windows version with WMP; as far as the legal theory of harm was concerned, that theory of harm was fully addressed by Microsoft providing Windows XP Edition N.

From an economic perspective, in order to address a concern that single-product media player suppliers could not compete effectively against WMP bundled with Windows, a remedy would ideally break the link between the tying and tied products entirely.

Viewed in this way, it is not clear that the WMP remedy was well-targeted at addressing the essential source of competition concerns. While the remedy required Microsoft to offer a non-tied product - Windows XP Edition N - it did not set any requirement on the price of that product. The remedy therefore allowed Microsoft to sell Windows XP (with WMP) and Windows XP Edition N (without WMP) at the same price, which was the strategy it indeed chose. In this scenario, the incremental cost to

45. *See* Decision, para. 829.
46. *See* Decision, Article 6.

Windows OS customers of purchasing WMP was zero. That is, a customer would have to make a specific choice to not receive WMP for no financial benefit. Given that use of WMP was optional for users, and did not preclude any choice to use an alternative media player product instead of or in parallel to WMP, there was no clear incentive for customers to consider not purchasing the tied product. Consequently, any anticompetitive concern arising from single-product rivals facing difficulties in gaining users against WMP would likely remain.

By contrast, Microsoft II was a commitment decision under Article 9 of Regulation 1/2003, in which Microsoft proposed a resolution to address the Commission's (by then preliminary) tying concerns, and negotiated that resolution with the Commission. On one hand, this enabled the Commission to accept and make legally binding remedies that it might not have been able to impose in a prohibition decision; on the other hand, it also enabled Microsoft and the Commission to consider solutions that better fit marker realities and the competitive concerns identified. Thus, rather than providing a version of Windows without IE, Microsoft offered – and the Commission accepted – a 'choice screen', which pro-actively alerted users to the existence of alternative browsers, and gave them an opportunity to download and install those alternative browsers. Under the settlement, Microsoft was not required to alter the pre-installation or prominent placement of IE, although the choice screen did contain instructions on how to disable IE if users wished to do so. The choice screen would be shown twice to users of new Windows PCs during a five-year period.

The IE remedy appears to have been better tailored to meet its objectives than the WMP remedy. Rather than relying on consumers to opt-out of a bundle without any benefit to doing so, the choice screen encouraged consumers to choose one or more of a series of pre-selected alternative browsers. This did not take away the option of users choosing to retain IE, but aimed to disrupt any default bias or inertia that might lead consumers to not consider alternatives by explicitly presenting alternative options.

The advantages of the IE Microsoft II remedy do indeed appear to be borne out in the evidence on market impact presented in the next section. The arguably more effective remedy in this case may have resulted from the Commission's experience of the impact of the Microsoft I WMP remedy, both in terms of specific remedy design, but also in terms of procedural approach with respect to the benefits of informal settlement.

Interestingly, Bellis notes that an informal settlement was also explored in the WMP case, Microsoft suggesting that three rival media players be bundled alongside WMP within Windows, allowing consumers to choose a default player.[47] Such an approach has clear parallels with that adopted in the IE case. Bellis explains that this proposal was seriously considered, but a settlement could not ultimately be reached, leaving the Commission feeling it could only address its tying concerns via an untying remedy.[48]

47. Jean-François Bellis, *EU Commitment Decisions: What Makes Them So Attractive?*, Concurrences 3-2015, para. 27 (2015).
48. *Ibid.*

[1] Browser Choice Screen Remedy

[a] Impact on Market Structure

The impact of the browser choice remedy can be assessed via a review of browser shares over time. Figure 2.5 shows browser shares for Europe over the period January 2009 to March 2015, five years after the introduction of the choice screen remedy.

The data show that IE's share of browser usage was declining throughout the period from January 2009. The rate of decline from early 2010, when the choice screen remedy was implemented, does accelerate to some extent. During 2009 IE's share of usage declined by 5.8 percentage points, representing an 11% decline in share. During the following three years however it lost an average of 7.3 percentage points of usage share per annum, equivalent to a 20% average annual decline.

By contrast, Google Chrome, which replaced IE as the leading browser in Europe in the first half of 2012, expanded rapidly following the introduction of the choice remedy. In 2009, it gained 4.4 percentage points of usage share. In the following three years, after the introduction of the browser choice screen, it grew at twice that rate, an average of 8.8 percentage points per annum.

Figure 2.5 Browser Shares, Europe

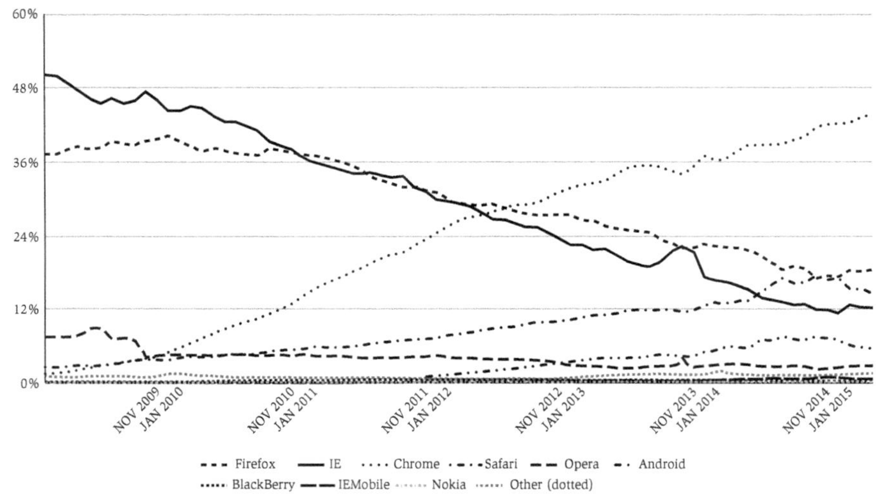

Source: Statcounter, *Browser Market Share in Europe: January 2009 – March 2015*, Global Stats (May 2021), https://gs.statcounter.com/browser-market-share/all/europe/#monthly-200901-201503.

These data demonstrate that IE declined markedly in the period since the introduction of the browser choice screen remedy; with that decline primarily benefiting Google Chrome. These trends may or may not be related to the browser choice screen remedy however. Indeed, the fact that there is no visible impact on market structure of Microsoft's non-compliance over the period May 2011 to July 2012 could be considered prima facie evidence that IE's decline was not necessarily due to the choice screen remedy.

In order to assess the extent to which this pattern may be related to the remedy, these data can be compared to market developments in the US, where no such remedy was implemented (*see* Figure 2.6).

Figure 2.6 Browser Shares, North America

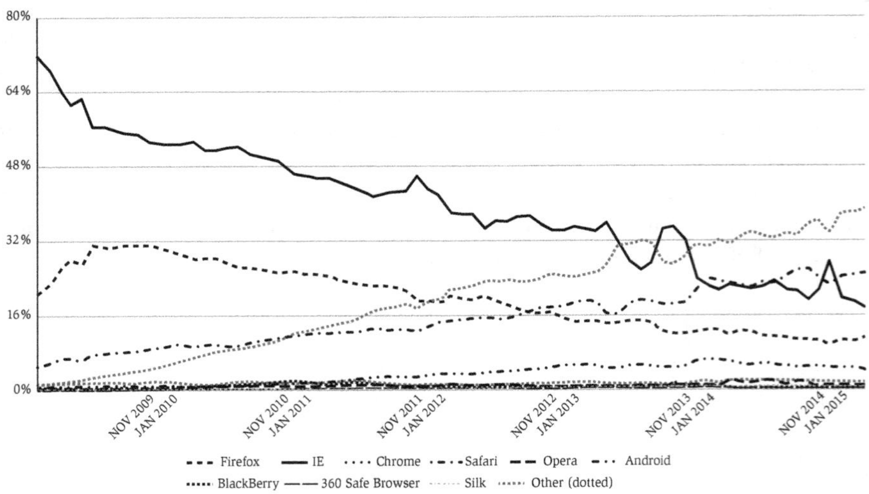

Source: Statcounter, *Browser Market Share in North America: January 2009 – March 2015*, Global Stats (May 2021), https://gs.statcounter.com/browser-market-share/all/north-america/#monthly-200901-201503.

Again, there is a pattern of decline for IE between 2009 and 2015, and of expansion for Google Chrome. The decline in IE's share following March 2010 is much less steep than in Europe however. During 2009, IE declined by 19.5 percentage points, equivalent to a 27% reduction in usage share. This rate of decline slowed in the following years however, to an average of 5.8 percentage points, or 13% of usage share, per annum in the following three years.

The data thus show that IE's share fell materially faster in Europe in the period following the introduction of the choice screen remedy than in the US during the same period. This is despite IE having entered that period in a more rapid state of decline in the US than in Europe.

Taken together, this pattern suggests that there was a Europe specific negative impact on IE's market position in the period following the introduction of the choice screen. The fact that differing rates of decline are observed in these two regions suggests that market developments in Europe are not solely due to inherent differences in the relative quality of different browsers. The evidence therefore suggests that the choice screen remedy served the intended purpose of addressing the Commission's theory of harm that IE's position within the browser market may have been boosted by tying to the Windows OS.

[b] Impact on Browser Quality

The evidence discussed above suggests that IE's market share may have declined as a result of the browser choice screen remedy.

From a competition policy perspective however market structure is a means to an end, and not the end itself. The purpose of a competitive market structure is to promote the process of rivalry that will produce lower prices and higher quality for consumers. It is therefore, instructive to consider the evidence on whether the browser choice screen could be considered to have generated greater competition amongst browsers that then led to improved market outcomes for consumers. As browsers are generally provided without monetary charge, any improvements would be expected to arise in terms of product quality.

At the time of the Microsoft II investigation, IE was widely considered to be inferior to alternative browsers such as Google Chrome and Firefox. As shown in Figure 2.7, IE 7 took significantly longer to perform Javascript tasks than other browsers. Some commentators also highlighted that despite IE 7 being better than its predecessor, it was still inferior in standards. In the words of Finley:[49]

> It was ... still not standards compliant, so designers kept jumping through hoops to have pages render correctly. Not until [IE] 8 landed in 2009 did Microsoft offer a browser that passed standards test Acid2, a widely used measure of how well browsers complied with the standards of the day, and the company lagged in adopting other standards, such as the 3D graphics technology WebGL.

49. Klint Finley, *The Sorry Legacy of Internet Explorer*, Wired (1 December 2016), https://www.wired.com/2016/01/the-sorry-legacy-of-microsoft-internet-explorer/.

Figure 2.7 Browser Speed Test Results, 2008

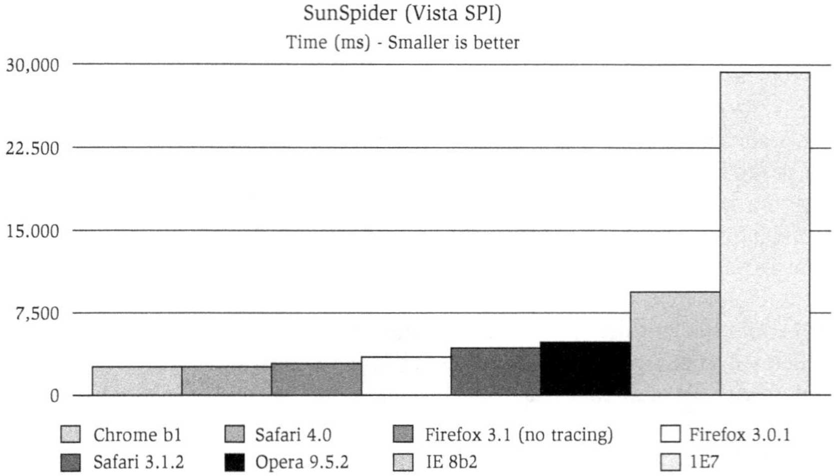

Source: John Resig, *JavaScript Performance Rundown*, johnresig.com (3 September 2008), http://ejohn.org/blog/javascript-performance-rundown.

In July 2010, PCWorld from International Data Group (IDG) reviewed key features of five leading browsers, including IE 8, which was introduced in March 2009.[50] This review found that IE 8 lacked many useful features that were available in other browsers, as set out in Table 2.1.

Table 2.1 Comparison of Key Features of Top Five Browsers as of July 2010

Browser	*Theme Support*	*Add-On Support*	*Bookmark/ Data Sync Support*	*Extra Security Features*	*Plug-In Crash Protection*	*Web Page Crash Protection*	*RSS Reader*
IE 8	No	Accelerators, toolbars, Web Slices	None	URL domain highlighting	No	Yes	Yes
Firefox 3.6	Yes	Extensions, toolbars	None	Plug-in update checker	Yes*	No	Yes
Chrome 5	Yes	Extensions	Google Bookmarks syncing	Sandboxing, URL domain highlighting	Yes	Yes	No

50. Nick Mediati, *Browser Blowout 2010*, PCWorld (26 July 2010), https://www.pcworld.com/article/200963/web_browser_reviews.html.

Browser	*Theme Support*	*Add-On Support*	*Bookmark/ Data Sync Support*	*Extra Security Features*	*Plug-In Crash Protection*	*Web Page Crash Protection*	*RSS Reader*
Safari 5	No	Extensions	MobileMe Bookmarks syncing	None	Yes	No	Yes
Opera 10.53	Yes	Widgets	Opera Link	None	No	No	Yes

Source: Nick Mediati, Browser Blowout 2010, PCWorld (26 July 2010), https://www.pcworld.com /article/200963/web_browser_reviews.html.

Note: *Crash protection introduced with Firefox 3.6.4.

Moreover, through lab-based tests and subjective examinations, this review found that:

- *Chrome* was the best browser in terms of interface and security, with impressive JavaScript handling performance but only a slight edge in page-loading speed.
- *Firefox* had the best extension support and library.
- *IE* nonetheless showed significant improvement in several areas. For instance:
  - historically IE had performed poorly in terms of security, but IE 8 added some 'solid security features';
  - although Chrome had the fastest page-loading time overall, IE was in fact the fastest browser in five out of the eight page-loading tests performed, and the speed differences between Chrome and IE were negligible.

More recently, Tamary and Feitelson (2015) performed a series of technical performance tests on various versions of IE, Chrome and Firefox. The results of these tests are summarized in Table 2.2. Overall, the Tamary and Feitelson results appear to suggest that Chrome has maintained its technical superiority in many aspects over time, but that IE and also Firefox had exhibited clear improvement.

Table 2.2 Comparison of Technical Performance and Conformance of IE (v8-v11), Chrome (v1-v31) and Firefox (v3-v26)

Type	*Benchmark*	*Content*	*Response*	*Result*
Performance	SunSpider	Javascript tasks	Time	Chrome was best until 2011, now IE is significantly better
	BrowserMark	General browser performance	Score	Chrome is best, IE worst
	CanvasMark	<canvas> tag	Score	Chrome is relatively good but inconsistent, Firefox worst
	PeaceKeeper	Javascript tasks	Score	Chrome is significantly better
	Start-up times	Cold start-up time	Time	initially Chrome was better but now Firefox is better, IE has deteriorated
Conformance to common standards such as HTML5 and CSS3	HTML5 Compliance	HTML standard	Score	Chrome is better, IE worst
	CSS3 Test	CSS standard	Score	Chrome is better
	Browserscope Security	Security-enhancing features	Tests passed	Chrome is better, Firefox worst

Source: Jonathan Tamary and Dror G. Feitelson. *The rise of Chrome, PeerJ Computer Science* 1: e28 (2015), https://peerj.com/articles/cs-28.pdf.

In fact, IE 9, released in March 2011, surpassed Chrome in the SunSpider speed tests, as illustrated in Figure 2.8. However, some industry commentators suggested that Microsoft might have specifically optimised JavaScript performance just to boost IE's SunSpider test performance.[51]

51. *See* Ricky, *Did Internet Explorer 9 Cheat in the SunSpider Benchmark?, Digitizor* (18 November 2010), https://digitizor.com/internet-explorer-9-caught-cheating-in-sunspider-benchmark/.

Figure 2.8 SunSpider Test Results

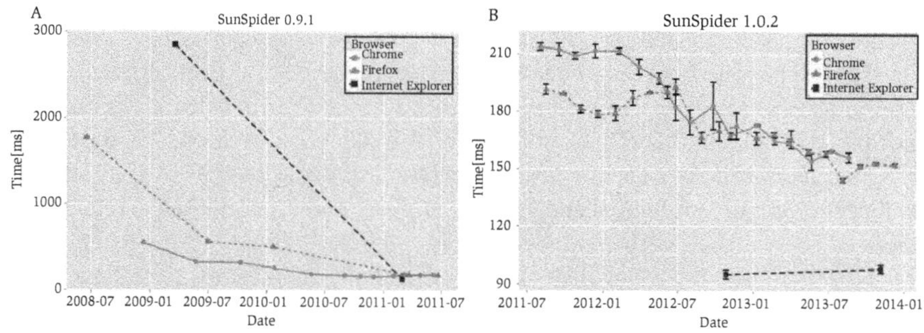

Source: Jonathan Tamary and Dror G. Feitelson. *The Rise of Chrome, PeerJ Computer Science 1: e28* (2015), https://peerj.com/articles/cs-28.pdf.

The observed improvements in IE's capabilities could potentially be attributed to greater competition within the browser market spurred by the Commission remedy promoting consumer choice. However, given that browsers are developed at a global, rather than regional level, it may be optimistic to attribute quality improvements to the Commission remedy specifically. It is possible that greater competitive intensity in Europe encouraged Microsoft to invest in improvements to IE globally; however those quality investments may equally have been driven by IE's declining position within the US, unrelated to the Commission remedy.

§2.04 CONCLUSIONS

The European Commission's cases against Microsoft have firmly established themselves among the landmark antitrust cases, in particular in relation to antitrust enforcement in the technology sector. However, these cases also highlight some of the challenges in designing effective remedies.

In the case of WMP, the 'untying' of WMP from Windows – while strictly speaking responsive to the legal concerns expressed by the Commission – did not result in an attractive remedy package: very few customers were interested in the unbundled version of Windows without WMP, perhaps unsurprisingly, given that the price was the same as that for Windows with WMP. These problems precluded a broad uptake of the WMP remedy, meaning that they were arguably never effectively put to the test.

In the workgroup server case, implementation of the remedies – provision of interoperability information to competing workgroup server OS developers – was similarly plagued by pricing concerns, which took several years to resolve. However, even after these concerns were resolved and more competitors obtained access to Microsoft's interoperability information, the structure of the workgroup server OSs market appeared not to be affected.

The remedy used in the IE case appeared to have a greater market impact. Europe saw a broader uptake of rival browsers after the implementation of the choice screen, and there is evidence that the Commission remedy made a positive contribution to browser competition when compared to the US, where there was no such intervention.

The Microsoft cases also demonstrate that the legal and procedural framework underlying the case can significantly affect the remedy. In particular, the European Commission is more constrained in the type of remedy it can impose in a prohibition decision than it is in the case of a settlement (commitment) decision. In the latter case, it is for the company under investigation to propose remedies, and those remedies may include measures the Commission would not have been able to impose unilaterally.

Nevertheless, the relevance of the Microsoft cases goes well beyond their remedies and the effectiveness of those remedies. These cases not only firmly established the European Commission as a global technology antitrust enforcer but also provided an analytical framework – upheld by the EU's General Court – that antitrust practitioners and enforcers can build on. Against a backdrop of increasing scrutiny of digital platforms, the Microsoft cases, and the lessons from those cases, will remain landmarks in the development of antitrust enforcement.

CHAPTER 3

Ex Post Assessment of European Competition Policy in the Payment Sector: The *Visa Europe* 2010 Commitments Decision*

Alen Veljan, Scott McInnes & Nicolas Petit

§3.01 INTRODUCTION

The payment sector has been subject to many European Union (EU) competition law decisions over the past twenty years. The decisions cover a wide range of competition law issues, from antitrust concerns (such as the European Commission's (EC) 2007 prohibition decisions against the GIE Cartes Bancaires about the so-called MERFA fee and against Visa Europe for having refused to grant a license to Morgan Stanley) to the review of proposed concentrations by the EC (amongst others in 2016 M.7873 Worldline/Equens/Paysquare; in 2018 Case M.9089 – Hellman & Friedman/Concardis Payment Group, in 2019 Case M.9452 – Global Payments/TSYS or in 2020 Worldline/Ingenico and Mastercard/Nets).

A particular focus of competition enforcement in the payment sector has concerned interchange fees (IF). Several competition law decisions by the EC and various national competition authorities (NCAs), as well as judgments from the EU courts, have sought to reduce IFs, before subjecting them to caps with the entry into force of the EU Interchange Fee Regulation (IFR) on 9 December 2015.[1]

---

* This report also benefitted from helpful comments and directions from Alfonso Lamadrid (Garrigues), Avantika Chowdhury (Oxera), Helène Bourguignon (MAPP Economics), and Dennis Carlton (University of Chicago Booth School of Business).

1. Regulation (EU) 2015/751 of the European Parliament and of the Council of 29 April 2015 on interchange fees for card-based payment transactions, OJ L 123/1, 19.5.2015.

This report ambitions to provide an *ex post* assessment of the EC's efforts to reduce IFs through competition enforcement. In particular, we focus on enforcement initiatives against Mastercard and Visa (Visa Inc. and Visa International, as well as Visa Europe) concerning IF. We study the economic impact of the EC Visa Europe 2010 commitment decision (the decision) with the support of a methodology known as Difference-in-Difference (DiD) analysis. Our ultimate goal is to get a first empirical sense of the decision's consequences on consumer welfare, and in turn to draw lessons for law and policy from this exercise.

A word on method. The report uses the Visa Europe 2010 commitments decision as the basis for an *ex post* economic analysis. The choice of this decision is based on the fact that it *covers both the IF applicable to cross-border transactions* within the European Economic Area (EEA), i.e., card issuer located in one EEA Member State and merchant located in another EEA Member State, *as well as the IF applicable to domestic transactions in nine EEA Member States (debit)*. In this, the Visa Europe 2010 commitments decision provides a better target than other decisions like the Visa 2002 and Mastercard 2007 decisions which only impacted the IF applicable to cross-border transactions within the EEA (which, at that point in time, only represented a very limited share of total payment transactions). Admittedly, the next EC decision of February 2014 regarding Visa Europe could have also been included in our *ex post* evaluation. But we considered that studying this last decision would create too much noise, given the then imminent implementation of the IFR (9 December 2015) and the inability to separate its impact from the latter event.[2]

Besides, we take a broad understanding of consumer welfare, not limited to price reductions towards customers. Instead of focusing on whether payment fees towards/single costs charged to merchants and subsequently cardholders have declined following enforcement, our analysis measures efficiency as a whole. Drawing on the premise that electronic payments constitute socially efficient and welfare-enhancing services,[3] several additional metrics can be used as proxies to measure the consumer welfare impacts of competition enforcement by the EC, namely size of card transactions and volumes, merchant acceptance, card issuing and the displacement of cash. With this background, our report thus aims to test whether the following hypothesis is true or not:

---

2. Visa Europe committed to a reduction of the IF applicable to cross-border acquired transactions, but this commitment was only effective as of 1 January 2015. Visa Europe also committed to a reduction of IF applicable to domestic credit card transactions in a number of EEA Member States, but those commitments were only meant to become applicable in approximately February 2016 and were therefore preceded by the IFR IF caps that became applicable as of 9 December 2015.
3. Proposal for a Regulation of the European Parliament and of the Council on interchange fees for card-based payment transactions, European Commission (24 July 2013), https://eur-lex.europa.eu/legal-content/EN/ALL/?uri=celex%3A52013PC0550. For the avoidance of doubt, we are not stipulating that card payments are socially efficient and welfare-enhancing, irrelevant of their price structure or level. Rather, by purposely disregarding the monetary characteristics (which, albeit altered post-enforcement, existed in both the pre-and post-enforcement environments) we aim to draw insights from other metrics, in order to subsequently assess any potential impacts of pricing alterations on system participants' behaviour.

The EC's competition enforcement has had a positive, statistically significant causal effect on the usage of consumer card payments, card issuance, merchant acceptance and cash displacement.

The report is structured as follows. Section §3.02 provides a brief introduction on the functioning of four-party card schemes (e.g., Mastercard, Visa, Cartes Bancaires, Bancontact), thereby highlighting the role of IFs. Section §3.03 provides a high level and selective review of the rich economic literature on two-sided markets. Section §3.04 offers a chronological overview of EU competition cases in relation to card payments between 2002 and 2019, highlighting the long-term evolution of the EC's thinking about IFs. This section also helps to lay down the factual background of the EC Visa Europe 2010 commitment decision, which forms the essence of our empirical analysis. Section §3.05 describes the data set and methodology used to perform our *ex post* evaluation of the decision. Section §3.06 presents our empirical results. Sections §3.07 and §3.08 discuss economic implications and look back in hindsight on the EC's 2002–2019 competition effort against IF. Section §3.09 concludes.

§3.02 THE FUNCTIONING OF FOUR-PARTY CARD SCHEMES

A transaction within a four-party card payment scheme involves five different parties: (1) the cardholder who uses a card to conduct a purchase; (2) the merchant (or retailer) who provides the goods or services, and accepts the card as a means of payment; (3) the card issuer (issuer) who issues the card to the cardholder, and is in charge of transferring funds for the purchased goods to the acquirer; (4) the acquirer who provides technical support to the merchant to allow it to accept card payments and thereupon receives the funds from the issuer, and passes those funds on to the merchant; and (5) the card scheme (e.g., Visa, Mastercard, Bancontact in Belgium, GIE Cartes Bancaires in France, Pagobancomat in Italy, Multibanco in Portugal, Dankort in Denmark, etc.) that, in particular, provides licences to issuers to issue cards with its brand, and to acquirers for the acquisition of transactions under its scheme/ brand.

The IF is a fee paid by the acquirer to the issuer on every single transaction. In the period preceding the regulation of the IF, fees could (i) either be determined by the card schemes, (ii) collectively by issuers and acquirers in a given country, or (iii) bilaterally between one issuer and one acquirer (although the cases of bilaterally agreed IF were relatively rare due to the arising complexities, in particular in a cross-border context where the issuer and acquirer were located in different countries). With this background, EC's enforcement only targeted the IF set by the schemes (rather than by issuers and acquirers, whether multilaterally or bilaterally). The fee set by the schemes have been referred to as multilateral IF (MIF), or fallback IF, or default IF. We call it the (default) IF.

The acquirer charges a fee to the merchant in relation to every transaction that it acquires for that merchant, typically referred to as the merchant service charge (MSC).

The MSC typically includes (1) the IF paid by the acquirer to the issuer, (2) the scheme fees paid by the acquirer to the card scheme, and (3) a service fee resulting in revenue/ a margin for the acquirer. The MSC is typically either a blended price (e.g., 2% of the amount of each transaction) or an 'IF plus' MSC (i.e., IF plus scheme fees plus an acquirer fee). The diagram below summarises the above.

It is noteworthy that, whilst interchange fee savings arising from reductions of the default IF by the schemes are automatically passed on by issuers to acquirers, it cannot be taken for granted that reductions of the default IF will be passed through by acquirers to merchants, and by merchants to their customers (e.g., consumers) in the form of lower (retail) prices. Multiple other factors (e.g., the scheme fees and the MSC) influence the intensity of pass-through from acquirers to third parties.

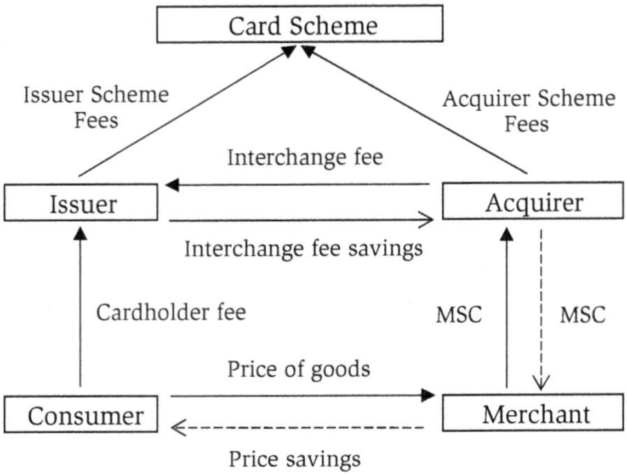

Two types of payment transactions can be distinguished: (1) domestic transactions which, at the time, were transactions where the issuer and the merchant were located in the same country; and (2) cross-border transactions which were transactions where the issuer and the merchant were located in two different countries. We refer to transactions involving an issuer located in one EEA Member State and a merchant located in another EEA Member State as Intra-EEA transactions. Transactions where the issuer is located outside of the EEA and the merchant located within an EEA Member State are referred to as inbound interregional transactions. The default IF set by Mastercard/Visa for Intra-EEA transactions applied to Intra-EEA transactions, but also as default for domestic transactions in EEA Member States unless a different domestic IF was applicable (either set by the scheme itself, or agreed bilaterally between an issuer and an acquirer, or agreed multilaterally by several issuers/ acquirers in that country).

To date, the entire body of EC enforcement initiatives against IF concerns consumer cards (cards issued to private individuals for personal expenses) at the point of sale.[4] The EC never issued any decision in relation to commercial cards (also known as corporate cards).[5] To our knowledge, the EC never publicly explained why it never issued a decision against the IF applicable to commercial cards. Some explanations may be drawn from the following facts. Commercial cards are less prevalent than consumer cards and therefore represent a lower amount of IF paid by acquirers (and often merchants) to issuers. In addition, American Express (Amex) is a significant player in the commercial card space, but the EC always took the view that competition law and in particular Article 101 TFEU (previously Article 81 EC) could not be enforced against Amex and its IF or equivalent fee arrangements since Amex was an independent company (Article 101 TFEU requires establishing existence of an 'association of undertakings', 'agreement', or 'concerted practice'). Therefore, a concern to maintain a level playing field between Mastercard/Visa on the one hand and Amex on the other, in the commercial card space, might explain the EC's forbearance towards Mastercard/Visa in relation to commercial cards IF.[6]

§3.03 LITERATURE REVIEW

The economic literature looks at card payment systems as a textbook model of 'two-sided market'. The model studies how platforms – here card payment systems – overcome the challenge of finding a 'viable business model' to bring distinct user groups – here merchants and cardholders – 'on board'.[7] A key insight from the economic literature is that the structure of prices on various sides of the market, rather than the (overall) price level, is what creates a possibility of economic exchange.

In the card payment case, systems that provide services to acquirers and issuers must set fees that allow simultaneous interactions between user groups. The platform can set a balancing mechanism, in our case an *interchange fee*, and thereby attempt to sponsor consumers' card usage with a cross-subsidy bearing on acquirers.[8] The impact of changes in the size and structure of the interchange fee will in turn depend on the pass-through behaviour of acquirers, merchants and issuers and is thus closely related to the competitive characteristics of the industry segment under consideration.[9] All network markets[10] exhibit externalities.[11] The most prominent externalities in payment

4. Not ATMs.
5. Essentially (pre-IFR) cards issued to companies (for onward distribution to their employees) or self-employed professionals for business expenses.
6. Throughout this report, we refer to credit/ debit/ prepaid cards for consumer cards, not for commercial cards.
7. Jean Tirole, *Market Failures and Public Policy*, 105(6) American Econ. Rev. 1665, 1682 (2015).
8. Jean-Charles Rochet and Jean Tirole, '*Platform Competition in Two-Sided Markets*', 1(3) J. Eur. Econ. Ass'n 990, 1029 (2003).
9. Alen Veljan, *Influence of Intra-and Inter-System Concentration on the Pre-regulated Setting of Interchange Fees Within Cooperative Card Payment Networks*, 21 J. Banking Reg. 139, 151 (2020).
10. Further examples include videogame platforms, newspapers and marketplaces. Jean-Charles Rochet and Jean Tirole, *Two-Sided Markets: An Overview*, Massachusetts Institute of Technology (12 March 2004), https://web.mit.edu/14.271/www/rochet_tirole.pdf.
11. Michael L. Katz and Carl Shapiro, *Systems Competition and Network Effects*, 8(2) J. Econ. Persps. 93, 115 (1994).

networks are adoption (card holding) and usage (card payment) externalities.[12] The value of membership to one user is affected by the addition or the loss of a marginal user. The demand for a network good is therefore a function of *both its price and the expected size of the network*. This is different from the demand for a standard good which is only a function of price.[13]

In a two-sided market, the platform sets prices in light of the demand elasticities of the various user groups. In card payment networks, the price will typically be set to maximise the overall profits to network participants, recover common costs, and provide the service to the largest possible number of members.[14] Economists and policymakers generally consider that a single interchange fee is more efficient to equilibrate payment markets than bilaterally negotiated agreements.[15] Accordingly, socially efficient pricing may result in fees for participants on a particular side (in our case card issuers) below marginal costs.[16] The economic literature suggests that this is not problematic even under an antitrust eye. In his Nobel Prize address, Jean Tirole cautioned against '*misleadingly complain about predation*' and called regulators to refrain from '*applying standard antitrust ideas where they do not belong*'.[17] The EC has followed Tirole's admonition by not raising a categorical objection against IF.[18]

Merchants' lower price elasticity relative to cardholders explains the allocation of IF costs to the acquirer side. Strong competition within the merchant sector and the convenience benefits cardholders reap when using card payments create strong incentives for merchants to accept card payments. Additionally, when cardholders collect rewards on certain cards, their willingness to pay with different means like cash or checks is even lower.[19] This signals that merchants *must take* cards and lack power to refuse card payments.[20] Some studies suggest that merchants might even accept cards in instances where the marginal costs exceed the marginal benefits of the card payment.[21] Last, demand elasticities of network participants are inversely related to the size of the platform. As the platform share of market output grows, network

---

12. Sujit Chakravorti, *Externalities in Payment Card Networks: Theory and Evidence*, Federal Reserve Bank of Chicago (18 November 2009), https://www.chicagofed.org/publications/policy-discussion-papers/2009/pdp-8.
13. Katz and Shapiro, *supra* n. 11.
14. Julian Wright, *The Determinants of Optimal Interchange Fees in Payment Systems*, 52(1) J. Indus. Econ. 1, 26 (2004).
15. William F. Baxter, *Bank Interchange of Transactional Paper: Legal and Economic Perspectives*, 26(3) The J. L. & Econ. 541, 588, (1983). In addition, an IF avoids the free-rider problem that arises when the number of participants within a network increase.
16. David S. Evans, *The Antitrust Economics of Multi-Sided Platform Markets*, 20(2) Yale J. Reg. 327, 379, (2003).
17. Tirole, *supra* n. 7.
18. *See* the EC's legal interpretation in Commission Decision 2002/914/EC of 24 July 2002 on COMP/29.373 – Visa International – Multilateral Interchange Fee (notified under document number C(2002) 2698), OJ L 318/17, 22.11.2002.
19. Jean-Charles Rochet and Jean Tirole, *Cooperation Among Competitors: Some Economics of Payment Card Associations*, 33(4) The RAND J. Econ. (2002).
20. John Vickers, *Public Policy and the Invisible Price: Competition Law, Regulation and the Interchange Fee*, 4(1) Competition L.J. 5, 21 (2005).
21. Jean-Charles Rochet and Jean Tirole, *Must-Take Cards: Merchant Discounts and Avoided Costs*, 9(3) J. Eur. Econ. Ass'n 462, 495 (2011).

participants become more dependent on the payment system and less elastic to pricing changes.[22]

Another important insight from the economic literature stresses the ambiguous contribution to social welfare of increased competition between payment schemes. When antitrust decision makers first laid their eyes on payment markets, they understandably hypothesised that blunted competition between card schemes was a possible cause for high (and above socially optimal) IF. Guthrie and Wright however showed that the reverse conclusion was plausible. As card schemes compete for partnerships with issuing banks, they increase benefits towards issuers. With increasing scheme competition, all things equal, IF rise, leading to inflated costs of card processing for merchants. Due to this dysfunctional competition, scheme competition can increase rather than decrease - as would be the predictable outcome with most industries - consumer prices. Further, the risk of a differentiated treatment of proprietary card schemes that are not utilising IF to achieve a desired fee structure and cooperative card schemes can ultimately result in a competitive advantage.[23]

Of course, the efficiency of the IF at 'bringing all sides on board' can be defeated in two sets of circumstances. First, the IF will not raise scheme output in instances where merchants can perfectly (without friction) surcharge consumers for the use of costly payment cards.[24][25] Second, the IF ends up being paid fully by consumers in all instances where perfectly competitive issuing, acquiring and merchant markets result in full pass-through of any interchange increases or decreases.[26] Leaving aside these mostly hypothetical scenarios, scholars and practitioners have spilt much ink trying to determine private and socially optimal IF levels. Initially, the EC endorsed an issuer cost methodology as a benchmark for compliant IF. The EC abandoned this approach after the Mastercard 2007 decision and adopted a new methodology known as the *tourist test* or *merchant indifference test (MIT)*.[27] Based upon the marginal costs and benefits of accepting a card payment, and under consideration of the applicable externalities, a level of IF is identified that makes the merchant indifferent between accepting card payments versus other payment instruments. When the tourist test is retained, any change in pricing within one side of the market will cause spillover effects on the other.[28] Due to the presence of multiple cost components within the network in addition to the interchange fee (such as scheme fees and acquirer processing fee that both typically form part of the MSC charged by the acquirer to the merchant as well as

---

22. Jean-Charles Rochet and Julian Wright, *Credit Card Interchange Fees*, ECB Working Paper Series (1138), 4, 30, (2009).
23. Graeme Guthrie and Julian Wright, *Competing Payment Schemes*, 55(1) The J. Indus. Econ. 37, 67 (2007).
24. Rochet and Tirole, *supra* n. 19.
25. Joshua Gans and Stephen King, *The Neutrality of Interchange Fees in Payment Systems*, 3(1) The B.E. J. in Econ. Analysis & Pol'y 1, 16 (2003).
26. Richard Schmalensee and David S. Evans, *The Economics of Interchange Fees and Their Regulation: An Overview*, MIT Sloan Working Paper No 4548-05, (23 May 2005), http://dx.doi.org/10.2139/ssrn.744705.
27. Rochet and Tirole, *supra* n. 21.
28. Glen Weyl, *A Price Theory of Multi-Sided Platforms*, 100(4) American Econ. Rev. 1642, 1672 (2010).

a cardholder fee that the issuer may charge to the cardholder), an alteration of other cost components can potentially neutralise any alterations of the interchange fee in terms of final pricing towards merchants and/ or cardholders.[29]

§3.04 OVERVIEW OF EU COMPETITION CASES IN RELATION TO CARD PAYMENTS: THE INTERCHANGE FEE 'SAGA'

The EC policy towards IFs has followed six consecutive 'waves'. Whilst our report seeks to evaluate the 2010 Visa Europe commitment decision, a brief summary of the other decisions adopted by the EC helps apprehend the context of the decision and the developmental path of competition policy towards IF. This section is likely to be of most interest to law minded readers:

(1) July 2002 - Visa International negative clearance decision.[30]
(2) December 2007 - Mastercard infringement decision.[31]
(3) December 2010 - Visa Europe (debit card) commitment decision.[32]
(4) July 2014 - Visa Europe (credit card and cross-border acquiring) commitment decision.[33]
(5) January 2019 - infringement decision against Mastercard in relation to cross-border acquiring (also sometimes referred to as central acquiring).[34]

29. Alen Veljan, *Regulating the Uncontrollable: The Development of Card Scheme Fees in Payments Markets in Light of Recent Policy Intervention*, 29 Res. in L. & Econ. (2020).
30. Commission Decision 2002/914/EC - Visa International - Multilateral Interchange Fee, *supra* n. 18.
31. Commission Decision 2009/C 264/04 of 19 December 2007, on Case COMP/34.579 — MasterCard, Case COMP/36.518 — EuroCommerce, Case COMP/38.580 — Commercial Cards (notified under document C(2007) 6474), OJ C 264, 6.11.2009.

    Earlier that year the Commission had issued Commission Decision 2009/C 183/05 of 3 December on Case COMP/D1/37860 - Morgan Stanley/Visa International and Visa Europe (notified under document C(2007) 4471), OJ C 183/6, 5.8.2009. That decision addressed the fact that Visa Europe had refused to grant Morgan Stanley a license to participate in the Visa scheme as acquirer due to the fact that Morgan Stanley was operating a competing card scheme in the US, called Discover. And a few dates later, the EC adopted another decision in the payment sectors involving the French domestic card scheme, GIE Cartes Bancaires (CB), and more particular a fee called 'MERFA' that some CB members were required to pay to other CB members (Commission Decision of 17 October 2007 on Case COMP/D1/38606 - groupement des Cartes Bancaires 'CB'). For the sake of (relative) brevity, we do not address those two decisions in the report.
32. Commission Decision of 8 December 2010 on Case COMP/39.398 — VISA MIF (notified under document C(2010) 8760 final). The commitments are available here: https://ec.europa.eu/competition/antitrust/cases/dec_docs/39398/39398_6186_3.pdf.
33. Commission Decision of 26 February 2014 on Case AT.39398 - VISA MIF (notified under document C(2014) 1199 final). The commitments are available here: https://ec.europa.eu/competition/antitrust/cases/dec_docs/39398/39398_9729_3.pdf.
34. Commission Decision of 22 January 2019 on Case AT.40049 - MasterCard II (notified under document C(2019) 241 final).

(6) April 2019 – two commitment decisions against Visa Inc./ Visa International and Mastercard in relation to inbound interregional transactions.[35]

Overview of EU competition cases in relation to card payments: the interchange fee 'saga'

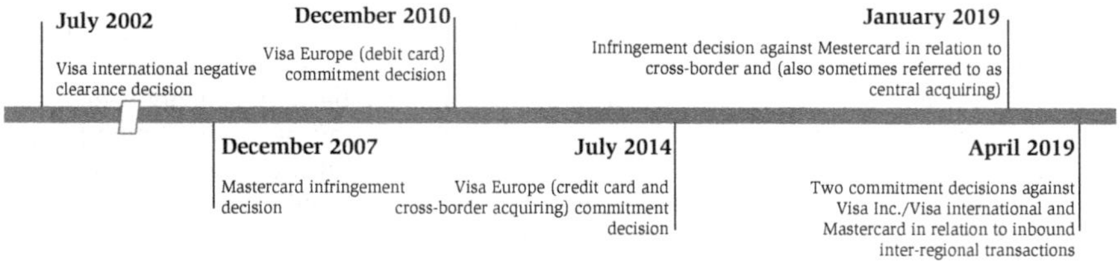

[A] The Background to the EC's Competition Law Enforcement

The history of the EC's enforcement against card schemes started in 1977, when Visa International notified its rules, including rules on IF, to the EC seeking prior approval of its IF arrangement. At the time, business and economic organisations participating in agreements with other firms could seek from the EC a negative clearance or, in the alternative, an exemption from antitrust liability under Article 101 TFEU (at the time, Article 81 EC). In 1985, the EC issued a comfort letter to Visa International. However, a complaint by the British Retail Consortium (BRC) against Visa's and Mastercard's default cross-border IFs in 1992 prompted the EC to re-open its investigation into Visa International. The comfort letter was withdrawn later that year. Between 1992 and 1995, Mastercard also made various notifications to the EC in relation to various schemes rules, including its IF arrangements.

In 1997, EuroCommerce lodged a competition law complaint against various aspects of the Visa and Mastercard scheme rules. The complaint focused on a range of issues including IFs but also the 'honour all' cards rule (HACR), the no-discrimination rule (NDR), etc. EuroCommerce alleged that the IF paid by the acquirer to the issuer was passed on by the acquirer to the merchant, thereby artificially inflating the level of MSC. The MSC overcharge was then typically passed on by the merchant to their customers (e.g., consumers) in the form of higher (retail) prices, ultimately resulting in consumers having to pay for an allegedly 'excessive' level of IF.

35. Commission Decision of 29 April 2019 on Case AT.40049 – MasterCard II (notified under document C(2019) 3033 final). The commitments are available here: https://ec.europa.eu/competition/antitrust/cases/dec_docs/39398/39398_14155_4.pdf. Commission Decision of 29 April 2019 on Case AT.39398 – Visa MIF (notified under document C(2019) 3034 final). The commitments are available here: https://ec.europa.eu/competition/antitrust/cases/dec_docs/39398/39398_14155_4.pdf.

The complainant wanted the EC to enforce its competition law powers to reduce the IF paid by acquirers to issuers, ideally to zero in the expectation that (1) acquirers would pass on to merchants this reduction of IF in the form of a lower MSC, and (2) in turn merchants would pass-on the reduction of the MSC to consumers in the form of lower retail prices. To that end, EuroCommerce argued before the EC that the IF was akin to a price-fixing cartel:

> the interchange fee as a mechanism to shift onto merchants (and indirectly onto customers who pay by means other than Visa card) the costs of free advantages offered to cardholders. Since the level of the fee is said to be agreed on between the banks without any pressure from the market, the setting of the MIF amounts, according to EuroCommerce, to a price-fixing cartel. EuroCommerce considers that the MIF is not indispensable for the Visa scheme to function successfully, and has provided examples of payment card schemes, which, it claims, function without a MIF.[36]

In turn, EuroCommerce requested that the EC impose on Visa and Mastercard to set the default Intra-EEA IF to zero. In 1999, the Commission launched proceedings against Visa International.

[B] Visa International 2001: Negative Clearance Decision

In 2001, the EC left the issue of IF on the backburner and issued a negative clearance decision covering the other rules contained in the Visa International scheme rules and subject to the EuroCommerce complaint, such as the HACR,[37] the NDR,[38] territorial licensing,[39] modified rules on cross-border issuing and cross-border acquiring[40] and the No Acquiring Without Issuing (NAWI) rule.[41] The EC concluded that those various rules did not restrict competition and therefore did not fall foul of Article 101(1) TFEU (previously, Article 81(1) EC); the only exception being the NDR which, according to the EC, did restrict competition, but not to an appreciable extent and therefore did not fall foul of Article 101(1) TFEU either.

---

36. Commission Decision 2002/914/EC – Visa International – Multilateral Interchange Fee, *supra* n. 18, at paras 27–28.
37. The Visa HACR required merchants to accept all valid Visa-branded cards, irrespective of the identity of the issuer, the nature of the transaction and the type of card being issued.
38. The NDR prevented merchants from surcharging card transactions or discounting for cash payments.
39. The licences granted by Visa International to issue cards or acquire transactions were granted country-by-country.
40. Initially, the Visa International rules did not allow Visa member banks to issue cards to cardholders outside their country of establishment or to acquire merchants in other Member States, except in very limited circumstances. However, Visa International had significantly increased the possibilities for cross-border issuing of Visa cards and cross-border acquiring of Visa transactions. Following the latest amendments, Visa International allowed cross-border issuing and cross-border acquiring without the prior establishment of a branch or subsidiary in the country concerned.
41. The NAWI rule required a financial institution to first issue a significant number of Visa cards before it would potentially be allowed to also acquire Visa transactions. This rule was there to promote the development of the system by ensuring a large cardholder base, thereby making the system more attractive for merchants.

In December 2001, EuroCommerce started annulment proceedings against the EC decision before the General Court (previously, the Court of First Instance),[42] which it later withdrew (the removal from the Court's register happened in March 2003).[43]

Whilst there is no need to discuss further the EC 2001 decision since it did not deal with IF, it is interesting to see that all the scheme rules under consideration were either amended and/or abolished by the card schemes as part of the EC's further competition law enforcement, and/or further to EU legislation proposed by the EC. This shows a clear evolution in the EC's position in relation to those rules over the years. For example:

- effective 1 January 2005, both Visa and Mastercard repealed their NAWI rule in the EEA;
- effective 1 January 2005, Mastercard also abolished the NDR in the EEA. Visa did not abolish that rule until EU legislation proposed by the EC, namely the 2007 Payment Services Directive (PSD1) allowed merchants to surcharge or discount for the use of a given payment instrument (unless prohibited or limited by each Member State's national legislation);[44]
- following a request from the EC, Mastercard also introduced a new cross-border acquiring license for its debit card 'Maestro'. As will be described below, the Visa and Mastercard rules on cross-border acquiring in particular were later on subject to further enforcement (resulting in the Visa Europe 2010 and 2014 commitment decisions, and an infringement decision against Mastercard in 2019 with a fine of approximately EUR 570 million);
- the 2015 IFR, as proposed by the EC in 2013, relaxed the HACR (more specifically the so-called 'honour all products' aspect of the HACR therefore allowing merchants to, for example, only accept Visa/Mastercard debit cards but not Visa/Mastercard credit cards, etc.), and prohibited territorial licences as well as any restrictions on cross-border issuing and cross-border acquiring.

[C] Visa International 2002 Exemption Decision

The EC position on IF became clearer in the course of events leading to the granting of an exemption to Visa International in 2002. During the procedure, the EC hinted that IFs could not be categorically deemed restrictive of competition, and *that this was a factual question requiring economic analysis.*[45]

---

42. Case T-336/01, *EuroCommerce A.I.S.B.L. v. Commission of European Communities* [2001] C 84, 06.04.2002.
43. Case T-336/01, *EuroCommerce A.I.S.B.L. v. Commission of European Communities* [2001] C 146, 21.06.2003.
44. Article 52(3) of Directive 2007/64/EC of the European Parliament and of the Council of 13 November 2007 on payment services in the internal market amending Directives 97/7/EC, 2002/65/EC, 2005/60/EC and 2006/48/EC and repealing Directive 97/5/EC, OJ L 319, 5.12.2007, pp. 1-36.
45. In a supplementary statement of objections as summarised in its 2002 decision, the EC defined the relevant markets, thereby hinting that an effects analysis was needed. The EC stated that the

In its decision, the EC concluded that the default Intra-EEA IF was not '*technically necessary for the operation of the Visa payment scheme. [...] The only provisions necessary for the operation of the Visa four-party payment scheme, apart from technical arrangements on message formats and the like, are the obligation of the creditor bank to accept any payment validly entered into the system by a debtor bank and the prohibition on (ex post) pricing by one bank to another.*'[46]

As regards the restriction of competition, the EC concluded that:

> 64. [...] *the MIF has a* ***restrictive effect*** *on competition among Visa issuers and among Visa acquirers.* [...]
>
> 67. [...] *Issuing banks are required to charge acquiring banks a certain fixed fee and are therefore prevented from developing at wholesale level an individual pricing policy vis-à-vis acquiring banks in so far as they provide services to them (for example a 'payment guarantee' for most transactions).*
>
> 68. The MIF moreover has as its effect to distort the behaviour of acquiring banks vis-à-vis their customers (at resale level), because it creates an important cost element (according to EuroCommerce on average approximately 80% of the merchant fee) which is likely to constitute a de facto floor for the fees charged to the merchants they acquire since otherwise, the acquiring bank would make a loss on its acquiring activity.
>
> 69. *However, the Commission does not consider the MIF agreement to be a restriction of competition by object, since a MIF agreement in a four-party payment system such as that of Visa has as its objective to increase the stability and efficiency of operation of that system (see section 8.1.1 below), and indirectly to strengthen competition between payment systems by thus allowing four-party systems to compete more effectively with three-party systems.*[47]

The EC held that the restrictive effect of the IF was enhanced by the implementation of other schemes rules and practices such as the HACR, the NDR and blended MSCs agreed between acquirers and merchants (instead of 'IF plus' MSCs) which hinder the merchants' ability to manage their payment costs. The restrictions of competition were appreciable and there was at least potentially an effect on trade between Member States.

Turning to the question of whether the default cross-border IF could benefit from an exemption under Article 101(3) TFEU (previously, Article 81(3) EC), the EC considered that a market analysis on a case-by-case basis was necessary:

> As a preliminary remark, it is not the case that an agreement concerning prices is always to be classified as a cartel and thus as inherently non-exemptible. Examples exist of agreements on prices which can meet the conditions for an exemption.

---

relevant markets (to be considered as part of the breach related to Article 101(1) TFEU were: (1) the markets for systems/networks where Visa International and Mastercard compete, as well downstream markets, i.e., (2) the intra-system market on the issuing side (where card issuers compete); and (3) the intra-system market on the acquiring side (where card acquirers compete). The geographic scope, whilst historically national, was left open by the EC.

46. Commission Decision 2002/914/EC – Visa International – Multilateral Interchange Fee, *supra* n. 18, at paras 59–60.
47. Commission Decision 2002/914/EC – Visa International – Multilateral Interchange Fee, *supra* n. 18, at paras 64 and 67–69.

> Furthermore, a MIF is not a price charged to a consumer, but a remuneration paid between banks who must deal with each other for the settlement of a card payment transaction and thus have no choice of partner. The absence of some sort of default rule on the terms of settlement could lead to abuse by the issuing bank, which is in a position of monopsony as regards the acquiring bank for the settlement of an individual payment transaction. Thus, *some kind of default arrangement is necessary, but the question of whether it qualifies for exemption or not will depend on the details of the arrangement.*[48]

In response, Visa International proposed a new (cost-based) methodology to determine a maximum level for its Intra-EEA IF, as well as maximum amounts. The EC found the proposed revisions to meet the conditions for an exemption.

Let us look closer at the changes introduced by Visa International. First, Visa International committed to reducing its cross-border credit IF from approximately 1.1% to reach a weighted average of *0.7%* by 2007. In addition, Visa International committed to reducing its cross-border debit IF to a yearly weighted average of *EUR 0.28* before the end of 2002. The average debit card transaction value in 2019 was EUR 57,[49] meaning that the average debit IF accepted by the EC was almost *0.5%*

Second, Visa International offered to introduce more objectivity in its Intra-EEA IF setting. To that end, Visa International committed to set the default Intra-EEA IF by sole reference to three costs components borne by issuers and that were considered by EC as benefitting merchants, i.e. (1) the cost of processing transactions; (2) the cost of providing the 'payment guarantee' to the merchant; and (3) the cost of the free-funding period extended by the issuer to the cardholder (for transactions related to credit cards).

Third, Visa International allowed acquirers to disclose the level of the IF and the cost components used for calculating the IF cap to merchants.[50]

The exemption was valid until 31 December 2007.

[D] Mastercard 2007 Infringement Decision

Following the Visa International 2002 decision, Mastercard informed the Commission in July 2003 of its intention to initiate proceedings against the EC under Article 232 EC (failure to act), unless the EC took a formal position with respect to Mastercard's Intra-EEA fallback IF. The EC then issued two SOs (2003, 2006) and a letter of facts (2007). There was no commitment in the Mastercard case – instead the EC reached an infringement decision against Mastercard Incorporated, Mastercard International Incorporated and Mastercard Europe SPRL (together Mastercard) in December 2007. The main conclusions reached by the EC are summarised hereafter.

First, the definition of relevant market was identical to the Visa 2002 decision.

---

48. Commission Decision 2002/914/EC – Visa International – Multilateral Interchange Fee, *supra* n. 18, at para. 79.
49. European Central Bank – Statistical Data Warehouse (https://sdw.ecb.europa.eu).
50. After the Visa 2002 decision, both Visa and Mastercard agreed to publish their intra-European cross-border interchange fees on their respective website (but not yet domestic IF).

Second, the EC concluded that Mastercard remained an association of undertakings subject to Article 101 TFEU (previously Article 81 EC). This conclusion was not a given, because Mastercard had gone through an initial public offering (IPO) in May 2006 so that issuers and acquirers no longer had ownership and control over Mastercard and in particular were no longer involved in the process of determining the level of the default Intra-EEA IF.

Third, since the Intra-EEA IF constituted an artificial, common de facto floor for the MSC charged by acquirers to merchants, it had the *effect* of restricting competition between acquirers; and that restrictive effect was appreciable and had at least a potential effect on trade between Member States. The EC left open the possibility that the Intra-EEA IF was a restriction of competition by object: '*[...] given that it can be clearly established that the MasterCard MIF has the effect of appreciably restricting and distorting competition to the detriment of merchants in the acquiring markets it is not necessary to reach a definite conclusion as to whether the MasterCard MIF is a restriction by object [...]*'.[51]

Fourth, the Intra-EEA IF was not objectively necessary to the operation of the Mastercard scheme and therefore could not be absolved as an 'ancillary restriction' of competition. The scheme could function on the basis of the remuneration of issuers by cardholders, and of acquirers by merchants. Unlike restrictions which are necessary for implementing a main operation, restrictions which are merely desirable for the commercial success of that operation, or which offer greater efficiency, can be examined only within the framework of Article 101(3) EC.[52]

Fifth, Mastercard therefore had to demonstrate that the level of the Intra-EEA IF met the conditions for an exemption under Article 101(3) EC. In the MEMO that accompanied the EC decision, the EC stated that '*The Commission sought to find an agreement with MasterCard on an acceptable MIF. However, the modifications proposed by MasterCard were not appropriate to bring its MIF in line with Article [101] 81 (3) of the EC Treaty. The Commission therefore continued its investigation.*'[53] The EC concluded in its decision that Mastercard had failed to demonstrate that its default Intra-EEA IF met the conditions for exemption, and therefore that it was in breach of Article 101 TFEU.[54]

---

51. Commission Decision on Case COMP/34.579—MasterCard, Case COMP/36.518—Euro Commerce, Case COMP/38.580—Commercial Cards, *supra* n. 31, at para. 407.
52. Commission Decision on Case COMP/34.579—MasterCard, Case COMP/36.518—Euro Commerce, Case COMP/38.580—Commercial Cards, *supra* n. 31, paras 526–527.
53. *Antitrust: Commission prohibits MasterCard's intra-EEA Multilateral Interchange Fees – frequently asked questions*, European Commission (19 December 2007), https://ec.europa.eu/commission/presscorner/detail/en/MEMO_07_590.
54. Note that the scope of the Mastercard 2007 decision was the same as the 2002 Visa International decision, i.e., the default IF applicable to Intra-EEA transactions. The EC 2007 decision states that it concerns the Mastercard default Intra-EEA IF as it applies not only to Intra-EEA transactions, but also to domestic transactions in a number of EEA Member States. However, in practice, and contrary to what the EC stated in its 2007 decision and its contemporaneous press release, by the time the EC decision was adopted in December 2007 the Mastercard-set default

Mastercard nonetheless benefited from an immunity from fines because it had notified its IF arrangements to the EC between 1992 and 1997. However, the EC requested that Mastercard brought the infringement to an end within six months of the notification of the decision, on threat of a daily penalty payment of 3.5% of Mastercard's daily consolidated global turnover in the preceding business year, which represented approximately USD 450,000 per day.

In the absence of guidance from the EC as to what level of default Intra-EEA IF it would consider exemptible, Mastercard first reduced the Intra-EEA IF to zero in June 2008.[55] Mastercard and the EC then started a dialogue as to the level of default Intra-EEA IF that the EC would consider exemptible. The EC requested that the IF be set on the basis of the *tourist test* methodology, which was later renamed and referred to as the MIT. The test seeks to set the IF at a level at which merchants are indifferent as to whether a payment is made by a card or by cash.[56] The discussions between the EC and Mastercard resulted in Mastercard offering '*Unilateral Undertakings*' to the EC in 2009,[57] including a weighted average default Intra-EEA IF level of *0.2%* for debit and prepaid cards and *0.3%* for credit cards. Those levels became the benchmarks for the future EC competition law enforcement (*see* below) as well as the enforcement by most (but not all) NCAs, as well as the levels that were proposed by the EC in the draft IFR that it published in July 2013 (and, which became applicable in December 2015 as far as IF are concerned).

In the meantime, Mastercard had appealed the EC's 2007 decision to the General Court, but the General Court upheld the EC's decision in its entirety in 2012. Mastercard then appealed the EC 2007 decision, as confirmed by the General Court, to the Court of Justice, which again upheld the EC's 2007 decision in its entirety in 2014.[58] The Courts upheld in particular the EC's finding that despite its 2006 IPO, Mastercard remained an association of undertakings because (1) the banks had retained certain decision-making powers on some key issues and (2) Mastercard, issuers, acquirers and Mastercard's new shareholders all had an interest in a high default Intra-EEA IF. The

---

Intra-EEA IF did not apply to domestic transactions in any EEA Member State; therefore, the practical scope of the decision was the same as the Visa 2002 decision: only Intra-EEA transactions.

55. *Antitrust: Commission notes MasterCard's decision to temporarily repeal its cross-border Multilateral Interchange Fees within the EEA*, European Commission (12 June 2008), https://ec.europa.eu/commission/presscorner/detail/en/MEMO_08_397.
56. Despite para. 38 of the Visa 2001 decision: 'The costs of accepting cash are largely administrative costs, and hard to compare with the cost of accepting cards.'
57. *Antitrust: Commissioner Kroes takes note of MasterCard's decision to cut cross-border Multilateral Interchange Fees (MIFs) and to repeal recent scheme fee increases*, European Commission (1 April 2009), https://ec.europa.eu/commission/presscorner/detail/en/IP_09_515; *Antitrust: Commissioner Kroes notes MasterCard's decision to cut cross-border Multilateral Interchange Fees (MIFs) and to repeal recent scheme fee increases – frequently asked questions*, European Commission (1 April 2009), https://ec.europa.eu/commission/presscorner/detail/en/MEMO_09_143.
58. Anecdotally, the hearing in the Court of Justice took place on 4th July, and the judgment was rendered on 9/11 (on the same day as the judgment in the *Cartes Bancaires* case – C-67/13 P), which are obviously dates that can make a US company wonder if the choice of dates by the Court is entirely accidental … .

Courts also upheld the existence of a restriction of competition by effect and the absence of objective necessity of the default Intra-EEA IF.

The EC's 2007 decision, as upheld by the EU Courts, is the decision that a number of merchants have relied upon since 2012 to seek damages from Mastercard and Visa as part of ongoing follow-on litigations, primarily (but not solely) in United Kingdom (UK) Courts. It also forms the basis for a consumer class action that is currently ongoing in the UK against Mastercard for an amount of GBP 14 billion.[59]

[E] December 2010: Visa Europe (Debit Card) Commitments

After the Mastercard 2007 decision, the EC 'turned back' once again to Visa. In 2009, the EC issued a Statement of Objections (SO) against Visa Europe, which based on the statements in the 2010 Visa Europe commitment decision, found that: (1) the relevant market in scope was the market for card acquiring services, and that those markets were still to be regarded as national; (2) Visa remained an association of undertakings (unlike Mastercard, Visa Europe was still owned and controlled by issuers and acquirers, so this qualification was not contested by Visa Europe); (3) Visa Europe's default debit IF, both for Intra-EEA as well as domestic debit card transactions in EEA Member States, restricted competition *by object* and effect; (4) those default IF were not objectively necessarily to the operation of the Visa Europe scheme; (5) they were capable of appreciably and negatively affecting cross-border trade between EEA Member States and; (6) Visa Europe had not demonstrated that the conditions for an exemption were met which, whilst not specifically addressed in the commitments decision, implicitly means that the EC no longer considered the levels of default debit card cross-border IF set out in the 2002 Visa International decision exemptible (presumably the EC was of the view that only the 0.2% weighted average applied by Mastercard since 2009 was exemptible).

Like Visa International earlier, Visa Europe offered commitments to the EC that were made binding in an EC decision dated 8 December 2010. Visa Europe committed to reducing the debit/prepaid Intra-EEA IF to 0.2% weighted average as it applied to cross-border transactions (thereby ensuring a level playing field with the Mastercard 2009 *Unilateral Undertakings* as far as debit/prepaid cards are concerned) but also potentially to domestic transactions in some EEA countries (although that was not the case in practice).

However, Visa Europe also committed to reducing to the same level debit IF applicable to *domestic* transactions in nine EEA countries where Visa Europe was in charge of setting the default domestic debit IF at the time.[60] This was a new approach since the EC had never before requested Visa Europe or Mastercard to reduce the levels

59. *See, e.g.*, Kristin Ridley, *UK Supreme Court Enables $18.5 Billion Class Action Against Mastercard*, Reuters (21 December 2020, 11:38 am) https://www.reuters.com/article/britain-mastercard-court/uk-supreme-court-enables-18-5-billion-class-action-against-mastercard-idUSKBN28L16J.

60. Greece, Hungary, Iceland, Ireland, Italy, Malta, Sweden, Luxembourg, Netherlands (in the last two countries, only Visa prepaid cards were issued by then – no Visa debit cards).

of domestic IF (it had left the issue of domestic IF entirely to NCAs). The EC reported that this represented a reduction of about 60% on average.[61] Visa Europe also committed to a few other measures reflecting what Mastercard had offered in its 2009 *Unilateral Undertakings*; however, we refrain from addressing those in detail here. The commitments were applicable for a period of four years from the notification of the decision (i.e., until approximately December 2014).

Interestingly, Visa Europe subsequently requested the EC to amend (i.e., to increase) the level of the above debit card IF caps that it had committed to, but the EC rejected Visa Europe's request by its decision of 31 July 2012. Visa Europe initially sought the annulment of that EC decision before the General Court on 10 October 2012. It would appear from the main pleas and arguments[62] that Visa Europe had submitted an economic study that resulted in higher levels of debit IF on the basis of the tourist test or MIT than the 0.2% weighted average that it had committed to - and, as a result, it sought an increase of those levels; which the EC refused. Visa Europe eventually discontinued its appeal in March 2014.[63]

[F] February 2014: Visa Europe Commitments

In July 2012, the EC issued a supplementary SO against Visa Europe in relation to its default credit IF, as well as its rules on which IF applies to domestic transactions that are processed by an acquirer located in another EEA country than the country where the merchant and issuer and located (i.e., cross-border acquired transaction). The SO apparently stated that: (1) Visa Europe was an association of undertakings (again, this was not disputed by Visa Europe); (2) its default cross-border and domestic credit card IF restricted competition by object and effect; same for the Visa Europe rule that stated that a cross-border acquirer should pay the IF of the country where the merchant and the issuer are located (it is not clear from the EC decision what the counterfactual is); (3) those default credit IF and the rule determining which IF should apply to a cross-border acquired transaction were not objectively necessary to the operation of the Visa Europe scheme; (4) whilst not specifically addressed in the commitment decision, implicitly it is clear that the EC no longer considered the level of default credit cross-border IF set out in the 2002 Visa International decision (i.e., 0.7%) exemptible. Visa Europe offered commitments to the EC, which were made binding in an EC commitment decision dated 26 February 2014. As part of those commitments, Visa Europe agreed essentially to the following (in chronological order).

First, Visa Europe committed to reducing its default Intra-EEA credit IF to a weighted average of 0.3% (i.e., the same level applied by Mastercard since its 2009 'Unilateral Undertakings', therefore ensuring a level playing field between the two competing schemes in relation to cross-border credit transactions).

---

61. *Antitrust: Vice President Almunia welcomes Visa Europe's proposal to cut interbank fees for debit cards*, European Commission (26 April 2010), https://ec.europa.eu/commission/presscorner/detail/en/IP_10_462.
62. https://eur-lex.europa.eu/legal-content/EN/TXT/?uri=CELEX%3A62012TN0447.
63. Case T-447/12 *Visa Europe Ltd and Others v. Commission*, 30.4.2014, ECLI:EU:T:2014:247.

Second, as of 1 January 2015, Visa Europe committed to a rule change in relation to cross-border acquiring. In the 2010 (debit card) commitment decision, Visa Europe had committed '*to continue to require Visa Europe members to register all MIF rates and apply them to cross-border issued and cross-border acquired transactions*' – i.e., the domestic IF of the country of the merchant/ issuer should apply to domestic transactions irrespective of whether the acquirer is a local/ domestic acquirer or a foreign/ cross-border acquirer.[64] Visa Europe committed to a change: in the case where a merchant relied on a cross-border acquirer, the applicable IF would be either the domestic IF of the country of the merchant/ issuer (as was the case until now) or 0.2%0.3% (knowing that, in practice, the latter would almost always be lower). This commitment was meant to encourage merchants to get connected to acquirers in other EEA countries than their own.

Third, as of 1 January 2015, Visa Europe accepted a reduction of the (credit and debit) IF paid by the acquirer of an EEA merchant to an issuer located in some select non-EEA countries (including Switzerland, Turkey and Israel), therefore giving the commitment decision a form of extra-territorial effect outside of the EEA.

Fourth, Visa Europe adopted a few other measures, including some that never became effective in practice with the IFR superseding them as from December 2015, including a reduction by Visa Europe of default domestic credit IF in ten EEA countries where Visa Europe set the rates (as opposed to local issuers or acquirers (either bilaterally or multilaterally) that should have happened approximately around February 2016.

The duration of commitments was four years from the notification of the decision (i.e., approximately December 2014).

[G] January 2019: Mastercard II Infringement Decision (Cross-Border Acquiring)

We saw above that in the EC commitment decision dated 26 February 2014, Visa Europe had given a commitment to the EC that allowed merchants to use an acquirer located in another country (i.e., a cross-border acquirer) and pay cross-border IF of 0.2%/0.3% which was lower than most domestic IF, therefore allowing merchants to normally pay lower IF as part of their MSC. Since Mastercard did not pro-actively offer the same commitment to the EC (despite the fact that the issue was going to be regulated by the, then, forthcoming IFR), in July 2015 the EC issued a SO to Mastercard which, based on the ultimate fining decision, apparently stated as follows, in summary.

64. 'The Commission's concern that certain cross-border acquirers could be foreclosed from competition with local acquirers due to different MIF rates applicable to the two groups has, however, been removed by the mandatory registration and application of domestic MIFs agreed by local acquirers. As regards the obligation for a cross- border acquirer to pay the MIF of the place of the transaction, the Commission has not investigated that point fully and reserves its right to investigate it further in the future.' Commission Decision on Case AT.39398 – VISA MIF, *supra* n. 33, at para. 49.

First, despite its 2006 IPO, Mastercard remained an association of undertakings in relation to its scheme rules on cross-border acquiring[65]

Second, '*Mastercard's cross-border acquiring rules meant that acquirers offering card payment transaction acquiring services in Member States where the domestic MIFs were lower were prevented from seeking to offer cheaper services based on the MIFs in their "home" countries in Member States where the domestic MIFs were higher. The merchants were also prevented from taking advantage of the internal market and benefiting from less expensive services from card acquirers established in low-MIF Member States. Therefore, the Commission concludes that Mastercard's cross-border acquiring rules created an obstacle to cross-border trade in the market for acquiring card payment transactions in the EEA. The rules shielded national markets from cross-border competition from acquirers established in other Member States. The rules reveal in themselves, and by their very nature, a sufficient degree of harm to competition to be considered a restriction of competition "by object".*'[66]

Third, the infringement period was 27 February 2014 (i.e., the day after the adoption of the Visa Europe commitment decision on *inter alia* cross-border acquiring) to 8 December 2015 (i.e., the day before the relevant IFR provisions became applicable). '*At least with the adoption of the Commission's 2014 Visa Europe Decision, Mastercard was aware, or should have been aware, that the cross-border acquiring Rules infringed the competition rules and it was reasonably foreseeable for Mastercard that it should be held responsible for an infringement if it continued to apply its cross-border acquiring rules. The Commission therefore concludes that as of that point in time Mastercard commitments an infringement intentionally, or at least negligently.*'[67]

After having responded to the SO, Mastercard submitted a formal offer of cooperation to the Commission ('Settlement Submission') in December 2018, in which it acknowledged in particular the breach of Article 101 TFEU. As a result, on 22 January 2019, the EC adopted an infringement decision against Mastercard imposing a fine of EUR 570,566,000 on Mastercard.[68]

[H] April 2019: Visa International and Mastercard Commitments on Inbound Interregional IF

In parallel to the above, the EC had opened investigations against Visa Inc. and Visa International Services Association (together Visa International), as well as three

65. Interestingly enough, the justification for Mastercard remaining an association is slightly different than in the January 2019 fining decision adopted just three months earlier. In the April 2019 Mastercard commitment decision, the EC relied on the two criteria as confirmed by the EU courts on appeal of the EC 2007 decision – whereas, as mentioned above, three months earlier, in January 2019 fining decision, the EC referred to Mastercard 'listening to its customers/ the market', etc.
66. Commission Decision on Case AT.40049 – MasterCard II, *supra* n. 34, at paras 62–63.
67. Commission Decision on Case AT.40049 – MasterCard II, *supra* n. 34, at para. 94.
68. Interestingly, consumer prepaid cards are not covered by the decision (*see* para. 22 of EC decision), unlike all previous, and future, EC competition enforcement that always treated consumer debit and prepaid together.

Mastercard legal entities (together Mastercard) in relation to the default IF applicable to inbound interregional transactions, i.e., transactions where the card issuer is located outside of the EEA and the merchant is located within the EEA. In essence, these investigations can be seen as complements to the IFR that had become applicable (in part) on 9 December 2015. Indeed, the IF caps set in the IFR only apply to transactions where the issuer, as well as the acquirer and the merchant, are located within the EEA – but not to inbound interregional transactions.

The EC issued several SOs against Visa International (in 2009, 2013 and 2017) and one SO against Mastercard (in 2015). The main allegations are as follows. First, Visa International and Mastercard, despite their respective IPOs, remain associations of undertakings as the two conditions mentioned in the Court of Justice of the European Union (CJEU) 2014 Mastercard judgment were met, i.e. (1) issuers and acquirers retained important decision-making powers in respect of essential aspects of the operation of the scheme; and (2) the existence of a commonality of interest between the scheme and issuers/acquirers on the issue of IF (read: a commonality of interest in a 'high' default IF).

Second, the interregional IF 'amount to *horizontal price-fixing* [...] Such *price fixing* is by its very nature harmful to competition and reveals in itself a sufficient degree of harm to competition to be considered a restriction of competition "by object".'[69] The Visa and Mastercard inbound interregional IF are not objectively necessary to the operation of the Visa and Mastercard schemes.

Third, The Visa and Mastercard inbound interregional IF did not meet the conditions for an exemption.

Visa International and Mastercard both offered commitments to the EC. Both schemes proposed to reduce the default IF applicable to inbound interregional transactions. The EC accepted the commitments and made them binding in two decisions dated 29 April 2019. More specifically, Visa International and Mastercard both gave identical commitments, including reductions of IF for:

- card-present (CP) transactions: the same level of IF as those applicable under the IFR since December 2015, i.e., 0.2% for consumer debit/ prepaid, 0.3% for consumer credit;
- card-not-present (CNP) transactions (e.g., online transactions): *1.15%* for consumer debit/ prepaid and *1.50%* for consumer credit. Those higher levels had generated critical comments from merchants and merchant associations during their market testing, but the EC accepted those levels and, in its press release, justified those higher levels as follows: '[...] *the Commission concluded that, with the proposed inter-regional MIFs caps, the cost for retailers of accepting inter-regional consumer card payments does not exceed the cost of accepting alternative means for such payments, such as cash for Card Present Transactions and e-wallets (digital wallets) funded via bank transfers for Card Not Present Transactions*'. Reading between the lines, it would appear that the

69. Commission Decision of 29 April 2019 on Case AT.40049 – MasterCard II, *supra* n. 35, para. 33. Commission Decision of 29 April 2019 on Case AT.39398 – Visa MIF, *supra* n. 35, para. 34.

> costs imposed by digital wallets, perhaps such as Paypal, to EEA-based merchants played a role in the EC accepting that the MIT resulted in higher levels of IF than the usual 0.2%/ 0.3%.

The commitments are valid for a period of, effectively, five years - which, depending on when the decisions were formally notified to Visa International and Mastercard, we expect to be approximately until May 2024. These two decisions mark the second time that the EC obtained commitments with an extra-territorial effect. The first time, as mentioned above, was in the Visa Europe 2014 commitments.

§3.05 DATA AND METHODOLOGY

The data set consists of 10,072 valid points, associated with twenty-one different variables. A total of twenty-seven Member States of the EU is covered over a time span of twenty years (2000–2019). The data is collected on an annual basis and all absolute variables are transformed into relative variables (*per capita* for instance) in order to reduce the impact of outliers and achieve a higher degree of normalisation with regard to distribution.[70] In addition to the two main data sources, namely the European Central Bank's (ECB) statistical data warehouse (https://sdw.ecb.europa.eu) and Eurostat's statistical database (https://ec.europa.eu/eurostat/data/database), IF are obtained from Veljan (2018).[71] A total of five outcome variables is tested. In addition to the descriptive variables *Country* and *Year* as well as the dummy variables required to conduct the DiD analysis (*Treatment period; Treated market; Treatment period and Treated market*), a mixture of nine control variables is considered for the analysis. The main driver behind the selected variables is in fact the rationale presented by the EC in relation to a market intervention. A competition enforcement (and ultimately regulation) is expected to lower the fees of card acceptance for merchants and thus drive higher merchant acceptance whilst passing a substantial amount of savings on to cardholders in form of lower prices. The increased acceptance is expected to drive higher overall card payment usage.[72]

Outcome Variable	*Label*	*Period*
Size (by number)	Number of total card payments per capita	2000–2019

70. Outliers are not subsequently removed; data is not normalised further; in cases of missing values these are not replaced.
71. Alan Veljan, *A Critical Review of the European Commission's Multilateral Interchange Fee Regulation*, 12(3) J. Payments Strategy & Systems (2018).
72. *Survey on merchants' costs of processing cash and card payments*, European Commission (March 2015), http://ec.europa.eu/competition/sectors/financial_services/dgcomp_final_report_en.pdf; Proposal for a Regulation of the European Parliament and of the Council on interchange fees for card-based payment transactions, European Commission (24 July 2013), https://eur-lex.europa.eu/legal-content/EN/ALL/?uri=celex%3A52013PC0550.

Outcome Variable	*Label*	*Period*
Size (by value)	Value of total card payments per capita [€]	2000–2019
Acceptance	Number of terminals installed per 1 million inhabitants	2000–2019
Issuance	Number of cards issued per capita	2000–2019
Displacement	Number of ATM cash withdrawals per capita	2000–2019

Due to the aforementioned characteristics of card payment markets and the ineffectiveness of assessing a single cost element in isolation, we deliberately depart from a monetary and one-sided analysis and focus on metrics that act as proxies for the success and efficiency of the network as a whole. We assume that increases in overall market size in terms of transaction numbers and volumes, as well as market participants (merchants on the acceptance and cardholders on the issuance side) and a displacement of cash are deemed favourable by the network participants. Further and disregarding the cost structure of card payments, electronic payments are regarded to be socially efficient and welfare optimising.[73] Based on these two premises, above variables can be utilised to assess the causal effects of the competition enforcement conducted by the EC by applying the DiD approach.

Control Variable	*Label*	*Period*
Productivity	Compensation of employees [€/ hour][74]	2004–2015
Poverty	People at risk of poverty or social exclusion [%]	2004–2015
Internet	Share of households with broadband access [%]	2004–2015
ATM	Number of ATMs installed per 1 million inhabitants	2000–2019
Inflation	Harmonised index of consumer prices [%]	2000–2019
Interchange	Weighted average interchange fee [%]	2007–2015
GDP	Gross Domestic Product per capita [€]	2000–2019
eCommerce	Online purchases made by individuals in the last 3 months [%]	2004–2015
Tourism	Nights spent at tourist accommodations [per capita]	2000–2019

The selection of control variables represents the degree of digitalisation within a country, the economic performance, stability and welfare distribution as well as access to banking and payment products. Whilst numerous initiatives have driven a harmonisation of the European card payment market, prevalent differences between the

73. Proposal for a Regulation on interchange fees for card-based payment transactions, *supra* n. 72.
74. Under consideration of purchasing-power-parity.

countries continue to exist. The selection of variables aims at identifying and controlling for these within the analysis.

We focus our analysis on the EC competition enforcement that led to the Visa Europe 2010 commitment decision. The period analysed spans from 2004 to 2015, with the exclusion of 2010 as this year can neither be classified as pre- nor post-enforcement.[75] The infringement period covers the years 2004–2009; the post-intervention period ranges from 2011 to 2015. Further, any confounding effects stemming from previous cases (34,579: Mastercard 2007) or the IFR can be minimised. Whilst the Mastercard 2007 case only applied to Intra-EEA[76] card transactions that, at the time, accounted for less than 5% of total card transactions across Europe,[77] the IFR came into effect on 9 December 2015 and should thus have not had any major impacts on the data either. The only remaining antitrust enforcement relates to Visa Europe's Intra-EEA and domestic fallback credit IF, which were amended on 14 May 2013. However, at this point in time, only a fraction (23 %) of European card transactions are completed using credit cards.[78]

During this period data availability is warranted for all countries; the variable *interchange* represents an exception. As part of the enforcement, the debit interchange fee was amended for all Intra-EEA card transactions within the EEA. The enforcement also applied to countries where Visa Europe was in charge of setting the domestic debit interchange fee. At this point in time, Visa Europe set the domestic debit interchange fee in Greece, Hungary, Iceland, Ireland, Italy, Malta, Sweden, Luxembourg and Netherlands. As these countries would have experienced a far greater impact of the enforcement, they are classified as the treated group, with all remaining countries representing the control group. This way cross-country variations can be exploited to provide insights into the effects of antitrust involvement.

In its simplest form, the DiD approach calculates the difference between the infringement and post-intervention periods for an outcome variable within the treated group and compares this with the obtained results for the same outcome variable within the control group, thereby enabling an assessment of the impacts.[79] The underlying methodology is a linear regression (OLS);[80] in our case conducted with the *Enter* method within the program *SPSS*. Initially all input variables[81] are selected and

75. On 26 April 2010 Visa agreed to trial the proposed interchange rate (0.2%) for debit card payments. On 8 December 2010 the EC makes Visa's commitments legally binding.
76. Intra-EEA transactions are transactions initiated with a card issued in country A within the EEA and utilised in country B. Card issuer and merchant are located in different countries but both within the EEA.
77. Commission Decision 2009/C 264/04 on Case COMP/34.579—MasterCard, Case COMP/36.518—EuroCommerce, Case COMP/38.580—Commercial Cards, *supra* n. 31.
78. European Central Bank - Statistical Data Warehouse (https://sdw.ecb.europa.eu).
79. A total of 5 regression analyses are run for the outcome variables. Additionally, 5 analyses are run to test the common trend hypothesis.
80. Ordinary Least Squares.
81. The analysis is run for the five selected output variables separately. In order to assess the main drivers of the movement in any outcome variable we also test the output variables' impact, i.e., initially select them as an input variable in each run. The rationale behind this can be exemplified as follows. For the outcome variable size (by number), we also test Acceptance and Issuance as input variables in order to evaluate if changes in the output variable are driven more

subsequently removed stepwise based on their significance. Significance is assessed via the t-test value and a confidence level of 95% is defined. In order to control for collinearity, the Variance Inflation Factor (VIF) is always kept below §3.05[E]. The behaviour of the outcome variable prior to the intervention needs to be assessed in order to establish a potential common trend. The common trend hypothesis can be accepted if the variable of interest is not statistically significant, i.e., different from zero. The significance of the enforcement can be visually interpreted and statistically assessed so as to complement the causal interpretation. For the sake of robustness, a separate analysis has been run whereby the pre-treatment period is extended by four years to cover the timespan 2000–2009. The results of this analysis do not yield significantly different results.

§3.06 RESULTS

The three variables Size (by number/ value) and Acceptance vary significantly across Europe. On the contrary, Issuance and Displacement exhibit a comparatively lower standard deviation. Both Size metrics are characterised by a positive/ right-skewed distribution, whereas Acceptance, Issuance and Displacement have a relatively symmetric distribution. A constant growth can be recorded for all outcome variables across the years (including infringement phase), except for Displacement which has remained relatively stagnant. This in itself requires a more profound investigation in order to enable an assessment if and to what extent the development of these variables was impacted by the competition enforcement.

Size (by number)[a]					
R^2 0.843	*Unstandardised Coefficients*		*Standardised Coefficients*	*t*	*Sig.*
	B	*Std. Error*	*Beta*		
(Constant)	108.600	14.237		7.628	.000
Compensation of employees under consideration of PPS [€/ hour]	–1.800	.422	–.201	–4.271	.000
People at risk of poverty or social exclusion [%]	–2.087	.337	–.237	–6.195	.000
Number of cards issued [per capita]	–18.146	7.240	–.136	–2.506	.013

by the merchant or cardholder side. We acknowledge the complexities this endogeneity problem can cause, especially in terms of establishing causality. However, this assessment is deemed essential for our analysis and is a prevalent problem within two-sided markets.

Size (by number)[a]					
R^2 0.843	*Unstandardised Coefficients*		*Standardised Coefficients*	*t*	*Sig.*
	B	*Std. Error*	*Beta*		
Number of ATM cash withdrawals [per capita]	–.078	.270	–.013	–.288	.774
Number of terminals installed [per 1m inhabitants]	.001	.000	.194	5.328	.000
Online purchases made by individuals in the last 3 months [%]	.674	.221	.185	3.046	.003
Nights spent at tourist accommodations [per capita]	–12.356	2.796	–.222	–4.420	.000
Value of total card payments [per capita]	.020	.001	.887	14.984	.000
Treatment period	1.987	4.984	.016	.399	.691
Treated market	–9.874	5.559	–.071	–1.776	.077
Treatment period and treated market apply	16.346	7.701	.088	2.122	.035

[a]. Dependent Variable: Number of total card payments [per capita].

The findings show that the *number of card payments per capita has significantly increased (by an average of 16 payments) as a result of competition enforcement.* Given that the mean (median) lies at 73 (49) payments per capita, this results in a 22% uplift. The model has a relatively strong explanatory power, characterised by a coefficient of determination of 0.843. Also, we can confirm a common trend in the development of the variable prior to the event date (2010).[82] A visual assessment of the trend confirms above findings. Whilst the treated and control groups exhibit a common trend prior to the competition enforcement in 2010, a discrepancy in developments is observable

82. The analysed coefficient was significant at the 95% confidence level so that a common trend cannot be assumed per se. However, although there was a significant divergence between the trends in the number of card payments per capita for the treated and control groups prior to the competition enforcement, this divergence was very small and close to zero (-0.005) so that the common trend assumption is (presumably) satisfied.

subsequently. A partial impact by the 2007 Mastercard decision, whereby a reduction of the Mastercard Intra-EEA IF to zero in April 2008 was followed by an increase to 0.2% for debit and 0.3% for credit cards as of July 2009, cannot be excluded. Also, it is observable that the positive trend was further amplified by the IFR which came into force on 9 December 2015. We can confirm a positive, statistically significant relationship between the size of the European card payment market (measured by number of transactions) and the EC's market intervention.

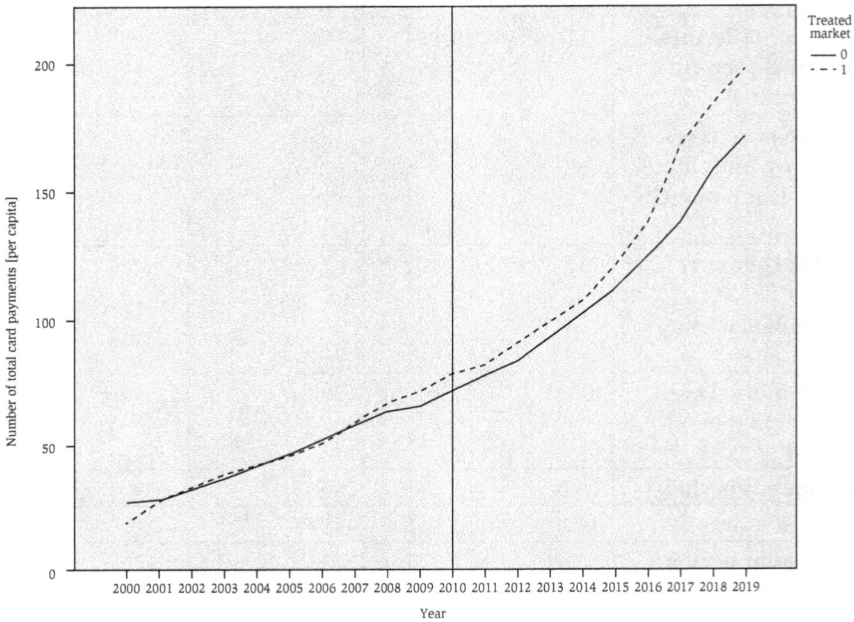

The majority of above findings hold for the second variable to be assessed, namely *Size (by value)*. Logically, one can assume that these two metrics will follow a similar trend as an increase in the number of transactions will, *ceteris paribus*, lead to an increase in card volume. However, whilst the number of total card payments is an evident proxy for payment card utilisation, card volumes can be impacted by confounding factors such as wealth, spending behaviour or other macroeconomic developments. A risk of misinterpretation is especially prevalent when analysing monetary values. In our model, we have tried to control for this by including control variables such as productivity (Compensation of employees under consideration of payment service providers (PPS)) or GDP per capita. The final model (shown below) only contains the aforementioned variable due to its comparatively higher explanatory power. The control variable GDP per capita has been removed due to collinearity issues.

Size (By Value)[a]					
R^2 0.911	*Unstandardised Coefficients*		*Standardised Coefficients*	*t*	*Sig.*
	B	*Std. Error*	*Beta*		
(Constant)	−3,134.403	473.121		−6.625	.000
Compensation of employees under consideration of PPS [€/ hour]	68.755	13.681	.166	5.026	.000
People at risk of poverty or social exclusion [%]	34.774	10.053	.093	3.459	.001
Share of households with broadband access [%]	−27.455	5.497	−.210	−4.994	.000
Number of cards issued [per capita]	2,006.217	182.115	.357	11.016	.000
Number of total card payments [per capita]	27.470	1.540	.547	17.836	.000
Online purchases made by individuals in the last 3 months [%]	42.655	7.280	.242	5.859	.000
Number of ATM cash withdrawals [per capita]	−9.401	7.791	−.031	−1.207	.229
Treatment period	302.060	211.494	.049	1.428	.154
Treated market	270.099	182.396	.040	1.481	.140
Treatment period and treated market apply	−550.065	257.737	−.063	−2.134	.034

a. Dependent Variable: Value of total card payments [per capita].

The model exhibits even stronger goodness of fit and is able to explain 91% of the total variance. Similarly, our findings show that the value of card payments is mainly driven by the number of card payments and vice versa. However, whilst the above results hint towards a positive impact of competition enforcement, the opposite is true with regard to the *Size (by value)*. In fact, the average cardholder spending has decreased by approximately EUR 550 annually subsequent to the market intervention. In comparison to the mean of EUR 3,469, this is equivalent to a reduction of 16%. This inconsistency can potentially be explained by the macroeconomic occurrences that have shaped the economy during the intervention period. The financial crisis and the subsequent credit crunch started in 2007 in the United States (US) and spilt over to Europe in late 2009. With increasing debt-to-GDP ratios and unemployment as well as significant drops in GDP and productivity rates, the overall spending had been impacted, which will – to a large degree – have impacted card spending as well.[83]

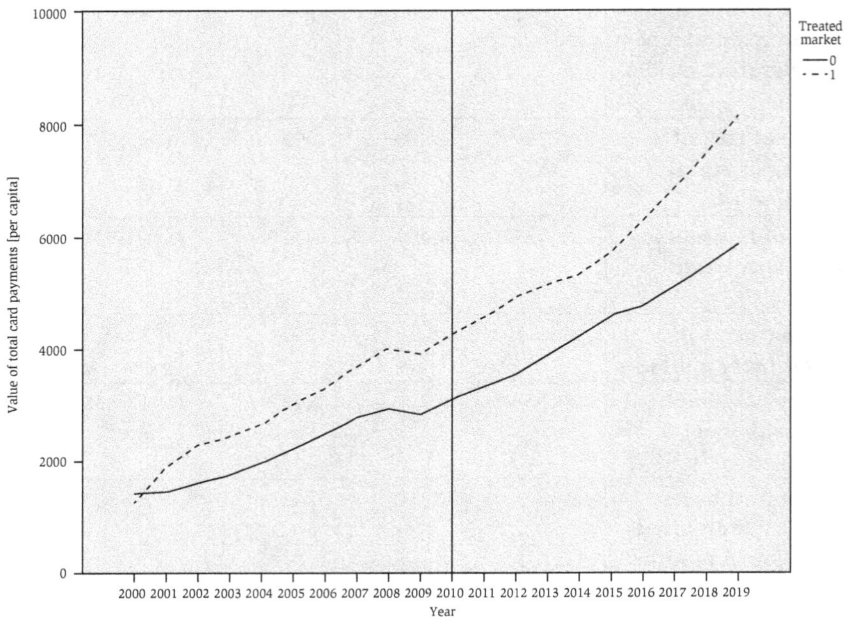

The above graph shows that whilst the growth momentum has continued for both the treated and control groups (driven by the other explanatory variables, rather than the policy intervention) subsequent to the downturn in 2009, the slope of the control group has increased, i.e., it has become steeper especially in the period between 2010 and 2015, whereas the slope for the treated markets has decreased, i.e., flattened, thereby resulting in a slower growth post-intervention. This is only the case between 2010 and 2015 which is the analysed period. Afterwards, and certainly post-IFR, the slope steepens significantly for the treated group whereas it remains relatively constant for the control group. A common trend between the control and treated groups cannot be confirmed for the infringement period.

The following two variables (*Issuance* and *Acceptance*) aim to assess in further detail the drivers of above findings. We look at whether the size of the network has increased and card payments are utilised in larger numbers and more often post-intervention. We seek to understand if this is driven either by an increased card issuance, by an increase in card acceptance, or by a mixture of both.

83. Hans-Werner Sinn, *The Euro Trap – On Bursting Bubbles, Budgets, and Beliefs* (Oxford University Press 2014).

Issuance[a]					
R^2 0.784	*Unstandardised Coefficients*		*Standardised Coefficients*	*t*	*Sig.*
	B	*Std. Error*	*Beta*		
(Constant)	.498	.063		7.951	.000
Number of ATMs installed [per 1m inhabitants]	.000	.000	.460	13.808	.000
Number of ATM cash withdrawals [per capita]	.008	.002	.148	3.933	.000
Number of total card payments [per capita]	.002	.000	.241	5.257	.000
Online purchases made by individuals in the last 3 months [%]	.020	.002	.613	10.905	.000
Nights spent at tourist accommodations [per capita]	–.121	.017	–.249	–7.160	.000
Share of households with broadband access [%]	–.004	.001	–.191	–3.066	.002
Treatment period	–.127	.056	–.113	–2.257	.025
Treated market	.273	.049	.225	5.519	.000
Treatment period and treated market apply	.225	.070	.141	3.212	.001

[a.] Dependent Variable: Number of cards issued [per capita].

The results obtained for the variable *Issuance* display a significant, positive impact of the market intervention on the number of cards issued per capita. Recall that a common belief was that card issuance would decrease as issuers would be less incentivised to invest in cards due to decreasing revenues stemming from a lower IF. In addition, it was also believed that increases in annual card fees or reductions in rewards programs would cause a deterioration in card payments. Our analysis suggests that the opposite is in fact the case. *Card issuance has continued to grow, and growth has actually been amplified by the EC antitrust intervention.* Although this could have manifold reasons, according to our model it is driven mainly by the emergence and growth of eCommerce and online purchases as well as continued card usage in relation to ATM withdrawals.

The fact that several European countries continue to rely on domestic (debit) card schemes for domestic transactions (e.g., Cartes Bancaires in France, Bancontact in Belgium, Girocard in Germany, PagoBancomat in Italy, Multibanco in Portugal, Dankort in Denmark, BankAxept in Norway), rather than Visa and Mastercard shall not be disregarded.[84] The model's overall goodness of fit is relatively strong with an R^2 of 0.784. On average an increased issuance of 0.225 cards can be recorded for the post-intervention period. This equates to an increase of 16% when compared to the average (mean) of 1.44 cards per capita.

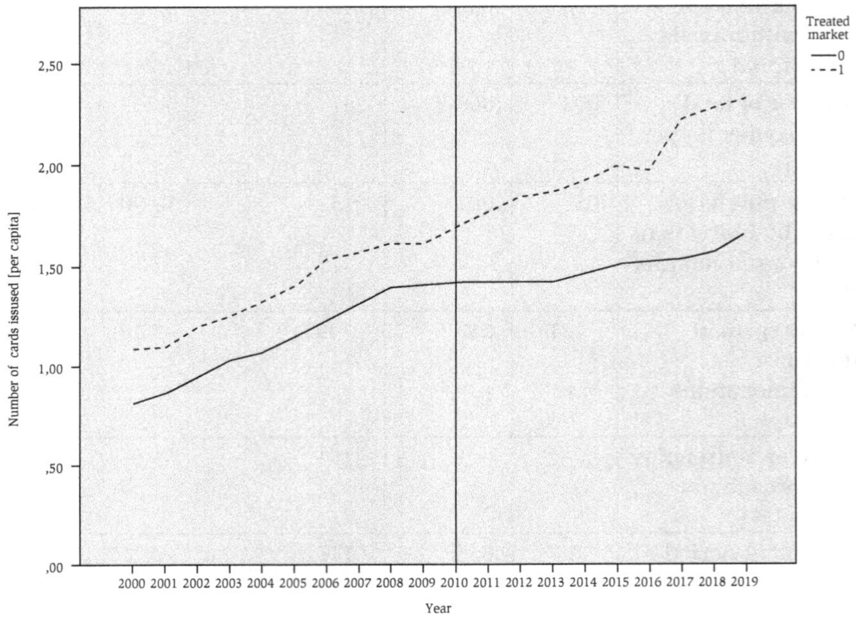

A visual representation of our results confirms our interpretation. A common trend prior to the event date can be observed and statistically confirmed. During the post-intervention phase, the slope for control markets flattens and even stagnates for a period, whilst a continued growth momentum can be observed for the treated group. A further anomaly is the slight dip in 2016 which may in fact be somewhat related to the IFR. However, this is overturned in 2017 where the growth is actually highest across all years. We can confirm that the increase in card payments has been (to a large extent) driven by an increase in average cardholding. From the set of outcome variables, *Acceptance* is the only one where a statistically significant impact of the intervention is not observable. Thus, we can conclude that *Issuance* has been the major

84. For a number of European economies, domestic debit card schemes continue to play a dominant role in terms of payment but also cash withdrawals. Visa and Mastercard hold a marginal share related to debit card circulation in several markets including Belgium (0%), Norway (0%), Portugal (0%), Germany (9%) and Italy (34%).

driver of increased card usage, alongside a mixture of potential other explanatory variables.

Displacement[a]					
R^2 0.514	*Unstandardised Coefficients*		*Standardised Coefficients*	*t*	*Sig.*
	B	*Std. Error*	*Beta*		
(Constant)	8.691	1.431		6.073	.000
Number of ATMs installed [per 1m inhabitants]	.000	.000	.260	4.233	.000
Number of total card payments [per capita]	.068	.011	.408	6.262	.000
Compensation of employees under consideration of PPS [€/hour]	–.553	.095	–.410	–5.825	.000
Number of cards issued [per capita]	8.282	1.383	.460	5.989	.000
Nights spent at tourist accommodations [per capita]	1.589	.461	.181	3.451	.001
Treatment period	–1.791	1.079	–.087	–1.660	.098
Treated market	–.845	1.399	–.038	–.604	.546
Treatment period and treated market apply	–3.811	1.892	–.130	–2.014	.045

[a]. Dependent Variable: Number of ATM cash withdrawals [per capita].

Finally, we try to assess whether we can see a displacement of cash usage in exchange for more sophisticated, electronic payment methods (including card payments). Our regression model is characterised by a medium goodness of fit, explaining 51 % of total variance. A statistically significant, negative impact is observable with regard to the number of ATM cash withdrawals per capita, resulting in an average decrease of four withdrawals across the treated group. Considering an average (mean) cash withdrawal of twenty-three, this results in a decrease of 17%. Further, cash usage seems to be positively related to the number of cards in circulation and the total number of payments, whereas an inversed relationship is observable with the productivity ratios within the market. This is in line with common belief that the level of productivity as well as other aspects of innovation and technological affinity will impact cash versus electronic payment usage. A common trend during the pre-intervention period is also observable and statistically confirmed.[85]

85. To reiterate in case of confusion: whilst the graphic depiction ranges from 2000–2019 to as to provide a longer-term view of the development of the metrics, the analysed period is defined from 2004–2015.

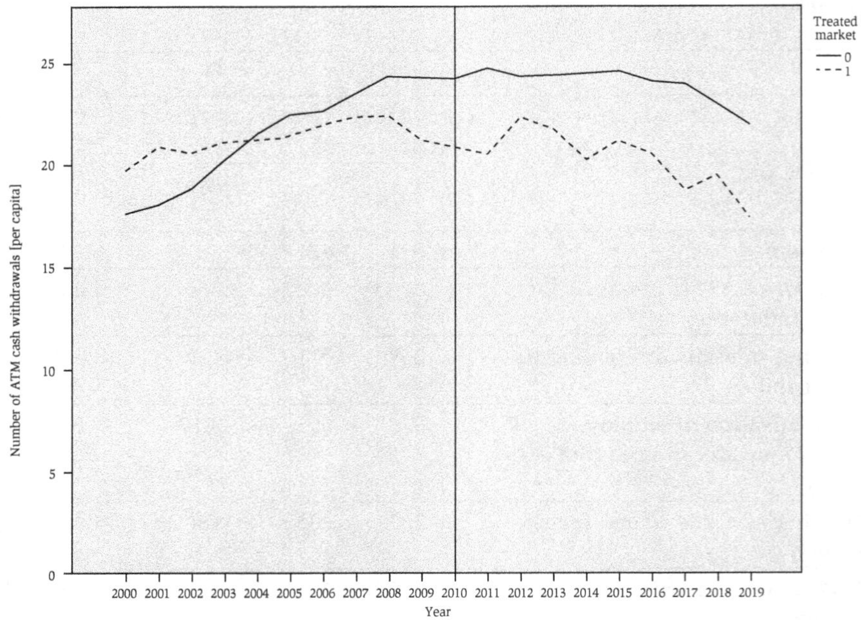

§3.07 DISCUSSION OF ECONOMIC FINDINGS

The focus of research in this paper differs from existing *ex post* impact assessments in relation to the IF. The vast majority of previous research,[86] including the EC's study on the application of the IFR,[87] predominantly focus on monetary redistribution effects, thereby aiming to assess the total impacts on the network, whilst facing the problem of limited empirical data for all market participants, in order to conduct a final interpretation. This problem is especially prevalent in two-sided markets as pass-through and pricing elasticity of participants becomes key. As a result, most research lacks a holistic assessment of the market or aims to bypass the problem with the usage of proxies or interviews; all of which are suboptimal and can in fact lead to detrimental policy decisions.[88] We deliberately depart from this approach and try to assess the impacts of antitrust intervention based on a set of metrics that represent overall network success. In this respect, our ambition is more in the line with traditional multisided market literature, which focuses on establishing functional relationships between price structures and output, leaving aside distributional concerns.

86. *See* David S. Evans, Howard H. Chang, and Steven Joyce, *The Impact of the U.S. Debit-Card Interchange Fee Regulation on Consumer Welfare*, 11(1) J. Competition L. & Econ. (2013); A Veljan and A Roaidi, *An Event Study Analysis of the Impacts of the European Interchange Fee Regulation*, 17(1) J. Competition L. & Econ. (2021).
87. *Study on the application of the Interchange Fee Regulation*, European Commission (11 March 2020) https://ec.europa.eu/competition/publications/reports/kd0120161enn.pdf.
88. Katz and Shapiro, *supra* n. 11.

Importantly, our analysis also operates on the assumption that card payments increase social welfare in comparison to non-digital payments such as cash. Put differently, we postulate that a larger utilisation of the service, driven by a mixture of increased merchant acceptance and/or cardholding, as well as an ultimate displacement of cash payments is beneficial. We ground this assumption on the widely documented inefficiencies and risks related to cash payments[89] but also on the overall digital finance strategy by the EC which includes payment services.[90]

Given the above, and from the perspective of overall market output, *our results are supportive of the policy expressed in enforcement initiatives like the Visa 2010 decision*. The hypothesis can only be partially confirmed as the variables Size (by number), Issuance and Displacement are significantly and positively impacted, whereas no confirmatory evidence can be obtained for Acceptance and Size (by value). This is of particular relevance, especially because prior to the IFR becoming applicable, the EC anticipated that issuer losses caused by the decrease in IF would in fact be compensated by increases in card spending, mainly driven by a growing acceptance rate on the merchant side.[91] In the case of the Visa 2010 enforcement initiative, this has not been the case.

Furthermore, and from a methodological perspective it is important to note that for the majority of tested outcome variables, only a relatively limited and specific set of explanatory variables led to above results. In many cases, the significance of findings depended on specific explanatory variables. Issuance was the only case displaying vastly stronger robustness. Also, one cannot fully exclude the potential impact of confounding events such as the Mastercard 2007 decision or the (amplifying[92]) impact of the IFR. Whilst we cannot state with certainty that the competition enforcement related to the Visa 2010 decision was the single and most significant driver of the observable impacts in relation to the outcome variables (an overall development trend is observable across the European payment landscape prior to this), we can affirm that the antitrust actions taken did not have a negative impact on welfare (measured by efficiency metrics such as total market output) and most likely amplified the previously observable positive trend.

Whilst our findings conform to standard cause-and-effect theories,[93] two prevalent sources of scepticism deserve to be considered. The first is related to issues arising

---

89. Transportation and security expenses as well as check-out times for cashiers at the end of the day are only a few examples. For further detail *see* Jean Tirole, *Payment Card Regulation and the Use of Economic Analysis in Antitrust*, 7(1) Competition Pol'y Int'l 137, 158, (2011).
90. *See Communication on Digital Finance package*, European Commission (24 September 2020) https://ec.europa.eu/info/publications/200924-digital-finance-proposals_en; European Commission: Digital Finance package, https://ec.europa.eu/info/business-economy-euro/banking-and-finance/consumer-finance-and-payments/payment-services/payment-services_en.
91. *See Survey on merchants' costs of processing cash and card payments*, European Commission (March 2015) https://ec.europa.eu/competition/sectors/financial_services/dgcomp_final_report_en.pdf; Proposal for a Regulation on interchange fees for card-based payment transactions, *supra* n. 72.
92. Due to its scope (all domestic and cross-border credit and debit transactions) as well as its size (IF were reduced in some regions by up to 80%).
93. It is noteworthy that whilst the utilised methodology by the EC to assess optimal interchange fees was developed by Rochet and Tirole, both authors clearly state that due to spillover effects,

out of cross-country examinations, namely reverse causality and omitted causal factors.[94] The second, inescapable in any *ex post* assessment, concerns the counterfactual. Would the growth momentum, observable for most countries during the infringement phase have continued (potentially at a slower rate) but for policy intervention? What impacts did the progressive reduction of IF have on innovation?[95] How has the reduction in IF, alongside other provisions and changes to (acquiring) rules, impacted market concentration? Would the development of scheme fees (charged by the card schemes to issuers and acquirers – i.e., the revenue of the card scheme) have been different in the absence of competition enforcement, and ultimately regulation, of IF?[96]

In light of the above and the fact that results obtained from other empirical research[97] show anomalies or contradictions in relation to economic (two-sided market) theory, we suggest further research in this field, in specific related to a potential tipping point within two-sided markets. We argue that whilst the economic notions related to card payment markets[98] are certainly logical, consumer payment behaviour continues to be highly (if not most significantly) influenced by cultural habits;[99] the IF remains a *hidden price* to consumers. Thus, the economic rationale for antitrust involvement needs to be re-assessed for markets that have surpassed a certain size. Once a card network adoption has reached a point known as tipping, price adjustments produce only insignificant or minimal effects on output. Most consequences will in turn become distributional, which confronts policymakers with hard questions. Often, congressional legislation is a more legitimate process to address distributional issues than decision or rulemaking by expert agencies.

In light of the above, let us now say a word about some of the controversies that have been associated with the IF 'saga'. Whilst contradicting views exist in terms of certain nuances of the tourist test/MIT methodology, a rather common agreement amongst scholars and practitioners is that cost-based approaches are suboptimal when

---

diverging demand elasticities and market power it is not in the interest of card associations to set interchange fees that deviate markedly from the social optimum. *See* Rochet and Tirole, *supra* n. 8.

94. Abhijit V. Banerjee and Esther Duflo, *Good Economics for Hard Times: Better Answers to Our Biggest Problems* (Juggernaut Books 2019).
95. Stuart E. Weiner and Julian Wright, *Interchange Fees in Various Countries: Developments and Determinants*, 4(4) Rev. Network Econ. 321 (2005).
96. Veljan, *Regulating the Uncontrollable: The Development of Card Scheme Fees in Payments Markets in Light of Recent Policy Intervention*, *supra* n. 29.
97. *See* Veljan, *A Critical Review of the European Commission's Multilateral Interchange Fee Regulation*, *supra* n. 71; Veljan and Roaidi, *An Event Study Analysis of the Impacts of the European Interchange Fee Regulation*, *supra* n. 86; *Study on the application of the Interchange Fee Regulation*, European Commission, *supra* n. 87.
98. These include but are not limited to following examples. A reduction in the MSC will c.p. drive increased card acceptance by merchants; a reduction of interchange fees will c.p. lead to reduced card benefits and lower card issuance and uptake; fee reductions for acquirers will c.p. lead to reductions in fees for merchants and subsequently consumers.
99. *Position on the Proposal for a Regulation of the European Parliament and of the Council on Interchange Fees for Card-Based Payment Transactions*, Die Deutsche Kreditwirtschaft (12 December 2013), https://die-dk.de/media/files/GBIC_Position_MIF_EN_20131212_dPNf1id_r8YBDbt.pdf. This includes exogenous influences such as a pandemic which has impacted the uptake of (contactless) card payments more than any other influence thus far.

determining IF.[100] What is more problematic is the non-transparent manner in which the EC has applied the methodology to determine the benchmark rates of 0.3% for credit and 0.2% for debit/ prepaid cards. From an economic perspective, these deviate from the results of EC's official publications about costs within European card payment markets.[101]

Further, the initial scope of antitrust intervention targeted only a minimal fraction of total payments made, i.e., less than 5%.[102] It took a decade to enlarge the scope of transactions that would fall under antitrust actions. A benefit of this is a rather incremental market impact, that minimises the costs of policy error, including by limiting the costs of reversibility. Moreover, *this suggests that the EC followed a pragmatic and evidence-based policy spirit based on learning from experience.* A downside for research lies however in the fact that the market interventions (up to the IFR) could not be evaluated accurately as the reductions in cross-border (and in certain countries domestic fallback) IF did not vastly impact the total costs of card acceptance. Within our models the variable Interchange was insignificant at all times. Other unintended consequences primarily stem from the characteristics of two-sided markets which are based on elements such as spillover effects, intra-and inter-system competition[103] as well as an inverted competition with regard to card schemes.[104]

When focusing on a single price component within card networks, we are confronted with two main limitations. On the one hand, reductions in IF can lead to (disproportionate[105]) increases in other fee components. Put more graphically, the various fees charged to merchants might be substitutes to each other, a problem known as the waterbed effect. On the other hand, the ultimate cost decrease for merchants and in turn for cardholders is dependent on the pass-through within acquiring as well as merchant sectors. This, again, is an empirical question.

One way to think about it is that competition in merchant markets plays a key role to ensure that reductions in IF fees are transferred to end-users. With this background, a historical analysis of industry concentration in merchant markets can provide a proxy for changes in demand elasticities, and in turn give economic insights on changes in pass-through rates. We try to shed light on this matter by analysing (1) the relationship between concentration and pass-through within the US acquiring market pre-and

---

100. Guthrie and Wright, *supra* n. 23.
101. *See Survey on merchants' costs of processing cash and card payments*, European Commission, *supra* n. 72.
102. Commission Decision 2009/C 264/04 on Case COMP/34.579—MasterCard, Case COMP/36.518—EuroCommerce, Case COMP/38.580—Commercial Cards, *supra* n. 31.
103. Alen Veljan, *Influence of Intra-and Inter-system Concentration on the Pre-regulated Setting of Interchange Fees Within Cooperative Card Payment Networks*, *supra* n. 9.
104. Guthrie and Wright, *supra* n. 23.
105. Fee amendments can follow an asymmetric development, meaning that scheme fees can increase on the acquirer side whilst potentially stagnating or even being reduced on the issuer side. This poses a risk to the effectiveness of the market involvement. This risk was ultimately recognised and circumvention prohibited as part of the IFR. *See* Regulation (EU) 2015/751 of the European Parliament and of the Council of 29 April 2015 on interchange fees for card-based payment transactions, *supra* n. 1. Also, cardholder fees on the issuing side as well as benefits associated to card usage can disproportionately deviate, i.e., increase due to interchange reductions so that the net cardholder impact may in fact be negative.

post-regulatory involvement and (2) the profitability of European acquirer's pre- and post-competition enforcement and regulation.

For the US acquiring market, the Herfindahl-Hirschman Index (HHI) did not significantly change between 2004 and 2016. HHI levels ranged between 1,046 in 2011 and 1,531 in 2005 and no trend development, apart from a relatively equal dispersion around the mean of 1,206 is observable during this period. What is interesting is the fact that the pass-through rates significantly decreased post implementation of the Durbin Amendment on 1 October 2011.[106] During the three years preceding the regulation the pass-through rate was on average 91 %, whereas in the five years post-regulation it averaged 81 %.

Year	*HHI*	*MSC Debit*	*IC Fee Debit*
2009	1150	1.63 %	1.49 %
2010	1078	1.59 %	1.40 %
2011	1046	1.39 %	1.31 %
2012	1062	0.78 %	0.65 %
2013	1071	0.76 %	0.60 %
2014	1153	0.75 %	0.60 %
2015	1152	0.74 %	0.60 %
2016	1229	0.73 %	0.59 %

As far as the European acquiring landscape is concerned, HHI levels ranged between 252 and 356 over the period 2004–2019.[107] Contrary to media reports[108] and large merger and acquisition (M&A) announcements, we do not observe clear concentrative trends in merchant markets. This can be attributable to the fact that the majority of M&A activity has spanned over multiple countries or even continents (Nets acquisition of Concardis; FIS acquisition of Worldpay) and involved companies with different roles within the payment chain (ACI acquires SpeedPay; Ingenico acquires Bambora and B + S Card Services).

That said, statistically significant results can be obtained in relation to the profitability of European acquirers. We have looked at a data set of three acquirers (two German acquirers and one pan-European acquirer; all within the top thirty European

106. Directed by the Durbin Amendment of the Dodd-Frank Act, the Federal Reserve Board caps interchange fees charged by financial institutions with more than USD 10 billion in assets for debit card payments. For further information *see Federal Reserve issues a final rule establishing standards for debit card interchange fees and prohibiting network exclusivity arrangements and routing restrictions*, Federal Reserve System (29 June 2011), Federal Reserve Board – Federal Reserve issues a final rule establishing standards for debit card interchange fees and prohibiting network exclusivity arrangements and routing restrictions.

107. For a detailed overview of in-market concentration within acquiring markets, please *see* Alen Veljan, *Influence of Intra-and Inter-system Concentration on the Pre-regulated Setting of Interchange Fees Within Cooperative Card Payment Networks*, *supra* n. 9.

108. *See Three M&A Waves Reshaping the Banking Payments Acceptance Segment*, Ernst & Young Global Limited (2 March 2021), https://www.ey.com/en_gl/banking-capital-markets/three-m-a-waves-reshaping-the-banking-payment-acceptance-segment.

acquirers by volume during the last two decades). Whilst this sample cannot be regarded as representative, we have been unable to gather a larger sample due to changes in ownership and corporate structure across the time span of fifteen years (2005–2019) and/ or the majority of acquiring firms either acting as card issuers simultaneously (*see* Crédit Mutuel or Barclays) or having a strong(er) presence in adjacent markets such as technical gateway services (*see* Ingenico or Adyen).

With these limitations in mind, our analysis suggests that the profits of every firm in the sample have significantly increased in both 2012 (post-enforcement related to Visa Europe 2010 decision) as well as 2016 (post- IFR).[109] For the two German acquirers, profits averaged EUR 12.9 million and EUR 4.7 million from 2005 (2006) to 2010. In 2011 these were EUR 19.5 and EUR 14.3 million respectively, i.e., 51% and over 300% higher. Similar results can be seen for the pan-European acquirer which averaged negative profits of EUR 9 million between 2006 and 2010 and recorded profits of EUR 14.6 million in 2011. A similar trend is observable for the first-year post-IFR implementation. Profits for the two German acquirers averaged EUR 89.6 and EUR 19.1 million respectively during the years 2012 to 2015. In 2016 these were EUR 115.6 million and EUR 89.6 million; up by 29% and 470%. The pan-European acquirer averaged profits of EUR 76.2 million during the four years preceding the IFR and EUR 305 million in 2016; an increase of 400%.[110] These findings suggest areas for future research. Our findings hint that *competition enforcement led to distributional effects favouring acquirers over merchants and subsequently end-users,* i.e., *consumers.* It would thus be helpful to assemble a more representative sample, to test whether this effect can be observed at a larger scale. Though the General Court in *Glaxo* confirmed that the benefits of enforcement under Article 101(1) TFEU need not accrue to end-users, it is always helpful to understand which categorical interests the policy tends to favour.

§3.08 DISCUSSION OF LEGAL CONSIDERATIONS

In this section, we provide some legal comments on the EC's enforcement of competition against IF between 2002 and 2019. We address in particular the fact that the baseline theory of harm changed from a restriction of competition by effect to a

---

109. According to The Nilson Report the selected firms had an average annual growth rate between 10% and 14% in terms of processed transaction numbers. A potential positive impact on revenues in 2016, caused by the Visa Inc. acquisition of Visa Europe cannot be excluded. *See Visa Inc. Completes Acquisition of Visa Europe,* Visa Inc. (21 June 2016), https://investor.visa.com/news/news-details/2016/Visa-Inc-Completes-Acquisition-of-Visa-Europe/default.aspx and Steve Slater, *European Banks Set for Windfall from Visa Europe Deal: Sources,* Reuters (16 October 2015, 18:45) https://uk.reuters.com/article/uk-visa-europe-banks/european-banks-set-for-windfall-from-visa-europe-deal-sources-idUKKCN0SA26M20151016.
110. Above profits may be slightly inflated due to the windfall from Visa Inc's acquisition of Visa Europe, which at the point in time was owned by more than 3,000 banks and payment firms. We tried to reduce this impact by avoiding the top acquirers (British banks alone would have accounted for 40% of the kick-back; much of the rest residing with French, Italian and Spanish payment providers) whilst selecting firms that would have been impacted by the regulatory enforcement. *See* Slater, *supra* n. 109.

restriction by object (which is not unusual per se), but also the manner in which the benchmark for setting the exemptible level of IFs (i.e., the tourist test of MIT) has left room for improvement (as well as other points – in no particular order).

[A] No Specification of Pass-Through Mechanisms

None of the above EC decisions contained a mechanism seeking to induce acquirers to pass on IF reductions (in whole) to merchants (whether in the form of a commitment in the Visa/ Mastercard commitment decisions, or a remedy in relation to the Mastercard infringement decisions). One exception though is the Visa Europe 2014 commitments decision in which Visa Europe committed to change its scheme rules so that an acquirer would be forced to charge a merchant an MSC on an 'IF plus plus' if that merchant requested such an MSC (as opposed to a blended MSC).

It is surprising that the EC did not require (in commitment decisions) or impose (as a remedy in infringement decisions) the card schemes to implement a rule change forcing acquirers to pass on the reduction of IF to merchants, much like in the Visa Europe 2014 commitments. Presumably the EC believed that market forces, and in particular, competition between acquirers, as well as transparency on the reduced levels of IF, would be enough to ensure a sufficient level of pass-through by acquirers to merchants?

With the benefit of hindsight, it would probably have been more effective for the EC to mandate such a requirement in all its decisions.[111]

As regards the reduction of MSC perceived by merchants, the EC never imposed a mechanism to ensure that merchants would in turn pass on that reduction of costs to their customers (e.g., consumers) in the form of lower (retail) prices. This makes sense since this would probably have been an impossible task for the EC to monitor. The EC assumed that the intensity of the competition between merchants would be enough to ensure a pass-through to consumers.[112]

---

111. Further to the IFR (rather the competition law enforcement against IF), it would appear from the EY study on the IFR commissioned by the EC (*Study on the application of the Interchange Fee Regulation,* EY on behalf of European Commission (2020), https://ec.europa.eu/competition/publications/reports/kd0120161enn.pdf) and the EC report on the IFR (Report on the application of Regulation (EU) 2015/751 on interchange fees for card-based payment transaction, European Commission (29 June 2020), https://ec.europa.eu/competition/sectors/financial_services/IFR_report_card_payment.pdf) that a significant proportion of the IF reduction caused by the IFR effective 9 December 2015 was not passed on to merchants: 'Acquirers have gained revenue of EUR 1,200 million per year coming from lower interchange fee savings and offset by larger scheme fees and pass-through to merchants, the latter likely to increase over time (gains to acquirers were calculated indirectly).' (page 6).

112. In relation to the IFR: For information, the EC's conclusion under the IFR is as follows: 'A key yardstick for the assessment of the effects of the IFR is its impact on retail prices for consumers. As the change in interchange fees induced by the caps of the IFR results in a very small impact per transaction, it makes it notoriously challenging to determine pass-through rates, which is the share of interchange fees reductions which are passed on as reductions of final consumer prices. However, since interchange fees transmitted through MSCs are one of several cost factors for merchants, competition between merchants should result – *in the longer run* – in interchange fee reductions being reflected in lower prices or improvement of services on the consumer side' (Report on the application of Regulation (EU) 2015/751 on interchange fees for card-based payment transaction, European Commission, *supra* n. 111, page 6).

[B] Mixed, but Non-simultaneous Enforcement

The chronological summary shows that the EC's policy towards payment systems has consisted in a mix of commitment decisions (against Visa and Mastercard), and of infringement decisions (against Mastercard only). This approach can be an efficient way for policymakers to reduce consumer harm due to competition law violations: infringement decisions provide clarity on the law and set a precedent, whilst commitment decisions enable the EC to shape markets going forward and suggest safe harbours for market participants.

At the same time, the main feature of the Commission's policy is one of asynchronous enforcement. Expecting that its decisions would generate industry-level guidance and compliance, the EC enforced competition law, one market player at a time, anticipating that the other market player would do the same. The facts at our disposal suggest that this is not the case. Visa and Mastercard pursued distinct legal strategies. In reality, we see here that the case-specific nature of competition enforcement produces limited effects on third parties.

More importantly, the fact that the EC never dealt with Visa and Mastercard at the same time (except in the April 2019 commitment decisions) means that the two competitors were never subject to the same 'rules of the game' and therefore to a level playing. Instead, since 2002, one organisation was always required to do more than the other – and it typically required quite a few years from the EC to get the competitor do so the same, but then even more than its competitor – before turning back (again) to the first competitor:

- Visa was at a competitive disadvantage between 2002 and July 2008 in relation to the level of its cross-border IF.
- Then Mastercard was at a competitive disadvantage between July 2008 and, respectively, 2010 for debit and 2014 for credit in relation to cross-border IF.
- And Visa was at a competitive disadvantage in relation to domestic IF since 2010, first in relation to debit only in 9 EEA countries, then in relation to all cards (credit and debit) as from January 2015 further to its commitment on cross-border acquiring. Clearly the commitments on cross-border acquiring put Visa Europe at competitive disadvantage as from 1 January 2015 since a Visa cross-border acquired transaction would attract less IF for the issuer (i.e., 0.2%/0.3%) than a Mastercard cross-border acquired transaction (that would attract the IF of the country of the merchant/issuer).

One can question whether this is optimal competition law enforcement. Arguably, the EC should have enforced competition law at the same time against both competitors, as it did in relation to the 2019 commitments on inbound interregional transactions. Or it could have used tools like sector inquiries to study industry-wide practices from distinct firms on equal footing.

Moreover, this is potentially unfair. As mentioned above, there has been no competition law enforcement against the IF, or equivalent fees to IF, that was being applied by three-party schemes like American Express (and a fortiori no private actions for damages against American Express, at least as far as we are aware). This situation is recognised today in the IFR, which seeks to ensure a level playing between traditional four-party card schemes such as Visa, Mastercard, Cartes Bancaires, Bancontact, etc., and three-party schemes sometimes operating as a four-party scheme.

[C] On Default IF as Restrictions 'By Object'

As was also hopefully clear from the above chronological summary, the EC's thinking, and indeed the EU Court's case law, has evolved over the years in relation to several issues, including the issue of restriction by object or by effect.[113]

Although the EC has relied on the same counterfactual for the default IF since 2002 (i.e., no default IF to be paid by acquirer to issuer, coupled with a prohibition of *ex post* pricing), the EC has evolved from 'no object - only effect' in its Visa International 2002, to 'effect - and perhaps object?' in its Mastercard 2007, to 'object and effect' in its Visa 2010 (which was before the EC won before the General Court, in 2012, in the Mastercard case) and Visa 2014 decision - to ultimately reach the qualification of 'horizontal price-fixing' arrangement in the Visa/ Mastercard 2019 commitment decisions.

Of course, since the Visa 2010, Visa 2014 and Visa/ Mastercard 2019 decisions were commitment decisions, the EC's object qualification was technically only preliminary. However when the EC reiterates an object 'preliminary assessment' across several decisions, over a period of nine years, we believe that one can legitimately draw the conclusion that the EC really is of the view that there is a restriction of competition by object. In particular when during that period, in 2018, as part of an amicus curiae submission made as part of the merchant lawsuits against Visa and Mastercard in the UK, the EC stated that '*As such, it is appropriate to draw an analogy with a cartel between all acquiring banks to charge their customers a substantially inflated fee.*'[114]

It is of course legitimate for the EC to change its policy over time, in particular in relation to complex topics such as the legal and economic assessment of IF in competition cases. However, when policy change occurs, one would expect the EC to (1) explicitly acknowledge in its decision a change in position and (2) to explain in its decisions what justifies the evolution in its position. This is not only a good rule of practice, but the case law of the CJEU actually requires accountability from the EC when it incrementally develops its decisional practice over a series of cases:

> Although a decision which fits into a well-established line of decisions may be reasoned in a summary manner, for example by a reference to those decisions, if

---

113. Not to mention that the EC seems to have steadily changed its position on the acceptable level of IF.

114. Written observations of the European Commission in *Mastercard Inc. and others, vs. Sainsbury's Supermarkets Limited,* para. 28, https://ec.europa.eu/competition/court/visa_mastercard_commission_observation1_en.pdf.

> it goes appreciably further than the previous decisions, the Commission must give an account of its reasoning.[115]

In so far as IF are concerned, the EC has not observed this rule of practice. There is no explanation in the various EC decisions as to what justified the evolution from effect to object (and in particular price-fixing).

Any antitrust observer looking at the latest EC pronouncement on IF will come away with more questions than answers. In 2019, the EC reached the somewhat puzzling finding that the default IF under investigation were tantamount to 'horizontal price-fixing'/'price fixing'[116] arrangement, but that they met the conditions for an exemption (again, after a committed reduction of the level).

Of course, it is not impossible in theory for a restriction by object to meet the conditions for an exemption under Article 101(3).[117] The Court has actually confirmed this in its 2020 judgment in *Budapest Bank.*[118] The hard question is, however, that the narrow circumstances in which a horizontal price-fixing arrangement can be found to meet the Article 101(3) TFEU conditions are left entirely underspecified in practice, leading to genuine legal uncertainty.

In effect, the EC granted exemptions on several occasions. In the Visa Europe 2010 and 2014 decisions, the EC found that a restriction of competition by object had met the conditions for an exception (albeit after a committed reduction of the level). And in its Mastercard/ Visa 2019 commitments decisions, the EC even concluded that a price-fixing arrangement had met the conditions for an exemption (albeit, again, after a committed reduction of the level).

What is more important, however, is that the substantial recourse to Article 101(3) TFEU begs the question whether the qualification of restriction by object is really adequate in the first place – in particular after the Court of Justice judgments in *Cartes Bancaires* (2014) and *Budapest Bank* (2020).

In its 2010 and 2014 Visa Europe commitment decisions, the EC stated that the default IF is a restriction of competition by object because '*The MIFs appeared to inflate the base on which acquirers set the MSCs by creating an important cost element common to all acquirers.*'[119]

---

115. Case 73-74, *Groupement des fabricants de papiers peints de Belgique and others v. Commission,* 26 November 1975, ECLI:EU:C:1975:160, para. 31.
116. Commission Decision of 29 April 2019 in Case AT.40049 - MasterCard II, *supra* n. 35, para. 33. Commission Decision of 29 April 2019 in Case AT.39398 - Visa MIF, *supra* n. 35, para. 34.
117. *See,* e.g., European Commission Guidelines on the application of Article 81(3) of the Treaty, OJ, C 101/97, 27.4.2004, para. 46; *See also* the EC Guidelines on the applicability of Article 101 of the Treaty on the Functioning of the European Union to horizontal co-operation agreements, OJ C11/1, 14.1.2011; *See also* Guidance on restrictions of competition 'by object' for the purpose of defining which agreements may benefit from the De Minimis Notice, accompanying Notice on agreements of minor importance which do not appreciably restrict competition under Article 101(1) of the Treaty on the Functioning of the European Union (De Minimis Notice), OJ C 291, 30.8.2014.
118. Case C-228/18, *Gazdasági Versenyhivatal v. Budapest Bank Nyrt. and Others,* 2.4.2020, ECLI:EU:C:2020:265, paras 41–42.
119. Commission Decision of 8 December 2010 in Case COMP/39.398—VISA MIF, *supra* n. 32, para. 21 and Commission Decision of 26 February 2014 in Case AT.39398 - VISA MIF, *supra* n. 33, para. 23.

In 2019, the EC went further by saying that:

> *rules on inter-regional MIFs amount to horizontal price-fixing. The inter-regional MIFs fix a significant component of the price charged to merchants for acquiring services through the MSCs. The Commission came to the preliminary conclusion that the restriction of competition on price follows from the very substance of [the] rules on inter-regional MIFs. The Commission also came to the preliminary conclusion that the objective of* [the] *rules on inter-regional MIFs is to fix a part of the price charged to merchants and to restrict competition to the benefit of* [the card scheme] *Mastercard and its members/licensees, primarily the issuers. Such price fixing is by its very nature harmful to competition and reveals in itself a sufficient degree of harm to competition to be considered a restriction of competition 'by object'*[120]

However, it appears from the *Budapest Bank* judgment that the mere fact that Hungarian issuers and acquirers had agreed to a MIF applicable to domestic transactions in Hungary, '*even assuming that the MIF Agreement had inter alia as its objective the fixing of a minimum threshold applicable to the* [MSC]', was not enough to qualify the restriction of competition between acquirers as a restriction by object. In other words, the justifications provided by the EC in its 2010, 2014 and 2019 decisions are (in our view) not sufficient, in light of *Budapest Bank*, to justify the existence of a restriction by object. Rather than paraphrasing, we think that a (fairly long) quote from the judgment is helpful:

> 51. [...] in order to determine whether an agreement between undertakings or a decision by an association of undertakings reveals a sufficient degree of harm to competition to be considered a restriction of competition 'by object' ... regard must be had to the *content* of its provisions, its *objectives* and the *economic and legal context* of which it forms a part. [...]
>
> 54. [...] *the concept of restriction of competition 'by object' must be interpreted restrictively.* The concept of restriction of competition 'by object' can be applied only to certain types of coordination between undertakings which reveal a sufficient degree of harm to competition for it to be found that there is no need to examine their effects, as otherwise the Commission would be exempted from the obligation to prove the actual effects on the market of agreements which are in no way established to be, by their very nature, harmful to the proper functioning of competition. [...]
>
> [...]
>
> 65. Although it is clear from the documents before the Court that specific percentages and amounts were used in the MIF Agreement for the purposes of fixing the interchange fees, the *content* of that agreement does not, however, necessarily point to a restriction 'by object', in the absence of proven harmfulness of the provisions of that agreement to competition. [...]
>
> 71. [...] certain information contained in the documents before the Court tends to indicate that *one objective* of the MIF Agreement was to ensure a degree of balance between the issuing and acquisition activities within the card payment system at issue in the main proceedings.

120. Commission Decision of 29 April 2019 in Case AT.40049 – MasterCard II, *supra* n. 35, para. 33. Commission Decision of 29 April 2019 in Case AT.39398 – Visa MIF, *supra* n. 35, para. 34.

[...]

73. It cannot be ruled out that such information points to the fact that the MIF Agreement was pursuing *an objective* consisting not in guaranteeing a minimum threshold for service charges but in establishing *a degree of balance between the 'issuing' and 'acquisition' activities* within each of the card payment systems at issue in the main proceedings in order to ensure that certain costs resulting from the use of cards in payment transactions are covered, whilst protecting those systems from the undesirable effects that would arise from an excessively high level of interchange fees and thus, as the case may be, of service charges.

[...]

76. Indeed, as the Advocate General has stated in points 54 and 63 to 73 of his Opinion, in order to justify an agreement being classified as a restriction of competition 'by object', without an analysis of its effects being required, there must be sufficiently reliable and robust experience for the view to be taken that that agreement is, by its very nature, harmful to the proper functioning of competition.

[...]

78 Second, as regards the acquiring market in Hungary, *even assuming that the MIF Agreement had inter alia as its objective the fixing of a minimum threshold applicable to the service charges* [read: the MSC]*, the Court has not been provided with sufficient information to establish that that agreement posed a sufficient degree of harm to competition on that market for a restriction of competition 'by object' to be found to exist.* It is, however, for the referring court to carry out the necessary verifications in that respect.

79 In particular, in the present instance, subject to those verifications, *it is not possible to conclude on the basis of the information produced for this purpose that sufficiently general and consistent experience exists for the view to be taken that the harmfulness of an agreement such as that at issue in the main proceedings to competition justifies dispensing with any examination of the specific effects of that agreement on competition.* The information relied on by the Competition Authority, the Hungarian Government and the Commission in that connection, that is to say, primarily, that authority's decision-making practice and the case-law of the Courts of the European Union, specifically demonstrates, as things currently stand, *the need to conduct an in-depth examination of the effects of such an agreement in order to ascertain whether it actually had the effect of introducing a minimum threshold applicable to the service charges and whether, having regard to the situation which would have prevailed if that agreement had not existed, the agreement was restrictive of competition by virtue of its effects.*

80. Finally, with regard to *the context of which the MIF Agreement formed a part,* in the first place, it is true that, as the Commission maintains, the complexity of the card payment systems of the type at issue in the main proceedings, the bilateral nature of those systems in itself and the existence of vertical relationships between the different types of economic operators concerned are not, in themselves, capable of precluding classification of the MIF Agreement as a restriction 'by object' [...]. That said, the fact remains that such an anticompetitive object must be established.

[...]

82 In the event that the referring court were also to find there to be, a priori, strong indications capable of demonstrating that the MIF Agreement triggered [...] upwards pressure [on the level of IF] or, at the very least, contradictory or

> ambivalent evidence in that regard, such indications or evidence cannot be ignored by that court in its examination of whether, in the present instance, there is a restriction 'by object'. *Contrary to what it appears may be inferred from the Commission's written observations in this connection, the fact that, if there had been no MIF Agreement, the level of interchange fees resulting from competition would have been higher is relevant for the purposes of examining whether there is a restriction resulting from that agreement,* since such a factor specifically concerns the alleged anticompetitive object of that agreement as regards the acquiring market in Hungary, namely that that agreement limited the reduction of the interchange fees and, consequently, the downwards pressure that merchants could have exerted on the acquiring banks in order to secure a reduction in the service charges.
>
> 83 In addition, *if there were to be strong indications that, if the MIF Agreement had not been concluded, upwards pressure on interchange fees would have ensued, so that it cannot be argued that that agreement constituted a restriction 'by object' of competition on the acquiring market in Hungary, an in-depth examination of the effects of that agreement should be carried out,* as part of which, in accordance with the case-law recalled in paragraph 55 of the present judgment, it would be necessary to examine competition had that agreement not existed in order to assess the impact of the agreement on the parameters of competition and thereby to determine whether it actually entailed restrictive effects on competition.

Put another way: if the above commitment decisions (2010, 2014 and two in 2019) had been infringement decisions rather than commitments decisions, and had been challenged by Visa and/or Mastercard before the EU Courts, they, based in particular on *Budapest Bank*, would likely have concluded that the mere fact that the IF (as set by Visa or Mastercard) sets a common de facto floor for the level of the MSC was not, in itself, sufficient evidence by the EC of the existence of a restriction of competition by object.

At the same time, *Budapest Bank* insists on the fact that an agreement can be named 'a restriction of competition "*by object*"' if there is '*reliable and robust experience for the view to be taken that that agreement is, by its very nature, harmful to the proper functioning of competition*'.[121] This requirement was recently tested in the *Lundbeck* pay-for-delay case.[122] What is clear from the pay-for-delay cases is that if a so-called new form of conduct is, in fact, disguising what amounts to a cartel arrangement such as market sharing, then there is sufficient accumulated experience for that conduct to be found restrictive of competition by object. Despite the EC finding in 2019 that the '*rules on inter-regional MIFs amount to horizontal price-fixing*', given its long-standing application of Article 101(3) would it be appropriate to say the rules were in fact analogous to a cartel? This seems doubtful. That said, our report shows that given the evolving decisional practice of the EC relating to Visa and Mastercard over the years, it is arguable that 'reliable and robust experience' now exists today. However, whether it can be said with confidence that a consensus has emerged that the IF is a restriction of competition by object, which has regularly weaved its way into

121. Case C-228/18, *Gazdasági Versenyhivatal v. Budapest Bank Nyrt. and Others, supra* n. 118, at para. 76.
122. Case C-591/16P, *Lundbeck v. Commission*, 25.3.21, ECLI:EU:C:2021:243.

decisional practice both in the EU Courts and EC, is not quite so clear-cut. Certainly, the EC has failed to produce, in the context of the proceedings, evidence showing that its own experience leaned in this direction and, likewise, failed to explain that its thinking has evolved and why.

Given the fact that IF is now regulated by the IFR in relation to consumer cards, the only way for the qualification of default IF as a restriction by object to be tested would be a legal challenge in relation to the IF applicable to commercial cards (which are not subject to caps under the IFR). However, to our knowledge there is no ongoing competition law enforcement against Visa or Mastercard (or domestic schemes') commercial card IF. This begs the question whether more frequent *ex post* assessment, and disclosure by the EC, might improve legal certainty, by providing competition law subjects with a better understanding of what the EC's 'experience' teaches them, and whether their agreement leans towards falling within the object box, or will be subject to a thorough market inquiry of its 'effects'.

[D] Evolution in the EC's Thinking Regarding the Methodology to Set the Exemptible Level of IF

Another evolution in the EC's approach concerns the methodology deemed suitable to set the level of exemptible IF. Whilst the EC initially considered some of the costs borne by issuers in 2002, it moved in 2009 to an evaluation based on the costs borne by merchants (in particular their cost of cash) under the so-called tourist test/MIT. Interestingly, the EU had explicitly discarded the cost of cash as a relevant benchmark in 2002, noting that '*… as concerns cash and cheques, neither of these can be considered as substitutable with payment cards, either from the point of view of merchants or that of consumers. For merchants first of all, such non-card payment instruments are not at all substitutable with cards, since the loss of revenue for merchants from ceasing to accept all cards would be far greater than the loss of revenue from increasing their general level of prices by the amount of any small but sustained increase in merchant fees for all cards …*'.[123]

The EC's methodological evolution has also been accompanied by an evolution of the IF levels deemed exemptible: from *EUR 28* cents (approximately 0.5%) for debit/ *0.7%* for credit in 2002, down to *0.2%* for debit and prepaid/*0.3%* for credit since 2009, and more recently in 2019 0.2%/0.3% for CP debit (including prepaid) and credit respectively and *1.15%/1.50%* for CNP debit (including prepaid) and credit.

For CNP transactions, the fact that the EC accepted that cash is not an appropriate comparator for inbound interregional CNP (e.g., online) transactions, but instead e-wallet transactions with higher costs such as Paypal for example were an appropriate comparator, and therefore, on the basis of the MIT, allowed higher levels that 0.2%/0.3%, is an interesting evolution. Surely cash was already not an appropriate comparator for CNP transactions in 2008 in relation to Intra-EEA transactions, whereas

123. Commission Decision 2002/914/EC – Visa International – Multilateral Interchange Fee, *supra* n. 18, para. 48.

e-wallets (e.g., Paypal) was. It therefore begs the question why the higher levels of 1.15%/1.50% were not already accepted in the 2009 Mastercard Unilateral Undertakings and/or in the 2015 IFR.

This problem of time inconsistency shines a bright light on the challenges of determining IF levels that are exemptible under Article 101(3) TFEU, and more generally, on the incredible level of uncertainty, discretion and subjectivity involved in any such exercise. It also highlights the risk of competition law potentially being used to regulate the level of fees.

Make no mistake. There is no suggestion here that the EC should stick to a given methodology. Rather, the point is that changes in methodology should be (1) explicitly acknowledged and (2) reasoned. Absent this, the evolution in the EC's position leaves itself open to an interpretation whereby the EC was in reality using its competition law powers to directly regulate fee levels (which is something that EuroCommerce itself was claiming in relation to the proposed Visa 2002 exempted levels, but which the EC denied in its 2002 decision – as well as later in the MEMO that accompanied the Mastercard 2007 decision[124]), which is an activity traditionally reserved to regulation/legislation.

[E] Legal Uncertainty

It is not an understatement to say that there has been substantial legal uncertainty for a very long time about the levels of IF deemed legal under competition law. The various points discussed above (e.g., no simultaneous enforcement, the evolution in the EC's thinking on the type of restriction, evolutions on the EC's thinking on exemption), as well as other factors such as the enforcement by NCAs in some EEA countries (but not all) which lead to different results and in particular different exemptible levels (e.g., 0.28% in France), have all combined to create an environment of considerable fluidity, complexity, and instability.

By contrast, it is harder to ponder about the consequences of legal uncertainty in relation to IFs. One conjecture, however, is that the ever-changing competition policy environment might have prevented markets from producing clear price signals that would have been needed to support the creation of a European version of Visa or Mastercard, despite various EC and ECB calls for the creation of such a European

124. 'The Commission considers that MIF's must be examined under Articles 81(1) and 81(3) of the EC Treaty on a case by case basis. However, like any other agreement that restricts competition, interchange fee agreements must fulfil the four cumulative conditions of Article 81(3) of the EC Treaty. This also holds for an entirely new (that means materially different) MIF in the MasterCard scheme should MasterCard choose to continue operating with this mechanism. Otherwise, the MIF is illegal. If the criteria of Article 81(3) of the EC Treaty are not met, the Commission would adopt a cease and desist order and, if appropriate, impose fines. *However, the Commission could not set a different level of interchange fee. The Commission does not apply competition rules to regulate the level of interchange fees.*' – *Antitrust: Commission prohibits MasterCard's intra-EEA Multilateral Interchange Fees – frequently asked questions*, European Commission (19 December 2007), https://ec.europa.eu/commission/presscorner/detail/en/MEMO_07_590.

scheme.[125] This issue is very topical at the moment with the renewed proposal to create a European Visa/Mastercard, referred to as the European Payment Initiative (EPI).

In addition, despite the above legal uncertainty that the EC competition law enforcement created for a number of years, Mastercard and Visa are facing very significant private actions for damages for hundreds of millions of pounds. Mastercard is also facing a very significant consumer class action in the UK for GBP 14 billion (as well as apparently in Portugal, as was recently announced in the press). It would seem that Visa and Mastercard are essentially being treated by claimants as if it had always been clear that they were acting in breach of competition law, and in particular were involved in so-called price-fixing to use the EC's 2019 terminology – whereas, as mentioned above, this understanding was of course not the case. There was genuine legal uncertainty in the market, for many years, as to the legality, or not, of IF up to certain, then undefined, levels.

[F] Evolution in the EC's Thinking Regarding Cross-Border Acquiring

In the early days, the EC considered acceptable the coherence rule that required similar IFs to be charged to foreign/cross-border acquirers and domestic acquirers. After exempting the Visa International rules on cross-border acquiring in 2002, in 2010 the EC blessed again the Visa Europe rule that required that a cross-border acquirer paid the same IF as a domestic acquirer, i.e., the IF of the country where the merchant and issuer are located.

Fast forward to 2014. The EC considered the same rule restrictive of competition by object and required that a cross-border acquirer paid either the domestic IF of the country of the merchant/issuer or 0.2%/0.3% (in practice, the latter was generally lower). The EC did not acknowledge the change in its position. Nor did it explain the reason for the change in its position.

The EC's intervention sought to encourage merchants to 'shop around' to get connected to an acquirer outside their own Member States in order to get access to lower IF (i.e., 0.2%/0.3%). The EC hoped this would increase competition between domestic and cross-border acquirers. Instead of this, we have seen a number of large acquirers re-locate to other EEA Member State and continue to serve merchants from that/those other Member States. For example, a number of UK merchants that were until then relying upon the acquiring services of WorldPay UK were suddenly acquired by WorldPay Netherlands, paying 0.2%/0.3% IF rather than UK domestic IF as they would have if they were still acquired by WorldPay UK. It is therefore not entirely clear to what extent merchants have really connected to new cross-border acquirers, rather than continued with the same acquirer but located in another EEA country.

125. *See, e.g.*, 'The Commission, like the ECB, would welcome the emergence of new pan-European schemes that would compete with international schemes such as MasterCard and Visa. This will require a level playing field between the potential newcomers and the incumbent schemes.' – *Antitrust: Commission prohibits MasterCard's intra-EEA Multilateral Interchange Fees – frequently asked questions*, European Commission, *supra*, n. 124.

However, in 2019, at the time of the Mastercard II decision, it would appear that the EC's counterfactual was no longer the same as in the Visa Europe 2014 decision – but instead was a counterfactual where the acquirer pays the domestic IF of its 'home' country. Again, this is a change in the EC's position without the EC (1) acknowledging it and (2) justifying it. But this decision also raises a number of other comments; we only address a few below for the sake of (relative) brevity.

First, since December 2015 and the IFR becoming applicable, the principle is that the cross-border IF and domestic IF are identical at 0.2%/0.3%, meaning that cross-border acquirers and domestic acquirers in principle pay the same IF. Therefore, given that regulatory position, it is curious that the EC identified as restrictive of competition (by object) a Mastercard rule that was essentially the same as the IFR regime. In other words, given that the Mastercard (and before it the Visa) rule on cross-border acquirers was found by the EC as restrictive of competition by object, this means that the IFR is always restrictive of competition by object and therefore the EC should propose an immediate legislative change to the IFR. But the EC recently announced, as part of a report on the IFR, that it was not going to propose changes to the IFR for now.[126] This seems contradictory on the part of the EC.

Second, the IFR allows a Member State to set lower domestic IF, a possibility that some Member States have used (e.g., Ireland has set a maximum debit IF cap for Irish domestic transactions at 0.1% rather than the standard 0.2% under the IFR). Domestic acquirers have access to those lower levels, whereas a cross-border doesn't have access to those but instead always pays the 0.2%/0.3% cross-border IF. For example, an acquirer located in Ireland acquiring an Irish domestic transaction (i.e., merchant and issuer both in Ireland) will pay a 0.1% IF, whereas an acquirer located in another Member State (e.g., a German acquirer) will pay cross-border IF, i.e., 0.2%, to acquire that same Irish domestic transaction – i.e., a higher level of IF than the local Irish acquirer This puts the German acquirer at a competitive disadvantage versus the local Irish acquirer.[127] Under the EC's logic, the IFR is even more restrictive of competition than the Mastercard rule (and before it the Visa rule) was. Again, this means that the EC should hurry to propose a chance to the IFR to fix this issue … but as mentioned above, the EC has recently announced it was not minded to change the IFR for now. Again, this seems inconsistent.

Third, in its 2019 decision, the EC used a counterfactual ('home' IF of the country of the cross-border acquirer) that was different not only from the commitment given by Visa Europe effective 1 January 2015 (i.e., domestic IF of the country of merchant/issuer or 0.2%/0.3%) but also different from the regulatory solution that the

126. *Antitrust: Commission publishes report on the impact of the Interchange Fees Regulation*, European Commission (29 June 2020), https://ec.europa.eu/commission/presscorner/detail/en/IP_20_1217.

127. Interestingly, the EC had already indicated in its Visa Europe 2010 commitment decision (Commission Decision of 8 December 2010 on Case COMP/39.398 – Visa MIF) that a mechanism that forced cross-border acquirers to pay higher IF than local acquirers '[…] *was considered as increasing the anti-competitive effect* […] *since it puts cross-border acquirers at disadvantage vis-à-vis their domestic competitors in case the* […] *domestic MIFs are lower than the Intra-Regional MIFs*'.

EU legislation had put in place since December 2015 under the IFR (i.e., cross-border acquirer pays cross-border IF). Shouldn't the EC have used as a counterfactual the regime adopted by the EU legislator to assess Mastercard's practices on cross-border acquiring? Granted, the infringement period in the EC 2019 decision relates to the period between February 2014 and 8 December 2015, i.e., pre-IFR. Granted too that the EC is given quite some flexibility in terms of determining what the relevant counterfactual or one of the relevant counterfactuals is.[128] But if the EU legislator, after having analysed various possible avenues during the legislative process including the counterfactual used by the EC in its 2019 decision (i.e., having the cross-border acquirer pays its 'home' domestic IF) decided not to follow that approach, but instead to regulate in a different way (i.e., cross-border acquirer pays cross-border IF), should the EC be allowed, more than three years after that regulation became applicable, to adopt a decision, even for past conduct pre-legislation, (1) to use a counterfactual different from what the legislation requires; and (2) that results in the EU legislation being considered anticompetitive/putting in place a restriction of competition even more severe than that allegedly put in place by the (association of) undertaking(s) under investigation? Should the EC not instead be required to enforce competition law for pre-legislation conduct in a way that makes it aligned with the legislation /that doesn't result in the legislative work of the Council and the EP being suddenly considered as anticompetitive and even more anticompetitive than the conduct pre-legislation?[129]

---

128. *See* for example the EU Courts in the Mastercard 2012 (T-111/08, *MasterCard and Others v. Commission*, 24.5.2012, ECLI:EU:T:2012:260) and 2014 (C-382/12 P, *MasterCard and Others v. Commission*, 11.9.2014, ECLI:EU:C:2014:2201) judgments: when Mastercard was arguing that the counterfactual used by the EC (i.e., no default IF and a prohibition of *ex post* pricing) was not one that would have resulted from market forces, but instead was merely the EC's preferred regulatory outcome, the Court of Justice stated that '[...] *the alternatives on which the Commission may rely in the context of the assessment of the objective necessity of a restriction are not limited to the situation that would arise in the absence of the restriction in question but may also extend to other counterfactual hypotheses based, inter alia, on realistic situations that might arise in the absence of that restriction. The General Court was therefore correct in concluding, in paragraph 99 of the judgment under appeal, that the counterfactual hypothesis put forward by the Commission could be taken into account in the examination of the objective necessity of the MIF in so far as it was realistic and enabled the MasterCard system to be economically viable*'. – para. 111 of Court of Justice judgement. General Court: 'while the terms of that comparison must be realistic ... [the EC] was not, however, obliged to demonstrate that market forces would compel the issuing and acquiring banks themselves to decide to adopt [that counterfactual]' (para. 99 – *see also* para. 132 where rather than 'realistic' the GC referred to 'economically viable').

129. Other aspects of Commission Decision of 22 January 2019 on Case AT.40049 – MasterCard II, *supra* n. 34, that we do not address here, again for the (relative) brevity, are the fact that the EC used 27 February 2014 as the beginning of the infringement period, where Visa Europe was allowed to continue to operate with the same rule until 1 January 2015 – this does not seem to ensure a level playing field between the two competitors? The Mastercard rule on cross-border acquiring was found to be in breach of Article 101 for partitioning the internal market by preventing merchants from working with acquirers in another EEA Member State, but a number of domestic card scheme (e.g., Bancontact in Belgium, Cartes Bancaires in France), to our knowledge, either did not allow cross-border acquiring at all, or if they did also apply the same IF to foreign/cross-border acquirers and domestic acquirers.

§3.09 CONCLUSIONS

In summary, we find that the policy intervention in relation to the Visa 2010 case has significantly impacted card payment markets across Europe. Whilst all markets were in scope in terms of the interchange fee reduction for Intra-EEA transactions, a subset of nine countries (eight of which form part of our analysis; Iceland has been omitted due to limited data) have also experienced reductions for domestic debit transactions. These countries have benefited from a comparatively higher card usage in terms of network size (by number), predominantly driven by an increased cardholding. Also, the displacement of cash by electronic payment methods (including card payments) has been expedited. Our findings are summarised in the table below:

Outcome Variable	*Significantly Impacted*	*Common Trend Confirmed*
Size (by number)	Yes, by 16 payments per capita (22%)	Yes
Size (by value)	Yes, by EUR 550 per capita (-16%)	No
Issuance	Yes, by 0.225 cards per capita (16%)	Yes
Acceptance	No	Yes
Displacement	Yes, by 4 withdrawals per capita (−17%)	Yes

Notwithstanding some methodological imperfections and seemingly contradictory findings (insignificant impact on variable Acceptance) our hypothesis that the EC's competition enforcement has had a positive, statistically significant effect on the usage of consumer card payments, card issuance, merchant acceptance, and cash displacement can be partially confirmed. From the perspective of overall market output, *our results are supportive of the policy expressed in enforcement initiatives like the Visa 2010 decision*. Whilst we cannot affirm with certainty that competition enforcement was the single and most significant driver of the observable impacts in relation to the outcome variables (an overall development trend is observable across the European payment landscape before this), we can state that the antitrust actions taken did not have a negative impact on welfare and market output and most likely amplified the previously observable positive trend.

From a legal standpoint, the evidence may suggest that the *EC has sought to follow a pragmatic and evidence-based policy spirit based on learning from experience*. However, the unstable ebb and flow of competition policy towards payment systems might have come at the price of substantial legal uncertainty, disincentivising entry from one or more European wide schemes.

With the benefit of hindsight, the clear consumer welfare benefits arising from antitrust intervention might have *justified faster regulation*. Although price regulation should only be a last resort, generalising the benefits of bilateral enforcement in a broadly applicable instrument would have avoided some of the potential legal issues that we flagged above. To draw a comparison, the EC moved much more quickly to regulate roaming charges in communications markets.[130] In relation to IF, the draft IFR proposed by the EC in July 2013 '*builds on 20 years of experience in competition cases*'.[131] Twenty years is obviously a very long time ... .

130. With SOs sent to mobile network operations (MNOs) in 2005 and 2006, and a proposed regulation already in 2006.
131. *Factsheet on the interchange fees regulation*, European Commission (https://ec.europa.eu/competition/publications/factsheet_interchange_fees_en.pdf.

CHAPTER 4

Ex Post Assessment of European Competition Policy: Buyer Power in Concentration Cases

Maurice de Valois Turk & Ignacio Herrera Anchustegui[*]

§4.01 INTRODUCTION

Buyer power effects remain a relatively unexplored area of the competition law literature and practice. Even more scarce are buyer power-related concentration cases - instances in which the ability of a buyer to decrease the prices it pays for a good by withholding demand or through bargaining tactics plays a major role in the assessment of a concentration.

In this contribution, we focus on the retrospective analysis of three landmark buyer power concentration cases from the late 1990s and early 2000s -*Kesko/Tuko,*[1] *Carrefour/Promodès,*[2] *and Enso/Stora.*[3] These cases represent interesting, rare and somewhat dissimilar examples of merger control in which buyer power has played a role - and does so in its different aspects. The presence of buyer power may lead to either declare a concentration compatible with the internal market as countervailing power, as in *Enso/Stora,* or prompt concerns due to its effects regarding upstream and downstream effects, as is the case in *Kesko/Tuko* and *Carrefour/Promodès,* two mergers in the flood supply sector. All of these mergers are horizontal, taking place between

* The authors would like to thank Nicolas Petit and John Kirkwood for their comments on earlier drafts. We would also like to express our gratitude to Aleksander Glapiak, Thierry Wetzel, Dr Timo Klein and Vesa Frijling for their research assistance, and to Reuben Oreffo for his linguistic and editorial suggestions. All errors and omissions are those of the authors alone.

1. COMP/M.784 - *Kesko/Tuko* (1996).
2. COMP/M. 1684 - *Carrefour/Promodès* (2000).
3. COMP/M.1225 - *Enso/Stora* (1999).

competing undertakings, and our analysis of buyer power effects reflects this transaction structure. That said, anticompetitive effects from changes in bargaining position are also assessed as part of non-horizontal mergers by the Commission, often under 'partial foreclose concerns'.[4]

The objective of our study is, beyond discussing the merits of the case and the analysis made by the European Commission (hereafter 'the Commission'), to illustrate the ways in which buyer power can be assessed in mergers. This is done as part of a review of the role of buyer power in mergers from an economic and legal perspective. Further, we make use of quantitative data to analyse the effect of buyer power in mergers and to evaluate the effects on rivals of the merging firms once a merger has been announced and then declared compatible with the market. Lastly, we look beyond the analysis of these three cases and discuss the adoption of the Unfair Trading Practices Directive[5] as a regulatory initiative undertaking by the European Union (EU) to deal with competition risks, in a wide sense, which bare similarities to concepts discussed in *Kesko/Tuko* and *Carrefour/Promodès*.

§4.02 BUYER POWER ECONOMICS IN A NUTSHELL

Buyer power concerns the position of the purchaser with respect to the supplier of goods and services.[6] Suppliers and purchasers need to agree on the terms of their contract, and a number of factors can influence these negotiations.

In this respect, the notion of buyer power is similar to the notion of market power, which typically describes the degree to which a supplier can act independently of its users (and could be more accurately referred to as 'seller power'). In other words, buyer power is a form of market power given from a purchasing perspective that may have effects typically in the upstream (purchasing market), as well as potentially in the downstream (retailing market). Their common background can be found in the definition of dominance adopted by the European Court of Justice (ECJ) in the seminal *United Brands v. Commission* case:[7] 'a position of economic strength enjoyed by an undertaking that enables it to prevent effective competition being maintained on the relevant market by affording it the power to behave to an appreciable extent independently of its competitors, its customers and ultimately of its consumers'.

---

4. Examples of mergers involving vertical buyer power effects are: M/7194 *Liberty Global/Corelio/W&W/De Vijver Media* (2015); M/8323 *AT&T/Time Warner* (2017).
5. Directive (EU) 2019/633 of the European Parliament and of the Council of 17 April 2019 on unfair trading practices in business-to-business relationships in the agricultural and food supply chain (OJ [2019] L 111/59).
6. Ignacio Herrera Anchustegui, *Buyer Power in EU Competition Law* (Institut de droit de la concurrence 2017); Zhiqi Chen, *Buyer Power: Economic Theory and Antitrust Policy*, 22 Res. L. & Ec. 17 (2007); Zhiqi Chen, *Defining Buyer Power*, 53 Ant. Bull. 241–249 (2008) Roger D. Blair and Jeffrey L. Harrison, *Monopsony in Law and Economics* (Cambridge University Press 2010); Roger G. Noll, *'Buyer Power' and Economic Policy*, 72 Ant. L. J. 589 (2005); OECD, *Policy Roundtables: Monopsony and Buyer Power, 2008* (2009).
7. Judgment of 14 February 1978, *United Brands v. Commission*, C-403/03, EU:C:1978:22.

While the ECJ does not refer specifically to suppliers, Article 2.1(b) of the Merger Regulation does so,[8] mentioning—among the different aspects to consider in a concentration case—'the market position of the undertakings concerned and their economic and financial power, the alternatives available to suppliers and users, their access to supplies or markets, any legal or other barriers to entry, [and] supply and demand trends for the relevant goods and services'.

[A] Two Different Economic Models

In discussing buyer power, we distinguish - in line with previous authors[9] - two different economic concepts or theories: the monopsony model and bargaining power.

The monopsony model describes the behaviour of a market where a sole purchaser faces an upstream market with perfect competition among suppliers.[10] In this model, there is an upward-sloping supply curve, meaning that the purchaser has an incentive to restrict its purchases as it can realise a lower price at lower quantities, implying a withholding effect. The monopsony model in its simplest form represents the mirror image of the monopoly model.[11]

The second model relates to bargaining power, also sometimes called 'countervailing power', identified as the newer approach to buyer power regulation by the Bundeskartellamt, the German national competition authority.[12] The notion of bargaining power describes the way in which the agreement between a purchaser and supplier differs depending on the characteristics of both parties.[13] Most bargaining models use a structure whereby both the supplier and the purchaser have an incentive to reach an agreement if, for each of them individually, it is more advantageous compared to the alternative of no deal (the so-called outside option). The combined benefit that an

---

8. Council Regulation No 139/2004 of 20 January 2004 on the control of concentrations between undertakings (the Merger Regulation).
9. Zhiqi Chen, *Defining Buyer Power,* 53 Ant. Bull. 241 (2008); OECD (2009); John B, Kirkwood, *Powerful Buyers and Merger Enforcement* 92 Boston U. L. Rev. (2012); and Dennis W. Carlton, Mary Coleman, and Mark Israel, *Buyer Power in Merger Review,* in R. D. Blair and D. D. Sokol (eds), *The Oxford Handbook of International Antitrust Economics,* Volume 1, pp. 529-550 (2014).
10. For a discussion on the monopsony model, *see also* Roger D. Blair and Jeffrey L. Harrison, *Monopsony in Law and Economics* (Cambridge University Press 2010); James P. Quirk, *Intermediate Microeconomics* (Science Research Associates 1987); Robert H. Frank and Amy J. Glass, *Microeconomics and Behavior* 503 (McGraw-Hill 1999); Hal R. Varian, *Intermediate Microeconomics: A Modern Approach* 471 (W. W. Norton & Co 2006); B. Douglas Bernheim and Michael D. Whinston, *Microeconomics,* 648 (McGraw-Hill Irwin 2008); Robert S. Pindyck and Daniel L. Rubinfeld, *Microeconomics,* 373 (Pearson Prentice Hall 2008)
11. For further examples of the use of this expression, *see* Roger D. Blair and John E. Lopatka, *Predatory Buying and the Antitrust Laws,* 2 Ut. L. Rev. 415 (2008); Cory S. Capps, *Buyer Power in Health Plan Mergers,* 6 J. of Comp. L. and Ec. 375 (2010); David Waterman, *Local Monopsony and Free Riders,* 8 Info. Ec. and Pol. 337 (1996); Steven C. Salop, *Anticompetitive Overbuying by Power Buyers,* 72 Ant. L. J. 669 (2005).
12. Bundeskartellamt, *Summary of the Final Report of the Sector Inquiry into the Food Retail Sector,* 9 (2014).
13. For a general discussion on bargaining power and the associated literature, *see* Ignacio Herrera Anchustegui, *Buyer Power in EU Competition Law* (Institut de droit de la concurrence 2017), at paras 92–114.

agreement brings to the purchaser and the supplier is referred to as the 'surplus'. Many models exist that aim to predict the division of this surplus based on the characteristics of the players.

[B] Buyer Power in Merger Control: Theories of Harm and Countervailing Effect

Following the reference to the position of suppliers in the Merger Regulation, it should come as no surprise that buyer power is also explored as part of concentration reviews.[14]

More specifically, buyer power is considered in two different ways – as figuring in a theory of harm, or as a (positive) countervailing effect. Looking at theories of harm, we *see* three broad groups:

(1) reduction of volume;
(2) reduction of choice;
(3) foreclosure effects.

The first theory of harm relates to a reduction of volume based on the monopsony model. From a welfare perspective, the reduction of output is a drawback – as the term 'deadweight loss' aptly suggests. Looking at the specific context of merger control, the fact that the monopsony model involves a single bidder means that any merger leading to such a position will raise competition concerns.

The second theory of harm relates to the reduction of choice. According to Inderst and Schaffer, following a merger, retailers limit their assortment in an effort to exercise increased buyer power—and this leads to a welfare-reducing loss of product variety for consumers.[15] This is the case as suppliers may reduce product differentiation in anticipation of consolidation. This theory has been empirically tested by Argentesi et al. using data from Dutch supermarket mergers.[16] The authors found a small negative effect of these mergers on choice.

The third theory of harm relates to foreclosure effects. These effects follow from an increase in bargaining power. A merger can lead to a shift in the outside options for one of the firms, leading to a different outcome. The most obvious example of this is where a merger of purchasers allows them to secure lower prices from their suppliers

14. Ignacio Herrera Anchustegui, *Buyer Power in EU Competition Law* (Institut de droit de la concurrence 2017), and *Buyer Power in Merger Control: An Overview of EU and National Case Law,* Concurrences: e-Competitions, 1–16 (2018); Ariel Ezrachi and Maria Ioannidou, *Buyer Power in European Union Merger Control,* 10 Eur. Comp. J. 69 (2015); Ioannis Kokkoris, *Buyer Power in UK Merger Control,* 4 Eur. Comp. L. Rev. 176 (2009).
15. Roman Inderst and Greg Shaffer Inderst, *Retail Mergers, Buyer Power and Product Variety,* 117 The Ec. J. 45 (2007).
16. Elena Argentesi, Paolo Buccirossi, Roberto Cervone, Tomaso Duso and Alessia Marrazzo, *The Effect of Retail Mergers on Prices and Variety: An Ex-post Evaluation,* DICE Discussion Paper (2016).

(who face a more negative outside option, as they would lose a larger volume due to the inability to reach an agreement).[17]

This result of lower prices may not immediately support a theory of harm in merger cases, where the most common concern in price increases following the transaction. However, we do have here grounds for accepting alternative theories of harm. A first such theory is that the better terms are passed on to consumers, but have the effect of pushing smaller purchasers out of the market as they struggle to match the lower consumer prices enabled by lower purchasing costs. Another theory is that suppliers, faced with lower margins from their sales to the merged entity, are forced to raise their prices to other purchasers, thus (as in the example above) creating a cost advantage for the merging firm, which could be applied anticompetitively. This is known as the 'waterbed effect'.[18] In both of these examples, the underlying assumption is that the short-term benefits of having lower prices are outweighed by the long(er)-term effect of having a market with fewer players. This theory of harm appears to be touched upon by the Commission in two of the cases discussed in this chapter: *Kesko/Tuko*[19] and *Carrefour/Promodès*.[20]

Finally, the notion of countervailing buyer power describes the case where the increased bargaining power of the merged entity is believed to be constrained by a powerful purchaser.[21] It is based on the same economic theory of bargaining power, being an expression of it.[22] If it can be showed that these purchasers can sufficiently constrain the merging parties, there may be grounds to consider that the effect of the concentration is not harmful. Additionally, EU competition law seems to require some form of spillover of the countervailing buyer power benefits to other buyers with respect to the supplier, as discussed extensively by Herrera Anchustegui.[23] This form of buyer power exertion is explored further in this chapter in relation to the *Enso/Stora* merger.

---

17. The output effects of such a change in agreed terms are (all things being equal) presumed to be neutral. Inderst and Wey (2007) present a model where this negative change in outside options can induce suppliers to increase their output.
18. *See*, for instance, Paul Dobson and Roman Inderst, *Differential Buyer Power and the Waterbed Effect: Do Strong Buyers Benefit or Harm Consumers?*, 28 Eur. Comp. L. Rev. 393 (2007); Roman Inderst and Tommaso M. Valletti, *Buyer Power and the 'Waterbed Effect'* 59 J. Indus. Econ. (2011); Paul Dobson and Roman Inderst, *The Waterbed Effect: Where Buying and Selling Power Come Together*, 2 Wisc. L. Rev. 331 (2008); Christos Genakos and Tommaso M. Valletti, *Regulating Prices in Two-Sided Markets: The Waterbed Experience in Mobile Telephony*, 36 Tel. Pol. 360 (2012); Ignacio Herrera Anchustegui, *Buyer Power in EU Competition Law* (Institut de droit de la concurrence 2017), at paras 149–159.
19. European Commission Decision of 20 November 1996 declaring a concentration to be incompatible with the common market (Case No. IV/M.784 – *Kesko/Tuko*) Council Regulation (EEC) No 4064/89.
20. European Commission Decision of 25 January 2000 declaring a concentration to be compatible with the common market (Case No. IV/M.1684 – *** *Carrefour/Promodes*) according to Council Regulation (EEC) No 4064/89.
21. John K. Galbraith, *The Affluent Society & Other Writings 1952–1967: American Capitalism; The Great Crash, 1929; The Affluent Society; The New Industrial State* (The Library of America 2010).
22. Ignacio Herrera Anchustegui, *Buyer Power in EU Competition Law* (Institut de droit de la concurrence 2017), at para. 1078.
23. *Ibid.*, paras 1175–1191.

§4.03 *EX POST* REVIEWS OF MERGERS INVOLVING BUYER POWER

While there are several papers on *ex post* review of mergers (e.g., Ilzkovitz and Dierx),[24] and papers that discuss buyer power in merger decisions (e.g., Carstensen,[25] Kokkoris,[26] Ezrachi and Iannadou,[27] Kirkwood,[28] Van Doorn,[29] Herrera Anchustegui[30]) our chapter is a first attempt to combine both fields from a law and economics perspective.

Ilzkovitz and Dierx[31] cite previous reports by the Canadian Competition Bureau[32] and the New Zealand Commerce Commission[33] that reviewed past merger decisions and also touched on buyer power.

Neumann and Sanderson review three past merger cases from the Canadian Competition Bureau, which all saw an extensive review of potential competition concerns and were all cleared unconditionally.[34] The three mergers related to horizontal transactions in the markets for commercial broadcast radio, coal, and finally concrete and other building materials. The authors indicate that countervailing buyer power plays a role in each of these three cases. Their assessment is limited to a review of the decisions taken as they cite challenges to obtain post-merger pricing data required to conduct their own analyses.

Csorgo and Chitale review eighteen past merger decisions from the New Zealand Commerce Commission.[35] Citing issues with the availability of data, the authors focus their review on whether anticipated market developments such as entry and/or increased imports did indeed materialise. In one of these decisions, the issue of entry sponsored by a purchaser was investigated. While such entry did not materialise, the

---

24. Fabienne Ilzkovitz and Adriaan Dierx (eds), *Ex Post Economic Evaluation of Competition Policy: The EU Experience* (Kluwer 2020).
25. Peter C. Carstensen, *Buyer Power and Merger Analysis: The Need for Different Metrics*, workshop on merger enforcement held by the Antitrust Division and the Federal Trade Commission, USA (2004); Carstensen, Peter C. Carstensen, *Buyer Power and the Horizontal Merger Guidelines: Minor Progress on an Important Issue*, 14 U. Penn. J. Bus. L. 775 (2012).
26. Ioannis Kokkoris, *Buyer Power Assessment in Competition Law: A Boon or a Menace?*, 29 W. Comp. 139 (2006); Ioannis Kokkoris, *Buyer Power in UK Merger Control*, 4 Eur. Comp. L. Rev. 176 (2009).
27. Ariel Ezrachi and Maria Ioannidou, *Buyer power in European Union Merger Control*, 10 Eur. Comp. J. 69 (2015).
28. John B. Kirkwood, *Powerful Buyers and Merger Enforcement*, 92 Bost. U. L. Rev. 1485 (2012).
29. Frederik van Doorn, *The Law and Economics of Buyer Power in EU Competition Policy* (Eleven International Publishing 2015).
30. Ignacio Herrera Anchustegui, *Buyer Power in EU Competition Law* (Institut de droit de la concurrence 2017); Ignacio Herrera Anchustegui, *Buyer Power in Merger Control: An Overview of EU and National Case Law*, Concurrences: e-Competitions, 1–16 (2018).
31. Fabienne Ilzkovitz and Adriaan Dierx (eds), *Ex Post Economic Evaluation of Competition Policy: The EU Experience* (Kluwer 2020).
32. Mark Neumann and Margaret Sanderson, *Ex Post Merger Review: An Evaluation of Three Competition Bureau Merger Assessments*, Competition Bureau, Canada (2007).
33. Lilla Csorgo and Harshal Chitale, *Targeted Ex Post Evaluations in a Data-Poor World*, 51 N. Z. Ec. P. 136 (2017).
34. Mark Neumann and Margaret Sanderson, *Ex Post Merger Review: An Evaluation of Three Competition Bureau Merger Assessments*, Competition Bureau, Canada (2007).
35. Lilla Csorgo and Harshal Chitale, *Targeted Ex Post Evaluations in a Data-Poor World*, 51 N. Z. Ec. P. 136 (2017).

authors indicate that the purchaser continues to take the view that it can (still) credibly sponsor entry should prices become too high.

This suggests that there is limited empirical work on the *ex post* assessment of buyer power in mergers.

§4.04 ASSESSING BUYER POWER AS A COMPETITION CONCERN IN SUPERMARKET MERGERS

Buyer power anticompetitive concerns have been particularly present in the supermarket sector.[36] Some of these concerns relate to alleged abusive or unfair purchasing practices by supermarkets with respect to food producers, while others have to do with risks of anticompetitive buyer power-related exclusions targeting rival supermarkets or affecting suppliers, including the complex issue of private labels.[37]

Concentration cases also display buyer power competition issues. Notable European examples are found in cases from the mid- and late-1990s in food retailing. For our study, we focus on two concentrations that provide distinct perspectives on the study of buyer power as an anticompetitive and exclusionary exertion of market power. First, we discuss the Finnish *Kesko/Tuko* merger – a case mixing concerns of both exclusionary and exploitative abuses – as it could have led to the creation of a dominant buyer.[38] We then turn our attention to the French *Carrefour/Promodès* merger – a case relevant due to what it tells us about anticompetitive and exploitative buyer power risks that arise at the 'threat point' – this being the proportion of sales that a buyer presents for a supplier and which makes it prone to have substantial buyer power. Unlike in the *Kesko/Tuko* case, this merger would not have led to the creation or strengthening of a dominant position.

---

36. Bob Young, *Supermarket Buyer Power*, Comp. L. Ins. 13 (2013); Javier Berasategi, *Supermarket Power: Serving Consumers or Harming Competition*, SSRN (2014); European Commission, *Green Paper on Unfair Trading Practices in the Business-to-Business Food and Non-Food supply Chain in Europe* (2013); Victoria Daskalova, *The New Directive on Unfair Trading Practices in Food and EU Competition Law: Complementary or Divergent Normative Frameworks?*, 10 J. Eur. Comp. L. and P. 281 (2019); Center for Antitrust and Regulatory Studies, *Legislation Covering Business-to-Business Unfair Trading Practices in the Food Supply Chain in Central and Easter European Countries* (2019); Hanna Schebesta et al., *Unfair Trading Practices in the Food Supply Chain: Regulating Right?*, 9 Eur. J. R. Reg. 690 (2018); Ronny Gjendemsjø and Ignacio Herrera Anchustegui, *The Scope for National Regulation of Unfair Trading Practices*, in Johan Giertsen et al. (eds), *Festskrift til 50-årsjubileet for jurist-utdanningen ved Universitetet i Bergen* (Fagbokforlaget 2019); Ronny Gjendemsjø and Ignacio Herrera Anchustegui, *Regulating the Food Supply Chain in Europe and the Unfair Trading Practices Directive*, Rev. eur. de dr. de la cons. 165 (2020).
37. Ariel Ezrachi, A. and Koen De Jong, *Buyer Power, Private Labels and the Welfare Consequences of Quality Erosion*, 33 Eur. Comp. L. Rev. 45 (2012); Wernhard Möschel, *Market Definition with Branded Goods and Private Label Products*, 35 Eur. Comp. L. Rev. 29 (2014); Sergio Meza and K. Sudhir, *Do Private Labels Increase Retailer Bargaining Power?*, 8 Quant. Mark. and Ec. 333 (2010); Paul Dobson and Ratula Chakraborty, *Assessing brand and private label competition*, 36 Eur. Comp. L. Rev. 76 (2015).
38. *See also* discussing the case: Ariel Ezrachi and Maria Ioannidou, *Buyer Power in European Union Merger Control*, 10 Eur. Comp. J. 69 (2015).

[A] *Kesko/Tuko*

[1] The Operation and the Parties

On 20 November 1996, the Commission declared the concentration between Kesko Oy and Tuko Oy incompatible with the common market. These two companies were incorporated and operating mostly in Finland in the 'retail sales of daily consumer goods and/or specialty goods'[39] and the 'wholesale and retail of daily consumer goods and speciality goods'[40] respectively. On 27 May 1996, 'Kesko acquired 56.3 % of Tuko's share capital, thereby obtaining 59.3% of the voting rights, and direct control of Tuko'.[41]

At the time, the operation constituted a concentration with no community dimension pursuant to Article 1 of the then Merger Regulation. However, the Commission found that '[t]he acquisition of Tuko by Kesko will *create foreclosure effects for new entrants*, including potential entrants from other Member States, in particular on the Finnish markets for daily consumer goods'.[42]

Both Kesko and Tuko were part of several 'international purchasing organisations' in the European Economic Area, reinforcing their buyer power as members of these alliances. [43]

Kesko and its affiliates, independent entrepreneurs but contractually bound to Kesko, operated through a collaboration scheme called the 'K-block'.[44] A similar approach was adopted by Tuko and its retailer agents.[45] Despite the agents being somewhat independent, the pricing, purchasing and retailing strategies were centrally planned. In this sense, the Commission concluded that for the K-block, 'Kesko, as the central organ of the Kesko group has responsibility for the planning and execution of changes to the overall group structure',[46] being all independent retailers bound and loyal to Kesko. A similar conclusion was reached regarding the Tuko retailers and its 'T-block' system.[47]

[2] Relevant Markets Assessed

The assessment of the relevant markets was particularly important for this case and its buyer power implications. *Kesko/Tuko* is a prime example showing the dualistic nature of buyer power cases and how the existence of selling market power in a retailing end consumers market exacerbates the risk of abuse of buyer market power by retailers.

---

39. Case No. IV/M.784 – *Kesko/Tuko*, para. 5.
40. *Ibid.*, para. 6.
41. Case No. IV/M.784 – *Kesko/Tuko*, para. 7 (punctuation updated).
42. *Ibid.*, para. 11 (emphasis added).
43. *Ibid.*, para. 12.
44. *Ibid.*, paras 5 and 39.
45. *Ibid.*, paras 6 and 39.
46. *Ibid.*, para. 63.
47. *Ibid.*, para. 65.

This logic was also stressed in the decision by the Commission when it maintained that:[48]

> the three daily consumer markets ... are vertically connected in such a way that the position of Kesko and Tuko on the retail market for daily consumer goods creates the basis for their positions on the procurement markets (e.g., vis-à-vis suppliers of daily consumer goods). Conversely *their position at the procurement level significantly affects their position at retail level.*

Kesko argued first that the operation was to be assessed at the wholesale but not at a retail level.[49] If accepted, this would not have fully captured all of the markets involved or the full effects of the merger. The Commission rejected this[50] and proposed the assessment in three markets- the retail market for daily consumed goods; the market for cash and carry sales of daily consumed goods as sellers; and the markets for procurement of daily consumer goods as buyers.

Selling Markets

The retail market for daily consumer goods was defined as comprising the provision for end consumers of fresh and dry food-stuffs and non-food household consumables sold in supermarkets - not including specialised stores, kiosks or petrol stations.[51] Geographically, this market was defined as covering all of Finland and was not based on national, regional or local levels as the market shares of Kesko and Tuko remained constant throughout the whole of the country.[52]

At the time of the merger, the Finnish retail market for daily consumer goods was one of the most concentrated in Europe.[53] If the concentration had taken place, the 'K-block would account for at least 55% ... of all sales of daily consumer goods in Finland'.[54] Not only would this have reached the presumption of dominance,[55] but the combined market share would have trebled the shares of the second-largest competitor, SOK, with 21.9% of the market share.

On the other hand, the *wholesale market* for cash and carry sales of daily goods was structured in such a way that 'customers provide the transport themselves, and pay for the goods in cash rather than on credit'. This market was particularly used by smaller buyers that will later resell to end consumers, typically represented by smaller companies and entities present in the industrial household business (hotels, restaurants, hospitals). In this market, the main purchases from both Kesko and Tuko were of dry food products, amounting to 60%-70% of the volume of sales.[56] Importantly, customers in this market were found to be captive. This was the case as they would not

48. *Ibid.*, para. 38, (emphasis added).
49. Case No. IV/M.784 - *Kesko/Tuko*, para. 14.
50. *Ibid.*, para. 15.
51. *Ibid.*, para. 20.
52. *Ibid.*, para. 22.
53. *Ibid.*, para. 93.
54. *Ibid.*
55. Judgment of 3 July 1991 in *AKZO v. Commission*, C-62/86, EU:C:1991:286, para. 60.
56. Case No. IV/M.784 - *Kesko/Tuko*, paras 24-28.

be able to switch easily to 'classic' wholesaling due to storage and financial means,[57] highlighting the dependence in which they were as buyers but not as sellers vis-à-vis the proposed merger parties. Geographically, the cash and carry market was assessed regionally and not nationally due to the long distances and low population density in Finland.

Only the market for procurement of daily consumer goods had a particular buyer-orientated analysis. This market involved the sale of daily consumer goods by producers to wholesalers, retailers and other businesses. Due to the specificity of the purchases, each product or product group was seen as 'an individual product market'.[58] However, the Commission concluded that it was 'not necessary to assess the impact of the concentration on each individual product or group of products. It is sufficient to assess the impact of the increased buying power, brought about by the new demand structure, across the whole range of daily consumer goods'.[59] This purchasing market was found to be Finland as a whole.

[3] Theor(ies) of Harm

Selling-Side Concerns

The Commission's investigation focused on the creation of what would have been at the time a dominant position in the retail market for daily consumer goods. Such a dominant position would have led to a price increase in the food retailing market, affecting end consumers. Unequivocally, the Commission stated that:[60]

> The combined market share of Kesko and Tuko of at least 55%, whether assessed at local, regional or national level creates a presumption of dominance. This presumption is further strengthened by Kesko's and Tuko's position as regards large retail outlets, their control of a significant part of all business premises suited for retail outlets in Finland, their customer loyalty schemes and private label products, their distribution systems and, not least, by the position of their central organs as buyers of daily consumer goods.

This large market power, reaching dominance, combined with the relatively small size of the rivals, led the Commission to conclude that no competitor would have been able to 'restrict Kesko's behaviour in the market in any significant way, and in particular if it were to increase consumer prices'.[61] This conclusion applied to Kesko as a retailer/seller but not as a buyer. In addition to pure market shares and the risk of a price increase without being constrained by its much smaller rivals, entry barriers were

57. *Ibid.*, para. 29.
58. Case No. IV/M.784 – *Kesko/Tuko*, para. 34.
59. *Ibid.*, para. 34.
60. *Ibid.*, para. 106. *See also* remarking this point in the decision and linking it buyer power: Ariel Ezrachi and Maria Ioannidou, *Buyer Power in European Union Merger Control*, 10 Eur. Comp. J. 69 (2015).
61. Case No. IV/M.784 – *Kesko/Tuko*, para. 137.

present in the market - preventing new entrants from accessing the market. We consider these entry barriers in our discussion below.

Entry Barriers

The Commission stressed that allowing such concentration would have led to the creation of significant entry barriers in the food retailing market, particularly because it would have permitted the merged entity to control and have a presence throughout Finland in large establishments, defined as those larger than 1,000 m^2.[62]

Furthermore, due to the nature of the food retailing business in Finland and the difficulty of acquiring the necessary authorisation from local governments to operate such a business, the control by Kesko and Tuko of a significant number of business premises was also seen as a way to 'maintain and increase the strength of the dominant position held by Kesko and Tuko'.[63]

The use of loyalty schemes, in the form of the K-advantage card - with 600,000 of them issued - created a loyalty-inducing effect for customers. Additionally, it provided Kesko with personalised information about its customers and their purchasing patterns to a 'level which none of its competitors can match'.[64]

The presence of Kesko's private brands, accounting for up to 20%-30% of its total sales, was seen as another key barrier to competition. Some of these products were found to be exclusive, which not only could have raised issues of entry barriers but also could grant Kesko the opportunity to 'price a greater proportion of its sales without having the need to take into account the reaction of its competitors in the same way as with branded products'.[65] This situation, along with the buyer power-related effects of private labels, was also seen as putting competition at risk in the food retailing market.

Lastly, the food retailing market was affected by the presence of Kesko's subsidiary as a distributor/transporter of goods, controlling the two only systems in Finland for the distribution of frozen foods. The acquisition would have allowed Kesko to influence the way in which frozen goods were transported, increasing third-party retailers' dependence on Kesko and constituting a 'significant barrier to entry on the retail market'.[66]

The analysis in the cash and carry market was not very different either. This was a 'very concentrated' market in which Kesko and Tuko clearly dominated the distribution outlets and in which there were very few other cash and carry outlets among three other groups. With the concentration, the merged entity would have reached a combined market share of over 80% across the country, and at least 50% in each of the different Finnish regions.

62. Case No. IV/M.784 - *Kesko/Tuko*, paras 106-112.
63. *Ibid.*, para. 118.
64. *Ibid.*, para. 121.
65. *Ibid.*, para. 130.
66. *Ibid.*, para. 132.

Buyer-Side Concerns

Buyer power was a factor when evaluating the merger and determining that it would have led to the creation of a dominant position in the three markets that were investigated. While these concerns were not the main reason to block the merger, they were of importance. As stressed in the decision, the 'main competitive concerns identified by the Commission concerns the retail market, which is the main market, in terms of turnover as well as [the] direct impact on Finnish consumers'.[67] That said, *Kesko/Tuko* illustrates well the complex relation of reinforcement that buyer power and seller power have when combined in a single entity, as remarked by the Commission.[68]

Buyer power concerns were raised by the Commission in all assessed markets. The focus of this analysis, however, was the markets for the procurement of daily consumer goods.

In the analysis of buyer power effects on food retailing and procurement of daily consumer goods the Commission combined concerns about possible exploitation of dependent suppliers, even though there was no mention of how this could have taken place, with effects against rival supermarket chains. According to the Commission, Kesko would have used its buyer power to the detriment of competitors as retailers in the downstream market to further weaken their position in the long term.[69] Additionally, the Commission directly linked seller market power to the granting of buyer power when it held that such a position 'guarantees Kesko *an extremely powerful negotiating position vis-à-vis the producers of daily consumer goods*'.[70]

In this setting, buyer power surges based on the volume of purchases and the centralised way Kesko acquires goods for its suppliers. The decision shows how 'the majority of the suppliers (including several major multinationals) that replied to the Commission's investigation indicated that *they depend* on Kesko and Tuko for approximately 50 %–75 % of their total sales in Finland'.[71] Furthermore, most of these suppliers would not have been able to switch to another buyer if *Kesko/Tuko* had exerted exploitative buyer power.[72] Dependence, therefore, was the crucial factor for assessing risks of buyer market power abuse – even though some large sellers were *not* as they had countervailing (seller) power.[73]

Private labels not only granted some market power vis-à-vis downstream consumers but also buyer market power in relation to the suppliers of the proposed entity,

67. Case No. IV/M.784 – *Kesko/Tuko*, para. 170.
68. Herrera Anchustegui refers to this as the 'hourglass effect' in his *Buyer Power in EU Competition Law* (Institut de droit de la concurrence 2017). *See also* Frederik van Doorn, *The Law and Economics of Buyer Power in EU Competition Policy* (Eleven International Publishing 2015), at 163–164.
69. Case No. IV/M.784 – *Kesko/Tuko*, para. 153.
70. *Ibid.*, para. 146 (emphasis added).
71. *Ibid.*, para. 148 (emphasis added).
72. *Ibid.*, para. 151.
73. *Ibid.*, para. 150.

especially in combination with loyalty scheme programmes.[74] This dual nature of supplier and retailer for private goods gave the merging parties privileged information about their rivals, who produced branded goods. For the Commission, this 'increases the leverage enjoyed by retailers over branded goods producers'.[75]

The Commission concluded that despite these concerns the buyer power risks pertaining to the procurement of daily consumer goods alone and in themselves do not appear to be sufficient to block the merger. Instead, and as we will *see* below, the emphasis seems to have been placed on the fact that 'given that the concentration would lead to dominant positions on the retail and cash and carry markets, the Commission is of the opinion that the increased buying power of Kesko would further reinforce the dominant position of Kesko on the retail and cash and carry markets'.[76]

In the retail of daily consumer goods - the core of the case - buyer power also played a role. If the merger had been approved, the new entity would have become a market gatekeeper and necessary trading partner, being a retailer with 55% of the market. This 'gatekeeper effect' would be further increased by the combination of Kesko and Tuko's private label products and their success. Such combination could have been used as a tool when negotiating with suppliers to achieve additional concessions on, *inter alia*, reduced prices or increased marketing support.[77]

In the market for cash and carry sales, similar buyer power issues as those discussed above (in the market of retail of daily consumer goods) would have arisen. This was due to the fact that the merged entity would have been able to foreclose its rivals and act as a gatekeeper.[78]

Lastly, buyer power was also a concern for potential competition from foreign undertakings. The buyer power of the proposed entity would have been 'one of the most significant barriers to foreign entry, since one of the key questions for any potential entrant will be to secure access to daily consumer goods at prices which allows such an entrant to effectively compete with Kesko' in the investigated markets.[79]

[4] Outcome

Despite commitments offered by Kesko involving the divestiture of its assets and the creation of a new block of retailers on the market,[80] the assessment by the Commission concluded that the merger was contrary to EU law. Therefore, it was declared incompatible with the internal market. In addition, as the concentration had been implemented *before* the Commission established its ruling on the case, measures to

74. *See also* on this p. 79 of Ariel Ezrachi and Maria Ioannidou, *Buyer Power in European Union Merger Control*, 10 Eur. Comp. J. 69 (2015).
75. Case No. IV/M.784 - *Kesko/Tuko*, para. 152.
76. *Ibid.*, para. 153.
77. *Ibid.*, para. 133.
78. *Ibid.*, para. 144.
79. *Ibid.*, para. 158.
80. Ariel Ezrachi and Maria Ioannidou, *Buyer Power in European Union Merger Control*, 10 Eur. Comp. J. 69 (2015).

restore the situation as if the merger had not taken place were implemented. Kesko appealed the decision before the General Court, but the action was dismissed in its entirety.[81]

[B] *Carrefour/Promodès*

[1] Operation and the Parties

In 1999, Promodès, a French food retailer with 8%–13% market share domestically, was acquired by its major rival Carrefour, another French food retailer with about 12%–17% of the French food retailing market share.[82] As we discuss in detail below, the merger assessment identified some market power abuse risks in two markets. Yet a dominant position would not have emerged in either the upstream or the downstream market.[83] A first market power abuse risk pertained to food distribution/retailing with respect to end consumers (downstream market) due to possible price increases and existing barriers of entry. A second market power risk affected the purchasing (upstream) market. Here, the merged entity could have abused its buyer power to the detriment to its suppliers. Additionally, buyer power could have created exclusionary risks for other large buyers that compete with the merging parties as food retailers in the downstream market. Despite the concerns in both markets, in which buyer power was one aspect but not the sole aspect considered, the operation was declared compatible with the market as it did not create or strengthen a dominant position in the French food retailing market.

As announced, the *Carrefour/Promodès* merger was launched to create a single group that would have control over more than a quarter of the French food retailing market and which would form the largest retail group in the European Community at the same time. The merger had a community dimension with an estimated combined worldwide turnover of EUR 5 billion.[84] Due to this, it fell within the scope of the Council Regulation on the control of concentrations between undertakings (Merger Regulation).[85] Pursuant to Article 4(1) of Merger Control Regulation of 1989, this acquisition was reported to the Commission to be assessed on 5 October 1999.[86]

At the time of the notification, Carrefour and Promodès were holding companies specialised in retail activities carried out across France, Spain, Italy, Greece and Portugal.[87] They centred their activities in large stores combining food and non-food products (predominantly hypermarkets and supermarkets) that covered a total area exceeding 4.1 m square metres – almost double of the shopping space of the largest

81. Judgment of 15 December 1999, *Kesko v. Commission*, T-22/97, EU:T:1999:327.
82. COMP/M. 1684 – *Carrefour/Promodès*, full (French version) of 25 January 2000.
83. *See* p. 81 of Ezrachi and Maria Ioannidou, *Buyer Power in European Union Merger Control*, 10 Eur. Comp. J. 69 (2015).
84. Decision 1999/C359/10, *Carrefour/Promodès* (2000), para. 6.
85. Council Regulation (EEC) No 4064/89 of 21 December 1989 on the control of concentrations between undertakings (OJ L 395, 30.12.1989, p. 1).
86. Decision 1999/C359/10, *Carrefour/Promodès* (2000), para. 1.
87. *Ibid.*, para. 8.

rival (Intermarket).[88] Through the similar business models of the merging retailers and the considerable gains resulting from the acquisition, Carrefour was set to take a leading role in the French market, increasing the number of its selling points by 150%.

Two main markets were affected by the operation, both related to food retailing[89] – the distribution market ('le marché aval'), in which supermarkets are in contact with end consumers as suppliers of food stuff (i.e., the downstream retailing market); and the purchasing market ('le marché amont'), in which supermarkets acquire goods from food suppliers and product producers. Such combination, as in *Kesko/Tuko*, reinforces buyer power exertion risks in both associated markets, as well as creating some gatekeeper effects.[90]

Relevant Market Delimitation

Both markets assessed were associated with food retailing. The investigation distinguished a distribution market in which both parties act as retailers with respect to end consumers.[91] Here, the decision distinguishes small local stores from medium and large stores (supermarkets and hypermarkets), the latter being the focus of the analysis.

However, unlike in the *Kesko/Tuko* case, the definition of the market was supplemented with groups of products.[92] The Commission subscribed to the catalogue of twenty-three groups suggested by the parties, simultaneously recognising the presence of different dynamics within each group.[93] The justification of this approach stems from the broad range of merchandise offered in supermarkets or big-box stores, including not only groceries but also department store goods.

In the national food retailing (distribution) market, the Commission assessed the market shares of Carrefour and Promodès by taking into account both the surface of shops in the country and the market shares as sellers. Carrefour had between 10% and 15% in surface, while in sales it represented 12%–17%. Promodès had 8%–13% and 8%–13% respectively. The resulting merged entity would have reached between 25% and 30% both in surfaces and sales.[94] Post merger, the joint entities would become France's largest food retailing distributor,[95] with Intermarché, Casino and Leclerc not too far behind in a market that is not very concentrated (with percentages between 10% and 20% of the market), in opposition to the *Kesko/Tuko* case.

---

88. Decision 1999/C359/10, *Carrefour/Promodès* (2000), para. 39.
89. *Ibid.*, para. 8.
90. For a discussion regarding gatekeeping and buyer power *see*: Warren S. Grimes, *Buyer Power and Retail Gatekeeper Power: Protecting Competition and the Atomistic Seller*, 72 Ant. L. J. 563 (2005); Ignacio Herrera Anchustegui, *Buyer Power in EU Competition Law* (Institut de droit de la concurrence 2017), at paras 440–448.
91. Decision 1999/C359/10, *Carrefour/Promodès* (2000), paras 9–13.
92. *Ibid.*, para. 16.
93. For instance, products categorised as appliances (RTV or household appliances) or textile comprised a fraction of hypermarket sales, and had other (specialised) outlets – contrary to most of the groceries (*see* Decision 1999/C359/10, *Carrefour/Promodès* (2000), para. 94).
94. Decision 1999/C359/10, *Carrefour/Promodès* (2000), para. 36.
95. *Ibid.*, para. 40.

Additionally, an upstream purchasing market – in which buyer power played a key role – was defined as the sale of goods by producers to the distributors, small retailers or other types of larger buyers (hotels or restaurants).[96] In this product market, the Commission took account of the degree of flexibility left to the suppliers' appreciation after the operation, as the flexibility varies from product to product (or sector to sector).[97] This level of discretion is crucial, as highlighted by the Commission and surveyed suppliers, as the change of distributor (buyer) would be troublesome (the change can be associated with modification to product size, package or label design) – and as a result, it would also require considerable investment.[98]

Market delimitation accounting for differences in each product group was particularly useful in assessing the position of suppliers confronted by the merger of Carrefour and Promodès – companies that jointly held 25%–30% of market share.

Regarding the geographical market, the assessment is based on a study at the national level of competition, in line with the views both of the parties and of the suppliers.[99] The Commission noted that activities such as advertising campaigns, launches of new products and customer loyalty policies are predominantly carried out at the national level.[100] Its decision reiterates findings of the case *Rewe/Meinl*,[101] stressing that the supply should be considered at the national level,[102] because distributors exercise their buyer power domestically, rather than locally or regionally.[103] On the other hand, for the downstream market, the Commission did not raise serious doubts, regardless of geographical delimitation.[104]

[2] Theories of Harm

As in *Kesko/Tuko*, the Commission assessed competitive risks both in the market regarding food retailing (distribution) and the purchasing market. This again supports the proposition that buyer power has a clear dual effect in markets, and that buyer market power typically reinforces seller market power.

We only discuss briefly here concerns regarding seller market power. In the downstream market, the fears were about price increases, as well as entry barriers and foreclosure effects vis-à-vis other food retailers. These concerns centred on the fact that: (i) Carrefour and Promodès were the only actors present in all the markets of different food distribution models (hypermarkets, supermarkets, large stores and small

96. *Ibid.*, para. 14.
97. *Ibid.*, para. 15.
98. *Ibid.*, para. 20.
99. *Ibid.*, para. 31.
100. *Ibid.*, para. 25.
101. *Rewe/Meinl*, Commission Decision 1999/674/EC (1999) OJ L274/1.
102. Decision 1999/C359/10, *Carrefour/Promodès* (2000), para. 28.
103. *Ibid.*, para. 30.
104. *Ibid.*, para. 27. For the analysis of catchment areas in local downstream markets in the present case, the Commission referred to the French and Spanish authorities, as they requested (Decision 1999/C359/10, *Carrefour/Promodès* (2000), paras 34 and 108).

proximity stores);[105] (ii) the new entity would be the leader of the hypermarket segment with a market share of 25%–35%;[106] (iii) the entity would have a particularly influential position regarding fidelity cards,[107] and a more integrated structure than its rivals;[108] and (iv) the new entity would have greater financial strength than its competitors.[109]

Concerning the purchasing market, the concern arose from the ability of the new entity to exert pernicious buyer market power over its providers, to the point that they could be exploited in a 'de facto situation of "economic dependence"'.[110] We discuss this in further detail below in this section.

The major anticompetitive effect preliminarily found in the assessment of the operation was the strengthening of Carrefour's position relative to its suppliers, as well as competitors – particularly in France. Two factors played a major role here.

On the one hand, Carrefour owned 42% of shares in Cora,[111] another food retailer present in the distribution/downstream market with a market share in France of about 5%–10%.[112] Even though Carrefour was not a majority shareholder, it could have considerable influence over the decision-making processes in Cora. Additionally, it could have undermined Cora's competitiveness in the retail markets, casting some doubts on Carrefour's position vis-à-vis its competitors (and suppliers). For that reason, the company committed to tender its Cora shares.[113]

The second concern regarded the situation of small- and medium-sized suppliers that could find themselves in a disadvantaged position after the acquisition. The Commission provided the detailed rationale and justification for this buyer power concern in its decision.

Buyer-Power Concerns: The Menace Point or Spiral Effect

Potential pernicious effects of the exertion of buyer power in the upstream purchasing market were the subject of extensive analysis in the decision, focusing on what the Commission called 'taux de "menace"' or the 'threat point',[114] also dubbed as the 'spiral effect'.[115] This concerns the ability to exert abusive buyer power on suppliers that could be in a situation of economic dependence. This phenomenon can be observed in another supermarket merger case – *Rewe/Meinl* – an operation that, despite concerns about buyer power abuse, was declared compatible with the internal

105. Decision 1999/C359/10, *Carrefour/Promodès* (2000), paras 56–59.
106. *Ibid.*, paras 57–63.
107. *Ibid.*, paras 63–65.
108. *Ibid.*, paras 63–69.
109. *Ibid.*, paras 70–75.
110. *Ibid.*, para. 52.
111. *Ibid.*, para. 83.
112. *Ibid.*, para. 36.
113. *Ibid.*, para. 90.
114. Decision 1999/C359/10, *Carrefour/Promodès* (2000), paras 52–55.
115. *See also* on this issue p. 81 of Ariel Ezrachi and Maria Ioannidou, *Buyer Power in European Union Merger Control*, 10 Eur. Comp. J. 69 (2015).

market.[116] According to this spiral or threat point effect theory, buyer power upstream increases market concentration downstream, leading to a vicious circle of more retailer power and the capacity later to reap monopoly profits from end consumers due to the creation of entry and exit barriers.[117]

The Commission consulted with the suppliers regarding the point at which they considered the loss of a customer to represent 'a threat for the existence of their business'. In this case, suppliers indicated that when a buyer represents 20%–22% of their turnover, they would be in a state of 'economic dependence' regarding said buyer. Interestingly, the same average threshold resulted from the surveys of suppliers in *Rewe/Meinl* case.[118]

Based on this, the Commission concluded that 'when a distributor exceeds such threshold [22%] of the turnover of one of its suppliers', there is a situation of economic dependence.[119] The figure here resembles that of national rules dealing with relative dominance, but such a concept does not exist in EU competition law.

This threshold was reached regarding some particular products related to the drugstore, hygiene, dry groceries and perfumery sectors.[120] None of the merging entity competitors as buyers and retailers would have achieved more than 20% of this turnover representation in most product groups, reinforcing the strong buying position of the merging parties.[121]

As remarked by Herrera Anchustegui before:[122]

> Importantly, and a factor that may easily be overlooked, is that this 22% does not represent the undertaking's market shares in the purchasing market but instead *represents the ratio of sales that a buyer signifies for a particular buyer*. However, this situation was not isolated concerning a single supplier of a single product (which qualifies as an individual market) but happened in at least ten of the markets affected by the merger. In practice, this may imply that even a buyer with a small total purchasing market share may still have *relative* buyer power vis-à-vis a particular supplier but not *general* buyer power. Yet and at least for concentration assessments, relative buyer power may be an issue that can, along with other circumstances, imply that the operation may not be compatible with the internal market.

Lastly, the Commission reinforced its argument by stressing the relationship between buyer power and seller power'. Explicitly, the Commission stated that due to Carrefour's specific advantages in the downstream markets, these could 'strengthen

116. Decision 1999/674/EC, *Rewe/Meinl* (1999). *See also*: Decision 1999/C359/10, *Carrefour/Promodès* (2000), para. 52.
117. Ignacio Herrera Anchustegui, *Buyer Power in EU Competition Law* (Institut de droit de la concurrence 2017), at 67.
118. Decision 1999/674/EC, *Rewe/Meinl* (1999), para. 101.
119. Decision 1999/C359/10, *Carrefour/Promodès* (2000), para. 52.
120. *Ibid.*, para. 53.
121. *Ibid.*, para. 54.
122. Ignacio Herrera Anchustegui, *Buyer Power in EU Competition Law*, para. 408 (Institut de droit de la concurrence 2017).

the new downstream entity and, consequently, have a significant impact on its position *vis-à-vis* its suppliers'.[123]

Two other linked to buyer power concerns were discussed. Firstly, after the acquisition, Carrefour was also expected to enjoy some specific advantages stemming from its new position in the market and reinforcing its buyer power. Chiefly, these advantages were linked to two determinants: the scale of the new group (the higher the purchase volume, the more preferential conditions offered by suppliers),[124] and a profitable emphasis on hypermarkets in the business model (the more substantial the area of a selling point, the broader range of suppliers' products that might be presented - hence, the greater interest in commercial relations with such a distributor).[125] Secondly, the substantial sales area allowed Carrefour to introduce profitable private labels. In principle, Carrefour's presence in the offer leaves the retailer greater room for manoeuvre and strengthens its power over suppliers.[126] Essentially, it allows the company to obtain more generous concessions from its suppliers as a part of the bargain offsetting private label policy.

Additionally, and as part of an analysis related to a possible existence of collective dominance that was dismissed, the Commission raised the fact that with respect to suppliers, other competitors of the merging parties reached the 'threat point'. The Commission then went further and argued that due to the new market structure after the concentration, many suppliers will be faced with at most two, three or four customers, each representing such a large part of their total sales that the refusal to purchase by just one of them would create insurmountable difficulties for the suppliers concerned.[127] As a consequence, suppliers would not only face a threat related to the loss of a single, large client, but the turnover in one product group might almost entirely depend on two or three players only. Therefore, it seems that the Commission makes use of the threat (risk) rate to determine and assess structural challenges in the market, while the meaning of this rate in individual merger cases is limited.[128]

Buyer power concerns were also briefly mentioned when reviewing the effects of the operation in Spain.[129] In the segments of 'drugstore', 'self-service perishable products' and 'dry groceries', the merging parties also reached the threat point, putting their suppliers in a situation of economic dependence. The Commission also stressed that competitors to the margining entities had a proportion of sales that did not reach the threat point between 20% and 22%.

Interestingly, the Commission did not discuss in the decision how this economic dependence could be exploited, either in the French or Spanish markets. However, it can be inferred that it would have been an exertion of buyer power with respect to

123. Decision 1999/C359/10, *Carrefour/Promodès* (2000), para. 55.
124. *Ibid.*, paras 45–46.
125. *Ibid.*, para. 63.
126. *Ibid.*, para. 75.
127. Decision 1999/C359/10, *Carrefour/Promodès* (2000), para. 97.
128. In this case, the French retail market after entry into force of the so-called *Galland Law*, *see* Decision 1999/C359/10, *Carrefour/Promodès* (2000), paras 100–104.
129. Decision 1999/C359/10, *Carrefour/Promodès* (2000), para. 127.

suppliers, akin to unfair purchasing practices that are often associated with food retailing, and which we will discuss further in section §4.07.

[3] *Searching for Solutions*

Despite the upstream and downstream competition risks that were generated by the proposed operation, the assessment made by the Commission indicates that, in general, this would have been a concentration not leading to the creation or strengthening of a dominant position. Regarding concerns about economic dependence in the upstream market, the decision indicates that the risks were limited to some types of products, and little was said about *how* such dependence could be abused. This leads us to infer that they were not particularly significant.

However, the merging parties offered a series of commitments to mitigate any risks associated with the concentration. As remarked by Herrera Anchustegui before, none of them was linked directly to buyer power abuses – instead '[t]he commitments addressed the buyer dependence indirectly as it was ordered to divest some stores that represented alternative buyers for the suppliers who would have been less dependent on the single entity'.[130]

In general, Carrefour pledged not to modify the contracts concluded with suppliers that were in force when the decision was adopted. Annex 2 outlines the main characteristics of that commitment, specifying which suppliers are subjects to it, the duration, as well as further details, the dispute resolution clause,[131] and exceptions.[132] This pledge was meant to serve as protection for small and medium suppliers,[133] the turnover of which did not exceed EUR 1.5 billion, and was designed to temporarily (and effectively) limit the exertion of buyer power by the new Carrefour/Promodès group vis-á-vis suppliers.

§4.05 COUNTERVAILING BUYER POWER AS A DEFENCE IN CARDBOARD MERGERS

Unlike in the previous two cases, buyer power arising in concentrations may also be used by merging parties and competition authorities to determine whether it may sufficiently neutralise or countervail risks of anticompetitive seller power. The

130. Ignacio Herrera Anchustegui, *Buyer Power in EU Competition Law*, pp. 186–187 (Institut de droit de la concurrence 2017).
131. Decision 1999/C359/10, *Carrefour/Promodès* (2000), Annex 2, para. B.
132. *Ibid.*, Annex 2, para. A2.
133. *Ibid.*, para. 135.

Enso/Stora merger,[134] between two entities involved in the forest industry and manufacturing of paper and pulp board, is a classic example of sufficient countervailing buyer power exerted by TetraPak (a buyer of liquid packaging board).[135]

[A] *Enso/Stora*: The Merging Parties and the Operation

On 18 June 1998, Enso Oyj ('Enso') and Stora Kopparbergs Bergslags AB ('Stora') notified the European Commission of their intention to fully merge to create a new company, Stora Enso Oyj ('Stora Enso'), pursuant to Article 4 of the then in force Regulation 4064/89 ('the Merger Regulation'). Enso and Stora were both involved in the forestry business. Enso, a company incorporated in Finland, and which operated and owned production plants in both Europe and Asia, was engaged in 'activities consist[ing] of wood procurement, paper and board manufacturing, pulp and sawmilling', as well as being a merchant.[136] Stora was a Swedish corporation with production plants in both Europe and Canada, which operated in the forest industry, particularly in the production of paper and board as well as in sawmilling.[137]

The concentration was configured as a public bid for all of Stora's shares and reaching a community dimension with a global turnover above EUR 5 billion. Upon acquisition, former Stora shareholders would receive newly issued shares in Enso, rendering Stora a subsidiary wholly owned by Enso. Interesting, the largest shareholder of the proposed entity was to be the Finnish State with 17.6% of the shares and 21% of the voting rights.[138]

[B] Markets Affected by the Concentration

As a whole, the operation had an impact in several markets: newsprint, magazine papers, fine papers, corrugating raw materials, consumer packaging, and pulp. In the assessment, the European Commission focused on some of these sub-markets: newsprint (paper for newspapers), magazine paper, and consumer packaging board. In the case of newsprint, magazine paper, and non-liquid packaging board, the Commission analysed concerns related to the creation of an 'oligopolistically dominant position' which was ultimately discarded.[139] In these assessments, countervailing buyer power was briefly taken into account.

134. Commission Decision of 25 November 1998, declaring a concentration to be compatible with the common market and the functioning of the EEA Agreement (Case No. IV/M.1225 – *Enso/Stora*) (OJ [1999] L 254/9).
135. *See also* highlighting this Ariel Ezrachi and Maria Ioannidou, *Buyer Power in European Union Merger Control*, 10 Eur. Comp. J. 69, 81 (2015); Simon Baker and Andrea Lofaro, *Buyer Power and the* Enso/Stora *Decision*, 21 Eur. Comp. L. Rev. 187 (2000).
136. Case No. IV/M.1225 – *Enso/Stora*, para. 3.
137. *Ibid.*, para. 4.
138. Case No. IV/M.1225 – *Enso/Stora*, para. 6.
139. *Ibid.*, paras 60–71.

Newsprint Market

In the case of newsprint, the proposed entity would have had between 20% and 30% market shares – with a few other competitors having market shares of 10%–20% such as UPM-Kymmene, or 10%–15% for Norske Skog. This led the Commission to conclude that this market was 'fairly concentrated. The six leading producers account for about 75%'.[140] Such concentration levels led the Commission to consider whether this selling market structure could constitute an oligopoly formed by the six largest newspaper sellers.[141] In contrast to the selling side, the Commission found that there were two large buyers, accounting for about 25%–35% of the market – who 'are a source of stability, and therefore security, since losing or partly losing a large customer could cause substantial problems for a supplier to fill its mill capacity. Suppliers are, therefore, very sensitive to losing large customers'.[142]

The Commission assessed whether the concentration in this oligopolistic market could lead to an increase in prices vis-à-vis the largest buyers, increasing the overall market price level. The Commission found that 'the characteristics of the newsprint market indicate a market with few incentives for the members of the oligopoly to compete'.[143] Moderate growth, supply-side concentration and therefore buyer power (although not discussed), product homogeneity, and technology maturity contribute to this, as well as an increase 'in the Herfindahl-Hirschman Index of 313 points'.[144] Despite this, the concentration was found 'not to lead to the creation or strengthening of an oligopolistically dominant position',[145] because there was no price market transparency, some potential competition from outside the Union, and some limited '*countervailing purchasing power of the largest buyers appears to exist*, too'.[146]

In the decision, there is no discussion of the assessment of said countervailing buyer power in the newsprint market. We assume that this passing mention was based on the relative concentration in the purchasing market with two large players in which size was the main factor to be evaluated as these buyers could 'buy volumes that could fill the complete capacity of some of the large producers'.[147]

Magazine Paper

Paper used for magazine and its production was another of the EEA-affected matters. The merging parties would have reached a market share of approximately 20%–25%. Based on these low thresholds and the market conditions, the Commissioned briefly concluded that the 'operation does not lead to the creation or strengthening of an oligopolistically dominant position in the market of magazine paper'.[148]

140. *Ibid.*, para. 61.
141. *Ibid.*, para. 65.
142. *Ibid.*, para. 64.
143. *Ibid.*, para. 67.
144. *Ibid.*
145. Case No. IV/M.1225 – *Enso/Stora*, para. 68.
146. *Ibid.* (emphasis added).
147. *Ibid.*, para. 63.
148. *Ibid.*, para. 71.

Non-liquid Packaging Board

In this market, after the concentration, the parties would 'only achieve a market share [of 25%-35%]* in the EEA'.[149] As the margining parties produced different goods with these characteristics, there would be very little overlapping in the specialised non-liquid packaging board products, leading to the conclusion that the merger would not create competition risks.

Liquid Packaging Board

Liquid packaging board was the focus of the case - concerning the merger leading to the creation or strengthening of a dominant position, as well as the reasons why countervailing buyer power could neutralise such dominance. Thus, our analysis of the merger and the effects of the measures focuses on this relevant product and geographic market.

Liquid packaging board was considered to be a type of consumer packing board different from non-liquid packaging board. These are boards made of virgin fibres, recycled fibres or a mix of the two. Board is converted into cartons, cups, boxes, etc., which are later sold to 'producers of food and non-food consumer products, including nonliquid and liquid foods, cigarettes, cosmetics and pharmaceuticals'.[150] In particular, liquid packing products are used to contain juices and milk, for example. Two types were identified, aseptic packaging systems and fresh packaging systems. The former has a long shelf life of up to two years, while the fresh packaging systems have a much shorter life of no longer than two weeks.[151] Board for packaging liquids contains a plastic coating or aluminium laminate. Further, the Commission found that these types of liquid packaging boards do have differences from other boards and are not interchangeable as 'liquid packaging board must have a particularly high absorption resistance'.[152] Also, since this type of packaging contains food, it must comply with food law and bacteriological and environmental requirements.

Customers for this kind of product are not diaries. Instead, they are converters and packagers, such as at the time Tetra Pak, SIG Combibloc and Elopak.[153] These buyers of boards do not switch between packing materials and stick to their chosen one, such that board is not substitutable for glass or plastic, for example.

Geographic Market for Liquid Packaging Board

Enso and Stora submitted in their request for evaluation of the concentration that the relevant geographical market for liquid packaging board be a global one, based on a high level of exports and imports in the EEA market.[154] Buyers of liquid packaging boards, however, argued that outsourcing these materials from outside of Europe was

149. *Ibid.*, para. 72.
150. Case No. IV/M.1225 - *Enso/Stora*, para. 18.
151. *Ibid.*, para. 22.
152. *Ibid.*, para. 25.
153. *Ibid.*, para. 33.
154. *Ibid.*, paras 52-53.

not cost attractive due to transport costs, duties and even environmental costs.[155] Furthermore, the Commission stressed that due to the existing European regulations, 'board grades in the EEA are developed to meet certain environmental requirements, which is not necessarily the case outside Europe'.[156] This, alongside costs, made imports to Europe of liquid packaging board from the United States (US) difficult and unlikely. Because of this, the relevant market for this product was defined to be only the EEA.[157]

[C] Theory of Harm That Would Have Prevented the Concentration to Take Place Absent Countervailing Buyer Power

As discussed, only the liquid packaging board relevant market as defined by the Commission raised anticompetitive concerns that could have led to declaring the merger as incompatible with the EU and EEA law.

In the EEA market, the Commission estimated that 'the parties' market share in liquid packaging board applications would be [between 50% and 70%],* a position far ahead of the other players in the market', which were much smaller.[158] Holding such market shares would usually be thought to confer dominance, leading the concentration towards being declared incompatible.

The Commission, in this case, did not propose a clear theory of harm for the case - arguably because under the operation, the merged entity would have become dominant. This would be sufficient for the concentration to be prohibited under the regime at the time.

Potential Competition

In this selling-market power-oriented assessment, the Commission stressed several factors that would have allowed the merged undertaking to behave independently of its competitors in the future.

Entry barriers in this market were high - the construction of a board machine, for example, reached 300m–400m European Currency Units. New entry was also seen to be precluded because of a lack of growth in demand which was aggravated by the need for economies of scale.[159] These observations led the Commission to affirm the existence of barriers of entry hindering the entrance of new rivals in this liquid packaging board market.

The position of potential rivals was also discussed. This included both current rivals in the European market and potential rivals from outside of the EEA. For both, one factor taken into account was the time needed to enter the market - several years due to the specificities of producing the board mill, combined with the need for

---

155. *Ibid.*, para. 56.
156. *Ibid.*, para. 57.
157. *Ibid.*, para. 59.
158. Case No. IV/M.1225 - *Enso/Stora*, para. 73.
159. *Ibid.*, para. 75.

investment into an item that would be a sunk cost.[160] Also, for both, neither the competitive risks of the merger nor the strategies to be adopted by rivals afterwards were thoroughly discussed.

In the case of existing rivals in the EEA, Korsnäs and AssiDomän, the merging parties argued that these entities had the capacity to increase their production and had recently done so. The Commission obtained evidence from them indicating that such an increase in production capacity was due to an increase in demand.[161] Additionally, the positions of other producers of boards – but not of liquid packaging boards – were evaluated and it was concluded that these entities would not enter this specific market.

One potential rival identified from outside of the EU was a Russian undertaking, which produced a product of inferior quality that was not suitable for the European market.[162] A Polish board producer was also evaluated (before Poland was an EU member), but this entity did not produce liquid packaging boards and could not export liquid packaging boards to the EEA for the foreseeable future.[163]

[D] Buyer Power to the Rescue?

The concentration appeared to be headed towards approval with serious commitments regarding the liquid packaging board market, if it would be declared compatible. However, the countervailing buyer power of a very large buyer, Tetra Pak, was considered crucial to conclude that it was capable to neutralise anticompetitive risks arising from the merger.[164] However, two other smaller buyers were also found to have some degree of buyer power.

The Commission stressed that:[165]

> Buyers of liquid packaging board are few and the market is *dominated by Tetra Pak*, which represents an estimated market share of *close to [between 60% and 80%].** The other main buyers of liquid packaging board are Elopak and SIG Combibloc with about [between 10% and 20%]* of the EEA market each. After the merger *the structure of the supply-side will mirror the structure of the demand-side of the market.*

The merging parties argued that in such a scenario, all their buyers (but particularly Tetra Pak) 'exercise considerable buyer power that prevents the producers of liquid packaging board from increasing prices'.[166]

In the analysis of the *sufficiency* of countervailing buyer power to offset the negative effects of the merger, the Commission adopted a comparison approach, inspired by the mirror image of the market structure with one very large buyer and one

160. *Ibid.*, para. 78.
161. Case No. IV/M.1225 – *Enso/Stora*, para. 81.
162. *Ibid.*, para. 79.
163. *Ibid.*, para. 80.
164. *See also* stressing this when discussing dominance as a concept: Giorgio Monti, *The Concept of Dominance in Article 82*, 2 Eur. Comp. J. 31, 36–38 (2006).
165. Case No. IV/M.1225 – *Enso/Stora*, para. 84 (emphasis added).
166. *Ibid.*, para. 85.

very large seller.[167] The Commission stressed that the existence of buyer power alone is not sufficient, but that such market power must be at least sufficient to 'neutralise the potential increase in market power of the merger between Stora and Enso'.[168]

Several factors were taken into account to conclude that Tetra Pak, as well as two other much smaller buyers Elopak and SIG Combibloc, had 'sufficient countervailing buyer power to remove the possibility of the parties exercising market power'.[169]

Dependence

The Commission discussed the existence of some form of dependence between the parties. The concept of economic dependence is not rare in buyer power cases. We discussed it in the two supermarket mergers analysed, and it is a concept linked to the idea of an uneven bargaining position in which one party can force the other into accepting some contractual condition.[170]

In this case, the Commission found that due to the mirror image, there was a *mutual dependence* between buyers and sellers that had become established over the years, which was of a 'long-term nature and [in which] switching supplier of liquid packaging board is rare'.[171] Buyers and sellers explained that switching suppliers of board was complex and time-consuming, besides being capital-intensive.

Long-term relationships, while not being a buyer power factor, were stressed in the analysis as connected to the idea of mutual dependence. Based on these types of relationships, producers of board tended to divide their production into specialised lines to supply specific buyers, tailoring their equipment to buyers' needs.

Proportion of Sales a Buyer Represents and Sponsoring of Entry as Measures of Countervailing Buyer Power

The role of Tetra Pak as a large buyer of liquid packaging board was highlighted. Tetra Pak acquired more than 50% of its demand from Stora and Enso. This represented 'the whole output of several board machines and about [more than 50%]* of the parties'

167. For a thorough discussion on the sufficiency needed for countervailing buyer power to offset benefits and the associated test found in the Commission's practice *see*: Ignacio Herrera Anchustegui, *Buyer Power in EU Competition Law* (Institut de droit de la concurrence 2017), at paras 1159–1174.
168. Case No. IV/M.1225 – *Enso/Stora*, para. 92.
169. *Ibid.*, para. 97 (emphasis added).
170. For some literature dealing with the issue of economic dependence in general, *see*: Pranvera Këllezi, *Abuse Below the Threshold of Dominance? Market Power, Market Dominance, and Abuse of Economic Dependence, in Abuse of Dominant Position: New Interpretation, New Enforcement Mechanisms?* 55 (Mark-Oliver Mackenrodt, Beatriz Conde Gallego and Stefan Enchelmaier eds, Springer 2008); Valeria Falce, *The Italian Regulation Against the Abuse of Economic Dependence*, in Fabiana Di Porto and Rupprecht Podszun (eds), *Abusive Practices in Competition Law* 375 (Edward Elgar Publishing 2018); Mor Bakhoum, *Abuse Without Dominance in Competition Law: Abuse of Economic Dependence and Its Interface with Abuse of Dominance*, in Fabiana Di Porto and Rupprecht Podszun (eds), *Abusive Practices in Competition Law* (Edward Elgar Publishing 2018).
171. Case No. IV/M.1225 – *Enso/Stora*, para. 86.

total output for the EEA',[172] in a 50-versus-50% scenario. Losing such a large customer was found to be a major issue; the industry is based on economies of scale in which large suppliers need high rates of capacity utilisation and in which finding new buyers in the short term is not feasible.[173]

Not only was Tetra Pak a buyer representing at least half of the sales of the merging parties, but due to its purchasing volume, it also 'would have the option of developing new capacity with other existing or new suppliers, should the parties attempt to exercise market power'.[174] This outside option tends to be the most important element for countervailing buyer power to be exerted.

Other Buyers' Situations

Instead of limiting the analysis to the sufficiency of countervailing by a single buyer, the Commission also assessed the purchasing power of two other much smaller customers of the merging entities, Elopak and SIG Combiblock. This is connected to the spillover effect requirement found in other countervailing buyer power cases.[175]

The Commission noticed that the merger could 'weaken the buyer power of Elopak' because it ran joint converting activities in Lahti in Finland with Enso.[176] Although they were much smaller buyers, their orders were able to fill the capacity of a board machine. Due to these large volumes, it would be difficult for these companies to find alternative suppliers, but this also meant that they could switch to other suppliers who would start producing liquid packaging boards.[177] Also, as these buyers had suppliers outside of the EEA, this 'strengthens their countervailing buyer power' through dual sourcing strategies.

However, unlike Tetra Pak, these small buyers would have had only one actual type of liquid packaging board in the EEA with much smaller volumes. So while they had some buyer power to counter a price increase, the merger would have shifted the balance (and arguably eliminated the sufficiency even if not discussed) between the parties.

At the same time, for the merging parties, it was important not to exert selling market power against these smaller buyers so as 'not to become completely dependent

---

172. Case No. IV/M.1225 - *Enso/Stora*, para. 90.
173. *Ibid. See also* stressing the importance of capacity in the *Enso/Stora* case: Massimo Motta, *Competition Policy: Theory and Practice* 122 (Cambridge University Press 2004).
174. Case No. IV/M.1225 - *Enso/Stora*, para. 91. *See also* the commentary on this aspect of the case in Baker & Lofaro (2000), p. 188.
175. For some cases requiring some degree of spillover of the countervailing power *see*: Commission Decision of 22 July 1992 relating to a proceeding under Council Regulation (EEC) No 4064/89 (Case No. IV/M.190 - *Nestlé/Perrier*) [1992] OJ L 356/1; Commission Decision of Non-opposition to a notified concentration M.4057 - *Korsnäs/Assidomän Cartonboard* [2006] OJ C 209/12; Commission Decision of 31 January 2001 declaring a concentration to be incompatible with the common market and the functioning of the EEA Agreement (Case COMP/M.2097 *SCA/Metsä Tissue*) [2001] OJ L 57/1; Commission Decision of 3 April 2001 declaring a concentration to be compatible with the common market and the functioning of the EEA Agreement (Case COMP/M.2139 - *Bombardier/ADtranz*) [2002] OJ L 69/50.
176. Case No. IV/M.1225 - *Enso/Stora*, para. 93.
177. *Ibid.*, para. 94.

on Tetra Pak'.[178] This was interpreted by the Commission as a side effect of Tetra Pak's countervailing buyer power that would 'to a certain extent, spill over to Elopak and SIG Combibloc as well'.[179]

Therefore, the Commission concluded that while the merger will create a large supplier in the liquid cardboard market with more than 50% of the market shares, the exceptional market structure present meant that buyers had 'sufficient countervailing buyer power to remove the possibility of the parties exercising market power'.[180]

[E] Remedies Adopted in the Concentration

Even if countervailing buyer power was able to remove the anticompetitive concerns raised by the merger (a price increase of liquid packing cardboard), the parties submitted measures to alleviate concerns. These commitments partially addressed issues related to the reduction in buyer power by the two smaller clients, Elopak and SIG Combiblock.

First, Enso and Stora committed to create 'a price protection mechanism for the smaller customers for a period of five years from the date of the completion of the merger'.[181] This mechanism implied that price increases to large buyers would not be smaller than to small customers in a percentage base, effectively neutralising the larger buyer power of Tetra Pak. Also, price decreases would follow the same patterns. Yet there could be some exceptions to this commitment (made upon notifying the Commission), and the price protection mechanism was to be audited annually.[182]

The merging parties also committed not to hinder the opening of a duty-free quota on imports of liquid packaging board within the Community.[183]

Lastly, Enso and Elopak had some joint activities in Finland, which were seen as detrimental to Elopak's exertion of buyer power. Because of this, Enso agreed to 'to sell its entire interest in these activities to Elopak. Such a sale would remove any concerns that this link would reduce the countervailing buyer power of Elopak',[184] if the merger were to be accepted.

§4.06 ROLE OF BUYER POWER IN MERGERS AND THEIR REVIEW

The study of the effect of buyer power presents a number of practical challenges. This relates to a number of methodological and practical issues.

The key methodological challenge is how to isolate the effect of any changes in buyer power from the wider effects of the merger. To date, most quantitative *ex post* reviews of merger decisions look at the effect of consumer prices. A good example is

178. Case No. IV/M.1225 – *Enso/Stora*, para. 96.
179. *Ibid.*
180. *Ibid.*, para. 97.
181. *Ibid.*, para. 101(a).
182. *Ibid.*, para. 101(a).
183. *Ibid.*, para. 101(b).
184. Case No. IV/M.1225 – *Enso/Stora.*, para. 101(c).

Allain et al.,[185] who discuss the effects of the *Carrefour/Promodès* merger on the French market for supermarkets. Similarly, Skrainka discusses the welfare effects of the supermarket merger between Morrisons and Safeway in the UK.[186]

Looking at the foreclosure theories of harm, the prediction is for prices to be lower post-merger as the predation strategy for the merging firms is implemented. But these prices may also be affected by efficiencies incurred as part of the merger.[187]

Similarly, the prediction of countervailing buyer power would be no effect on prices post-merger; but this could equally be explained by the merging firms not being able to exploit an (expected) increase in market power.

This implies that any comparison of prices before and after the merger will not yield specific insights related to buyer power. Difference-in-difference would be an option. However, we *see* similar challenges, as to isolate the effect of buyer power, one needs similar mergers that differ only with respect to the degree of buyer power (and not market power). For instance, in both the *Kesko/Tuko* case and the *Carrefour/Promodès* case, the Commission identified (unilateral) competition concerns related to the market for the provision of daily consumer goods. Our research suggests that this theory of harm is common amongst transactions in this time period (applying also, for instance, to the *Rewe/Meinl* buyer power case) and which, despite some concerns related to the spiral effect, was declared compatible with the internal market.[188]

However, it follows from the discussion of buyer power above that the effect of buyer power may not be on consumer prices but on other elements such as assortment. Argentesi et al. investigate the effect of a Dutch supermarket merger on assortment.[189]

The second issue is that buyer power is typically one of the theories of harm in a concentration. To measure the effect of a merger on buyer power based on bargaining theory, one would ideally understand the change in outside options for both firms to then be able to establish whether the merger has led to a change in the distribution of the surplus. With some exceptions for raw materials that are traded,[190] most data on procurement terms are private.

Finally, we note that in one of the two cases in our sample where buyer power was a theory of harm, *Kesko/Tuko*, is a prohibition case, meaning that there is no clear counterfactual to study.[191]

---

185. Marie-Laure Allain, Claire Chambolle, Stéphane Turolla and Sofia B. Villas-Boas, *Retail Mergers and Food Prices: Evidence from France*, 65 J. of Ind. Ec. 469–509 (2017).
186. Benjamin S. Skrainka, *The Geography of Grocery Demand in the UK: An Evaluation of the 2003 Morrisons-Safeway Merger*, SSRN (2012).
187. Petro P. Barros, Duarte Brito and Diogo de Lucena, *Mergers in the Food Retailing Sector: An Empirical Investigation*, 50 Eur. Ec. Rev. (2006).
188. For discussion of this case, *see* Ariel Ezrachi and Maria Ioannidou, *Buyer Power in European Union Merger Control*, 10 Eur. Comp. J. 69, 76 (2015); Ignacio Herrera Anchustegui, *Buyer Power in EU Competition Law* (Institut de droit de la concurrence 2017).
189. Elena Argentesi, et al., *The Effect of Retail Mergers on Prices and Variety: An Ex-post Evaluation*, DICE Discussion Paper (2016).
190. *See*, for instance, Lloyd et al. (2009) for a number of food items.
191. We note that the merger was implemented ahead of the Commission's prohibition decision, meaning that there was a period in which the firms were merged. However, we consider that

Nonetheless, we combine a number of strands of economic research to provide an overview of the role of buyer power in mergers. First of all, we present an overview of literature investigating the determinants of merger decisions. A number of these papers also touch on buyer power, thus providing insight into how prevalent the topic of buyer power is and the effect it had on the outcome of a merger review. Second, we discuss a number of papers that aim to quantify the effect of a merger on suppliers of the merging firms. Finally, we discuss a number of papers on the rationale for mergers and acquisitions to explore the extent to which the pursuit of an increased bargaining position versus suppliers is an objective. We use this research as a backdrop for a discussion of increased concentration in the European food retailing industry.

[A] Quantitative Analyses of Past Merger Decisions

To assess the prevalence of buyer power in merger reviews and the effect of buyer power on the outcome of merger cases, we have completed a review of a group of papers that analyse past EU merger decisions to assess which elements are relevant in determining their outcome (*see* Table 4.1).

These papers use different case studies of various types (EU only, versus EU and USA; phase 1, versus phase 2, versus both). The common thread is that each study identifies a dependent variable on the basis of which the merger is challenged – where to 'challenge' a merger is to issue a prohibition, a conditional approval, or a withdrawal. These papers use a range of explanatory variables. The most frequent are *market share*, *concentration levels* and *barriers to entry*. Beyond that, there is variation between the studies with respect to variables such as whether they occurred before or after the 2004 reform of the EU Merger Regulation (EUMR), and 'political' factors such as the nationality of the firms involved. Some of the papers also include explanatory variables that relate to buyer power.

Table 4.1 Analyses of Past EU Merger Decisions

Author(s)	*Sample*	*Selected Parameters*
Lindsay et al. (2003)	245 EU merger decisions between 2000 and 2002	Market share, HHI, barriers to entry, buyer power
Bergman et al. (2005)	96 EU merger decisions between 1990 and 2002	Market share, vertical mergers, collusion, nationality, undertakings
Fernandez et al. (2008)	50 EU merger decisions between 2005 and 2006	Market share, vertical mergers, entry barriers, nationality

this period of several months during a competition investigation was not sufficient for us to study the effect of the combination.

Author(s)	*Sample*	*Selected Parameters*
Bergman et al. (2010)	109 EU phase II horizontal merger decisions between 1990 and 2004	Market share, entry barriers, unilateral effects, buyer sophistication
Szuecs (2012)	309 EU mergers between 1991 and 2007	Dominant firm, entry barriers, HHI
Mai (2016)	341 EU horizontal merger decisions between 1990 and 2012	Market share, entry barriers, 2004 EUMR reform
Mini (2018)	13,818 horizontally affected markets in 1,670 EU merger decisions between 1990 and 2013	Market share, HHI, IP, industry
Bergman et al. (2019)	151 EU phase II mergers between 1990 and 2013	Market share, entry barriers, unilateral effects, buyer sophistication
Cottyn (2019)	1,113 horizontally affected markets from 160 EU phase 1 merger decisions between 1992 and 2013	Market share, entry barriers, industry, countervailing effects
Affeldt et al. (2020)	30,995 markets from 5,109 EU merger decisions between 1990 and 2014	HHI, markets with concerns, entry barriers

Lindsay et al. used a random sample of 245 European Commission merger decisions between 1 January 2000 and 30 June 2002. One of the hypotheses the authors test relates to countervailing buyer power:[192]

> (H4) Buyer power arises when customers can readily adopt strategies which would defeat any attempt by the merged group to exercise market power. We expected that buyer power itself would rarely be sufficient to justify clearing a transaction without undertakings when the merger resulted in high market shares because, in such cases, customers generally cannot defeat attempts by the merged group to exercise market power. We therefore expected the study to show that buyer power was relevant in moderate to highly concentrated markets or in combination with other factors which together serve as a competitive constraint on the activities of the merged group.

192. Alistair Lindsay, Emanuela Lecchi and Geoffrey Williams, *Econometrics Study into European Commission Merger Decisions Since 2000*, 14 Eur. Comp. L. Rev. 673, 675 (2003).

The authors conclude that the buyer power variable is not significant in any of the model specifications and suggest that these results are surprising in view of a qualitative analysis conducted for the UK competition authority.

Bergman et al. aim to compare the outcomes of merger review by the European Commission versus the US Federal Trade Commission (FTC). Their dataset includes horizontal mergers between 1990 and 2004, which have been subjected to a full review (e.g., phase II review with the Commission and/or second request with the FTC). Their model includes a parameter called 'Sophistication', which appears to relate to the scope for buyers to exercise countervailing buyer power:[193]

> Sophistication denotes that the decisions or memoranda highlighted the potential for buyers to affect the competitive process in their markets. Because sophisticated buyers might disrupt anti-competitive price increases, a negative impact on the probability of challenge is expected for this variable.

Whereas the Sophistication variable is significant for the US models, it is not for the EU models. The authors offer no explanation for this difference.

Mini derive his dataset from all EU decisions between 21 September 1990 (the start date of the EUMR) and 31 December 2013.[194] After filtering for horizontal overlap markets and decisions with sufficient information, he secures a sample of 1,670 distinct mergers. He then aims to separate out cases where the effect on the position of the merging firms as buyers (as opposed to sellers) was discussed (e.g., monopsony) by introducing a dummy variable.

This Procurement variable appears to be significant (either at the 1% or the 5% level – *see* Table 4 in Mini's paper) for all of his regressions.[195] Interestingly, the sign switches from positive to negative (with the difference also being significant) between the subset of cases before and after the 2004 reform of the EUMR. This suggests that following the 2004 EUMR reform, the cases in which buyer power was explored were less likely to be challenged. The authors suggest that the limited number of observations may explain this change in sign.

Following Bergman et al.,[196] Bergman et al. study a sample of EU 151 phase II merger decisions, as well as 260 FTC decisions from the period from 1999 to the end of 2013.[197] As before, their model includes an explanatory variable '*Customer Sophistication*' – we consider this variable to aim to capture a review of countervailing buyer power.

Bergman et al. go on to conclude that the Customer Sophistication variable does not have a significant effect on the EU outcome. However, the authors do find a

193. Mats A. Bergman, Malcolm B. Coate, Maria Jakobsson and Shawn W. Ulrick, *Comparing Merger Policies in the European Union and the United States*, 36 Rev. Ind. Org. 305 (2010), p. 314.
194. Federico Mini (2018), *Fifty Is the New Forty: EU Merger Policy Permits Higher Market Shares after the 2004 Reform*, 53 Rev. of Ind. Org. 535 (2018).
195. *Ibid.*
196. Mats A. Bergman, Malcolm B. Coate, Maria Jakobsson and Shawn W. Ulrick, *Comparing Merger Policies in the European Union and the United States*, 36 Rev. of Ind. Org. 305 (2010).
197. Mats A. Bergman, Malcolm B. Coate, Anh T.V. Mai and Shawn W. Ulrick, *Does Merger Policy Converge after the 2004 European Union Reform?*, 15 J. of Comp. L. & Ec. 664 (2019).

significant result for their sample of FTC cases.[198] These results are in line with also previous results found in the literature.[199]

Cottyn uses a sample of 160 randomly selected EU phase I decisions from the period 1992–2013.[200] For each of these decisions, she collects data on the relevant markets discussed in these decisions leading to a sample of 1,113 horizontally affected relevant markets.

Cottyn introduces an explanatory dummy variable to capture a collection of countervailing factors, including - but not limited to - countervailing buyer power. Other factors considered are efficiencies and the failing firm defence. Cottyn's results show that this variable had a significant negative sign (i.e., supporting clearance) for the models based on cases from after the 2004 reform of the EUMR. This effect is so large that a further simulation shows that the inclusion of this variable had a similar effect on the likelihood of clearance compared to a reduction in combined post-merger market share of 40%.

This summary highlights that the limited body of empirical papers that investigate (countervailing) buyer power appear to give mixed results with respect to its significance.

[B] The Effect of Merger Announcements on Suppliers

There exists a large body of economic literature looking at the effects of various types of announcements on share prices. Where this methodology was initially developed to research the level of efficiency of financial markets in absorbing new information, the outcomes are also used to establish the significance of the effect itself. For example, an event study looking at the development of the share prices of firms announcing acquisitions is used to reflect on the benefits of mergers.

Various authors have also explored and/or applied the event study methodology to the competitive assessment of mergers. For example, an increase in the share price of a firm announcing an acquisition may reflect that investors believe the merged entity will see improved performance following an increase in market power.

In a similar vein, there are several papers that investigate the effect of merger announcements on the share price of suppliers of the acquirer/merging firms. Like in the previous example, these results could indicate whether investors consider that the outlook for these suppliers would change as a consequence of a merger involving their clients.

Fee and Thomas,[201] and Shahrur[202] present similar analyses. These authors aim to infer the objective of the transaction by measuring the share price effect around the

198. *Ibid.*
199. Mats A. Bergman, Malcolm B. Coate, Maria Jakobsson and Shawn W. Ulrick, *Comparing Merger Policies in the European Union and the United States*, 36 Rev. of Ind. Org. 305 (2010).
200. An-Sofie Cottyn, *An Interdisciplinary Analysis of the More Economic Approach in EU Competition Policy at the Crossroad of Markets and Governments*, doctoral dissertation, Ghent University, Belgium (2019).
201. C. Edward Fee and Shawn Thomas, *Sources of Gains in Horizontal Mergers: Evidence from Customer, Supplier, and Rival Firms*, 74 J. of Fin. Ec. 423 (2004).

announcement. Fee and Thomas also look at the subsequent performance of suppliers.[203] For the purposes of our discussion on the role of buyer power in mergers, we combine the hypothesis identified in both papers. The authors explore the effect on suppliers in the following scenarios.

The first scenario is called 'Productive Efficiency' and is used to describe the outcome of a merger aimed at improving efficiencies within the merging firms. Both papers suggest that this should not affect suppliers in the first instance. The authors do suggest a second-order effect in that the performance of the merged firm may lead it to increase or decrease its output.

The second scenario is called 'Collusion' and is used to capture those mergers that aim to restrict competition and thus increase monopoly rents. Fee and Thomas,[204] and Shahrur[205] predict a negative result for suppliers in this scenario, as the merged firm is expected to reduce its output following its improved market position.

The third and fourth scenarios concern buyer power. Shahrur presents only one scenario, 'Monopsonistic Collusion', to describe those mergers that create a larger buyer that intensifies competition amongst suppliers.[206] Fee and Thomas present two scenarios for two possible outcomes of a merger for suppliers of the merging firms.[207] The first is 'Buying Power' and indicates an outcome where the merging firms use their improved bargaining position to extract better terms for their (remaining) suppliers. While we discussed monopsony and bargaining position separately in the earlier part of this chapter, we consider that the two scenarios here are similar in that they both predict suppliers to be negatively affected by a merger. Fee and Thomas also include a fourth scenario, 'Purchasing Efficiencies', to describe an outcome where the merging firm and the (remaining) supplier(s) benefit from economies of scale post-merger.[208]

Fee and Thomas use a database containing 554 transactions between 1980 and 1997 – looking only at transactions where both the bidder and the target are listed on a US stock exchange.[209] Customers are identified based on the requirement that publicly traded firms disclose customers representing more than 10% of total sales

---

202. Husayn Shahrur, *Industry Structure and Horizontal Takeovers: Analysis of Wealth Effects on Rivals, Suppliers, and Corporate Customers*, 76 J. of Fin. Ec. 61 (2005).
203. C. Edward Fee and Shawn Thomas, *Sources of Gains in Horizontal Mergers: Evidence from Customer, Supplier, and Rival Firms*, 74 J. of Fin. Ec. 423 (2004). The other relevant methodological difference relates to the classification of suppliers. Where Fee and Thomas (2004) use company disclosures indicating significant suppliers, Shahrur (2005) uses benchmark input–output accounts of the US economy (i.e., which SIC codes buy/sell from which SIC codes), meaning that all firms with the same SIC industry code are considered to be suppliers of the merging firms.
204. C. Edward Fee and Shawn Thomas, *Sources of Gains in Horizontal Mergers: Evidence from Customer, Supplier, and Rival Firms*, 74 J. of Fin. Ec. 423 (2004).
205. Husayn Shahrur, *Industry Structure and Horizontal Takeovers: Analysis of Wealth Effects on Rivals, Suppliers, and Corporate Customers*, 76 J. of Fin. Ec. 61 (2005).
206. Husayn Shahrur, *Industry Structure and Horizontal Takeovers: Analysis of Wealth Effects on Rivals, Suppliers, and Corporate Customers*, 76 J. of Fin. Ec. 61 (2005).
207. C. Edward Fee and Shawn Thomas, *Sources of Gains in Horizontal Mergers: Evidence from Customer, Supplier, and Rival Firms*, 74 J. of Fin. Ec. 423 (2004).
208. *Ibid.*
209. *Ibid.*

(avg. 0.40 customers per deal). Suppliers are identified by inverting this relationship (avg. 1.09 suppliers per deal).

In terms of effects on customers, the authors find no significant effects for their entire sample in terms of abnormal share price returns around the announcement date or cash flow to sales in subsequent years. This would support the 'Productive Efficiency' scenario where suppliers are not affected by mergers.

However, a further test for the distribution of this result suggests that the average contains a relatively high proportion of cases where suppliers see a negative share price result and a relatively lower number of cases where suppliers' share price benefits. The authors consider that these results could indicate that the suppliers will be able to mitigate any longer-term negative consequences (for instance by merging themselves). In terms of cash flows, there is a significant negative effect for the first year.

One subgroup showing significant negative results both in terms of share price response and cash flow is the group of 'Terminated Suppliers' – firms that are not listed as suppliers in the financial disclosure of the merged firm in the year following the merger.

The second set of supplier results aims to explain these effects by looking at a set of explanatory variables such as the percentage of sales for the merging firms, the status of Terminated Supplier, and market concentration. The overall regression results are weak, but the model includes variables for each of these three elements with significant values.

The third set of supplier results is based on similar regressions, but for subgroups of the sample. The explanatory value of the model now increases, in particular for the set of mergers where pre-merger, the market in which the merging firms operate in is already concentrated (defined as value of industry Herfindahl–Hirschman Index (HHI) over 2,000). This result suggests that the negative effects for suppliers are more pronounced for markets that are already concentrated. The authors go on to conclude that this result suggests that the efficiency gains of mergers come to some extent at the expense of suppliers.

The fourth set of analyses looks at which factors explain whether a supplier continued to work with the merging firms or not (and thus end up as a Terminated Supplier). Their results show that suppliers serving only the target have a lower chance of staying on compared to those firms supplying the bidder. Firms supplying both the bidder and the target have the highest probability of staying on (as opposed to supplying only the bidder or the target). Other elements that increase the likelihood of staying on as a supplier are the percentage of sales and continuity (i.e., the number of years as a supplier).

Shahrur uses a dataset of 463 horizontal transactions involving US-listed bidders and targets between 1987 and 1999.[210] Suppliers are defined using input–output tables, meaning that these relate to a group of firms with the same industry code, which is earmarked as an industry supplying the merging firms.

210. Husayn Shahrur, *Industry Structure and Horizontal Takeovers: Analysis of Wealth Effects on Rivals, Suppliers, and Corporate Customers*, 76 J. of Fin. Ec. 61 (2005).

The overall results for share price effect (cumulative average return) are not significant for a short window around the announcement date. However, the authors find significant negative results for two subsets in one of the periods considered.[211] The first subset is referred to as 'Main Suppliers' and relates to the industry (Standard Industrial Classification (SIC)) code for which the dollar amount of output sold to the merging firms' industry is divided by the merging firms' industry's total output. The second subset is referred to as 'Dependent Suppliers' – and relates to the SIC code for which the dollar amount of output sold to the merging firms' industry divided the suppliers' industry's total output. These are –0.48% for the Main Suppliers group of firms and –0.95% for the Dependent Suppliers group of firms. However, the results for both of these groups show a significant spread with 45% of the observations being positive. Looking at the different scenarios for mergers discussed above, the overall results would support the 'Productive Efficiency' scenario, whereas the results for the subgroups suggest otherwise and point to either of the scenarios related to buyer power.

The authors go on to divide their total sample is transactions where the overall share price response (defined as positive combined market value effect or combined wealth effect or CWE) was positive or negative. The share price effect for suppliers was significantly negative for the group of negative CWE mergers. The result for 'Main Suppliers' was -2.76% and for 'Dependent Suppliers' -4.23% for the same announcement window as referred to above. However, the variation of positive and negative results in this average continues to be significant, suggesting that this division may explain only part of the effect. The share price effect in the case of positive CWE mergers was + 1.06% for 'Main Suppliers' and + 1.28% for 'Dependent Suppliers' for the same announcement window. The variation effect for these findings is less pronounced as compared to the negative CWE mergers group. Overall, these results suggest that suppliers are expected to do as well as the merging firms. In other words, if the markets expect the merger to generate positive effects (as measured by a positive CWE), suppliers as a group are believed to profit as well.

In a next step, the authors aim to explain the share price effect for the groups of 'Main Suppliers' and 'Dependent Suppliers' using a number of parameters as explanatory variables in a regression model. This model includes one significant variable that captures both the level of concentration in the supplier industry and the change in concentration in the (downstream) market of the merger. This combined variable has a negative coefficient. This suggests that mergers leading to a large change in the HHI of the (downstream) industry of the merging firms combined with a concentrated suppliers' industry leads to a large negative share price effect for suppliers. These results suggest that the relative market share/position of suppliers and their customers matters in terms of the bargaining outcome post-merger – or more specifically, a merger leading to customers significantly increasing in size compared to their large suppliers is expected to lead to a negative share price effect for these suppliers.

211. This period runs from ten days before the announcement date to ten days after.

Bernile and Lyandres use a dataset of 480 horizontal mergers between 1996 and 2005.[212] For this dataset of mergers, they have identified 1,523 suppliers to the bidder and/or the target firm.

The authors find a significant negative share price effect for suppliers, which are identified on an individual level as Fee and Thomas earlier did in 2004.[213] The percentage range between -1.57% for the period covering one day before and after the announcement date (–1,1), and -4.26% for the period (–20,20). However, these results represent the average of unweighted observations. When the relative size of suppliers' market value is used to calculate weighted average results, these are closer to zero and not consistently significant. This latter finding is in line with the findings of Fee and Thomas,[214] and Shahrur.[215]

When looking to explain these results using regression analysis, a number of explanatory variables generate statistically significant effects. The first variable is the present value of the expected efficiency gains from the merging firms, which has a positive coefficient. This appears to be in line with the findings of Shahrur for the subgroup of mergers with a positive combined wealth/market capitalisation effect.[216] The second relates to the degree of product similarity between bidder and target. The sign of the coefficient is positive, suggesting that the higher the degree of similarity, the higher the degree of a positive share price response for suppliers. The authors acknowledge that this finding does not align with a buyer power explanation, which would see increased product similarity lead to an improved bargaining position post-merger. This latter effect may well be captured by the third significant variable: the change in HHI, which has a negative coefficient. The final significant variable is linked to the size of the supplier measured as the logarithm of sales. This variable has a positive coefficient, meaning that the share price response is more positive with the suppliers' sales. Looking at Fee and Thomas,[217] this variable may be a proxy for the likelihood of the supply relationship continuing or the bargaining power of the supplier.

One article that employs an event study approach but does not measure share price effects is Bhattacharyyaa and Nain.[218] The authors study the effects on supplier profitability and prices following US horizontal mergers. The authors use transaction data between 1984 and 2003 to select 259 industries that have experienced one or more

212. Gennaro Bernile and Evgeny Lyandres, *The Effects of Horizontal Merger Operating Efficiencies on Rivals, Customers, and Suppliers*, 23 Rev. of Fin. 117 (2019). Although the authors are silent on this point, we deduct from the various data sources used that these mergers were between US-listed firms.
213. C. Edward Fee and Shawn Thomas, *Sources of Gains in Horizontal Mergers: Evidence from Customer, Supplier, and Rival Firms*, 74 J. of Fin. Ec. 423 (2004).
214. C. Edward Fee and Shawn Thomas, *Sources of Gains in Horizontal Mergers: Evidence from Customer, Supplier, and Rival Firms*, 74 J. of Fin. Ec. 423 (2004).
215. Husayn Shahrur, *Industry Structure and Horizontal Takeovers: Analysis of Wealth Effects on Rivals, Suppliers, and Corporate Customers*, 76 J. of Fin. Ec. 61 (2005).
216. *Ibid.*
217. C. Edward Fee and Shawn Thomas, *Sources of Gains in Horizontal Mergers: Evidence from Customer, Supplier, and Rival Firms*, 74 J. of Fin. Ec. 423 (2004).
218. Sugato Bhattacharyyaa and Amrita Nain, *Horizontal Acquisitions and Buying Power: A Product Market Analysis*, 99 J. of Fin. Ec. 97 (2011).

significant jumps in horizontal merger activity in a specific quarter during the research period.

The authors find a significant negative effect of downstream consolidation on the cash flow margins of suppliers to the merging firms. These suppliers are grouped in supplier industries using the same approach as Shahrur.[219] To establish whether this negative profitability is driven by increased buyer power from the merged customers of the supplying firm, the authors go on to look for changes in the level of prices. The authors find that price levels for firms affected by downstream consolidations decrease in the years of the merger compared to a sample of suppliers that are not dependent on the merging firms. The difference over the entire three-year period is estimated to be 3.6%.

In a subsequent analysis, the authors aim to establish whether the negative price effect can be explained by increased bargaining power from their merged customers. The authors find that the negative price effect is more pronounced for supply industries with relatively higher levels of concentration (measured either in terms of HHI or combined market share of the largest four firms).

Finally, the authors look at whether there is a link between the negative price effect and changes in concentration in the supply industry. They find that the price decline following downstream consolidation is larger when the level of concentration in the supply market had been increasing in the period up to the downstream merger. Similarly, suppliers experiencing increased horizontal merger activity prior to downstream consolidation see larger negative price effects following from this downstream consolidation.

This latter finding introduces a dynamic element in that it considers how upstream consolidation and downstream consolidation interact, which is the key topic of the next section.

[C] Buyer Power as a Driver for Concentrations

Another perspective on buyer power is to reflect the extent to which it could be the driver for merger activity. Unlike the more general question of why firms pursue acquisitions, the effect of buyer power on the occurrence of concentrations has received little attention in the literature. It is believed that Galbraith already predicted such a pattern as part of his work on buyer power.[220]

---

219. Husayn Shahrur, *Industry Structure and Horizontal Takeovers: Analysis of Wealth Effects on Rivals, Suppliers, and Corporate Customers*, 76 J. of Fin. Ec. 61 (2005).
220. John K. Galbraith, *The Affluent Society & Other Writings 1952–1967: American Capitalism; The Great Crash, 1929; The Affluent Society; The New Industrial State* (The Library of America 2010).*See* making this claim the work of Kenneth R. Ahern and Jarrad Harford, *The Importance of Industry Links in Merger Waves*, 69 J. Fin. 527 (2014), who indicate that Galbraith predicted that that industry consolidation in an upstream industry leads to consolidation in a downstream industry to counteract the monopoly power created through the initial consolidation.

Öberg and Holstrom discuss the notion of parallel M&A and explore how mergers among customers lead to mergers among suppliers, and reverse.[221] Their article uses empirical data from six case studies, including the *Enso/Stora* merger. The authors consider that mergers are contagious.

Ahern and Harford investigate the role of inter-industry relations in explaining merger waves.[222] Their research also covers a scenario where merger waves do not move through industries via vertical mergers, but instead, concentration amongst suppliers prompts increased concentration amongst customers.

The authors develop a sample of 51,002 transactions between US firms from 1986 to 2010 and overlay this with US data on industry linkage (input–output data tables from the Bureau of Economic Analysis).

The authors find that the merger activity in what they label as 'close' industries (i.e., a lower number of links in the input–output tables) has a strong positive effect on an industry's level of merger activity one year later. They also find an effect for 'distant' industries where the effect is relatively muted and has a larger time lag (i.e., two to three years).

Moreover, and in contrast to the notion of parallel M&A, the authors find that the effect is stronger in one direction. Their results show that this effect is stronger coming from supplier links as opposed to customer links: in other words, firms appear to respond more to upstream consolidation compared to downstream consolidation.

Hui et al. investigate the effect of consolidation amongst customers on the supplying firm's profitability.[223] They find that major customer concentration is negatively associated with the supplier firm's profitability but positively associated with the major customers' profitability. They go on to demonstrate that these effects weaken as the supplier firm's own power grows over its relationship with major customers.

The authors use two datasets: the first uses static industry data and the second uses data from horizontal customer mergers. The conclusions are supported by both data sets.

[D] Further Analysis

We have further explored this hypothesis for the industries involved in the three mergers that are the focus of this chapter. To this end, we have investigated whether a Granger causality exists in the series of mergers in two sets of industries. Granger causality shows whether one time series (for instance, upstream mergers) precedes another time series (downstream mergers). This method allows us to explore whether the two-time series are related without the need to populate a broader model aimed at

221. Christina Öberg and Johan Holstrom, *Are Mergers and Acquisitions Contagious?* 59(12) J. Bus. Res. 1267–1275 (2006).
222. Kenneth R. Ahern and Jarrad Harford, *The Importance of Industry Links in Merger Waves*, 69 J. Fin. 527 (2014).
223. Kai Wai Hui, Chuchu Liang and P. Eric Yeung, *The Effect of Major Customer Concentration on Firm Profitability: Competitive or Collaborative?*, 24 Rev. Acc. St. 189 (2019).

explaining the (other) drivers of upstream or downstream merger activity as is the case with much of the research discussed above.

The first set of industry pairs we explored relates to the (downstream) supermarket sector and the (upstream) food and beverage industry, in line with the *Kesko/Tuko* case and *Carrefour/Promodès* merger. The second set relates to the (downstream) market of packaging and the (upstream) market of paper products in line with the role of TetraPak as the firm exercising countervailing buyer power in the *Enso/Stora* merger.

The aim of this analysis is to explore whether there exists an *ex post* effect of these transactions, in that they are linked to further consolidation amongst the parallel industry.

We use a dataset of completed mergers obtained from Dealogic between 1995 and 2020 for each of the four industries.[224] Following the focus on European Commission cases, we selected transactions where the bidder and/or target are active in Europe.[225] Finally, we deploy a number of filters to arrive with a set of horizontal transactions[226] leading to a transfer of control.[227] Table 4.2 contains an overview of the number of mergers in the dataset for each sector.

Table 4.2 Overview of Number of Mergers in Dataset

Industry		*Number of Mergers in Dataset*
Industry pair 'Food retailing'	Food and Beverage (upstream)	7,643
	Supermarket (downstream)	899
Industry pair 'Forestry and Paper'	Forestry and Paper – Pulp and Paper (upstream)	233
	Forestry and Paper – Packaging (downstream)	465

The mergers in the dataset for each sector are grouped using the announcement date.

---

224. Using the field 'Announcement Date'.
225. Using the fields 'Bidder Region' or 'Acq Subsidiary Region' and 'Target Region'.
226. Mergers involving at least one vertically integrated firm (e.g., active in both Supermarket and Food and Beverage) are removed from the data. Horizontal mergers are then identified by selecting those transactions for which the industry classification for the target, as well as the acquiring firm, are the same. For acquirers, this is done using the fields 'Acq Subsidiary Specific Industry Group' if subsidiary information is available and 'Acq Specific Industry Group' if subsidiary information is not available, and for targets the 'Target Specific Industry Group'. Note that if a firm is active in multiple industries, but is not a vertically integrated firm (e.g., Supermarket as well as finance), it is treated as a firm active in the downstream Supermarket industry.
227. Transactions leading to a chance of control are identified by selecting those transactions where the share interest transferred exceeds 50% using the field 'Acquired Stake' and where the share interest passes the 50% mark following the transaction using the fields 'Initial Stake' and 'Final Stake'.

We also collected data on transaction values. However, due to limited disclosure, the resulting data sets are significantly smaller and more sporadic, and so unfortunately are not suitable for inclusion in the analysis.

Figure 4.1 Overview of Number of Transactions Per Quarter: Forestry and Paper

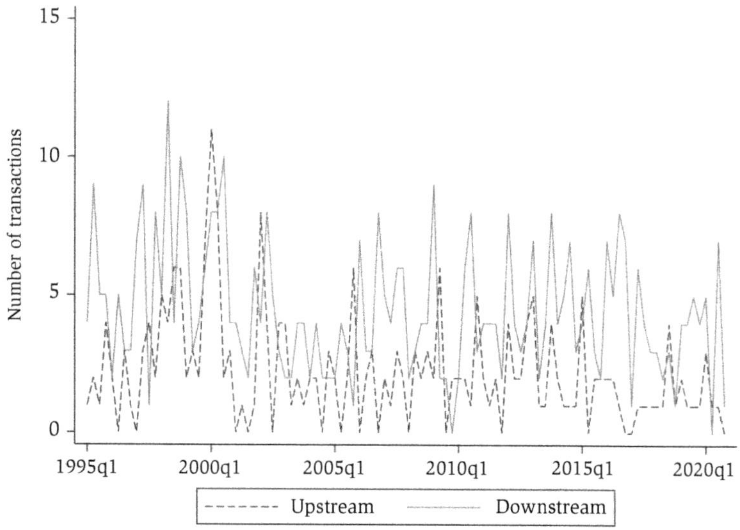

Source: Dealogic.

Figure 4.1 shows the number of transactions for the pair of Forest and Paper industries with horizontal mergers in the Pulp and Paper industry sector earmarked as 'Upstream' and 'Downstream' containing horizontal mergers in the Packaging industry sector.

Figure 4.2 shows a similar overview with horizontal mergers in the Food and Beverage industry sector earmarked under 'Upstream' and horizontal supermarket mergers grouped as 'Downstream'.

An immediate observation is that the number of upstream transactions in the food retailing example is much higher than the number of downstream transactions. This can be explained by the fact that supermarkets have a wide range of suppliers (as opposed to producers of cardboard packaging).

Figure 4.2 Overview of Number of Transactions Per Quarter: Food Retailing

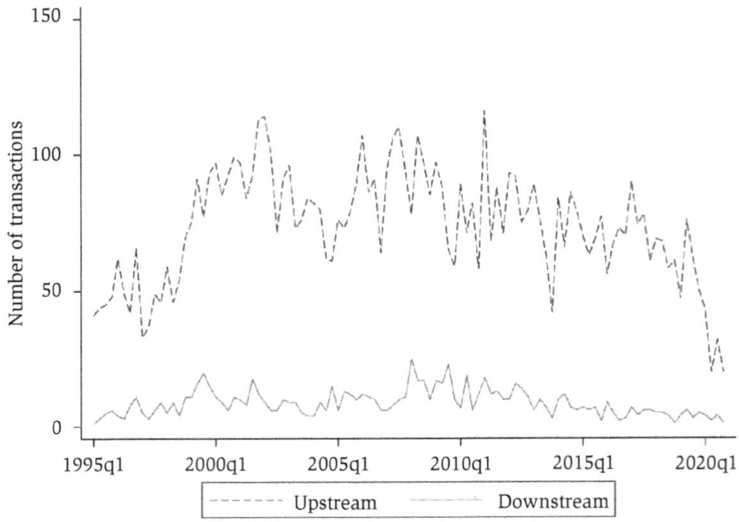

Source: Dealogic.

Econometric Analyses

To be able to find support for our hypothesis that there is a link between the pace of upstream merger activity and downstream merger activity, we perform a Granger causality test.

Before a Granger causality test can be deployed, the underlying statistical assumptions of this test have to be shown to hold. A core assumption of the Granger causality test is *stationarity* – this entails that the statistical properties of each of the time series are constant over time. If one of these time series were non-stationary, then any relationship with another time series found in the Granger causality test would be considered weaker. To test for stationarity, we deploy the augmented Dicky–Fuller test.

We perform these tests at different time periods. The Granger causality test explores the link between two-time series of data. First, we have grouped the merger data in the number of transactions in two time intervals: per month as well as per quarter. In a second step, we explore different lags to explore Granger causality for different combinations of time periods (i.e., one up to six monthly and quarterly periods back).

Finally, we have explored Granger causality not only between individual time periods but also between the sum of transactions in combined periods (moving sum) and the average number of transactions in past periods. These additional time periods were included to explore whether merger activity in one part of the value chain may be driven more by sustained levels of merger activity over multiple time periods as opposed to a single period. We find that these results for these modified time periods generate significant results for the Dicky–Fuller test and Granger causality; the patterns found in these results across the different time periods tested leads us to conclude that these results are not meaningful.

We find that both the monthly and quarterly time series for both upstream and downstream mergers in the Forest and Paper industry pair are stationary. In the case of food retailing, the quarterly time series for Food and Beverage firms shows relatively high p-values, suggesting that the upstream time series is non-stationary. As such, any further results using this quarterly time series require more cautious interpretation. An overview of the results of the various augmented Dicky–Fuller tests can be found in Annex 1.

Now that the degree to which the underlying assumptions hold has been established, the Granger causality test can be performed. The test itself focuses on the interplay between the time series for upstream and downstream horizontal merger activity for both industries using a Granger causality test. This test allows us to explore the relationship in either direction (whether upstream granger causes downstream or vice versa). The test also allows us to look at different time lags (e.g., upstream merger activity leads to downstream merger activity x periods later). Here we have tested for periods up to six months, as well as three quarters of a year. The results of the various Granger tests are summarized in Annex 1.

The results for food retailing show statistically significant results using the monthly time series for both directions, as well as with multiple lag periods. This provides support for the starting hypothesis. The results for the different lag periods are statistically stronger for the direction in which upstream causes downstream horizontal mergers. This result also supports the notion of circularity, as suggested in Öberg and Holstrom.[228] Looking at the quarterly time series for food retailing reveals that the results are statistically weaker across the board. While we would accept granger causality at the 10% statistical significance level, the upstream series is non-stationary, as previously explained. A single quarter produces the most statistically robust outcome.

The results for the Forest and Paper industry are weaker across the board for both directions and various time lags. One possible explanation is that these time series have fewer observations. The most robust results for the monthly and quarterly time series relates to upstream causing downstream horizontal mergers in the very short term (i.e., with a lag of one period).

Whilst our dataset is limited as it focuses on only two pairs of upstream and downstream sectors, the results do provide support for the hypothesis and/or intuition raised in the literature that mergers in connected parts of the value chain lead to consolidation amongst suppliers and customers.

228. Christina Öberg and Johan Holstrom, *Are Mergers and Acquisitions Contagious?* 59(12) J. Bus. Res. 1267–1275 (2006).

§4.07 BEYOND AN *EX POST* ANALYSIS, MEASURES TAKEN, AND LESSONS LEARNT? THE UNFAIR TRADING PRACTICES DIRECTIVE AS A SPILLOVER?

[A] Unfair Trading Practices and Their Connection to the Cases of *Kesko/Tuko* and *Carrefour/Promodès*

Buyer power concerns are still rarely discussed in the enforcement of competition law, both in Europe and in the USA.[229] However, the food retailing sector is perhaps a rare exception. *Kesko/Tuko* and *Carrefour/Promodès*, alongside the case of *Rewe/Meil*, are examples from the late 1990s and early 2000s that generated a competition policy-related buzz relating to the negative and exploitative effects of buyer power - on end consumers but even more so with respect to small food producers.

Concerns regarding the imposition of exploitative or *unfair* purchasing practices by supermarket chains and food distributors over small food producers have been voiced at the national and European levels. These debates have taken place inside and outside of the EU competition law/policy agenda. Despite the competition policy debate and interest, European (but also national) cases relating to breaches of competition (antitrust) law have remained scant.[230]

Instead, these issues have been approached from the perspective linked to *unfair* competition, contractual fairness and ethical purchasing.[231] These discussions have also been centred on imbalances in the relations between small food suppliers and large food distributors and supermarket chains that allow these latter to impose unfair contractual and non-contractual conditions.

229. For a global perspective on buyer power matters *see*: Peter C. Carstensen, *Competition Policy and the Control of Buyer Power: A Global Issue* (Edward Elgar Publishing 2017).
230. *See* Alexander Italianer (Director-General for Competition, European Commission) at https://ec.europa.eu/competition/speeches/text/sp2014_04_en.pdf (accessed 11 January 2021): 'A third, more general question that had to be kept in mind is: to what extent are we really dealing with problems of competition, and to what extent with unfair trading practices? Simply put, competition law deals with overall effects on the markets. Consumers suffer because a lack of competition leads to higher prices, stifles innovation and reduces choice. Unfair trading laws deal with fairness in individual business relationships, for instance, when a big supplier bullies a retailer into stocking a product'.
231. *See, e.g.*, Ignacio Herrera Anchustegui and Ronny Gjendemsjø, *Unfair Trading Practices in the Food Supply Chain*, 5 Conc. N. 3 On-Topic (Special Issue Editors 2019), and the contributions included therein; Ronny Gjendemsjø and Ignacio Herrera Anchustegui, *Regulating the Food Supply Chain in Europe and the Unfair Trading Practices Directive*, Rev. eur. de dr. de la cons. 165 (2020); Victoria Daskalova, *The New Directive on Unfair Trading Practices in Food and EU Competition Law: Complementary or Divergent Normative Frameworks?*, 10 J. Eur. Comp. L. & P. 281 (2019); Hanna Schebesta et al., *Unfair Trading Practices in the Food Supply Chain: Regulating Right?*, 9 Eur. J. R. Reg. 690 (2018); European Commission, *Report from the Commission to the European Parliament and the Council on unfair business-to-business trading practices in the food supply chain* (2016); European Commission, *Study on the Legal Framework Covering Business-To-Business Unfair Trading Practices in the Retail Supply Chain* (2014); European Commission, *Tackling Unfair Trading Practices in the Business-to-Business food supply chain* (2014).

Unfair purchasing practices take place in contractual and extra-contractual relationships in which there is a transfer of profit or risk without adequate compensation, to such a degree that it becomes unfair and contrary to good commercial practices. These practices take many forms and shapes, as discussed in the literature:[232]

> Some of the practices deal with imposition of charges, others with delays in payment and other contractual obligations, some with refusing to purchase a good or deciding to terminate a contractual relationship with no or inadequate grounds, while others deal with vagueness in contractual terms, intellectual property-related abuses or conduct as refusing to have the contract in writing.

In the *Kesko/Tuko* and *Carrefour/Promodès* merger decisions, there was no extensive or explicit analysis concerning unfair purchasing practices. However, implicitly in *Kesko/Tuko* and more directly in *Carrefour/Promodès*, relating to the 'threat point' concept, there is a connection between the risks of buyer power exertion and economic dependence with unfair trading practices. If a supplier is dependent on a buyer, then the latter would be able to extract extraordinary price or risk concessions, for example, to avoid being delisted. In this sense, *Carrefour/Promodès* considers some of the unfair practices in the relation between the new group and its suppliers. The Commission noted prospectively that a downstream merger might lead to a dominant position of the new entity in terms of the information it can gather about suppliers. Subsequently, it would affect the negotiation of purchasing conditions between the two parties, where one of them has considerably more data at its disposal.[233] More related to risks of imposing unfair purchasing are the commitments made in which the merging entity agreed not to delist products or suppliers,[234] and not to modify contractual conditions on volume, price or delivery times.[235]

[B] The Directive in a Nutshell

After some years of political discussions, the European Commission's DG Agriculture (and not DG Competition) proposed a Directive on Unfair Trading Practices in the Agricultural and Food Supply Chain that ultimately came into force in 2019.[236]

The Directive is an instrument that proposes a regulation of contractual and non-contractual practices – prohibiting some and subjecting others to a previous agreement in clear and unambiguous terms among the parties in the supply or a subsequent arrangement. As designed, the Directive is a minimum protection standard or minimal set of harmonisation instruments, and each Member State 'may introduce

232. Ronny Gjendemsjø and Ignacio Herrera Anchustegui, *Regulating the Food Supply Chain in Europe and the Unfair Trading Practices Directive*, Rev. eur. de dr. de la cons. 165, 167 (2020).
233. Decision 1999/C359/10, *Carrefour/Promodès* (2000), para. 104.
234. *Ibid.*, Annex 2, para. 1.
235. *Ibid.*, Annex 2, para. 2.
236. Directive (EU) 2019/633 of the European Parliament and of the Council of 17 April 2019 on unfair trading practices in business-to-business relationships in the agricultural and food supply chain (OJ [2019] L 111/59).

stricter rules against unfair trading practices to ensure a higher level of protection of food suppliers, as long as those provisions are compatible with the internal market'.[237]

Such protection is achieved by 'creating a list of prohibited practices and secondly by making other practices subject to a previous and unambiguous agreement between the supplier and the buyer. The Directive also requires the designation of an enforcement agency with sufficient powers to ensure compliance with the norms'.[238] All these practices are said to deviate grossly from good commercial conduct, being contrary to good faith and fair dealing and unilaterally imposed by one trading partner on another.[239] Nine practices are included in the 'black list' of the Directive, implying that they would not be allowed in bilateral relations. These include late payments, cancelling orders of perishable foods, unilateral and retroactive changes of the terms of the supply agreement, and requesting that payments related to deterioration or loss (or both) that occurs on the buyer's premises or after ownership has been transferred to the buyer. Six other practices are prohibited unless the parties have agreed to them clearly and unambiguously, in either the original supply agreement or in a subsequent one. These practices are related to issues such as requiring payments, imposing charges or foregoing payments from the buyer to the supplier, all of them shifting the profit distribution in a contract.

Concerning the scope of application of the Directive, some resemblance can be shed to these food retailing mergers by focusing on the relationship between big versus small undertakings in the value chain, which is an element of economic dependence. The Directive seeks to target the bargaining power differences between large and powerful buyers with respect to smaller suppliers based on a 'cascade' system in which turnover has been used as a proxy for bargaining power.[240] However, unlike in *Kesko/Tuko, Rewe/Meinl* or *Carrefour/Promodès*, no references to a threat point or a specific percentage of sales a buyer represents for a supplier is made.

[C] Influence of the Merger Decisions in the Directive?

The use of economic thresholds serves to illustrate a similar concern as expressed in these merger cases, relating to the possibility of abuse of economic dependence or even risks of relative dominance – issues that do not fall within the scope of EU competition law but which are covered under antitrust provisions in some Member States, with Germany providing the most salient example. It is, therefore, through the associated risk of imposing unfair trading practices and this link to the idea of economic dependence and imbalance that a connection is made between the foreseen risks in

237. Ignacio Herrera Anchustegui and Ronny Gjendemsjø, *Unfair Trading Practices in the Food Supply Chain*, 5 Conc. N. 3 On-Topic (Special Issue Editors 2019), para. 10.
238. Ronny Gjendemsjø and Ignacio Herrera Anchustegui, *Regulating the Food Supply Chain in Europe and the Unfair Trading Practices Directive*, Rev. eur. de dr. de la cons. 165, 179 (2020).
239. Article 1 of the Directive 2019/633.
240. Ignacio Herrera Anchustegui, *Buyer Power in EU Competition Law* (Institut de droit de la concurrence 2017); foreword of Ignacio Herrera Anchustegui and Ronny Gjendemsjø, *Unfair Trading Practices in the Food Supply Chain*, 5 Conc. N. 3 On-Topic (Special Issue Editors 2019), para. 7.

food retailing – as identified explicitly in *Carrefour/Promodès* and *Rewe/Meinl*, and hinted at in *Kesko/Tuko* – and unfair purchasing practices can be made.

In the cases assessed in this chapter, buyer power concerns were found to be affecting not only the upstream (purchasing market) but also, directly or indirectly, the downstream market. In the retailing market, the competitive risks arose from the fact that as a powerful buyer with also market power in a related downstream market, buyer power could be used to foreclose other rivals – with less buyer market power – as they would receive worse purchasing conditions, for example. In the upstream market, the concerns raised in both cases were linked to the ability of a powerful buyer to extract better and presumably exploitative rents from their suppliers. This was the point made by the Commission regarding the threat point in which the main issue was the existence of a *relative* dominant position generated by the fact that a supplier is in economic dependence with respect to a buyer when the latter provides at least 22 % of the former's turnover.

Economic dependence related to this threat point might be the main reason why powerful buyers are able to impose on certain suppliers conditions that appear to be unfair in a bilateral relationship because they are not properly compensated or retributed. In case the supplier does not agree to the buyer's requirement, the buyer may delist its products or simply stop purchasing goods from it.

Accordingly, the Commission's theory about the threat point used in these merger cases appears to have served as both an example of rules regarding unfair competition and inspiration for solutions to the particularities of food retailing from a wide competition policy perspective. Curiously, and as mentioned before, no examples of possible unfair (and anticompetitive) purchasing practices were explicitly discussed.

Likewise, in the Directive, there is no explicit mention of the idea of the threat point. Instead, the Directive adopts a 'cascade system' to signal when a difference in volume (turnover) is representative of bargaining power. However, the threat point is probably a better indicator as it measures a degree of dependence between the buyer and the supplier and not the turnover of firms in general.

[D] A Change of Regulatory Tactic?

The Unfair Trading Practices Directive marks a stricter and different method for dealing with risks associated with buyer power exertion in the food retail chain that were generally not captured by EU competition (antitrust) law. Such exclusion from the antitrust scope was – either because the buyer was not dominant, or because (in the case of concentrations among undertakings with large buyer power) it did not significantly impede effective competition in the upstream market (or the downstream market due to associated risks of buyer power advantages).

The Directive combines both 'blacklisted' practices with others available only upon previous agreement between the parties, creating, therefore, a distinction on the severity and *unfairness* among them. Connected to this, the Directive through *ex ante* regulation would address risks that have been associated in the past with the merger of large buyers in the supermarket chain, which could narrow even further the quite limited role that buyer power has played as a source of competition risks in food retailing cases.

Interestingly, this change in regulatory tactics to address buyer power issues in food retailing does not seem to arise from a significant amount of European or even national competition law cases in which risks of monopsony or bargaining power have been brought forward, nor *true* antitrust concerns. They are not very common, in fact. Thus, the Directive does not seem to be a regulatory response linked to an unusually large amount of anticompetitive buyer power cases or future anticompetitive buyer power risks associated with food retailing mergers.

§4.08 CONCLUSION

Buyer power concerns in competition law are rare - even though there have been waves of interest on an industry level. For the most part, buyer (bargaining) power tends to be welfare-enhancing as parties to a bilateral commercial relationship negotiate terms of the trade and the buyer power extracts supra-competitive profits that would have been kept by the supplier. If competition downstream for that buyer exists, at least part of those supra-competitive profits will be passed on to end consumers in the form of lower prices and/or better products. However, buyer power can also lead to instances in which it can be detrimental to competition and welfare. This may be because there is a reduction of demand to also reduce purchasing prices - as it occurs in the monopsony model - or because there is abusive or unfair purchasing behaviour. Mergers are no exception, as we discussed in section §4.03 above. The literature and antitrust practice in Europe show how buyer power effects are factored into the analysis of whether a concentration is compatible with the internal market. However, despite being mentioned fairly often, buyer power is rarely a key aspect of the outcome of a decision.

In this chapter, we have discussed three landmark buyer power-related concentration cases which are exceptional in the practice due to the importance given to purchasing-side competition concerns. These are the two food retailing cases of *Kesko/Tuko* and *Carrefour/Promodès*, and the cardboard case of *Enso/Stora*. We discussed these cases to understand which theories of harm and market effects were raised by the Commission in the assessment and the strength of such analysis.

On the one hand, in the food retailing cases, we see how the Commission's concerns regarding buyer power are focused on downstream effects and foreclosure of rivals of what would have been a dominant buyer and retailer in *Kesko/Tuko*. In this case, the Commission resorted to buyer power risks as an additional concern related to selling-side competitive issues. In this light, buyer power reinforced seller market power as the proposed entity would have been able to act as a gatekeeper, foreclosing food retailers downstream through their use of buyer power and purchasing volume. Also, due to their large buying power and proportion of market shares, *Kesko/Tuko* would have been able to extract very advantageous bargaining terms from *dependent* suppliers.

The idea of buyer power-induced dependence was again discussed in *Carrefour/Promodès*, also in food retailing. Unlike in *Kesko/Tuko*, the concentration was not likely to lead to the creation or strengthening of a dominant position in the food retailing sector. However, it could lead to some exploitative and unfair exertion of buyer power abuse against food suppliers. The Commission resorted to a *threat point* theory according to which when a buyer represents 22 % of a supplier's business, the supplier becomes dependent and likely to be in a situation of economic dependence. Economic dependence shares similarities with relative dominance: not all suppliers are dependent on the same buyer and this is, therefore, anchored in a bilateral situation and not a market-wide one. Being dependent and under the risk of the *threat point*, a buyer could impose unfair trading practices on its suppliers. Also, in *Carrefour/Promodès*, the Commission stressed the connection existing between seller and buyer power in a reinforcing mechanism by referring to the 'spiral effect'.

Both *Kesko/Tuko* and *Carrefour/Promodès* were buyer power pioneer cases in the food retailing sector – alongside *Rewe/Meinl*. In these cases, the commonality is the risk of exerting exploitative and to some degree 'unfair' bargaining power over a weak and dependent supplier. In none of these cases were buyer power concerns in and of themselves sufficient to render the concentration incompatible with the internal market. The buyer power risks were seen as an additional factor to the seller and downstream concerns. Also, the discussion in the analysed cases remained somewhat superficial yet logically sound. The Commission does not seem to have needed a very detailed analysis of buyer power effects because this was not crucial to the investigation, even in the case of *Kesko/Tuko*. Furthermore, the buyer power analysis did not hinge on concerns about monopsony power exertions. Rather, the discussion was mostly tied to two concepts: (i) the idea of economic dependence of weak suppliers – with some hints to unfair purchasing practices; and (ii) the issue of gatekeeping and use of buyer power to reinforce a strong position in a retailing market – issues that with the surge in online retailing and antitrust are starting to resurface again.

Enso/Stora constitutes perhaps the most representative of merger cases related to the topic of countervailing buyer power as this neutralising power was the main reason for allowing a merger between sellers of cardboard to take place. The Commission evaluated the position of TetraPak as a large purchaser with sufficient buyer power to offset any potential risks of selling-side market power abuses. Doing so, it applied a comparison test that, in this particular case, was centred on the market symmetry between one very large buyer and one future very large seller. Interestingly, the Commission also required countervailing buyer power to be sufficient to benefit other smaller buyers, with the spillover effect. In retrospect, *Enso/Stora* represents a very rare case of a mirror market structure, providing an example of a somewhat limited and simplified analysis of countervailing buyer power. Other cases have gone beyond this and brought further finesses to the discussion on the sufficiency of countervailing buyer power. However, in this case, the Commission does not seem to have needed a much more complex analysis to reach a similar conclusion.

In section §4.06 we go on to establish the wider prominence of buyer power considerations in EU merger decisions. Our review of the economic literature highlights that buyer power is not a standard component of the (empirical) research. Moreover, those papers in which buyer power or a combination of elements including buyer power are discussed do not appear to consistently show a significant effect.

We consider that these findings help to illuminate the topic of buyer power: while the concept is well understood, it appears more difficult to quantify and/or research. Unfortunately, the three horizontal merger cases at the focus of our review presented challenges in establishing the effect of buyer power and its role in *ex post* effects of these mergers. This is confirmed by those *ex post* reviews of merger decisions that touch on the topic of buyer power in mergers.

This prompted us to shift perspective in an attempt to better understand how other parties reflect on the role of buyer power in mergers. First, we looked at the investment community, discussing a number of papers that look at the share price response of suppliers to mergers of their (downstream) clients. We found there to be a body of literature, though focused on US firms and transactions. This suggests that shareholders do actively consider the fate of suppliers in mergers.

Second, we looked at the business community and discussed a number of papers that look at the role that buyer power plays as a driver of merger waves. Research using US transaction data suggests that this is the case. As part of this paper, we conducted a similar experiment using data on EU transactions in the two industry pairs focused on in our three cases. The first set of the two industries looked at relates to the (downstream) supermarket sector and the (upstream) food and beverage industry, in line with the *Kesko/Tuko* case and the *Carrefour/Promodès* merger. The second set relates to the (downstream) market of packaging and the (upstream) market of paper products, in line with the role of Tetra Pak as the firm exercising countervailing buyer power in the *Enso/Stora* merger. Our experiment also establishes a link between merger activity in one layer of the value chain and subsequent merger activity in the related upstream or downstream industry layer. This appears to support the prediction attributed to Galbraith (1952) that mergers from clients would spur consolidation amongst suppliers, which would in turn spur further consolidation amongst clients.

Furthermore, in our article, we found a link between buyer power concerns observed in the two food retailing cases studied and the relatively new rules on the food supply chain. While the adoption of the Unfair Trading Practices Directive cannot be said to derive from these concentrations, its content tallies with the concerns raised by the Commission in these cases. The Directive seeks to prevent instances of unfair or exploitative buyer power exertion from food retailers over food suppliers. This is done by prohibiting some conducts and subjective others to previous agreements between the parties effectively restricting buyer power exertion. These measures were adopted not on the basis of antitrust rules but as a result of unfair competition law, showing a closer link to the idea of fairness rather than economic efficiency.

Our contribution to the literature has been to establish the gap between the various strands of economic research on mergers and buyer power. Somewhat ironically, these findings suggest that the topic of buyer power would benefit from further research to better understand the effect of buyer power on the post-merger performance of firms. We will leave this challenge to (more) resourceful researchers.

Lastly, as mentioned at the start of this section, the topic of buyer power has been explored in the context of food retailing, as well as more recently in the digital/online industry. In both of these cases, the relative size of downstream retailers and upstream producers appears to be a key driver, and the discussion is focused on the gatekeeper role of large buyers. It appears that this discussion, in particular related to the digital/online sector as illustrated by the 'Proposal for a Regulation on Contestable and Fair Markets in the Digital Sector',[241] has generated increased policy debate on the notion of relative market power and issues of unfairness.

ANNEX 1 RESULTS OF DICKY–FULLER TEST FOR STATIONARITY

Industry	Time interval	Lags	Upstream mergers (p-value)	Downstream mergers (p-value)
Supermarket/Food	Monthly	1	0%	0%
Supermarket/Food	Monthly	2	0%	0%
Supermarket/Food	Monthly	3	1%	0%
Supermarket/Food	Monthly	4	1%	0%
Supermarket/Food	Monthly	5	11%	0%
Supermarket/Food	Monthly	6	8%	0%
Paper/Packaging (update)	Monthly	1	0%	0%
Paper/Packaging (update)	Monthly	2	0%	0%
Paper/Packaging (update)	Monthly	3	0%	0%
Paper/Packaging (update)	Monthly	4	0%	0%
Paper/Packaging (update)	Monthly	5	0%	0%
Paper/Packaging (update)	Monthly	6	0%	0%
Supermarket/Food	Quarterly	1	12%	0%
Supermarket/Food	Quarterly	2	27%	4%
Supermarket/Food	Quarterly	3	61%	9%

241. European Commission, *Proposal for a Regulation on contestable and fair markets in the digital sector* (Digital Markets Act) COM/2020/842 final (2020).

Industry	Time interval	Lags	Upstream mergers (p-value)	Downstream mergers (p-value)
Paper/Packaging (update)	Quarterly	1	0%	0%
Paper/Packaging (update)	Quarterly	2	0%	0%
Paper/Packaging (update)	Quarterly	3	0%	0%

P-values below or equal to 1%, 5% and 10% indicate significance at the 1% level, 5% level and 10% level, respectively.

Results of Granger Test for Causality

Industry	Time interval	Lags	U granger causes D (p-value)	D granger causes U (p-value)
Supermarket/Food	Monthly	1	0%	0%
Supermarket/Food	Monthly	2	0%	0%
Supermarket/Food	Monthly	3	0%	0%
Supermarket/Food	Monthly	4	1%	2%
Supermarket/Food	Monthly	5	1%	19%
Supermarket/Food	Monthly	6	0%	0%
Paper/Packaging (update)	Monthly	1	0%	15%
Paper/Packaging (update)	Monthly	2	14%	4%
Paper/Packaging (update)	Monthly	3	17%	10%
Paper/Packaging (update)	Monthly	4	15%	7%
Paper/Packaging (update)	Monthly	5	0%	17%
Paper/Packaging (update)	Monthly	6	19%	32%
Supermarket/Food	Quarterly	1	1%	1%
Supermarket/Food	Quarterly	2	3%	7%
Supermarket/Food	Quarterly	3	8%	0%

Industry	Time interval	Lags	U granger causes D (p-value)	D granger causes U (p-value)
Paper/Packaging (update)	Quarterly	1	0%	3%
Paper/Packaging (update)	Quarterly	2	2%	29%
Paper/Packaging (update)	Quarterly	3	85%	68%

P-values below or equal to 1%, 5% and 10% indicate significance at the 1% level, 5% level and 10% level, respectively.

CHAPTER 5

Ex Post Assessment of European Competition Policy: The Pharmaceutical Parallel Trade Cases

Jan Blockx & Benoît Durand[*]

§5.01 INTRODUCTION

This chapter presents an *ex post* assessment of the enforcement of competition law regarding restrictions targeting the parallel trade of pharmaceuticals in the European Union (EU). Parallel trade is the activity of re-selling pharmaceuticals in another country without the express consent of the company that holds the marketing authorisation. This trading activity is driven by the price difference that exists between countries. Specifically, traders purchase the medicine at a low price in one country to resell it at a higher price in another country. In many developed countries parallel imports of pharmaceuticals are illegal. For example, pharmaceuticals sold abroad cannot legally be imported in the United States (US) where prices tend to be higher than the rest of the world. However, within the European Economic Area (EEA), once the holder of the marketing authorisation for a medicine (either granted centrally by the European Medicines Agency (EMA) or by a national competent authority) supplies that product in one Member State, this medicine can be resold in other Member States without its authorisation.

In a number of cases in the first decade of the twenty-first century, the Court of Justice of the European Union (CJEU) has considered whether the use of trade restrictions by the holder of the marketing authorisation to prevent distributors from

* This report benefitted from helpful comments and directions from Paolo Buccirossi, Ángel Givaja Sanz, Margaret Kyle and Laura Lasio, as well as from Pedro Caro de Sousa, Luc Gyselen, Assimakis Komninos and Patrick Rey. The authors also wish to thank Alexander Eroshenko, Bernardo Silva and Steffen Wyngra for excellent research assistance.

engaging in parallel trade within the EEA, infringes EU competition rules (in particular what are now Articles 101 and 102 TFEU). These rules have the objective of facilitating the creation of the EU Single Market and of promoting consumer welfare through the prevention of inefficient business practices. The CJEU held that restrictions of parallel trade may breach the EU competition rules in certain circumstances.

This chapter starts with a brief description of the characteristics of the pharmaceutical sector, in particular as regards distribution and pricing (section §5.02) before discussing the role of the Single Market imperative in EU law (section §5.03). Section §5.04 contains a succinct description of the case law of the CJEU on parallel trade in pharmaceuticals. Section §5.05 presents the *ex post* assessment of this case law, in particular the extent to which the judgements have affected the development of the parallel trade of pharmaceuticals in the Single Market, and further the effects of parallel imports on prices and innovation. Section §5.06 concludes.

§5.02 BACKGROUND TO THE PHARMACEUTICAL SECTOR

[A] Pharmaceutical Distribution

The distribution and sale of pharmaceuticals are heavily regulated, principally at a national but to some extent also at a European level. This regulation has several, sometimes conflicting, goals, including ensuring the safety and quality of drugs, controlling the health care expenditure on drugs whilst guaranteeing access to patients, and encouraging innovation.[1]

Medicinal products reach consumers essentially in two ways: either as part of a treatment in a hospital, or as a product sold in community pharmacies (or, in some EU Member States, in other retail outlets). Some pharmaceutical products can be freely purchased by consumers in community pharmacies (over-the-counter (OTC)). However, most pharmaceutical products sold in pharmacies can only be purchased if a medical doctor has provided the consumer with a medical prescription for that drug.[2] In the case of such prescription-only medication, just like for pharmaceuticals administered in hospitals, the decision to procure a drug is not really made by the patient, but rather by the physician. There are differences between Member States as to which

1. *See* OECD, *Competition and regulatory issues in the pharmaceutical industry* 21 (2000). *See* also Elias Mossialos, Tom Walley and Monique Mrazek, *Regulating Pharmaceuticals in Europe: An Overview*, in *Regulating Pharmaceuticals in Europe: Striving for Efficiency, Equity and Quality* 1, 22 (Elias Mossialos, Monique Mrazek and Tom Walley eds, Open University Press 2004) who list additional objectives.
2. Article 71(1) of Directive 2001/83/EC of the European Parliament and of the Council of 6 November 2001 on the Community code relating to medicinal products for human use, OJ L 311, 28.11.2001, provides that this is for medicinal products which are (i) likely to present a danger either directly or indirectly, even when used correctly, if utilised without medical supervision, or (ii) are frequently and to a very wide extent used incorrectly, and as a result are likely to present a direct or indirect danger to human health, or (iii) contain substances or preparations thereof, the activity and/or adverse reactions of which require further investigation, or (iv) are normally prescribed by a doctor to be administered parenterally.

drugs are available in community pharmacies and in hospitals, as well as to which drugs are OTC and prescription only.

It is rare for manufacturers of pharmaceuticals to supply community pharmacies directly. In all EU Member States, wholesalers supply a full line of products from multiple manufacturers to pharmacies. The distribution channel is vertically integrated into some countries, where wholesale activities are run by large pharmacies, and in other countries, there are independent players at each step of the distribution chain. Hospital pharmacies generally tender supply contracts to pharmaceutical manufacturers and wholesalers, often through purchasing alliances.

[B] Pharmaceutical Pricing

As indicated above, most pharmaceutical products are administered based on the decision of a doctor, who is not paying for the product. Furthermore, although consumers usually pay for OTC drugs, all or a large extent of the cost of prescription drugs is usually covered, depending on the Member State, by (private or public) health insurance. In those circumstances, final consumer demand for pharmaceuticals tends to be inelastic.[3]

To limit the burden that this would pose on health insurers, Member States use regulatory intervention, which comes in a variety of ways. These include demand-side tools which aim to reduce the consumption of reimbursed drugs, such as excluding certain drugs from formularies of approved and reimbursed drugs (e.g., where cheaper equivalents are available) and requiring a co-payment from consumers (i.e., where only part of the price of the drug is reimbursed). Some EU Member States also incentivise or require physicians to limit the total amount of drugs (in monetary terms) they prescribe, and incentivise or require physicians and/or pharmacists to prescribe or dispense cheaper (e.g., generic) variants of drugs if these are available.

One important tool available to limit expenditure on pharmaceuticals is price control. In that case the (public) insurer usually negotiates a maximum price or a maximum profit margin with the manufacturer, or limits the reimbursement provided to the consumer (reference pricing). EU law merely requires that the way prices are set is (to some extent) transparent,[4] but otherwise leaves the Member States a free choice of techniques to do so. As a result, and despite the incorporation of international price comparisons in many national price-setting mechanisms, there are significant price differences between different EU Member States.

Some EU Member States do not merely regulate drug prices but also the margins which pharmacies and wholesalers can earn on pharmaceutical sales (or their profits

3. OECD, *Competition and regulatory issues in the pharmaceutical industry* 40 (2000); Benoît Durand, *Competition Law and Pharma: An Economic Perspective*, in *EU Law of Competition and Trade in the Pharmaceutical Sector* 1, 6 (Pablo Figueroa and Alejandro Guerrero Perez eds, Edward Elgar 2019).
4. Pursuant to Council Directive 89/105/EEC of 21 December 1988 relating to the transparency of measures regulating the prices of medicinal products for human use and their inclusion in the scope of national health insurance systems, OJ L 40, 11.2.1989.

more generally), thereby diminishing their ability and incentive to negotiate prices with manufacturers. There are nevertheless schemes in some Member States to incentivise wholesalers and pharmacies to negotiate rebates on their purchase prices, for example by paying pharmacies (partially) per item dispensed. Cheaper parallel imports are also more attractive under such schemes than in situations where the margin of the pharmacy increases with its purchase price. In many Member States, pharmacists are required to dispense cheaper versions of drugs if these are available, including from foreign sources. In Germany, pharmacies are furthermore required by law to dispense drugs that come from parallel imports until a certain target saving has been achieved.[5] Insurers may in turn claw back some of the extra profit pharmacies earn this way.

§5.03 EU SINGLE MARKET IMPERATIVE

[A] General Description

The European Economic Community was created to establish a common market, including through the abolition of restrictions on the free movement of goods between EU Member States.[6] This entailed the elimination of tariffs between the Member States as well as the removal of any quantitative restrictions on imports and exports and measures having equivalent effect, unless such restrictions are justified by public interest concerns.[7]

[B] Restrictions on Parallel Trade Imposed by Member States and IP Rights

In the pursuit of this objective, European law requires the Member States to abolish any restrictions on the parallel trade of pharmaceutical products, except if such restrictions are justified by public interest concerns such as the health and life of humans. The CJEU has multiple times found that restrictions on the import of pharmaceuticals fail to be justified in this sense,[8] but the prohibition of exports is similarly problematic.

The requirement that drugs marketed in EU Member States receive a marketing authorisation is as such not a restriction of trade. Indeed, EU law requires that drugs benefit from a marketing authorisation before they are marketed.[9] However, once such an authorisation has been granted, national legislation cannot prevent parallel traders

---

5. Dimitra Panteli et al., *Pharmaceutical Regulation in 15 European Countries: Review 59 and 65* (European Observatory on Health Systems and Policies 2016).
6. *See* in particular Articles 2 and 3 of the Treaty establishing the European Economic Community.
7. *See* Article 30ff EEC, currently Article 34ff TFEU.
8. *See*, for example, Case C-215/87, *Schumacher v. Hauptzollamt Frankfurt am Main-Ost*, ECLI:EU:C:1989:111; Case C-62/90, *Commission v. Germany*, ECLI:EU:C:1992:169; and Case C-387/18, *Delfarma*, ECLI:EU:C:2019:556.
9. *See* already Article 3 of Council Directive 65/65/EEC of 26 January 1965 on the approximation of provisions laid down by Law, Regulation or Administrative Action relating to proprietary medicinal products, OJ 22, 9.2.1965 and currently Article 5(1) of Directive 2001/83/EC of the

from importing the product in question.[10] The European courts have also required the Member States to grant market authorisations to parallel importers under a proportionally simplified procedure when the information necessary for the purposes of protecting public health is already available to the competent authorities of the Member State of destination, and the Commission has even issued guidelines to that effect.[11] In some circumstances, parallel import licences must be maintained, even after the holder of the original market authorisation requests the withdrawal of the authorisation.[12]

The EU has furthermore taken positive harmonisation steps through the adoption of common rules regarding the adoption of marketing authorisations (a decentralised but uniform marketing authorisation system) as well as a centralised marketing authorisation procedure for European market authorisations processed by the EMA.[13]

Parallel imports are further aided by the application of the principle of exhaustion of intellectual property (IP) rights across the EU. The CJEU indeed established that a holder of a patent or trademark exhausts his rights across the whole of the EU by voluntarily placing a product on the market in any one of the Member States.[14] Provided certain conditions are met, IP rights therefore cannot prevent the commercialisation of a drug that is sold in one Member State, also in other Member States.[15]

Beyond marketing authorisations, Member States regulate pharmaceutical sales in other ways. For example, Member States in the past imposed various packaging requirements on drugs sold in their territory: this was allowed to the extent that such requirements were essential to protect human health.[16] Member States are also allowed

---

European Parliament and of the Council of 6 November 2001 on the Community code relating to medicinal products for human use, OJ L 311, 28.11.2001.

10. Case C-104/75, *De Peijper*, ECLI:EU:C:1976:67.
11. Commission communication on parallel imports of proprietary medicinal products for which marketing authorisations have already been granted (COM(2003) 839 final).
12. Case C-172/00, *Ferring*, ECLI:EU:C:2002:474.
13. *See* Articles 6–39 of Directive 2001/83/EC of the European Parliament and of the Council of 6 November 2001 on the Community code relating to medicinal products for human use, OJ L 311, 28.11.2001, and Regulation (EC) No 726/2004 of the European Parliament and of the Council of 31 March 2004 laying down Community procedures for the authorisation and supervision of medicinal products for human and veterinary use and establishing a European Medicines Agency, OJ L 136, 30.4.2004.
14. Case C-15/74, *Centrafarm BV and Others v. Sterling Drug*, ECLI:EU:C:1974:114 and Case C-16/74, *Centrafarm BV and Others v. Winthorp BV*, ECLI:EU:C:1974:115. In the case of trademarks, the principle is currently included in Article 15 of Directive (EU) 2015/2436 of the European Parliament and of the Council of 16 December 2015 to approximate the laws of the Member States relating to trade marks, OJ L 336, 23.12.2015.
15. In the case of repackaging, these conditions include that the repackaging must be necessary, that the new packaging clearly states who repackaged the product and the name of the manufacturer, that the repackaged product is not liable to damage the reputation of the trade mark and of its owner, and that the importer gives notice to the trade mark owner before the repackaged product is put on sale. *See* Case C-436/93, *Bristol-Myers Squibb v. Paranova*, ECLI: EU:C:1996:282.
16. *See* Article 6 and 7 of the Second Council Directive 75/319/EEC of 20 May 1975 on the approximation of provisions laid down by Law, Regulation or Administrative Action relating to proprietary medicinal products, OJ L 147, 9.6.1975. These requirements are currently mainly regulated through European law in Directive 2001/83/EC of the European Parliament and of the Council of 6 November 2001 on the Community code relating to medicinal products for human use, OJ L 311, 28.11.2001.

to grant pharmacies a monopoly to sell pharmaceutical products[17] and to regulate other aspects of the sale of pharmaceuticals, if this does not disadvantage foreign products.[18]

The institution of price control mechanisms for pharmaceuticals is in principle a prerogative of the Member States. However, the CJEU has taken issue with features of price control systems which restrict trade between the Member States, such as a differentiated system of price controls for imported pharmaceuticals as opposed to medicines produced domestically.[19] Also the extension of price controls for prescription-only drugs to products procured by consumers from mail-order pharmacies in other Member States is considered to be an unjustified restriction on the free movement of goods.[20]

[C] Interaction with Public Health Policy

Whilst European law only allows restrictions on the free movement of pharmaceuticals if these are required to protect the health and life of humans, public health policies also pursue other objectives such as guaranteeing access to medicines whilst controlling health care expenditures and encouraging innovation.

The European Commission has argued that the creation of a Single Market in pharmaceuticals would also facilitate the achievement of these other policy objectives. The divergences between regulatory regimes in different Member States may create delays in the marketing of drugs, whilst a Single Market may encourage R&D investments in Europe.[21]

On the other hand, the effects of policy on health care mainly arise at a national level. In this respect, different Member States make different choices and are confronted with different realities, in terms of what are acceptable health care costs both for their public finances and their respective population. This is reflected in the different regulatory requirements individual Member States have established, including for pricing and reimbursement.

The free movement of pharmaceuticals across EU Member States may therefore both facilitate and obstruct public health policies.

17. Case C-369/88, *Delattre*, ECLI:EU:C:1991:137.
18. Case C-322/01, *Deutscher Apothekerverband*, ECLI:EU:C:2003:664.
19. Case C-181/82, *Roussel*, ECLI:EU:C:1983:352.
20. Case C-148/15, *Deutsche Parkinson Vereinigung*, ECLI:EU:C:2016:776.
21. *See*, in particular, the Commission Communication on the single market in pharmaceuticals (COM(1998) 588 final) and the Commission Communication on safe, innovative and accessible medicines: a renewed vision for the pharmaceutical sector (COM(2008) 666 final).

[D] The Single Market Objective, Economic Efficiency, and the Parallel Trade of Pharmaceuticals

In the middle of the 1980s, when the European Commission published its *White Paper on Completing the Internal Market*,[22] it noted the clear economic benefits that an internal market brings: 'The creation of a true European internal market will, on the one hand, suppress a series of constraints that today prevent enterprises from being as efficient as they could be and from employing their resources to the full, and, on the other hand, establish a more competitive environment which will incite them to exploit new opportunities.'[23]

By creating a free trade area, the Single Market objective seeks to increase the prosperity of the EU by allowing consumers to buy more, better-quality products at lower cost. In particular, free trade within the Single Market is expected to improve economic efficiency, notably by shifting resources to more productive uses, and thereby fuelling economic growth. Free trade also imposes competitive discipline on firms, given them further incentives to minimise costs and keep prices low.

In principle, market integration could deliver a more efficient allocation of resources, more quantity produced and sold, and low prices. However, when firms set different prices in different countries, this can improve economic efficiency too. This is the case when differences in demand across countries are large, such that so-called price discrimination enables firms to sell more products than they would otherwise. Indeed, such a pricing policy allows consumers in low-price countries to acquire the product in question, whilst if the price were the same everywhere, these would not be served. Malueg and Schwartz (1994) formalises this argument.[24] Naturally, this pricing policy can work only if there is no arbitrage. That is, the goods sold in the low-price countries cannot be resold in the high-high price countries. In other words, restricting parallel trade is required to achieve this type of efficiency gain.

Given the importance of R&D investments and innovation in the pharmaceutical sector, the question of parallel trade and market integration must also be examined with this aspect in mind. Whilst low medicine prices generate cost savings for national health insurance and contribute to maintaining affordable health care, at the same time, they reduce the incentives of pharmaceutical companies to invest in R&D, potentially limiting the pace of innovation. Because the industry is heavily regulated, each Member State can set the cursor depending on its preference, either to favour innovation or to select low prices. However, as shown by Rey (2003), in theory parallel trade can challenge the ability of Member States to make such a choice, and result in inefficient outcomes.

22. White Paper from the Commission to the European Council 'Completing the internal market' COM(85) 310 final.
23. European Commission, *The economics of 1992*, 35 European Economy 17 (1988).
24. David A. Malueg and Marius Schwartz, *Parallel Imports, Demand Dispersion and International Price Discrimination*, 37 J. Int'l Econ. 167 (1994).

§5.04 HISTORICAL DEVELOPMENT OF THE CASE LAW

[A] Article 101 TFEU

In line with the Single Market imperative discussed above, agreements which restrict parallel trade have been found to amount to a restriction of competition in the sense of (what is now) Article 101 TFEU since the 1970s. In particular, the CJEU has held that 'by its very nature, a clause prohibiting exports constitutes a restriction on competition'.[25] This principle was also applied in the pharmaceutical sector.[26]

[1] Bayer Adalat

In 2000, the Court of First Instance (CFI) nevertheless created an opening for restrictions of parallel imports imposed by suppliers of pharmaceutical products in its *Bayer (Adalat)* judgment. This judgment concerned a Commission decision of 1996 which had found that Bayer had infringed what is now Article 101 TFEU by reducing supplies to the French and Spanish distributors of its Adalat drug to prevent them from exporting to the United Kingdom (UK), where prices were higher. Bayer did not inform the French and Spanish distributors that the volume reduction was due to concerns about parallel trade (it cited 'stock shortages') but the distributors nevertheless guessed the real motives and reduced their orders, whilst at the same time increasing purchases through other wholesalers, in order to continue exporting.[27]

In its 2000 judgment, the CFI annulled the Commission decision on the basis that it was not established that there was an 'agreement' in the sense of Article 101 TFEU between Bayer and its distributors. According to the CFI, there was no evidence of acquiescence of the distributors with Bayer's policy of reducing exports: on the contrary, the fact that the distributors sought alternative sources of supply showed that they did not agree with Bayer's attempts to restrict exports.[28] The CFI's judgment was subsequently confirmed by the CJEU.[29]

Some *dicta* of the CFI suggested that its ruling was informed by the specific characteristics of the pharmaceutical markets,[30] but the principle that acquiescence by distributors cannot simply be presumed was confirmed in later case law in other

25. Case C-19/77, *Miller International Schallplatten GmbH v. Commission*, ECLI:EU:C:1978:19, para. 7.
26. *See* Case C-277/87, *Sandoz Prodotti Farmaceutici v. Commission*, ECLI:EU:C:1990:6. Note that only a summary of this judgment was published.
27. Commission Decision of 10 January 1996 in case 34.279 Adalat.
28. Case T-14/96, *Bayer v. Commission*, ECLI:EU:T:2000:242.
29. Joined Cases C-2/01 and 3/01, *BAI v. Bayer and Commission*, ECLI:EU:C:2004:2.
30. *See* Case T-14/96, *Bayer v. Commission*, ECLI:EU:T:2000:242, paras 179–181. *See* also Patrick Rey and James S. Venit, *Parallel Trade and Pharmaceuticals: A Policy in Search of Itself*, 29 Eur. L. Rev. 153 (2004) and Urs Wickihalder, *The Distinction Between an 'Agreement' Within the Meaning of Article 81(1) of the EC Treaty and Unilateral Conduct*, 2 Eur. Competition J. 87 (2006).

sectors.[31] This case law therefore allowed suppliers of pharmaceuticals which were not dominant to unilaterally limit supplies to wholesalers. It did not, however, permit them to agree with their distributors to limit exports.

[2] Glaxo Spain *(Object Infringement)*

The CFI created another opening for possible restrictions of parallel trade in pharmaceuticals in 2006, when it ruled in *Glaxo Spain* that a restriction of parallel trade in pharmaceuticals is not necessarily a restriction by object and considered that the Commission had not correctly assessed the possible justification for such a restriction under what is now Article 101(3) TFEU.

In this case, GlaxoSmithKline (GSK) had notified[32] the Commission of proposed contracts with its Spanish wholesalers which contained a clause providing for differentiated pricing for medicinal products financed by Spanish social security funds and subsequently marketed in Spain, on the one hand, and other medicinal products, on the other hand. In 2001, the Commission decided that this dual pricing system amounted to a restriction of competition in the sense of Article 101 TFEU both by object and effect.[33]

Following an application for annulment by GSK, the CFI upheld the Commission's finding of a restriction by effect but annulled the qualification of a restriction by object. The CFI considered that, whilst restrictions of parallel trade must 'in principle' be regarded as having as their object the prevention of competition, this was only in so far as such restrictions can be presumed to deprive the 'final consumer' of the benefit of competition. The 'special and essential characteristics' of the pharmaceutical sector, however, imply that the benefits of parallel trade may to a large extent be kept by parallel traders.[34] As a consequence, the prices of medicines 'are to a large extent shielded from the free play of supply and demand' and 'it cannot be taken for granted at the outset that parallel trade tends to reduce those prices and thus to increase the welfare of final consumers.'[35]

However, the CJEU did not agree with the CFI's analysis and instead adhered more closely to the Single Market imperative. It held that the principle that restrictions

---

31. *See* in particular Case T-368/00, *General Motors Nederland and Open Nederland v. Commission*, ECLI:EU:T:2003:275, confirmed in Case C-74/04 P, *Commission v. Volkswagen*, ECLI:EU:C:2006:460.
32. Pursuant to the notification procedure which existed under Council Regulation 17/62 of 6 February 1962: First regulation implementing Articles 85 and 86 of the Treaty, OJ 13, 21.2.1962, but which was abolished by Council Regulation (EC) No 1/2003 of 16 December 2002 on the implementation of the rules on competition laid down in Articles 81 and 82 of the Treaty, OJ L 1, 4.1.2003.
33. Commission Decision of 8 May 2001 in cases 36.957 Glaxo Welcome (notification); 36.997 Aseprofar and Edifar (complaint); 37.121 Spain Pharma (complaint); 37.138 BAI (complaint) and 37.380 EAEPC (complaint), recitals 115–143.
34. These characteristics include the fact that the prices for pharmaceuticals are fixed by national authorities (although the Spanish legislation did not impose a system of differentiated prices), that the latter also bear the essential part of the cost of the medicines and that there is little harmonisation in this field.
35. Case T-168/01, *GlaxoSmithKline Services v. Commission*, ECLI:EU:T:2006:265, paras 114–147.

of parallel trade have as their object the restriction of competition also applies to the pharmaceutical sector. According to the CJEU, such a finding is not dependent on the requirement that final consumers be deprived of the advantages of effective competition. The differentiated pricing used by GSK therefore amounted to a restriction of competition by object.[36]

[3] Glaxo Spain *(Article 101(3) TFEU)*

As indicated above, the CFI was also critical of the Commission's assessment of the application of paragraph 3 of what is now Article 101 TFEU. GSK had raised a number of arguments in this respect but the focus of the CFI was on GSK's reasoning that restricting parallel trade contributed to technical progress because it stopped the erosion of profits caused by parallel trade, which in turn reduced the funds pharmaceutical companies had available for R&D. The Commission had dismissed this argument in its decision on the basis (i) that there was no guarantee that any additional profits obtained by these restrictions would actually be invested in R&D (rather than simply being retained as additional profits) and (ii) that the impact of parallel trade on profits was in any event small.[37]

The CFI considered that the Commission had not properly examined all the arguments GSK had made in this respect and in particular (i) that the Commission's analysis of the link between parallel trade and R&D expenditure was not 'rigorous' and 'thorough' enough and (ii) that the Commission did not seriously examine whether the losses as a result of parallel trade were significant.[38] Since the remainder of the Commission's argumentation on the application of what is now Article 101(3) TFEU rested on the conclusion that the restrictions did not provide a gain in efficiency, the CFI concluded that the Commission's decision needed to be annulled on this basis as well.

In its appeal to the CJEU, the Commission argued that the CFI had misallocated the burden of proof for the establishment of the conditions of Article 101(3) TFEU, had distorted the arguments made by the parties in this respect, and had exceeded the limits of its judicial review. However, the CJEU dismissed all these arguments.[39]

[4] EAEPC v. Commission

Following the CJEU's judgment in 2009, GSK withdrew its notification to the Commission of the contracts with the Spanish wholesalers. One of the complainants in the case,

36. Joined Cases C-501/06 P, C-513/06 P, C-515/06 P and C-519/06 P, *GlaxoSmithKline Services and Others v. Commission and Others*, ECLI:EU:C:2009:610, paras 54–67.
37. Commission Decision of 8 May 2001 in cases 36.957 Glaxo Wellcome (notification); 36.997 Aseprofar and Edifar (complaint); 37.121 Spain Pharma (complaint); 37.138 BAI (complaint) and 37.380 EAEPC (complaint), recitals 154–169.
38. Case T-168/01, *GlaxoSmithKline Services v. Commission*, ECLI:EU:T:2006:265, paras 247–303.
39. Joined Cases C-501/06 P, C-513/06 P, C-515/06 P and C-519/06 P, *GlaxoSmithKline Services and Others v. Commission and Others*, ECLI:EU:C:2009:610, paras 68–168.

the European Association of Euro-Pharmaceutical Companies (EAEPC), requested the Commission to nevertheless adopt a new decision on the pricing practices of GSK in Spain. By a decision in 2014, the Commission rejected EAEPC's complaint on the basis that GSK was not using the dual pricing system anymore, that there were no persistent effects of the dual pricing system practised by GSK in Spain more than a decade before, and that national competition authorities and courts were in any event well placed to deal with EAEPC's complaints, such that the Commission did not need to prioritise it.[40]

EAEPC brought an application for annulment before the General Court against this Commission decision. The General Court rejected that application, holding that the Commission was not required to adopt a new decision following the withdrawal of GSK's notification and that it did not make a manifest error of assessment when concluding that the union interest did not require further action on its part.[41] No appeal was brought against this judgment to the CJEU.

[B] Article 102 TFEU

The CJEU has for a long time considered that the creation of barriers to parallel trade can constitute an abuse of dominance in the sense of Article 102 TFEU.[42] The question of whether this was also the case for trade in pharmaceuticals products did not reach the CJEU before the *Glaxo Greece* case.

This case arose because the exports by pharmaceutical wholesalers in Greece had led to shortages of certain medicines in the Greek market. GSK had therefore started distributing its products itself and, after the conditions on the Greek market stabilised, it limited the quantities it supplied to Greek wholesalers. In an interim judgment, the Hellenic Competition Commission considered that this amounted to an abuse of dominance and requested a preliminary ruling from the CJEU, but that request was rejected as inadmissible.[43] However, in the parallel cases before the civil courts, the Athens Court of Appeal referred the same questions to the CJEU.

In a Grand Chamber judgment, the CJEU considered that intrabrand competition may be the only form of competition for patent-protected pharmaceuticals and that therefore it is not permissible for dominant pharmaceutical undertakings to stop all parallel trade. On the other hand, a dominant undertaking should be allowed to counter in a reasonable and proportionate way the threat to its own commercial interests potentially posed by significant orders that are essentially destined for parallel exports. The Court, therefore, considered that a dominant undertaking abuses its

40. Commission Decision of 27 May 2014 in case 36.957 Glaxo Wellcome (complaint).
41. Case T-574/14, *EAEPC v. Commission*, ECLI:EU:T:2018:605. The General Court nevertheless also ruled that the Commission had 'mischaracterised' its 2001 decision as being 'null and void'. The General Court clarified that the CJEU had in 2009 upheld the Commission's conclusion that dual pricing constituted a restriction of competition by object, and had only annulled the decision in relation to the Commission's insufficient assessment of GSK's efficiency defence under Article 101(3) TFEU.
42. *See*, for example, Case C-27/76, *United Brands v. Commission*, ECLI:EU:C:1978:22 and Case C-226/84, *British Leyland v. Commission*, ECLI:EU:C:1986:421.
43. Case C-53/03, *Syfait and Others*, ECLI:EU:C:2005:333.

position if it refuses to meet 'ordinary orders' from its customers but, it seems, not if it refuses to meet orders that are out of the ordinary. What 'ordinary' means, the Court left for the national court to decide 'in the light of both the size of those orders in relation to the requirements of the market ... and the previous business relations between that undertaking and the wholesalers concerned.'[44]

§5.05 *EX POST* ASSESSMENT

As indicated above, the most significant developments in the enforcement of the EU competition rules on the parallel trade in pharmaceuticals are the CJEU judgments in *Glaxo Spain*[45] and *Glaxo Greece*.[46] In the former, the CJEU held that restrictions of parallel trade, such as dual pricing, have as their object the restriction of competition, but that such restrictions may be justified under Article 101(3) TFEU. In *Glaxo Greece*, the CJEU held that a dominant undertaking abuses its position if it refuses to meet orders from wholesalers that are 'ordinary' in the light of both the size of those orders in relation to the requirements of the (national) market and the previous business relations between that undertaking and the wholesalers concerned, but not if it refuses to meet orders that are out of the ordinary. As is apparent from this description, the case law neither entirely bans restrictions of parallel trade in pharmaceuticals, nor always permits such restrictions.

In this section, we aim to assess the extent to which these judgments have had an effect on parallel trade in pharmaceuticals in recent years. Unfortunately, the lack of detailed data on the volume and evolution of parallel trade over time prevents us from drawing any conclusions on the causal effects of judgements on the parallel trade of medicines in the EU. In particular, our assessment is somewhat limited by the lack of available data on quantity sold. For instance, to determine whether progress has been made towards the market integration objective, we consider the effect of parallel trade on prices. However, we have no information on whether parallel trade has caused an increase in quantity sold within the EEA, which is relevant to determine whether these activities have delivered efficiency gains.

That said, our analysis provides some evidence regarding the importance of parallel imports in the European pharmaceutical market. Our assessment further considers evidence on the impact of parallel trade on the price of pharmaceutical products and innovation. This analysis also takes into account the role of national regulations and their interplay with parallel trade.

We combine the analysis of publicly available data and a review of recent works on parallel trade, published in economic journals. Specifically, we have relied on the following data sources:

44. Joined Cases C-468/06 to C-478/06, *Sot. Lélos kai Sia and Others*, ECLI:EU:C:2008:504, paras 33–77. The final ruling on the merits of this case in Greece is discussed below.
45. Joined Cases C-501/06 P, C-513/06 P, C-515/06 P and C-519/06 P, *GlaxoSmithKline Services and Others v. Commission and Others*, ECLI:EU:C:2009:610.
46. Joined Cases C-468/06 to C-478/06, *Sot. Lélos kai Sia and Others*, ECLI:EU:C:2008:504.

- Information on parallel import licences from the EMA. The EMA, founded in 1995, is a body that evaluates applications for the marketing authorisation of medicines submitted through the so-called centralised procedure for all EU countries. This centralised procedure, however, is not available for all medicines.[47] The EMA also grants parallel distribution licences for medicines approved through the centralised procedure.
- Information on parallel import licences from national registries of the three most important destination countries for parallel imports in the EU, namely Denmark, Germany and Sweden.
- Eurostat data on pharmaceutical prices.
- A review of the relevant economic literature concerning the impact of parallel trade on price and on innovation.

In addition, we conducted a survey in September and October 2020 amongst the most significant pharmaceutical originators and wholesalers in the EU. The survey asked the respondents' views on the clarity and suitability of the latest EU antitrust case law on parallel trade in pharmaceuticals, as well as their experience of the existence and extent of parallel trade in pharmaceuticals in the EU and its effects. The response rate of the survey was poor: only a handful of the companies contacted submitted their answer. Amongst the companies that responded, none seemed to have fundamental objections to the case law, although some decried the lack of clarity on certain aspects of the current rules (such as the conditions for the application of Article 101(3) TFEU and the notion of 'ordinary orders' in the CJEU's *Glaxo Greece* judgment). Because of the limited response we received, it is not possible to identify any statistically significant patterns in the responses as to the existence and extent of parallel trade, but we have used the responses to interpret and colour some of the data obtained elsewhere.

Our *ex post* assessment of the EU case law on parallel trade in pharmaceuticals will start with a discussion of the scale of parallel trade in the EU (section §5.05[A]) and the evolution of that trade over the years (section §5.05[B]). Subsequently, we will look at pharmaceutical pricing in the EU and in particular the absence of convergence of pricing and the literature on the effects of parallel trade on pricing (section §5.05[C]). In section §5.05[D], we will discuss a number of explanations of the perceived (lack of) effects of parallel trade. The section concludes with a discussion of the literature on the effects of parallel imports on innovation (section §5.05[E]).

47. The centralised procedure is compulsory for human medicines containing a new active substance to treat HIV, cancer, diabetes, neurodegenerative diseases, auto-immune and other immune dysfunctions, and viral diseases. It is also compulsory for medicines derived from biotechnology, advanced-therapy medicines and orphan diseases. The centralised procedure is optional for other medicines.

[A] The Existence of Parallel Trade in the EEA

The data available to us clearly show that parallel imports of pharmaceutical products continue to be important within the EEA, although the precise volume movements cannot be deduced from the publicly available data which are at our disposal.

The EMA data indicate that for a very large proportion of centrally authorised medicines, a parallel distribution licence was granted. Figure 5.1 presents the proportion of medicines authorised between 1995 and 2017 with at least one parallel distribution licence.[48]

Figure 5.1 Proportion of Market Authorisation for Which There is Parallel Distribution (1995–2017)

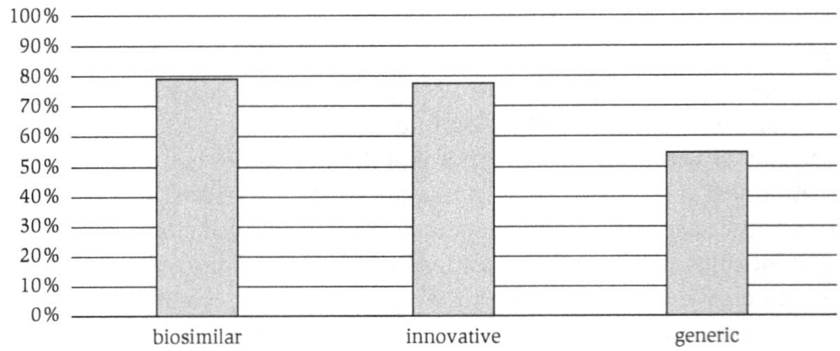

According to the data, for 77% of the innovative medicines approved by the EMA, there is at least one parallel distribution licence. Interestingly that proportion is 79% for bio-similar and 55% for generic. This indicates that parallel distribution does not affect only originator medicines.

Parallel distribution licences affect some categories of medicines more than others. As can be seen in Figure 5.2, the EMA data at the Anatomical Therapeutic Chemical (ATC) code level show that 90% of medicines in the respiratory system category have at least one licence whilst that proportion falls to 53% for the blood and blood forming organs category.

48. We have data until 2020 but excluded the most recent data to alleviate measurement bias. Indeed, a parallel distribution licence can be granted several years after the marketing authorisation.

Figure 5.2 MA (1995–2017) Which Get PD by ATC-Code

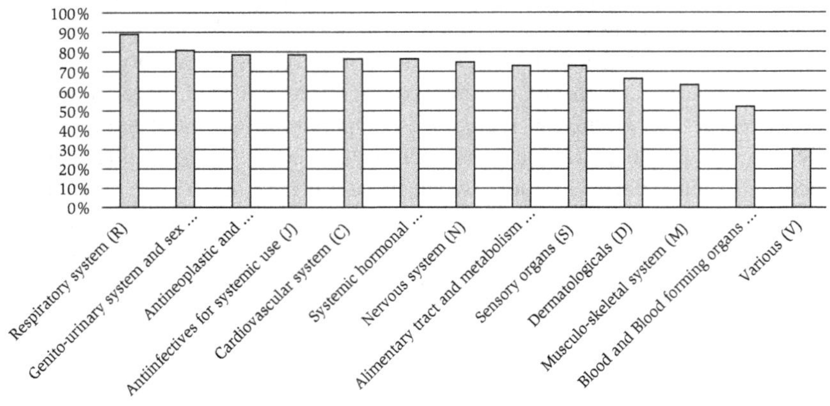

The EMA data also provide a clear picture of the countries that can expect to benefit from parallel imports in the EU, namely the destination countries. Figure 5.3 presents the ranking of all EU countries according to the number of medicines that are parallel imported in each country.[49] There is a distinct group of Northern European countries that represent the major destinations: Germany, Denmark, Sweden, the Netherlands and Austria. In addition, we note that the UK, Ireland, Finland as well as Malta have a large number of medicines that are parallel imported.

Figure 5.3 Number of Medicines That Are Parallel Imported

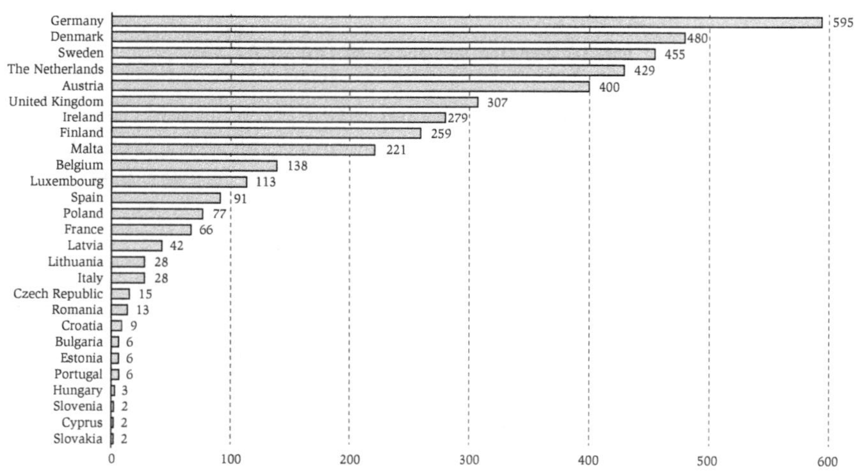

49. There is no record of registered parallel import licences for Greece as a destination country.

It is important to stress that the major destination countries have a regulatory system and rules in place that encourage parallel imports. First, in these countries, pharmaceutical companies have certain freedom in setting prices, which may attract parallel imports if prices are higher than those in other EU Member States where the regulator fixes prices at a lower level. Furthermore, in these destination countries rules have been set up that stimulate price competition and thus parallel imports. As discussed earlier, in Germany, regulation compels pharmacies to source a share of medicines sold from parallel imports. Until July 2019, German pharmacies were obliged to dispense parallel imports when these are 15% or EUR 15 cheaper than the price of the reference product, until they reach 5% of the total volume. The system has been amended recently but continues to compel pharmacies to use parallel imports until some target savings have been achieved.

In Denmark, pharmacies are required to dispense the cheapest product among available substitutes, unless the patient or the doctor explicitly request otherwise.[50] This provision encourages the sales of generic instead of off-patent products as well as parallel imports. Note that competition from generic and parallel imports is further encouraged by the fact that the patient's co-payment is greater when the more expensive solution is selected.[51]

In Sweden, there is no specific policy encouraging parallel imports. However, regulation encourages switching to cheaper products, including parallel imports. Since October 2002, Sweden has established the 'product of the month', which compels pharmacies to offer the equivalent of the prescribed medicine with the lowest price.[52] The Medical Products Agency decides and publishes the list of interchangeable medicines. That list is updated regularly. Each month the Dental and Pharmaceutical Benefits Agency (TLV) informs which product has the lowest retail price. If the patient refuses the product of the month, she will bear the extra cost.[53]

[B] The Evolution of Parallel Imports in the EEA

The most obvious way in which the enforcement of the EU competition rules in the area of parallel trade in pharmaceuticals could have an observable effect, would be through the evolution of parallel trade in the EEA. In particular, if the case law described above

50. The pharmacies are obliged to dispense the cheapest product with the same active substance. *See* Safiye Özer, Elisabeth Thomsen and Paul Schüder, *PHIS Pharma Profile Denmark 2011*. Pharmaceutical Health Information System; Commissioned by the European Commission, Executive Agency for Health and Consumers and the Austrian Federal Ministry of Health (2013).
51. Patients who have a supplementary private insurance may have less incentive to accept the substitution if their insurance covers the extra cost.
52. The Medical Products Agency (Läkemedelsverket) defines substitution groups that contains all products that are medically equivalent. Each group contains the originator medicines but also parallel imports and generics for off-patent medicines. Every month, the Dental and Pharmaceutical Benefits Agency (TLV) organises an action for each substitution group, and the winner is the product of the month. The pharmacy is compelled to supply the product of the month, irrespective of whether it was prescribed.
53. Johan Pontén, Gunilla Rönnholm and Peter Skiöld, *PPRI Pharma Profile Sweden 2017*, TLV Dental and Pharmaceutical Benefits Agency (2017).

would have effectively reduced the use of restrictions on parallel trade, this should result in an increase in parallel trade. If, on the other hand, the case law would have become more permissive in respect of restrictions of parallel trade, this should be apparent through a decrease in the volumes of parallel trade.

There is no publicly available information on the trade volume of pharmaceutical products within the EEA. As a proxy, we have considered the annual number of parallel distribution licences granted by the EMA, as reflected in Figure 5.4.

Figure 5.4 Parallel Distribution Licences Granted by the EMA

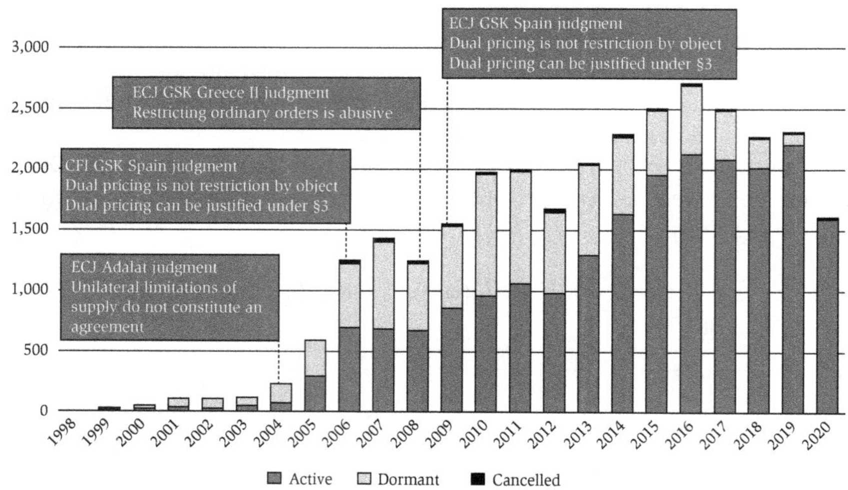

Whilst the data show a growing trend in the number of licences, it is important to note that this accompanies a similar trend in centralised authorisation. When the EMA was established in 1995, it was approving less than twenty medicines in the first couple of years of operations. Still in 2005, ten years later, it granted only eighteen authorisations. After 2005, the number of centrally approved medicines started to grow rapidly, however.

The two charts below present separately the total number of market authorisations granted by the EMA each year since 1995 (*see* Figure 5.5) and the total number of parallel trade licences. As can be seen below the number of licences has started to grow sharply after 2004, which corresponds to the time the number of market authorisations has also started to increase significantly.

Figure 5.5 EMA Authorisations and Licences

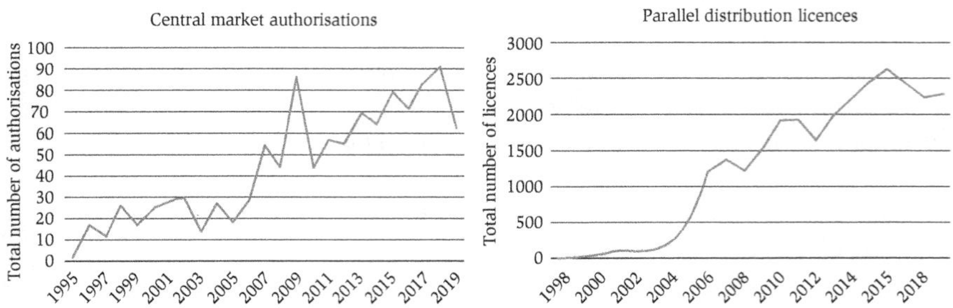

Against this background, we do not think it possible to draw any conclusions about the impact of judgments like *Bayer Adalat, Glaxo Greece* or *Glaxo Spain* on the number of parallel distribution licences granted by the EMA.

The next three figures present the number of annual licences for Denmark, Germany and Sweden, based on publicly available data contained in their national medicine registries.

Figure 5.6 PT Licences Granted by Denmark

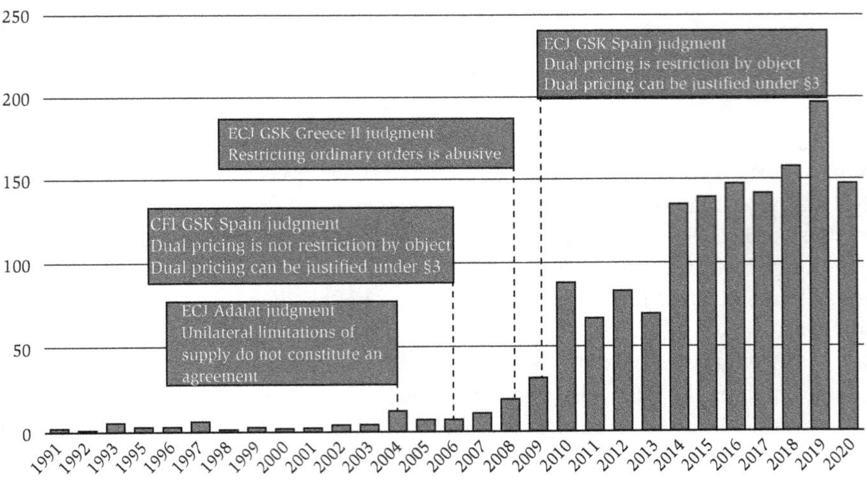

In Denmark, the data shows an apparent increase in the intensity of parallel imports towards the end of the first decade of the twenty-first century (*see* Figure 5.6). However, it is important to note that this increase is not recent. Indeed, regulation in Denmark has promoted the growth of parallel imports since the 1990s and expenditures of parallel imported medicines were reported to have increased by 9.5% on average between 2000 and 2009. In 2009, sales of parallel imported products in the so-called primary sector, which concerns treatment and care as well as prevention provided outside the hospital sector, accounted for approximately 8% in volume and 20% in value.[54] Another fact that highlights the importance of parallel imports in that country is that, in 2006, Orifarm, a parallel importer, recorded the largest amount of sales among all pharmaceutical companies.[55]

Figure 5.7 shows the number of licences for biomedicines in Germany.[56] There does not appear to be a clear trend in this data.

Figure 5.7 PT Licences Granted by Germany

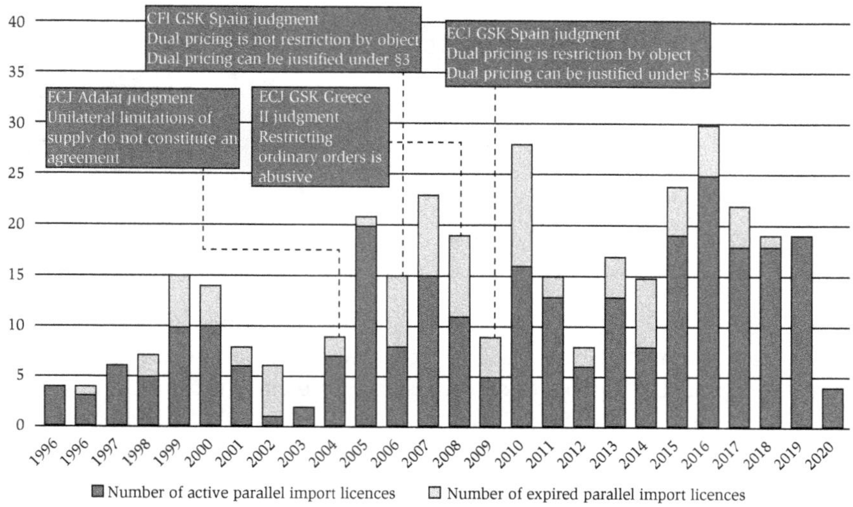

Figure 5.8 presents similar data for Sweden. Like for Germany, there is no apparent pattern in the data suggesting that the antitrust case law on restrictions of parallel trade in pharmaceuticals had any effect on parallel imports.

54. Safiye Özer, Elisabeth Thomsen and Paul Schüder, *PHIS Pharma Profile Denmark 2011*. Pharmaceutical Health Information System; Commissioned by the European Commission, Executive Agency for Health and Consumers and the Austrian Federal Ministry of Health (2013).
55. *Ibid.*, footnote 49.
56. The data on Human Biomedicines which are parallelly imported since 1995 are provided by the German Paul-Ehrlich-Institut.

Figure 5.8 PT Licences Granted by Sweden

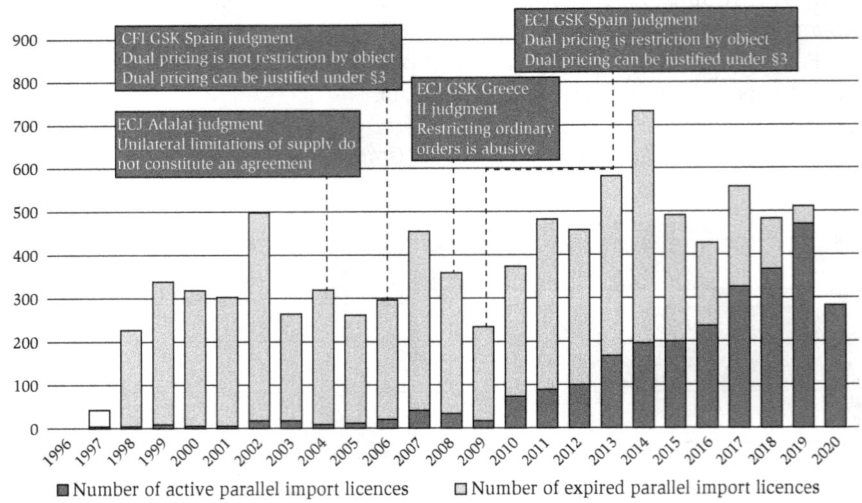

On the basis of this data, therefore, it is not possible to conclude that the antitrust case law on parallel trade in pharmaceuticals discussed above has had any positive impact on the development of parallel trade in these countries. At the same time, as the data show that the number of licences has not declined, this would be consistent with the view that the judgements have not had any negative effects on parallel trade. However, other factors also affect parallel imports, and notably national regulations, therefore, it is difficult to draw any strong conclusion about the impact of the judgements from this analysis.

Another source to assess the evolution of parallel trade is the estimate the European Federation of Pharmaceutical Industries and Associations (EFPIA) has been producing over the last fifteen years of the share of parallel imports as a proportion of pharmacy sales in a number of European countries (*see* Figure 5.9). Whilst these estimates may not be totally accurate, they represent the only publicly available estimate of the penetration of parallel imports in the destination countries.

Figure 5.9 Share of Parallel Imports

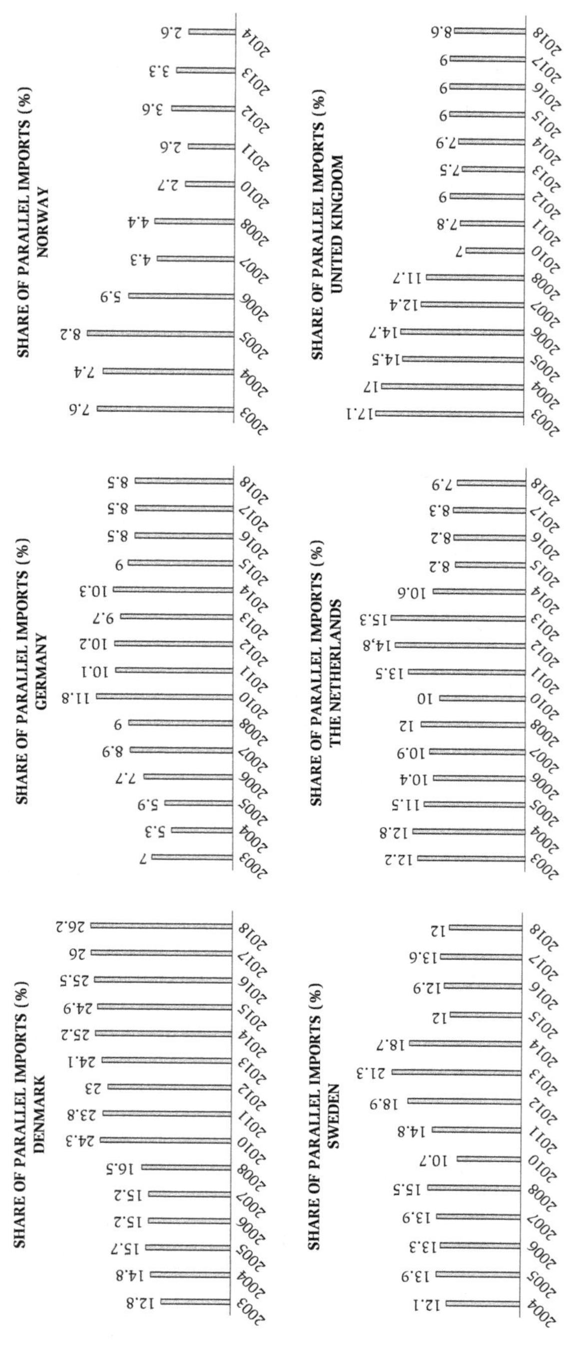

These data are consistent with the data on trade licences we discussed above, in that they show that the importance of parallel imports is not the same across all destination countries. As discussed earlier, this appears to be the result of different regulatory systems in individual Member States.

There are also significant changes over time. In three countries, namely the Netherlands, the UK and Norway, the proportion of parallel imports has decreased significantly over the time period. Note however that the change in the UK and in Norway is likely to be caused in part by currency fluctuations. The value of the British Pound against the Euro fell sharply starting in the summer of 2007, and this is likely to have affected parallel imports.[57] The value of the Norwegian krone against the Euro started to fall sharply in 2008, which may have contributed to slow down parallel imports.[58]

In sharp contrast, the share of parallel imports has increased substantially in Denmark in 2010 and since then these imports represent about a quarter of total pharmacy sales. In Germany and even more so in Sweden, the proportion of parallel trade has fluctuated over the years, but in both countries parallel imports account for a significant share of pharmacy sales.

Specifically, for the purpose of this chapter, the data we present do not suggest a clear effect of the *Bayer Adalat, Glaxo Greece* or *Glaxo Spain* cases, neither in facilitating parallel trade, nor in preventing it.

[C] The Effects of Parallel Trade on Prices

In unregulated markets, and in the absence of restrictions to trade, we expect significant differences in the price of a product sold in different countries to spur arbitrage, and thus parallel trade.[59] Arbitrage would cause the price of the product in question to fall in the high-price countries, leading to higher consumption (the extent to which depends on the price elasticity of demand). However, parallel imports could also lead to higher prices in the source countries. As distributors re-export the product from the low- to the high-price countries, supply is restricted in the low-price countries, leading to upward pricing pressure. Ultimately, the absence of trade restrictions would lead to price convergence.

As the antitrust case law on parallel trade in pharmaceuticals does not permit the wholesale restriction of parallel trade within the EEA, we could expect parallel imports to have had some price effects, notably in the destination countries, and to contribute to price converge across the EEA countries. With this in mind, we present below the

57. The value of the British Pound against the Euro dropped significantly between the summer of 2007 and the beginning of 2009, and the Pound did not fully recover for some time. The Pound rose again in the second half of 2015 but fell again.
58. The value of the Norwegian krone has declined sharply in 2008, and then rose back to fall again in 2012. Since then, the krone has steadily lost ground against the Euro.
59. Naturally, it must be the case that distributors would engage in parallel trade activities if the price difference is larger than the cost of re-exporting the product from the low-price to the high-price country.

evidence we have collected on the price effects of parallel imports of pharmaceutical products.

[1] Prices in Destination Countries

Economic theory predicts that parallel trade should reduce prices in destination countries, because of increased competition from lower-cost alternatives. Several empirical studies have investigated the extent to which parallel imports of particular medicines in the EEA have caused (or have been associated with) price reduction in the destination countries.

We understand that typically the price of parallel imports just undercuts that of the manufacturer's direct exports. This is confirmed by Duso et al (2014) and Mendez (2017) for oral anti-diabetic medicines in Germany and statin products in Denmark, respectively.[60] The price-reducing effect of parallel imports on the market is therefore expected to be significantly less than those of generic products, which are priced at substantially lower levels.

These two studies, which are conceptually similar, provide some insights on the effects of parallel imports, but are based on medicines for different diseases:

- Duso et al. (2014) studies the effect of parallel imports on the price of about 700 oral anti diabetic medicines that belong to six chemical groups. The data cover the period 2004–2010.
- Mendez (2017) investigates the effect of parallel imports for 213 products of the statins family (therapeutic group HMG CoA reductases inhibitors) sold in Denmark between May 2003 and March 2005.

The method employed is based on a structural economic model, which is then used to generate a counterfactual scenario in which parallel imports are banned. Prices in the counterfactual and actual scenarios are then compared.[61] Interestingly, both studies find that the market average price is lower in the counterfactual scenario without parallel imports. However, this is because part of the consumption of parallelly imported medicines would move to generic alternatives, which are substantially cheaper than both the direct and parallel imports. Naturally, this effect is not present for on-patent medicines.[62]

---

60. Tomaso Duso, Annika Herr and Moritz Suppliet, *The Welfare Impact of Parallel Imports: A Structural Approach Applied to the German Market for Oral Anti-diabetics*, 23 Health Econ. 1036 (2014) and Susan J. Méndez, *Parallel Trade of Pharmaceuticals: The Danish Market for Statins*, 27 Health Econ. 333 (2017).
61. These analyses rest on the econometric estimation of a nested logit demand model. Using the parameter estimates and assuming a Nash Bertrand model on the supply side with constant marginal cost, these studies simulate the equilibrium price without parallel imports.
62. In Mendez (2017), three molecules are off-patent and three are on-patent. The results show clearly that the average price of off-patent molecule is substantially lower without parallel imports as some consumption is directed to generic. In contrast, the average price of on-patent medicines is increased in a situation without parallel imports. We note that the nested logit demand in Duso et al. (2014) and Mendez (2017) assume that within each molecule substitution

That said, most economic studies we have seen, except for one notable exception, find that parallel imports compete with the manufacturer's direct exports, which is to be expected. These studies concern the price of medicines sold in Sweden, Denmark and Germany. We summarise these results below.

First, Ganslandt and Maskus (2004) is one of the first economic studies that investigated this question.[63] Their study is based on the price of 164 medicines (covering 50 molecules) sold in Sweden between 1994 and 1999. This study develops a simple reduced-form regression model and finds that the entry of parallel imports (which originated mostly from Italy and Spain) had a significant impact on the manufacturers' prices in Sweden. The price-reducing impact ranges from 12% to 19%.

Second, Hostenkamp et al. (2012) studies the effect of parallel imports on the price paid by hospitals in Denmark.[64] The sample of data covers 347 products representing 89 substances from 2005 to 2009. That study estimates that parallel imports have a price-reducing effect on statins. The estimated price effect is 11% on average, but this effect is smaller, 4%, when regional tenders instead of national ones were used.

Finally, the two studies mentioned above, Duso et al. (2014) and Mendez (2017), based on simulated equilibrium prices find that parallel imports have a reducing effect on the manufacturer's price, although the magnitude of their results differs:

- Duso et al. (2014) shows that the manufacturer price of oral antidiabetic medicines in Germany is higher by 11% on average without parallel imports. The simulated equilibrium price of generic products, however, is the same with and without parallel imports.
- Mendes (1017) finds without parallel imports the simulated manufacturer's price of statins in Denmark is about 2.5% higher. The simulated price of generic products is also 3.5% greater in the absence of parallel trade.

Another study, Kanavos and Vandoros (2010), find no significant impact on the price of medicines sold in destination countries.[65] This study is based on data from nineteen medicines in six therapeutic categories, which have high volume and high price products, mostly on-patent, sold in six countries, the UK, Germany, Sweden, Denmark, The Netherlands, and Norway. The sample period runs between 1997 and 2002. This study finds no evidence that parallel trade promotes price competition in the six destination countries: no downward effects on the retail price of locally sourced

---

patterns are proportional to market shares, irrespective of whether the product are direct exports, parallel imports or generics. A richer and more complex model may provide different results.

63. Mattias Ganslandt and Keith E. Maskus, *Parallel Imports and the Pricing of Pharmaceutical Products: Evidence from the European Union* 23 J. Health Econ. 1035 (2004).
64. Gisela Hostenkamp, Christian Kronborg and Jacob Nielsen Arendt, *Parallel Imports of Hospital Pharmaceuticals: An Empirical Analysis of Price Effects from Parallel Imports and the Design of Procurement Procedures in the Danish Hospital Sector*, Discussion Papers on Business and Economics No 16 (2012).
65. Panos Kanavos and Sotiris Vandoros, *Competition in Prescription Drug Markets: Is Parallel Trade the Answer?*, 31 Managerial & Dec. Econ. 325 (2010).

medicines is recorded. Further, as penetration of parallel imports increases, their retail price converges upward, toward the price of locally sourced originator medicines.

The supply of pharmaceuticals is regulated as discussed above. In particular, in the destination countries, rules have been put in place to encourage the development of parallel imports, with the objective of reducing prices. Had pharmaceutical companies been successful at quashing parallel imports, the regulator could have sought other ways to contain medicine prices. In other words, whist parallel imports have contributed to lower manufacturer's prices in destination countries, this is not to say that regulators could not use other levers to keep prices in check. Furthermore, as we discussed below, there is a complex interplay between regulation and parallel imports, and tighter price regulation can contribute to reduced prices, possibly at the expense of the distributors (wholesalers and pharmacies) and with little impact on manufacturers' profit.

These studies only concern prices in destination countries. As indicated earlier, parallel trade could also influence prices in origin countries. We are not aware, however, of any studies analysing such effects. We therefore turn to look at price convergence (regardless of whether prices change in the destination or in the origin countries).

[2] Price Convergence

We have indirect evidence, using information on parallel trade licences (*see* §5.05[A]. above), that parallel trade of authorised medicines is a significant phenomenon in the EU. In the absence of barriers to trade, parallel trade is expected to lead to price convergence between the importing and exporting countries within the Single Market. Even if not all authorised medicines are subject to parallel distribution, in principle we would expect that the most popular medicines be affected, which would influence aggregate measures of prices.

[a] Evidence from Eurostat

Eurostat compiles an average annual price index (HICP) on pharmaceutical products comprising medicinal preparations, medicinal drugs, patent medicines, serums and vaccines, vitamins and minerals, cod liver oil and halibut liver oil as well as oral contraceptives.[66] Whilst this is an imperfect measure in several ways, it nevertheless should provide an indication of the relative movement of the price of authorised medicines. Figure 5.10 and Figure 5.11 present the price index of pharmaceutical products for a select group of countries.

66. As indicated by Eurostat, the prices used in the HCIP (harmonised index of consumer prices) should be the price paid by households. The HCIP is calculated according to a harmonised approach and a single set of definitions. One of the aims of the HCIP is to assess price convergence. For more information, *see* https://ec.europa.eu/eurostat/documents/3859598/9479325/KS-GQ-17-015-EN-N.pdf/d5e63427-c588-479f-9b19-f4b4d698f2a2.

Figure 5.10 Price Index in High-Income Countries

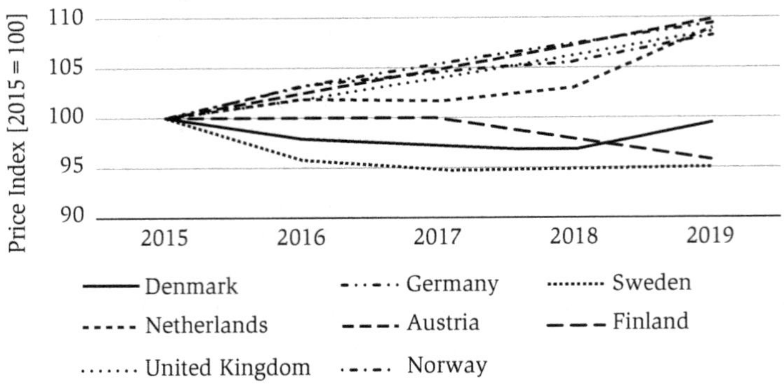

Figure 5.11 Price Index in Low-Income Countries

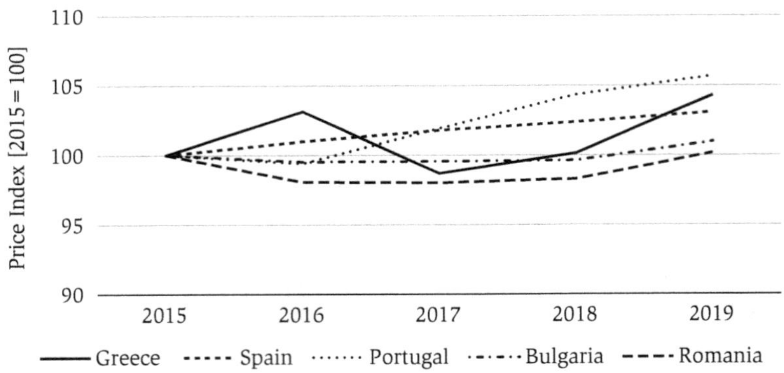

In recent years, the national indices have evolved in a way that is not consistent with price convergence across exporting and importing countries. Inflation in the high-income countries, which are usually the destination countries of parallel imports, move in different ways. Inflation is significantly higher in some high-income countries (Austria, Germany, UK) than in some low-income countries, which is not consistent with convergence. In most Nordic countries, however, prices have been falling (Denmark, Sweden and Finland), a pattern that is consistent with convergence.

Evidence from the Literature

Few studies have examined the extent to which prices of pharmaceutical products have been converging in the EU. We are aware of three studies whose results indicate the absence of convergence.

In a study covering twenty EEA countries using prices from IMS (MIDAS dataset) that range from 2002 to 2016, Kyle (2019) finds significant price dispersion of originator medicines in the EEA.[67] Based on a comparison of medicines widely distributed, the study shows that prices in Germany, Ireland, Sweden and Austria are about 10% higher than the EU average, and 8% and 6% for Finland and the UK respectively. In sharp contrast, prices of originator drugs in Greece, the Czech Republic, Hungary and Spain are at least 20% cheaper than the EU average, and 18% and 15% cheaper in Poland and Bulgaria respectively.

A study by Timur et al. (2011) assesses the extent of price convergence for 124 molecules that treat cardiovascular diseases between 1994 and 2003.[68] Specifically, this study benchmarks prices in Germany against four other EU countries, controlling for quality (pack size, strength, molecule age, etc.) and market characteristics. Regression results indicate price convergence relative to Germany. The convergence, however, between Germany on the one hand and France, Italy and Spain on the other is mostly due to reduction in the 'quality' of products sold in Germany.

Kyle et al. (2008) compares ex-manufacturer price dispersion in the EU with non-EU countries as control.[69] This study is based on 1,023 prescription medicines in 36 categories sold in 30 countries. The data sample runs from 1993 to 2004. The study finds no evidence that price dispersion is lower in EU countries than in non-EU countries. If parallel imports would affect prices, we would expect to observe less price dispersion in the EU, where such imports are legal, whereas they are not in non-EU countries.

Both the Eurostat data and the literature therefore suggest significant price dispersion across Member States of the EU, and contain little indication that prices have been converging. This cannot be explained by the absence of parallel trade since, as we have seen above, parallel trade is clearly taking place and in some countries in significant amounts as well. The lack of price convergence must therefore be explained, *despite the existence of parallel trade*. We will discuss possible explanations for this in §5.05[D]. below.

[D] Factors That May Explain the (Limited) Effects of Parallel Trade

There are various factors that can explain why parallel trade of pharmaceutical products in the EEA has not led to a clear-cut significant price effect in destination countries, and in particular has not led to price convergence.[70]

---

67. Margaret K. Kyle, *The Single Market in Pharmaceuticals*, 55 Rev. Indus. Org. 111 (2019).
68. Aysegul Timur, Gabriel Picone and Jeffrey DeSimone, *Has the European Union Achieved a Single Pharmaceutical Market?*, 11 Int'l J. Health Care Fin. & Econ. 223 (2011).
69. Margaret K. Kyle, Jennifer S. Allsbrook and Kevin A. Schulman, *Does Re-importation Reduce Price Differences for Prescription Drugs? Lessons from the European Union*, 43 Health Servs. Res. 1308 (2008).
70. There are other reasons not discussed in this section that can explain the absence of significant effect of parallel imports on price convergence. For instance, Kyle (2011) shows that pharmaceutical companies can develop strategies to mitigate the effect of parallel trade. In particular, to limit parallel trade, firms can diversify their product offering, and specifically increase product differentiation between source and destination countries. In simple terms, pharmaceutical companies tend to supply different versions of the same medicines in source and destination countries, which reduces arbitrage opportunities.

[1] The Case Law Allows Manufacturers to Limit Parallel Imports to Some Extent

The case law of the European courts in cases such as *Bayer Adalat, Glaxo Greece* and *Glaxo Spain* may provide part of the explanation for the lack of (or, least, limited) effect of parallel imports on prices within the Single Market. Whilst the CJEU has stated in these judgements that restrictions on parallel trade in pharmaceuticals may infringe EU competition law in some circumstances, it also allowed manufacturers to impose restrictions on parallel trade in other circumstances. In other words, as we explain below, manufacturers have the possibility to limit parallel imports, which might explain in particular the lack of price convergence.

The combined effect of *Bayer Adalat* and *Glaxo Greece* has mainly been to confirm the practice of pharmaceutical companies to introduce stock management systems to ensure the continued supply of authorised medicines to wholesalers and pharmacies, in accordance with the requirements of Article 81 of Directive 2001/83/EC (*see also* section §5.05[D][3] below). In order for these systems to work, pharmaceutical companies need to adjust orders to the expected consumption requirements of the countries in question.

In *Glaxo Greece* the CJEU accepted that a dominant undertaking could refuse to satisfy the orders of wholesalers which are out of the ordinary, in light of (i) the requirements of the market in question and (ii) the previous business relations with the wholesaler concerned. These two factors may not be easily applied in practice to distinguish between ordinary orders and those which are out of the ordinary. Furthermore, the domestic requirements of a specific country may not be established precisely, as these can change over time. In addition, a pharmaceutical supplier may err on the side of caution not to undersupply a market. Nevertheless, stock management systems precisely aim to ensure that supply is made in accordance with the requirements of the market concerned and are therefore based on at least one of the considerations accepted in *Glaxo Greece*. That said, because the system is not precise, parallel trade can still exist, but manufacturers may be able to limit the volumes available to be re-exported.

How this works in practice is apparent from a decision of the Hellenic Competition Commission in 2015 applying the criteria of the *Glaxo Greece* judgment. The authority ruled that a refusal by a dominant pharmaceutical supplier to supply a wholesaler is not an abuse if the quantities of the orders in question are disproportionate relative to the needs of the domestic market, and as a consequence unusual based on the previous trading relationships of the parties and the needs of the national market. To refuse to supply reasonable orders was considered abusive, however, even if the wholesalers in question, whilst focusing on the domestic market, also engage in some exports.[71]

The *Glaxo Spain* judgment is less explicit in this respect, but it does not exclude that restrictions of parallel trade can be justified under Article 101(3) TFEU. Moreover,

71. Decision 608/2015 of the Hellenic Competition Commission of 1 April 2015.

the Spanish legislator has approved price-setting rules facilitating the implementation of dual pricing in Spain.[72] Pharmaceutical suppliers have used these rules to set the prices for products exported by wholesalers at a higher level, thereby significantly reducing arbitrage opportunities. However, the interpretation of these rules and their interaction with EU competition law are still the subjects of disputes before the Spanish Courts.

[2] National Regulation Is a Major Determinant of the Price of Pharmaceuticals and Contributes to Maintaining Price Differences Between Member States

The role of parallel imports of pharmaceutical products in the Single Market may be better evaluated by accounting for the fact that the supply and pricing of medicines are highly regulated by the Member States. As discussed in section §5.02 above, the regulation of medicine prices varies across European countries and in fact appears to be an important factor that contributes to explain existing price differences, which in turn contribute to the persistence of parallel trade.

The prices of medicines in European countries are not typically the outcome of market forces, but are mostly the result of a combination of regulation and negotiation between each country and pharmaceutical companies. In some countries, the regulator exerts a strict control to keep the price of new medicines low, making medicines affordable. In general, national regulators, even in countries where pricing rules are less strict, use various tools to control prices, including price freezes and price cuts.

Kyle (2011) notes that large price differences between Member States are in part due to price controls.[73] Costa-Font (2015) further argues that parallel imports in the Single Market are largely a regulation induced phenomenon.[74] In low-price countries in particular price control tends to be stricter. In this context, distributors have an incentive to resell pharmaceuticals in high-price countries. As these price differences persist, so do parallel imports. After all, if prices could freely adjust, we would expect significant price convergence, arbitrage opportunities would diminish, ultimately reducing the importance of parallel imports. However, price and distribution margin differences across countries arise in large part because of the way each Member State regulates its pharmaceutical markets.

To support the thesis that parallel import is 'regulatory arbitrage', Costa-Font (2015) shows that statutory distribution margins are a major factor, and not price difference, that explain the volume of parallel imports of statins (a medicine that is

72. *See* currently Article 90 of the *Ley 29/2006, de 26 de julio, de garantías y uso racional de los medicamentos y productos sanitarios*, as amended.
73. Margaret K. Kyle, *Strategic Responses to Parallel Trade*, 11 B.E. J. Econ. Analysis & Pol'y: Advances 1 (2011).
74. Joan Costa-Font, *Is Medicines Parallel Trade 'Regulatory Arbitrage'?*, 16 Int'l J. Health Econ. & Mgmt. 321 (2016).

used to lower cholesterol) between the source countries and the Netherlands.[75] This study shows that in France, which was the major source country between 1997 and 2002), wholesaler margins were the lowest, and in the Netherlands, they were the highest. Dubois and Sæthre (2020) finds similar results using Norwegian data on all prescription medicines on-patent between 2004 and 2007.[76] The study shows that the extent to which pharmacy chains in Norway steer demand toward parallel imports depends on the difference in margin between parallel and direct imports. The higher the margin earned on parallel imports, the greater the share of parallel imports.

[3] The Impact of the Regulation of Drug Shortages

Pharmaceutical regulation does not merely cover the price of medicines but also their availability. Indeed, under Article 81 of Directive 2001/83/EC, pharma companies and distributors are required to 'ensure appropriate and continued supplies of [their] medicinal product[s] to pharmacies and persons authorised to supply medicinal products so that the needs of patients in the Member State in question are covered.'[77]

Several EU Member States have tried to set up further legislative frameworks to ensure the availability of medicines and to avoid shortages. Parallel trade is often pinpointed as a cause for such shortages and some Member States have therefore introduced measures to avoid that the export of pharmaceuticals would lead to shortages.[78] One measure that is often introduced is the possibility for the relevant health authorities to issue temporary bans on the export of certain drugs, as in the Czech Republic, Estonia, France, Greece, Italy, Poland, Slovakia, Spain and Romania.[79] In addition, several EU countries have tried to stop community pharmacists from selling drugs to wholesalers (so-called reverse distribution). Finally, in many Member States a monitoring system has been set up to create early warnings for medicines which are running short. This has not stopped significant shortages from arising. In

75. Statutory distribution margins are determined by Member State regulation, which is specific to each country.
76. Pierre Dubois and Morten Sæthre, *On the Effect of Parallel Trade on Manufacturers' and Retailers' Profits in the Pharmaceutical Sector*, 88 Econometrica 2503 (2020).
77. Article 81(2) of Directive 2001/83, introduced by Directive 2004/27/EC of the European Parliament and of the Council of 31 March 2004 amending Directive 2001/83/EC on the Community code relating to medicinal products for human use, OJ L 136, 30.4.2004.
78. Affordable Medicines Europe, an association of wholesalers, lists Austria, Belgium, Bulgaria, the Czech Republic, Estonia, France, Germany, Greece, Hungary, Italy, Latvia, Norway, Poland, Portugal, Romania, Slovakia, Spain and the UK. *See* Affordable Medicines Europe, *Medicine Shortages: Position Paper* of 28 May 2020. <https://affordablemedicines.eu/wp-content/uploads/2020/06/Position-Paper-on-Medicine-Shortages.pdf>.
79. *See* Tomasz Bochenek et al., *Systemic Measures and Legislative and Organizational Frameworks Aimed at Preventing or Mitigating Drug Shortages in 28 European and Western Asian Countries*, 8 Frontiers in Pharmacology 942 (2018). A legislative initiative to introduce a similar system in Belgium was annulled by the Belgian constitutional court in October 2019.

Poland, for example, all pharmacists which responded to a recent survey testified to the existence of shortages.[80]

The fear of shortages was of course amplified by the COVID-19 pandemic and the European Parliament has issued a resolution in that context which argued that 'parallel exports can in some cases have the unintended consequence of creating disruptions in supply across Member States'.[81] The European Commission also stated in 2019 that parallel trade may be one factor creating pharmaceuticals shortages,[82] but at the onset of the pandemic, it argued that export restrictions imposed by some Member States 'contribute to the risk of shortages in other Member States, thereby putting at risk the health of people living in Europe' and were contrary to the free movement of goods.[83] Wholesalers have similarly argued that parallel trade is a balancing force that can resolve shortages in destination countries.[84] In its Communication on a *Pharmaceutical strategy for Europe* of 25 November 2020 again listed parallel trade as a possible cause of shortages but this alongside other factors such as supply quotas and issues linked to pricing and reimbursement.[85]

A major study on the effect of parallel trade on shortages has only recently been launched, again in the context of the COVID-19 pandemic, so it is hard to say whether parallel trade may cause or may alleviate medicine shortages. In any event, any national rules that prevent or disincentivise exports may limit the volumes available for parallel trade. This in turn may mute the price effects of parallel trade.

[E] In the Presence of Parallel Imports Tighter Price Regulation, Which Would Reduce Expenditures, Would Mostly Hurt Distributors' Profit

Parallel imports play an important role in the price negotiation between manufacturers and distributors/pharmacies. Specifically, parallel imports represent an alternative to the products supplied by manufacturers, and thereby they enhance distributors/pharmacies bargaining power against pharmaceutical companies. In this setting stricter price regulation could hurt distributors more.

80. Tomasz Zaprutko et al., *Drug Shortages as a Result of Parallel Export in Poland – Pharmacists' Opinions*, 124 Health Pol'y 563 (2020). Most pharmacists surveyed blamed parallel trade for the shortages.
81. European Parliament Resolution of 17 September 2020 on the shortage of medicines – how to address an emerging problem (P9_TA(2020)0228).
82. *See* Answer given in the European Parliament on 23 August 2019 by Mr Andriukaitis on behalf of the European Commission to question E-002284/2019. Other causes mentioned are manufacturing problems, industry quotas, and economic reasons such as the price of medicines.
83. Communication from the Commission to the European Parliament, the European Council, the Council, the European Central Bank, the European Investment Bank and the Eurogroup 'Coordinated economic response to the COVID-19 Outbreak' COM(2020) 112 final at p. 4.
84. *See*, for example, Affordable Medicines Europe, *Trade Flows of Parallel Imported Medicines* of June 2020. <https://affordablemedicines.eu/wp-content/uploads/2020/06/Trade-Flow-Study-FINAL-big-file.pdf>.
85. Communication from the Commission to the European Parliament, the Council, the European Economic and Social Committee and the Committee of the Regions 'Pharmaceutical Strategy for Europe' COM(2020) 761 final at p. 17.

A study by Brekke et al. (2015) builds on the fact that parallel imports affect the price negotiation between pharmaceutical companies and domestic distributors (e.g. pharmacy chains).[86] Clearly, parallel imports improve the bargaining position of distributors because, if the manufacturer seeks to raise its price, the distributor can switch to parallel imports. This change can have a profound impact on the effect of price regulation. Consider that the retail price of the pharmaceutical product is capped. A reduction in that cap would weaken the competitive constraint exerted by parallel imports. Indeed, the retail price of the original product is reduced, making parallel imports less attractive. This, in turn, weakens the bargaining power of the distributor, enabling the manufacturer to raise the price it charges the distributor. These predictions are supported empirically with Norwegian data. The study shows that for medicines with parallel imports, a lower retail price cap does not reduce the producer price and profit as much as when there are no parallel imports. In fact, in the case of medicines for which parallel imports are persistent, the reduction in the retail price cap benefit the pharmaceutical manufacturer. This finding also suggests that when price regulation is tightened, and perhaps counter-intuitively, parallel imports may help manufacturers keep their share of the industry profit, thereby maintaining innovation incentives. (*See* below for a more extensive discussion analysis of the effects of parallel imports on innovation.)[87]

Dubois and Sæthre (2020) builds on the notion that parallel imports is a critical factor that affects the outcome of the negotiation between manufacturers and distributors. Using the parameter estimates of a sophisticated structural model that accounts for consumer behaviour as well as the strategic interaction between the manufacturer and distribution chains, they run some simulations to show that parallel imports allow pharmacy chains to capture a substantial share of industry profit regarding the supply of Lipitor (a statin product) in Norway between 2004 and 2007. Their results indicate that a ban on parallel imports would increase manufacturer's profit (in this case Pfizer). Interestingly, and in line with the finding of Brekke et al. (2015), their simulation also shows that a tightening of price regulation (i.e. a reduction in the retail price cap of Lipitor) would erode mostly the profit of the distribution chains and parallel importers. In other words, the savings achieved by the Norwegian government with tighter price regulation would not be a transfer from the profit of the pharmaceutical manufacturer but rather come from a significant reduction in the distributors' share of industry profit. In fact, Dubois and Sæthre suggests that the Norwegian government and Pfizer could negotiate a lower price cap, agreeing on a lump sum payment that would compensate the reduction in the manufacturer's profit, and still achieve significant savings for the taxpayers. Such a move would reduce arbitrage opportunities causing a fall in parallel imports.

---

86. Kurt R. Brekke, Tor Helge Holmas and Odd Rune Straume, *Price Regulation and Parallel Imports of Pharmaceuticals*, 129 J. Pub. Econ. 92 (2015).
87. This study does not consider innovation and its impact on welfare. In theory, the regulator would consider not only the price of medicines but its impact on further R&D investments. Hence, it is not possible to draw any robust conclusion about the effect of parallel imports on innovation here.

[F] The Effects of Parallel Imports on Innovation

Evaluating the impact of the case law on parallel trade in pharmaceuticals also requires an assessment of its effect on innovation.

Pharmaceutical companies have consistently argued that parallel trade undermines their incentives to make R&D investments and this issue has received much attention in the case law. The point is quite clearly made by Advocate General Jacobs in his opinion in the *Glaxo Greece* case: 'Innovation is an important parameter of competition in the pharmaceuticals sector. Substantial investment is typically required in the research and development of a new pharmaceutical product. The production of a pharmaceutical product is usually characterised by high fixed costs (to research and develop the product) and comparatively low variable costs (to manufacture the product once developed).'[88] In the *Glaxo Spain* case, the CFI accepted that parallel trade 'leads to a loss in efficiency for interbrand competition, in so far as it reduces GSK's capacity for innovation' whereas restrictions of parallel trade 'will lead to a gain in efficiency for interbrand competition in so far as it will enable GSK's capacity for innovation to be increased.'[89]

As indicated earlier, the European Commission has argued that a Single Market in pharmaceuticals may encourage R&D investments in Europe. Nevertheless, it accepts in principle that restrictions of intrabrand competition (through restrictions of parallel trade) could reduce incentives for innovation, although it found in its decision in *Glaxo Spain* that the causal link between parallel trade and the loss in efficiency had not been established in practice. More precisely, and as we saw above, the Commission considered that the profits foregone through parallel trade were limited and that there was in any event no certainty that these would be invested in R&D (rather than simply being retained as additional profits).[90] The scepticism about the causal link between parallel trade and the loss in efficiency was shared by Advocate General Ruiz-Jarabo Colomer in the *Glaxo Greece* case who considered this argument 'misleading, since it is aimed only at seducing public opinion, which is sensitised to the vital importance of R&D for competitiveness.'[91]

To the best of our knowledge, no empirical research has been conducted concerning the impact of parallel imports on innovation in the pharmaceutical sector. Nonetheless, the economic literature provides theoretical insights, based on stylised models, about the potential effects of parallel trade on R&D investments. We will summarise the key conclusions from these models, noting that we cannot draw any robust conclusions on this important question.

---

88. AG opinion in Case C-53/03, *Syfait and Others*, ECLI:EU:C:2004:673, para. 89. Note that this was the opinion in the first preliminary reference in this case, which was declared inadmissible by the CJEU.
89. Case T-168/01, *GlaxoSmithKline Services v. Commission*, ECLI:EU:T:2006:265, para. 255.
90. As we saw earlier, the Court of First Instance considered that the Commission should have investigated this point in more detail and this point of view was confirmed by the CJEU.
91. AG opinion in Joined Cases C-468/06 to C-478/06, *Sot Lelos and Others*, ECLI:EU:C:2008/108, para. 113. Note that this was the opinion in the second preliminary reference in this case, which was declared admissible by the CJEU.

We start this discussion by setting out the argument put forward by the pharmaceutical companies that parallel imports are likely to cause a reduction in innovation. This is because, in unregulated markets, parallel imports are expected to prevent pharmaceutical companies from pursuing Ramsey pricing, i.e. price discrimination, which would allow them to recoup more efficiently the fixed cost of R&D investments.[92] In other words, parallel imports erode the ability to price discriminate between markets (i.e. countries), which in turn reduces the returns that pharmaceutical companies can expect from their risky investments, notably in high price countries. Valletti and Szymanski (2006) shows that arbitrage dilutes the incentive of manufacturers to invest in higher quality products.[93] At the end of the day, consumers may benefit from parallel trade thanks to lower prices, but in the longer run, they will not have the opportunity to acquire improved products. Parallel imports, therefore, can have negative welfare effects as they reduce pharmaceutical companies' incentive to invest in developing new medicines and treatments.[94]

As pharmaceutical companies operate globally, their R&D investments can be recouped by sales made everywhere around the globe. This raises the question about the extent to which parallel trade in the EEA would have decreased global revenue (and profit) of pharmaceutical companies. There is evidence that pharmaceutical innovation responds to changes in revenue. For example, Dubois et al. (2015) shows that innovation, measured by the number of new chemical entities launched in fourteen countries, responds to expected revenue.[95] In other words, as companies expect a drop in revenue from selling future new medicines, they would cut in their investments to develop new molecular entities.

According to the EFPIA the European market is an important source of the manufacturers' revenue. Figure 5.12 provides estimates of the share of total revenue

---

92. For an introduction on standard economic principles on parallel trade in pharmaceuticals, *see* Patricia M. Danzon, *The Economics of Parallel Trade*, 13 Pharmaco Econ. 293 (1998).
93. Tommaso M. Valletti and Stefan Szymanski, *Parallel Trade, International Exhaustion and Intellectual Property Rights: A Welfare Analysis*, 54 The J. Indus. Econ. 499 (2006).
94. The basic intuition is that because parallel imports is expected to reduce the manufacturer's profit, the marginal return to investment becomes smaller, which in this case lowers the incentive to commit funds to R&D projects. That said, this need not always be the case. It depends in part on consumer preference for innovative medicines (i.e. the extent to which consumer willingness to pay for innovative medicines is increased compares to present-day medicines). It could be the case that the willingness to pay for better treatment is much higher in the low-price country, whilst in the high-price country, consumers would not be willing to pay more for innovation. In this setting, in theory parallel imports would impose the price in the low-price country on the high-price country, and the marginal return to investment would be higher than that in a situation without arbitrage. Indeed, the manufacturer's incremental profit depends on the higher price it can charge for the new, innovative product, which in turn depends on the willingness to pay for innovation of consumers in the low-price country. Because consumers in the low-price country value more innovation, the manufacturer could expect higher returns in a regime with parallel imports than without.
95. Pierre Dubois, Olivier de Mouzon, Fiona Scott-Morton and Paul Seabright, *Market Size and Pharmaceutical Innovation*, 46 The RAND J. Econ. 844 (2015) estimates an average elasticity of 0.23. This means that as expected revenue increases by 10%, this stimulates innovation, raising the number of new molecular entities by 2.3%. However, this study shows that the elasticity varies across ATC classes.

generated in Europe.[96] Whilst the North American market (USA and Canada) is clearly the world's largest, accounting for roughly 50% of global pharmaceutical sales, Europe still contributes significantly with around EUR 200 billion (or more than 20%) to global sales. This suggests that if parallel trade decreases profits in the EEA, it is also making a dent in global revenue and profit because the European market is relevant on a global scale. In turn, parallel trade could discourage manufacturers to engage in risky innovative investments to discover new treatments. Importantly, EFPIA also notes that for new medicines, Germany, France, Italy, Spain and the UK account for about 20% of global sales. In this context, EU policies related to parallel trade might have an impact on global R&D spending.

Figure 5.12 World Pharmaceutical Sales

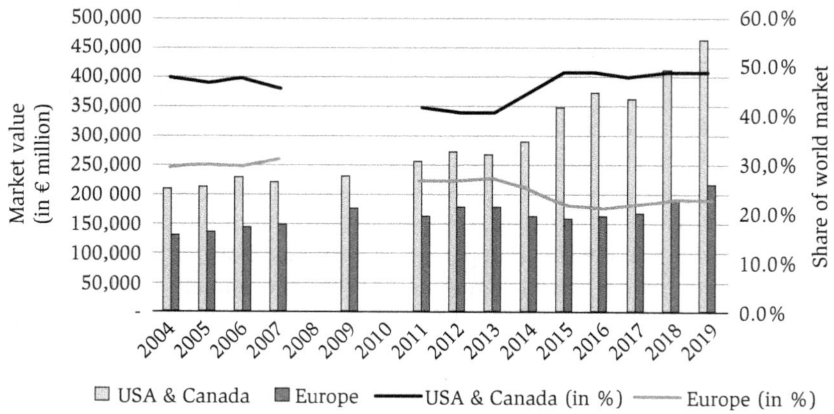

However, because prices of medicines are regulated (or indirectly controlled), the effect of parallel imports on innovation is more complex than the basic economic logic that would have prevailed in the absence of regulation.

Grossman and Lai (2008) provides a first contribution that challenges the notion that parallel imports have a negative impact on innovation.[97] Using a stylised economic model, where the world is divided into high- and low-income countries, they show that when parallel trade is allowed to flow from the low-income to the high-income countries, the rate of innovation is improved. This is because the government in the low-income country would raise the regulatory price cap, which ultimately benefits R&D investments globally. The logic goes as follows. When parallel trade is prohibited, the pharmaceutical companies, which are located in the high-income country, will sell in the low-income country so long as the price cap is above its marginal cost of

96. EFPIA relies on the IQVIA-MIDAS database (data relate to the audited global retail and hospital pharmaceutical market at ex-factory prices). Europe includes here Turkey and Russia, which are concerned by parallel imports.
97. Gene M. Grossman and Edwin L.-C. Lai, *Parallel Imports and Price Controls*, 39 The RAND J. Econ. 378 (2008).

production. This allows the regulator to set relatively low prices for the benefit of consumers in that country. When parallel trade is allowed, however, the regulator in the low-income country will have to set a price that is sufficiently high to encourage the pharmaceutical companies to export in it. Otherwise, the manufacturers may walk away if the regulated price is too low, as in that case there is a significant risk that parallel imports would undercut the price of medicines in the high-income country. At the end of the day the regulator in the low-income country will set a price cap that is high enough such that the medicines are not re-exported to the high-income country.[98]

Parallel imports force the regulator in the low-income country to set high regulated prices, and this benefits the high-income country as this promotes innovation. In other words, the low-income country no longer free rides on the high-income country, which was paying for most of the R&D investments.

Bennato and Valletti (2014) challenges the finding of Grossman and Lai (2008).[99] This theoretical study shows that in some settings parallel trade may reduce innovation. This is the case when the government in the (small) low-income country cannot commit fully to a price cap (i.e. before the manufacturer decides to invest in R&D).[100] Ultimately, the regulator sets a price cap that is sufficiently high to ensure that the innovative medicine is delivered in the low-income country. However, the lack of commitment by the low-income country results in a hold-up problem, which lowers the pharmaceutical company incentive to engage in sunk R&D investments.

Reisinger, Sauri and Zenger (2019) also extends the results of Grossman and Lai (2008) by showing that the effects of parallel imports on innovation hinge on the degree of similarity between the trading countries.[101] When the demand for medicines in the high- and low-income countries are very dissimilar, parallel imports would reduce innovation. In such a case, the regulator in the low-income country would not be able to set a price cap that is sufficiently high, and thus attractive for the pharmaceutical companies to serve that country. As the manufacturer will supply only the high-income country, its returns on R&D depend on sales in that country. Instead, if parallel imports are restricted, the manufacturer will serve the low-income country, even if the regulated cap is low (but higher than the manufacturer's marginal cost). In that case, the returns on investment are higher as the innovative treatment will also be sold in the low-income country. In cases when the two countries are dissimilar, but the manufacturer serves the low-income country, parallel trade reduces innovation. This is because

---

98. In this setting, the immediate consequence is that parallel imports harm consumers in the low-income country. Indeed, if parallel imports were not allowed, the regulator would be able to set a lower price and the manufacturer would sell at any price above marginal cost, as there is no risk that the products be re-exported in the high-income country.

99. Anna Rita Bennato and Tommaso Valletti, *Pharmaceutical Innovation and Parallel Trade*, 33 Int'l J. Indus. Org. 83 (2014).

100. In this set-up the government in the low-income country set the price for delivery after the manufacturer sinks its R&D expenditures but before it decides whether to deliver the new medicine in the low-income country. The government commits to a regulated price that ensures delivery, yet it does not eliminate totally the hold-up problem as this decision is made after the manufacturer decision to invest.

101. Markus Reisinger, Lluís Saurí and Hans Zenger, *Parallel Imports, Price Controls, and Innovation*, 66 J. Health Econ. 163 (2019).

the price cap in the low-income country also applies in the high-income country (the price cap is exported), which dampens the incentive of the manufacturer to innovate.

On the basis of the literature review, we unfortunately cannot come to conclusive statements on the impact of parallel trade on innovation.

§5.06 CONCLUSION

Health policies, including the pricing and reimbursement of pharmaceuticals, are the prerogative of Member States. In fact, the distribution and pricing of pharmaceuticals are heavily regulated in order to ensure the safety and quality of drugs, to control health care expenditures whilst guaranteeing access to patients and to encourage innovation.

The EU Single Market objective requires the abolition of restrictions on the free movement of goods between EU Member States. In line with this policy objective, the CJEU has stated that restrictions on parallel trade in pharmaceuticals may infringe EU competition law, but it has also accepted that manufacturers impose restrictions on parallel trade in some circumstances. In particular, the CJEU has ruled that restrictions of parallel trade have as their object the restriction of competition, but that such restrictions may be justified under Article 101(3) TFEU. As regards Article 102 TFEU, it has held that a dominant undertaking abuses its position if it refuses to meet orders from wholesalers that are 'ordinary' in the light of both the size of those orders in relation to the requirements of the market and the previous business relations between that undertaking and the wholesalers concerned, but not if it refuses to meet orders that are out of the ordinary.

The data available to us clearly shows that parallel imports of pharmaceutical products continue to be significant within the EEA. For instance, the data show that for a very large proportion of authorised medicines, a parallel distribution licence was granted. In addition, estimates show that parallel imports represent a small but significant proportion of medicines sold in Nordic countries, Germany, the UK and the Netherlands. However, it is not possible to conclude from this data whether parallel trade has actually increased (or decreased) as a result of the CJEU's case law.

We have drawn on a review of the economic literature as well as a review of Eurostat price indices to assess the price effect of parallel imports. There is some evidence that parallel imports have contributed to reducing manufacturer's prices in destination countries: this may be explained by the fact that in these destination countries, regulation has encouraged the development of parallel imports as a way to contain expenditures. On the other hand, there is no evidence of price convergence, which is consistent with the view that parallel imports have limited price effects.

We consider that the limited price effects can be explained by at least three factors:

- The first factor is the case law. Whilst the CJEU has ruled that restrictions on parallel trade in pharmaceuticals may infringe EU competition law in some circumstances, it also allowed manufacturers to impose restrictions on parallel trade in other circumstances.

- Second, regulation is a major determinant of prices of pharmaceuticals, and therefore price differences between Member States have persisted, whilst contributing to encourage parallel trade too.
- A third factor, finally, may be regulations aimed at preventing drug shortages both at an EU and at a national level. These regulations may reduce the volume available for parallel trade.

Importantly, the existence of parallel imports affects price negotiation between manufacturers on the one hand and distributors and pharmacies on the other. Specifically, parallel imports improve the bargaining position of the latter, enabling them to earn higher margins. Tighter price regulation in destination countries, on the other hand, would mostly erode the profit of distributors, and reduce total expenditures on medicines, without necessarily harming the returns of pharmaceutical companies.

This leads to the final critical issue, i.e., the extent to which parallel trade reduces the incentives of pharmaceutical companies to invest in R&D. In principle, as parallel imports erode the manufacturers' profit, they could reduce their incentive to fund risky innovative projects. However, given the interplay between price regulation, investment incentives and trade, parallel imports do not necessarily lead to reduced innovation. As we present in this chapter, advances in economic theory show that the net effect will depend on the circumstances. There is unfortunately no data available to assess this issue empirically. As a result, we cannot come to conclusive statements on the impact of parallel trade on innovation.

CHAPTER 6

Conditional Rebates under EU Competition Law: A Retrospective on *Michelin I*, *Michelin II* and *BA/Virgin*

Christian Ahlborn, Xavier Boutin, Verity Egerton-Doyle & Nayantara Ravichandran[*]

§6.01 INTRODUCTION

This chapter was part of a wider project on the *ex post* assessment of landmark competition cases for discussion at the 2021 GCLC conference. It focusses on three of the key cases in the evolution of European Union (hereinafter 'EU') law on the treatment of conditional rebates[1] under Article 102 of the Treaty on the Functioning of the European Union (hereinafter 'TFEU') (hereinafter 'Article 102 TFEU') and its precursors (Article 82 and Article 86 of the Treaty Establishing the European Community):[2] *Michelin I*,[3] *Michelin II*,[4] and *BA/Virgin*[5] (our 'Focus Cases'). The objective of this paper is to consider how these three significant cases should be viewed with the

* The authors acknowledge and thank the members of their 2021 GCLC conference working group for their contributions: Lars Kjolbye, Damien Neven, Claire Simpson and Denis Waelbroeck. We also thank Jean-François Bellis and Nicolas Petit for their comments. Finally, we are grateful to our colleagues, Dasha Konnova, Benjamin Sidbury and Pauline Bruant for their help with this paper. Needless to say, any remaining errors are the authors' alone.

1. The terms 'discount' and 'rebate' refer to different forms of discounting practices, which can have different or similar effects on the incentives of purchasers depending on the market context. It is common to refer to 'discounts' as conditional price reductions typically paid upfront while 'rebates' are paid once the condition has been fulfilled (they could also be paid upfront on the assumption that they will be repaid if the condition is not met). In this paper, we refer to the latter when we use the term 'conditional rebates'.
2. All references to Article 102 in this paper should be understood as a reference to the equivalent provision in force at the time.
3. Case C-322/81, *Nederlandsche Banden-Industrie Michelin NV v. Commission of the European Communities*, 9.11.1983, ECLI:EU:C:1983:313 (hereinafter '*Michelin I*').

benefit of over twenty years of hindsight and in light of more recent developments in case law and economic literature.

More specifically, the authors have reviewed the legal and economic framework applied in each case and considered whether the approach taken was the correct one; both at the time and with the benefit of hindsight of further developments in legal and economic thought. The remainder of the paper is structured as follows. *Section §6.02* briefly summarises each Focus Case. *Section §6.03* provides a general framework for analysis of conditional rebates outlining: (i) their classification; (ii) the economic framework for analysis; and (iii) the legal framework for analysis and the object/effect distinction as a framework for understanding treatment of rebates under Article 102 TFEU; and (iv) the economic building blocks for an effects-based analysis. *Section §6.04* describes the Focus Cases in depth, looking at: (i) the conduct under consideration; (ii) the legal test applied, (iii) the theories of harm; and (iv) the evidence considered. *Section §6.05* evaluates the approach taken in the Focus Cases and considers: (i) whether the right framework and theories of harm were applied; (ii) whether, on the basis of the evidence, the Focus Cases reached appropriate conclusions; (iii) their internal consistency; and (iv) whether important relevant facts have been considered. *Section §6.06* concludes.

§6.02 THE FOCUS CASES: IN A NUTSHELL

[A] *Michelin I*

Michelin I concerned a system of rebates applied by Nederlandsche Banden-Industrie Michelin (hereinafter 'Michelin NV') between 1975 and 1980. The European Commission (hereinafter 'EC') issued its decision on 7 October 1981,[6] which Michelin NV subsequently appealed to the European Court of Justice (hereinafter 'ECJ'). The ECJ issued its judgment on 9 November 1983.[7] The case arose following a complaint from an association of tyre dealers.[8]

Michelin NV was found to have held a dominant position in the market for replacement tyres for trucks and buses in the Netherlands. It offered various rebates to dealers, each linked to increasing the number of purchases from Michelin NV either explicitly or through the setting of targets (so-called target rebates).

The impugned rebates were often informally negotiated with dealers without written confirmation. In particular, Michelin NV offered a bonus to individual dealers who purchased a target volume of tyres. The target increased year on year. Michelin

4. Case T-203/01, *Manufacture Française des Pneumatiques Michelin v. Commission of the European Communities*, 30.9.2003, ECLI:EU:T:2003:250 (hereinafter '*Michelin II*').
5. Case C-95/04 P, *British Airways Plc v. Commission of the European Communities*, 15.3.2007, ECLI:EU:C:2007:166 (hereinafter '*BA/Virgin*').
6. Commission Decision 81/969/EEC of 7 October 1981 on IV.29.491 – Bandengroothandel Frieschebrug BV/NV Nederlandsche Banden-Industrie Michelin, OJ L 353, 9.12.1981 (hereinafter '*Michelin I (EC)*').
7. Case C-322/81, *Michelin I*.
8. Case C-322/81, *Michelin I*, page 3467.

NV's internal documentation showed a large degree of variation in the rebates and bonuses that Michelin NV paid to its dealers.

The EC condemned these practices as abusive. It considered that Michelin NV's conduct restricted the dealers' freedom of choice and resulted in inequality of treatment between tyre dealers.[9] The EC imposed a fine of EUR 0.68 million. The ECJ agreed that Michelin NV's practices were abusive and tended to bind the dealers to Michelin NV by virtue of the uncertainty of the arrangements.[10] It reasoned that Michelin NV's rebate system was calculated to prevent dealers from being able to select the most favourable of the offers made by the various competitors freely at any time and to change suppliers without suffering any appreciable economic disadvantage.[11] The fine was reduced to EUR 0.3 million by the ECJ on appeal.

[B] *BA/Virgin*

On 14 July 1999, the EC issued an infringement decision against British Airways (hereinafter 'BA') in relation to commissions that BA offered to travel agents.[12] The case arose following a complaint made by Virgin Atlantic (hereinafter 'Virgin'). BA appealed the EC's decision to the Court of First Instance (hereinafter 'CFI')[13] and later the ECJ, but both appeals were dismissed, on 17 December 2003,[14] and 15 March 2007[15] respectively.

The rebate schemes under scrutiny comprised (as in *Michelin I*) of target rebates (i.e., retrospective payments that travel agents could earn based upon increasing their sales of BA tickets compared to the previous year, quarter and month). The EC found that the schemes were abusive in two ways. First, they rewarded and encouraged the loyalty of travel agents for selling and increasing their sales of BA tickets.[16] This restricted the freedom of agents to sell their services to the airlines of their choice and hindered the access of competing airlines to the United Kingdom ('UK') market for air travel agency services.[17] Second, the schemes were held to be discriminatory since, contrary to Article 102 TFEU, they had the effect of imposing dissimilar conditions to equivalent transactions on the agents in question.[18]

9. Commission Decision 81/969/EEC, *Michelin I (EC)*, para. 37.
10. Case C-322/81, *Michelin I*, para. 86.
11. Case C-322/81, *Michelin I*, para. 85.
12. Commission Decision 2000/74/EC of 14 July 1999 on IV/D-2/34.780 – Virgin/British Airways (notified under document number C(1999) 1973), OJ L 030, 4.2.2000 (hereinafter '*BA/Virgin (EC)*').
13. The CFI later became the General Court. In this paper, we use the name at the relevant time.
14. Case T-219/99, *British Airways Plc v. Commission of the European Communities*, 17.12.2003, ECLI:EU:T:2003:343 (hereinafter '*BA/Virgin (CFI)*').
15. Case C-95/04 P, *BA/Virgin*.
16. Commission Decision 2000/74/EC, *BA/Virgin (EC)*, para. 102.
17. Commission Decision 2000/74/EC, *BA/Virgin (EC)*, para. 102.
18. Commission Decision 2000/74/EC, *BA/Virgin (EC)*, para. 107.

The EC also synthesised the case law from *Hoffmann-La Roche*[19] and *Michelin I* to establish a general principle that a dominant company can give rebates that relate to efficiencies (e.g., on large orders) but not those that encourage loyalties (i.e., for avoiding purchases from the dominant supplier's competitor).[20] The EC fined BA EUR 6.8 million, which was upheld on appeal.

[C] *Michelin II*

Twenty years after its *Michelin I* decision, on 20 June 2001, the EC issued a second decision against Michelin – this time relating to a complex system of rebates, discounts and financial benefits offered by Manufacture Française de Pneumatiques Michelin (hereinafter 'Michelin France') for a period of nineteen years, starting in 1980 (soon after the end of the Michelin NV rebate system).[21] Again, the EC's investigation followed a complaint by one of Michelin France's competitors – Bandag.[22] Like *Michelin I*, the scheme of rebates was offered to dealers in new replacement tyres and re-treaded tyres, but this time in France. Michelin France subsequently sought the annulment of the EC's decision in the CFI. The CFI upheld the EC's decision on 30 September 2003.[23] There was no further appeal to the ECJ.

The EC scrutinised a number of different schemes administered by Michelin France, which were again linked to increasing purchases. The various schemes entered into were retroactive volume rebates with a reference period of one year. The quantity rebate was calculated on the basis of all sales made during the reference period rather than the incremental sales.[24] These schemes, which had previously been considered lawful, were considered by the EC to be loyalty-inducing and to place Michelin France's dealers in a position of dependence, whilst simultaneously foreclosing competing tyre manufacturers.

The EC fined Michelin France EUR 19.76 million and ordered Michelin France to refrain from repeating any of the abusive conduct or from adopting any measure having equivalent effect. This finding was upheld on appeal.

---

19. Case C-85/76, *F Hoffmann-La Roche & Co AG v. Commission of the European Communities*, 13.12.1979, ECLI:EU:C:1979:36 (hereinafter '*Hoffmann-La Roche*').
20. Commission Decision 2000/74/EC, *BA/Virgin (EC)*, para. 101.
21. Commission Decision 2002/405/EC of 20 June 2001 on COMP/E-2/36.041/PO—Michelin (notified under document number C(2001) 1582), OJ L 143, 31.5.2002 (hereinafter '*Michelin II (EC)*').
22. The complaint came in the context of a broader trade dispute between Michelin, Bridgestone /Firestone Inc. and Bandag, which included litigation in the US: for more detail *see*, Timothy Aeppel, *Michelin Units Add Firestone to Lawsuit Against Bandag*, Wall Street Journal (1 February 2001), https://www.wsj.com/articles/SB981039581655735863.
23. Case T-203/01, *Michelin II*.
24. Case T-203/01, *Michelin II*, paras 218 and 224.

§6.03 GENERAL FRAMEWORK: PUTTING THE FOCUS CASES IN CONTEXT

This section provides some of the necessary context for the detailed description and in-depth analysis of the Focus Cases that follows in *sections §6.04* and §6.05. *Section §6.03[A]* outlines the various kinds of conditional rebates, highlighting those that were considered in the Focus Cases. *Section §6.03[B]* considers the economic aspects of conditional rebates, namely the main theories of harm and efficiencies associated with conditional rebates. *Section §6.03[C]* gives an overview of the framework for analysing the legal treatment of rebates under Article 102 TFEU, based upon the possible distinction between 'by object' and 'by effect' abuses. Finally, *section §6.03[D]* shows how these economic considerations can be used as a basis for building blocks for legal tests.

[A] Types of Conditional Rebates

[1] Scope

The Focus Cases - and thus this paper - consider '*pricing structures offering lower prices in return for a buyer's agreed or de facto commitment to source a large and/or increasing share of his requirements from the discounter*'.[25] In other words, rebates refer to forms of non-linear pricing which are dependent on the customer meeting certain conditions, and we refer to them generally as 'conditional rebates'.

It is also important to outline what is *not* within the scope of this paper. First, this paper focuses on single-product rebates only and does *not* consider multi-product rebates, which generally fall under a bundling analysis (we note that in *Michelin I* bundling rebates are briefly considered and then dismissed). Second, since the Focus Cases consider pricing abuses, this paper does not deal with related non-pricing abuses except to the extent relevant in evaluating the approach taken in the Focus Cases. In particular, rebates, even those offered with the aim or explicit objective of generating customer fidelity, must be distinguished from contractual exclusivity (i.e., agreements to purchase exclusively from the supplier as a *condition* of sale). While rebates can have exclusivity-inducing effects, the two must be assessed separately, because contractual exclusivity *guarantees* exclusivity (unless the contract is breached /risk of damages for breach of contract does not act as a sufficient deterrent for such a breach) in a way that a rebate does not.[26] Contractual exclusivity is therefore outside the scope of this paper.

Following the Focus Cases, as well as other cases considering rebates, four broad 'kinds' of categories of rebates have emerged. Despite the limitations of a strict

---

25. *Loyalty and Fidelity Discounts and Rebates*, OECD Report, 4 February 23 (DAFFE/COMP(2002)21), 7.
26. For more on the distinction between 'exclusivity obligations' and 'exclusivity options' and its relevance to assessment of different restraints, *see*: Nicolas Petit, *Intel, Leveraging Rebates and the Goals of Article 102 TFEU,* 11(1) Eur. Competition J. 26–68 (2015).

taxonomy from both a legal and economic perspective,[27] employing this broader classification of rebates may help in identifying a scale of competition concerns. We outline these and consider how they can be seen to have developed through the Focus Cases, as a useful framework for our analysis in *section §6.05* below.

[2] Classification

[a] Rebates (Explicitly) Linked to Exclusive or Near-Exclusive Dealing

Under such a rebate, a purchaser is given a discount on the condition of obtaining all or most of its requirements from the dominant firm: the rationale for competition concerns is that such rebates may have a similar competitive effect to a contractual exclusivity obligation. This was first considered in *Hoffmann-La Roche* (where it was considered unlawful).[28] The rationale for this rule, and the precise bounds of what can be considered to fit into this category, is one of the key controversies in the case law on rebates over the past forty years.[29] Notwithstanding this controversy, the principle that rebates explicitly conditioned on exclusive or near-exclusive dealing are presumed to constitute an abuse (albeit that if the dominant firm seeks to rebut this presumption, the burden shifts to the EC to establish an anticompetitive effect) remains part of the law at the time of writing.[30] This will be discussed at length in this paper.

A common feature of the Focus Cases is that none of the rebate systems considered imposing an explicit exclusivity commitment. But in all the Focus Cases, the various systems of rebates were considered (in some cases, cumulatively) to be fidelity-inducing, and thus prohibited under Article 102 TFEU. In particular, in both *Michelin* cases, there was a focus on the complexity and opacity of the rebate schemes, meaning that dealers felt compelled to purchase all or most of their requirements from Michelin. It is arguable that the features of the Michelin Friends Club considered in *Michelin II* were capable of promoting near-exclusive dealing, but the EC (endorsed by the CFI) considered the Michelin Friends Club cumulatively with the other rebates offered by Michelin France.

27. Robert O'Donoghue and Jorge Padilla, *Law and Economics of Article 102 TFEU*, 1174 (Hart Publishing 2020).
28. Case C-85/76, *Hoffmann-La Roche*, para. 89.
29. Case T-155/06, *Tomra*, 6.9.2010, ECLI:EU:C:2012:221 (hereinafter '*Tomra*'); Case C-413/14 P, *Intel Corp Inc v. European Commission*, 6.9.2017, ECLI:EU:C:2017:632 (hereinafter '*Intel*'); *see* also the extensive writings on this topic, for example: Damien Geradin, *Loyalty Rebates after Intel: Time for the European Court of Justice to Overrule Hoffman-La Roche*, J. Competition L. & Econ., George Mason Law & Economics Research Paper, No 15-15 (2015); Damien Neven, *A Structured Assessment of Rebates Contingent on Exclusivity* 1(1) Competition L. & Pol'y Deb. 86–96 (2015); Pablo Ibáñez Colomo, *Intel and Article 102 TFEU Case Law: Making Sense of a Perpetual Controversy*, LSE Law, Society and Economy Working Papers 29/2014; Nicolas Petit, *Intel, Leveraging Rebates and the Goals of Article 102 TFEU*, 11(1) Eur. Competition J. 26–68 (2015).
30. Case C-413/14 P, *Intel*, paras 137–139.

[b] Target Rebates

Under a target rebate system, a purchaser is granted a retroactive rebate, i.e., a rebate across all units purchased during the reference period once a certain condition (generally a purchase volume condition) is met. Target rebates (as we refer to them in this paper) are set individually. The objection to this form of rebate is that it can generate strong incentives for the purchase of incremental volumes and can have foreclosure effects if it makes it difficult for competitors to match the effective price.[31] Such an effect can be observed where a certain portion of a purchaser's demand is captive to the dominant supplier (i.e., non-contestable), which prevents competitors, even competitors that are as efficient in all other ways, from profitably serving the contestable segment of demand. However, such effect does not necessarily hold true in all circumstances, as described further below. *Michelin I* and *BA/Virgin* most neatly fit into this category.

Most cases dealing with target rebates have considered schemes where the purchase volumes that needed to be achieved were growth targets from one period to the next (though the category also includes individualised volume rebates that do not represent growth targets). Historically, the EU courts took a cautious approach to the circumstances in which individualised target rebates could be considered unlawful. In *Michelin I*, it was considered that the opacity of the system meant that dealers would not know the actual amount of the rebate (and consequently the effective price per unit) until the end of the period. Given this uncertainty, it was considered that dealers would be averse to buying from other suppliers since this could risk not achieving the target threshold. However, the EC did not assess qualitatively or quantitatively the likely effect of the rebates on customers' behaviour, and in particular, the materiality of the customers' loss aversion that would justify such a conclusion.

The approach to target rebates grew more hostile as the EC and the EU courts seemed prepared to assume anticompetitive effects (and therefore presume illegality) without any detailed analysis. In *BA/Virgin*, while the nominal percentage of the discounts offered by the rebates was quite low, the EC highlighted that BA's large sale base meant that in practice the rebates resulted in large monetary benefits for dealers.[32] The progressive nature of the system meant that rebates were capable of rising exponentially from one reference period to another, with the risk of a disproportionate decrease if sales declined even slightly.[33]

In some respects, *BA/Virgin* can be viewed as the 'high water mark' for hostility towards target rebate systems. In *Tomra*, while the EC and EU courts still applied the strict approach of considering target rebates to be presumed anticompetitive, the Advocate General (hereinafter 'AG') emphasised the correctness of the EC's approach in assessing the potential for anticompetitive effects '*in the circumstances of the case*' as

---

31. Robert O'Donoghue and Jorge Padilla, *Law and Economics of Article 102 TFEU*, 1196 (Hart Publishing 2020).
32. Commission Decision 2000/74/EC, *BA/Virgin (EC)*, para. 30.
33. Case C-95/04 P, *BA/Virgin*, paras 272–273.

opposed to in the abstract.[34] Subsequent cases – albeit dealing with retroactive quantity rebates in the case of *Post Danmark II* and exclusivity rebates in the case of *Intel* – moved away from the strict approach taken in these cases and, as discussed later in this paper, the EU courts have over the past two decades begun to adopt a more effects-based approach to such rebates.[35]

[c] Retroactive Quantity Rebates

Under a retroactive quantity rebate system, a rebate is granted on conditions that apply to all customers (i.e., standardised conditions), for example, based on meeting a generally applicable sales threshold. In contrast to the above categories, where the relevant threshold is set on an individual (purchaser-by-purchaser) basis, retroactive quantity rebates are offered on the same basis to all (or the entirety of a group/the whole category of) purchasers. In principle, therefore, any anticompetitive effect of such a system is 'blunted' because of the inability to target individual purchasers' volume requirements.[36]

These kinds of retroactive quantity rebates have generally been considered to be lawful,[37] though, as will be discussed, retroactive quantity rebates were impugned as 'loyalty inducing' in one of the Focus Cases: *Michelin II* (in a divergence from precedent).[38] The EC based its findings, among other things, on the fact that the *number* of these retroactive quantity rebates (nearly sixty in some years), meant that it could have effectively corresponded with dealers' maximum requirements.[39] The EC did not analyse whether these thresholds were used to deal with any particular business reality nor whether they were targeting particular groups of dealers. Moreover, tiered rebates have also generally been considered as less restrictive and closer to incremental rebates, since each step in the tariff is likely to be smaller.

The EC also found that the structure of the system meant that dealers risked making an overall loss unless they obtained the highest rebate.[40] Rebates with a relatively long (one year) reference period were presumed to be abusive, absent economic justification. The CFI noted that towards the end of the reference period, buyers would face increased pressure to reach the target threshold in order to secure a rebate for the entire period. However, the CFI did not consider whether economic theory would support the increase in such pressure, nor did it seek to identify its source

---

34. Opinion of Advocate General Mazak in Case C-549/10 P, *Tomra Systems ASA and others v. Commission*, 2.2.2012, ECLI:EU:C:2012:55, paras 43–44.
35. *See* e.g., Case C-23/14, *Post Danmark A/S v. Konkurrenceradet*, 6.10.2015, ECLI:EU:C:2015:651 (hereinafter '*Post Danmark II*'); Case C-413/14 P, *Intel*, para. 29.
36. Robert O'Donoghue and Jorge Padilla, *Law and Economics of Article 102 TFEU*, 1228 (2020).
37. Case C-85/76, *Hoffmann-La Roche*; Case C-23/14, *Post Danmark II*; Case C-413/14 P, *Intel*; Case C-310/93 P, *BPB Industries Plc and British Gypsum Ltd v. Commission of the European Communities*, 6.4.1995, ECLI:EU:C:1995:101 (hereinafter '*British Gypsum*').
38. Case T-203/01, *Michelin II*, paras 64–66.
39. Robert O'Donoghue and Jorge Padilla, *Law and Economics of Article 102 TFEU*, 1232 (2020).
40. Commission Decision 2002/405/EC, *Michelin II (EC)*, para. 218.

or make any qualitative or quantitative analysis of the influence of this factor on merchant's behaviour (in particular in terms of risk or loss aversion).

In line with the trend across all conditional rebate cases (and the Priorities Guidance[41]), more recent cases have moved towards an effects-based approach to the assessment of retroactive quantity rebates. In *Post Danmark II,* which concerned retroactive (standardised) all-unit rebates, while the ECJ recognised the potential for all-unit rebates, especially those based on annual reference periods, to have a strong marginal impact, it nonetheless emphasised the need to consider the actual effect of the rebate and, in particular, noted that the as efficient competitor (hereinafter 'AEC') test as an important tool in assessing such effect.[42]

[d] Incremental Rebates

Under an incremental rebate system, the meeting of the condition for a rebate to be applied does not result in a discount on *all* units, but only on those within the relevant tranche or increment. Incremental rebates could be individualised or standardised. The effect of the rebate on the customer's incentives inevitably depends upon the conditions by which it is met and the level at which it is set (as well as what proportion of the customer's own demand is captive to the dominant supplier).

These kinds of rebates – which do not feature in the Focus Cases – have generally been considered to present a lower foreclosure risk than target rebates. For example, in *Michelin II,* the CFI stated that '*the incentive to purchase created by a quantity rebate system is therefore much greater when the rebates are calculated on total turnover achieved during a certain period than when they are calculated only tranche by tranche*'.[43] The EC has expressed the same view, first in its 2005 Discussion Paper,[44] with the position confirmed in its Priorities Guidance, which indicates that for incremental rebates, a predatory pricing analysis has generally been used to determine their effect.[45] In 2009, the year after the Priorities Guidance was published, the EC closed its investigation into *Velux* over its incremental rebate scheme, concluding they were '*very unlikely to bar competitors from access to the market*', noting the incremental nature of the rebates and the relatively short reference periods in question.[46]

[3] The Merits and Limitations of Classification

While the above framework is useful for classifying and understanding different kinds of rebates, the categories are not strict in reality. At least three of the four categories

---

41. Guidance on the Commission's enforcement priorities in applying Article 102 to abusive exclusionary conduct by dominant undertakings (OJ 2009 C45/7) (hereinafter 'Priorities Guidance').
42. Case C-23/14, *Post Danmark II,* para. 61.
43. Case T-203/01, *Michelin II,* para. 88.
44. DG Competition discussion paper on the application of Article 82 of the Treaty to exclusionary abuses (2005), para. 166 (hereinafter 'Discussion Paper').
45. Priorities Guidance, para. 42.
46. Commission Decision C(2018) 3864 of 14 June 2018 on AT. 40026 – Velux, para. 8.

identified are not mutually exclusive: (i) standardised rebates linked to exclusive or near-exclusive dealing may be de facto exclusive (although that is unlikely, as they are standardised); (ii) target rebates may also be de facto exclusive; and (iii) retroactive quantity rebates may become de facto close to target rebates if you have multiple thresholds.

In addition, a significant number of landmark cases have each created their own categories, including two of the three Focus Cases, namely *Michelin I* (which created a new category of target rebates) and *BA/Virgin* (for retroactive quantity rebates). This classification is therefore often not the result of an *ex ante* analysis of the effects of non-linear prices based on experience, but rather an *ex post* rationalisation based on the concerns that emerged in the context of a few very specific cases brought to the attention of the EC by complainants. As such, the classification is liable to evolve and, while useful for understanding historical cases, does not in itself provide a sound basis for assessment.

[B] Economic Assessment of Conditional Rebates

[1] Procompetitive Rationales

The terms 'retroactive' or 'loyalty enhancing' are not economic terms. Therefore, the classification presented in *section §6.03[A][2]* does not correspond to an economic categorisation. Rather, economists naturally classify prices according to their dependencies. In particular, prices can be:

(i) related to the identity of the buyer;
(ii) related to the quantities bought from competing suppliers (this includes exclusivity conditions and market share thresholds); and/or
(iii) related to the quantities purchased (such aspect is generally referred to as 'not conditional' by economists).

Prices can fall within several categories at the same time. For instance, an individualised quantity discount added to a rebate conditional on a market share threshold falls in all three categories. There has to be a reason why all these features are used together. Therefore, it would be artificial to assess these aspects independently of each other. In fact, these features are complementary, and they have an effect that goes beyond the sum of their parts.

The type of tariff that will appear optimal from the perspective of the supplier (and possibly to both the supplier and the buyer) will naturally depend on the issue that the tariff intends to address. However, it will also depend on the type of information that is available and can be legally included in a contract. For instance, if prices have to be based on general terms of sale, the ability to propose completely different price structures will be limited. In such a situation, it will be necessary to alter the *shape* of a general tariff to provide different prices to actors in different situations. This will be necessary when the factors that are relevant for the supplier cannot be observed (e.g., the sales effort of a dealer) or when they cannot be put in a contract (e.g., the retailer's downstream prices).

Non-linear prices expose buyers to different parts of the tariff. They can be useful from the perspective of the seller offering prices to buyers who have different characteristics. It is also useful when buyers have the ability to behave in qualitatively different ways. Exposing buyers to different kinds of prices gives them the incentives to self-select.

These different motives will lead to different kinds of prices. In particular, optimal prices could either be continuous or not. EU case law has regularly referred to rebates as being 'retroactive' when total prices showed a disparity with the quantity purchased. In our opinion, this is a misleading term, as it implies that buyers make sourcing decisions without anticipating the influence of their choices.

EU case law has also emphasised that such disparities lead to negative prices and suction effects, which necessarily correspond to an intent to foreclose. While such a disparity could be intentional, using a few examples in this Section, we will show that it could also be a by-product of the necessity to design tariffs with different levels and slopes. Moreover, as we discuss in *section §6.03[B][2]* below, such disparities should be assessed by taking into account the characteristics of demand and of the types of strategic decisions that the parties are likely to take. It is particularly important to assess whether some customers are likely to cross the thresholds where such discontinuity occurs and, if they do, by what magnitude.

It is generally possible to divide the purposes of non-linear tariffs into two broad categories: (i) prices that respond to asymmetric demands and competitive conditions; and (ii) prices that intend to modify the strategic decisions of the buyer on factors that affect the supplier. In this Section, we refer to 'price discrimination' motives for the first category, and to 'alignment of incentives' motives for the second.

[a] Price Discrimination

Customers may have different characteristics of demand, in their outside options or their bargaining powers. Being able to propose different prices to different customers is always more profitable for sellers. The effects on buyers are more ambiguous. However, in general, economic theory regards price discrimination that allows a producer to increase its total sales as likely to be welfare-enhancing when compared to uniform pricing, as it leads to higher overall output. On that basis, prohibiting the firm from price discriminating would harm consumers, as it would lead to a decrease in the total output.

Price discrimination can also be a response to competitive pressure. A seller may not find it profitable to reduce their price uniformly when dealing with economies of scale. However, they can decide to respond to a rival's aggressive pricing strategy by setting a price closer to their marginal cost through an incremental quantity rebate scheme. This logic could apply either to different customers or to different parts of the demand of a given customer. In this context, if price discrimination can increase the total output sold on the market, it will benefit both sellers and final consumers. This is particularly relevant where price discrimination allows a supplier to recover their fixed costs more efficiently using demand elasticities (this is known as 'Ramsey pricing').

On balance, the benefits of price discrimination to consumers depend on the level of sales with uniform prices and the strength of competition.

It is also important to note that price discrimination could be implemented through any of the types of non-linear prices presented above.[47] It could, in particular, require rebates that appear retroactive (i.e., that are discontinuous). Imagine that two types of buyers can use a seller's product: (small) independent repair shops and (large) industrial manufacturers. Imagine as well that industrial manufacturers have stronger outside options (they could use a wider variety of inputs for instance). Then, competition would lead to higher unit prices for small manufacturers than for larger industrial manufacturers. If the seller cannot propose two different price structures to the two different types of buyers, the optimal tariff is discontinuous. In particular, imposing an incremental discount is logically equivalent to imposing a two-part tariff with a positive fixed fee to the industrial manufacturers, which would reduce the aggregate price they pay.

[b] Alignment of Incentives

In addition, non-linear prices are a natural answer to various types of coordination issues that can emerge in the context of vertical chains. Non-linear prices can therefore correspond to any of the procompetitive rationales of vertical restraints.

Reducing double marginalisation. One of the most common issues that can emerge in the context of vertical chains is double marginalisation. This happens when an intermediary firm earns a positive margin on top of the margin already earned by its supplier. This double marginalisation translates to higher final prices for consumers as compared to the same situation absent an intermediary. Double marginalisation requires significant market power both upstream and downstream. This is not necessarily a very common phenomenon, but it is more likely to emerge in the context of dominant undertakings. Double marginalisation mostly emerges with linear prices. The most natural theoretical answer to it is a tariff that contains a fixed fee and a unit price closer to marginal cost of production. In a context where larger buyers are more likely to have downstream market power (e.g., in local markets) and the supplier cannot offer different price structures to different types of buyers, the optimal price structure will also appear to be 'retroactive'.

Facilitating procompetitive vertical cooperation. In addition, non-linear prices can align the distributor's and the sellers' incentives and induce forms of vertical cooperation that benefit all parties, including consumers. The simplest example of such vertical cooperation concerns joint investments in the quality of service to final consumers. This might require suppliers' investing in their distributors such that better service can be offered to ultimate customers, without concerns about whether the investment will

47. For a general discussion on the use of non-linear prices for price discrimination, *see* Mark Armstrong, *Nonlinear Pricing*, 8(1) Annual Rev. Econ. 583–614 (2016).

be recouped (i.e., avoiding a potential moral hazard where the supplier's investment is relationship-specific). This can also concern incentives that need to be given to sellers to provide an adequate level of service themselves. Sellers add value to suppliers' products when they provide complementary services (e.g., product promotion, after-sales services, ensuring that there is the appropriate stock such that it fits the demand). These complementary services are valuable for both upstream firms and final consumers but are costly for the intermediary customer. As customers choose the level of services related to their private marginal benefit and marginal cost, they do not take into account the benefits to the supplier. By exposing sellers to different levels of unit and aggregate prices depending on their actions (e.g., if they manage to sell larger quantities), non-linear prices are useful to align all parties' interests. In some instances, in particular when final demand is uncertain, or when it is difficult to relate sold quantities to cooperation efforts, aligning all parties' interests will require tariffs that are truly conditional in the sense presented in this introduction, e.g., exclusivity conditions or rebates based on market share thresholds.

That such mechanisms could be procompetitive is not equally plausible in any market context. In addition, they could limit *ex post* competition, for instance by limiting buyers' ability to renegotiate contracts or switch suppliers. The form of protection they provide can however be necessary to preserve *ex ante* incentives to invest.

[2] Theories of Harm

While conditional rebates of any form can correspond to procompetitive rationales, they can also lead to anticompetitive outcomes through various mechanisms whose effects are described as 'theories of harm'. As non-linear prices are intrinsically related to price discrimination, the first theory of harm is that the dominant company is exploiting market power. While such harm is always possible, it is difficult to establish. For this reason, the focus of our paper is on exclusionary conduct. Most of the corresponding theories of harm involve various categories of non-linear pricing identified in the case law and described above. These different theories of harm are likely to emerge under different circumstances and market conditions (e.g., dominance, barriers to entry, economies of scale, levels in the supply chain, degree of downstream competition). Consequently, the economic assessment has to be based on the most likely theory of harm in the legal and economic contexts in which the relevant practice takes place; rather than on the mere form of the practice.

Conditional rebates have most commonly been seen through the lens of naked exclusion:[48] the incumbent finds a way to pay its customers (e.g., through discounts or rebates) to suppress their incentive to switch to a rival.[49] However, other relevant theories of harm include predatory pricing, raising rivals' costs and demand boost. We

48. Ilya R. Segal and Michael D. Whinston, *Naked Exclusion: Comment*, 90(1) American Econ. Rev. 296–309 (2000).
49. Eric B. Rasmusen, J. Mark Ramseyer and John S. Wiley, Jr, *Naked Exclusion*, 81(5) American Econ. Rev. 1137–1145 (1991).

outline the main theories here in turn and analyse how they should be assessed in the context of our economic framework. We then make a similar assessment of the potential procompetitive rationales for non-linear pricing.

[a] Predation

First, non-linear pricing could be used to implement predation. Predation is where a firm sacrifices short-term profits to foreclose rivals, generally by setting a price that no competitor could profitably match in the long term. The company engaging in the predatory strategy must have an advantage which enables it to exclude competitors, and buyers also need to abide by such a coercing scheme. For example, the company may have more resources (liquidity, inputs, capacity or technology), may be an unavoidable trading partner (on the same market or a related one), or there could be asymmetry of information between the different parties. Indeed, predation is generally only capable of having anticompetitive effects where pursued by a dominant firm.

For predation to succeed, the company needs to keep prices lower than would be justified by short term equilibrium conditions for a sufficiently long period to effectively harm and thereby exclude its rival(s). Then, during the recoupment period, it enjoys the release of competitive constraints and recoups the profit lost during the predatory phase. The strategy is profitable only if the expected long-term profit outweighs the short-run profit lost. This requires a sufficient future margin as well as a high chance of succeeding in the rival's foreclosure. A predation strategy is unlikely to succeed in markets with low barriers to entry, because new firms could easily enter and resurrect competition.

Predation in the form of generalised low prices is very expensive for the dominant company. A predatory pricing strategy through rebates directed towards critical parts of the demand is less costly (e.g., because the discount is only offered to customers who are most likely to buy from rivals and/or quantities that are most likely to be addressed by such rivals). However, the assessment of predation with selective prices is largely similar to the assessment of predation with generally low prices (with the exception of coverage, discussed below).

Finally, for the predation theory of harm to hold, the low prices need to prevent access to a sufficient number of customers to be capable of anticompetitively foreclosing competitors. Where general price levels are reduced, in the most classical predation cases, coverage (i.e., the proportion of the customer base covered by the strategy) is sufficient to be capable of generating harm (since it covers all the products and customers that the firm addresses). This is not the case if low prices only cover certain products or customers. And this is generally the case for predation through selective prices. In this context, it needs to be assessed whether these products or customers are sufficiently strategic to allow for competitors to compete effectively on the market (which we discuss in the context of naked exclusion below).

[b] Naked Exclusion

Instead of recouping the sacrificed profit on future sales, it is also possible for dominant firms to recoup these lost profits on certain sales or for certain customers. Such a mechanism is typically defined in the economic literature as 'naked exclusion'.[50]

Buyer coordination. In basic terms, naked exclusion arises when a putative market entrant needs to secure a minimum number of customers to be able to operate, and the incumbent needs to exclude a potential entrant through exclusive dealing. In this setting, the incumbent is able to lock in enough buyers or volumes purchased into the exclusive system to prevent the entrant from achieving the minimum sales it needs to operate profitably. From a first principles approach, this situation would appear most likely to arise where buyers are unable to coordinate themselves 'against' such a strategy and towards a preferred equilibrium.

The incumbent, in such cases, may not need to engage in a below-cost pricing strategy to foreclose competitors. Rasmussen, Ramseyer and Wiley (1991)[51] and later Segal and Whinston (2000)[52] explored the conditions necessary for such naked exclusion to emerge. Segal and Whinston found that when an incumbent firm is able to secure exclusive contracts with buyers, it does not need to rely on buyers' lack of ability to coordinate in order to successfully exclude potential rivals. They also showed that, through the exploitation of buyers' externalities, the incumbent could also profitably exclude the entrant.

Downstream competition. Various papers have taken different views on the importance of downstream competition to the ability of a dominant entity to execute a naked exclusion strategy. Fumagalli and Motta in 2006[53] and Wright in 2009[54] explored the role of downstream competition in a mechanism close to that considered by Segal and Whinston.[55] Their findings were ambiguous. In fact, Fumagalli and Motta found that, when there is strong downstream competition, retailers have a strong incentive not to participate in the exclusive dealing system and to buy from a more efficient supplier. By contrast, Abito and Wright in 2006[56] found that overall, more intense downstream competition seems to favour naked exclusion. With strong competition, downstream firms make very low margins. Therefore, the incumbent and downstream retailers can both increase their profit through exclusive deals that prevent entry and

---

50. The term 'naked exclusion' in this section refers to a particular strand of economic theory. The term also has a narrower meaning in EU law. For example, *see* Eric B. Rasmusen, J. Mark Ramseyer and John S. Wiley, Jr, *Naked Exclusion*, 81(5) American Econ. Rev. 1137–1145 (1991).
51. Eric B. Rasmusen, J. Mark Ramseyer and John S. Wiley, Jr, *Naked Exclusion*, 81(5) American Econ. Rev. 1137–1145 (1991).
52. Ilya R. Segal and Michael D. Whinston, *Naked Exclusion: Comment*, 90(1) American Econ. Rev. 296–309 (2000).
53. Chiara Fumagalli and Massimo Motta, *Exclusive Dealing and Entry, When Buyers Compete*, 96(3) American Econ. Rev. 785–795 (2006).
54. Julian Wright, *Exclusive Dealing and Entry, When Buyers Compete: Comment*, 99(3) American Econ. Rev. 1070–1081 (2009).
55. Ilya R. Segal and Michael D. Whinston, *Naked Exclusion: Comment*, 90(1) American Econ. Rev. 296–309 (2000).
56. Jose Miguel Abito and Julian Wright, *Exclusive Dealing with Imperfect Downstream Competition*, 26(1) Int'l J. Indus. Org. 227–246 (2008).

share the resulting monopoly profits. A few years later in 2009, Wright concluded that downstream competition changes the economics of exclusive dealing but does not make anticompetitive exclusive deals less likely.[57]

Rebate systems can include conditions on buyers to purchase solely or mostly from the dominant supplier. However, such rebates differ from contractual exclusivity in that customers can - at least nominally - freely choose their suppliers. They can decide to fulfil the condition to get the rebate or not. Therefore, the foreclosure theories in cases of rebates linked to exclusive or near-exclusive dealing rely on the price incentives rather than on contractual clauses.

It is important to note that the literature on naked exclusion points towards two versions of this theory of harm. In the first, competitors are naturally prevented from entering due to lack of ability to coordinate among buyers. This outcome could emerge due to market circumstances (including competition law, that prevents buyers from entering into contracts to coordinate their sourcing decisions). This version of the theory of harm does not require large rebates, but successful foreclosure is not certain. In addition, for such a theory to be plausible, buyers' ability to renegotiate needs to be limited. If buyers are able to renegotiate, they could reject exclusivity once other customers do so as well, which would foster entry. For this reason, this theory of harm is unlikely to be plausible, unless potential competitors are very small and contracts (or reference periods of rebates) are particularly long.

The second version of this theory of harm arises in a scenario where a dominant supplier makes coordination difficult for buyers by making selective offers to a particular group (or groups) of customers. Such a strategy is easier to implement, but it requires the existence of one customer, or a group of customers, whose cooperation is sufficient to have a wider impact on the whole market. It is more certain, but it is also more costly: such strategic customers need to be paid a foreclosure premium (i.e., an inducement to accept reduced competition).

[c] Other Theories of Harm Related to Quantity and Target Rebates

Another strand of the literature explores how rebates can be used for downstream firms to coordinate on a less competitive equilibrium and keep out upstream entrants.[58] Rebates can also be used to foreclose a new entrant when there is uncertainty.[59]

---

57. Julian Wright, *Exclusive Dealing and Entry, When Buyers Compete: Comment*, 99(3) American Econ. Rev. 1070–1081 (2009).
58. John Asker and Heski Bar-Isaac, *Raising Retailers' Profits: On Vertical Practices and the Exclusion of Rivals*, 104(2) American Econ. Rev. 672–686 (2014); Patrick DeGraba, *Naked Exclusion by a Dominant Input Supplier: Exclusive Contracting and Loyalty Discounts*, 31(5) Int'l J. Indus. Org. 516–526 (2013); John Simpson & Abraham L. Wichelgren, *Naked Exclusion, Efficient Breach, and Downstream Competition*, 97(4) American Econ. Rev. 1305–1320 (2007).
59. Philippe Aghion and Patrick Bolton, *Contracts as Barrier to Entry*, 77 American Econ. Rev. 388–401 (1987); Philippe Choné and Laurent Linnemer, *Nonlinear Pricing and Exclusion: I. Buyer Opportunism*, 46(2) RAND J. Econ. 217–240 (2015); Philippe Choné and Laurent Linnemer, *Nonlinear Pricing and Exclusion: II. Must-Stock Products*, 47(3) RAND J. Econ. 631–660 (2016).

According to Carlton and Waldman (2008),[60] quantity discounts and bundled pricing mechanisms can benefit consumers by generating efficiency gains or enabling the company to increase its total output through price discrimination. However, they find that quantity discounts can also harm competition to the extent that they deprive rivals of the minimum scale of operation necessary to be efficient and succeed on the market. They propose a test to assess the effect of the discount systems on competition. This test mainly focuses on whether competitors are able to survive and serve their customers as efficiently as they could have in the absence of a potentially abusive pricing scheme.

Regarding quantity discounts, in 2011, Calzolari and Denicolò[61] found that the exclusionary effect of rebate systems on social welfare is ambiguous and depends upon the degree of market asymmetry (in particular, the differences in efficiencies among the market players) and the extent of product substitutability. Indeed, they found that quantity discounts that facilitate the exit of less efficient firms offering close substitutes have a positive effect on social welfare. However, they also observed that quantity discounts reduce consumer surplus and harm rivals in highly asymmetric markets or when products are weak substitutes. To deal with these two opposing effects, they used the Carlton and Waldman test and established market conditions 'thresholds' for which kinds of quantity discounts ought to be prohibited. They conclude that when the market is highly asymmetric and products are fairly close substitutes, authorities should prevent dominant undertakings from offering quantity discounts because it reduces social welfare. This approach certainly requires a detailed assessment.

Salinger in 2017[62] and Chao, Tan and Wong in 2018[63] show that dominant firms can partially foreclose rivals by using target rebate schemes. These models are dependent on the structure of demand being such that customers *must* source some but not all products or volumes from the dominant incumbent (i.e., there is a portion of demand which is captive to the dominant incumbent, and another portion which is 'contestable'). Chao, Tan and Wong developed a model in which an incumbent firm designed a target rebate system that allowed it to tie part of the contestable share of demand to its captive demand. More precisely, for target rebates, a dominant company can use the inelastic part of the demand to induce buyers to purchase a larger proportion of their needs (in the competitive portion of demand) from the incumbent. By using this mechanism, an incumbent firm is able to leverage its market power from the captive to the competitive portion of the demand. They find that these schemes have potential foreclosure effects on the competitive portion of the market.

In Chao, Tan and Wong's model, there are no fixed costs, buyers have no ability to negotiate, and the dominant firm enjoys a captive demand because the capacity of its

60. Dennis W. Carlton and Michael Waldman, *Safe Harbors for Quantity Discounts and Bundling*, EAG Discussion Papers, 200801 (2008).
61. Giacomo Calzolari and Vincenzo Denicolò, *On the Anti-competitive Effects of Quantity Discounts*, 29(3) Int'l J. Indus. Org., 337–341 (2011).
62. Michael A. Salinger, *All-Units Discounts by a Dominant Producer Threatened by Partial Entry*, 81(2) Antitrust L. J, 507–536 (2017).
63. Yong Chao, Guofu Tan and Adam Chi Leung Wong, *All-Units Discounts as a Partial Foreclosure Device*, 49(1) RAND J. Econ, 155–180 (2018).

rival is constrained. They find that in these circumstances, target rebates offered by the dominant firm always harm the rival, the effect on consumer welfare is negatively correlated with the level of the rival's capacity constraint, and that the dominant firm increases its profit only if the pricing scheme does not foreclose the whole demand. Salinger analysed a similar setting and found that cliff discounts could have procompetitive effects but that the harm arose from the resulting decrease in market competition, rather than from exclusion by itself.[64] Salinger also indicated that an optimal target rebate contract did not result in exclusivity.

Therefore, under both Salinger and Chao, Tan and Wong's models, target rebates are seen to have potentially anticompetitive effects, but neither establish that such effects will arise in all circumstances.

[d] Raising Rivals' Costs

Some authors have argued that rebates should not only be seen as a profit sacrifice intended to directly foreclose rivals, but more generally as a strategy to raise rivals' costs. This view was put forward by Moore and Wright in 2015[65] and Salop in 2017.[66] According to this theory, exclusive dealing does not necessarily remove rivals from the market. Rather, it can serve to reduce rivals' economies of scale and, consequently, increase their costs, hindering their competitiveness and reducing competition on the market. While this can cause harm to competitors, the main criticism of this approach is that there is no limiting principle that allows a determination of when consumer harm is likely. Consequently, it is very difficult to imagine how this theory of harm could be translated into a structured rule, like the as efficient principles presented in *section §6.03[D]*.

[e] Demand Boost

Finally, yet another strand of literature promoted by Calzolari and Denicolo in 2015,[67] 2018[68] and 2020,[69] analyses how a dominant company can boost demand for its products through rebates without necessarily sacrificing any profit. Loyalty enhancing rebates, in this case, would have a similar effect to exclusive dealing. They deprive customers of variety and compensate them by lowering the final price. Then, instead of

---

64. Michael A. Salinger, *All-Units Discounts by a Dominant Producer Threatened by Partial Entry*, 81(2) Antitrust L. J. 507–536 (2017).
65. Derek W. Moore and Joshua D. Wright, *Conditional Discounts and the Law of Exclusive Dealing*, 22(5) Geo. Mason L. Rev. 1205–1246 (2015).
66. Steven C. Salop, *The Raising Rivals' Cost Foreclosure Paradigm, Conditional Pricing Practices, and the Flawed Incremental Price-Cost Test*, 81(2) Antitrust L.J., 371–422 (2017).
67. Giacomo Calzolari and Vincenzo Denicolò, *Exclusive Contracts and Market Dominance*, 105(11) Am. Econ. Rev., 3321–3351 (2015).
68. Giacomo Calzolari and Vincenzo Denicolò, *Price-Cost Tests and Loyalty Discounts*, CEPR Discussion Papers, 12924 (2018).
69. Giacomo Calzolari and Vincenzo Denicolò, *Exploring Rivals' Strengths*, CEPR Discussion Paper, DP15520 (2020).

competing on the marginal unit price, the companies compete for a whole market, which eliminates the importance of price differentiation.

This theory of harm assumes that authorities will declare exclusive dealing unlawful when some conditions are satisfied even without applying price cost tests. Indeed, in 2018, Calzolari and Denicolo found that price-cost tests are not relevant to assessing this theory of harm and may be misleading.[70] Moreover, Calzolari and Denicolo (2020) also found that when the dominant company has a strong competitive advantage, exclusive dealing is profitable for the dominant firm and always harms rivals and final consumers.[71] However, when the dominant firm has only a weak advantage, exclusive dealing is not profitable and increases consumer welfare. Indeed, when it holds strong competitive advantages, the dominant company does not need to lower its prices significantly. Then exclusive dealing produces anticompetitive effects because it forces consumers to increase their demand for the dominant firm's product in preference to smaller rivals.

[f] Other Theories

Edlin and Farell[72] add an additional theory of harm to the discussion of anticompetitive rebates. They write that a '*monopoly may not block improving trade between customers and rivals who would offer customers a better deal*'. In a monopoly setting, this can happen because rivals may have to compete against a virtual price lower than the actual price paid by the customers of the dominant firm. To explain this, Edlin and Farell propose the simple following model. The monopolist 'M' charges a high price 'H' but would cut it to a low price 'L' in case of entry. Rival(s) 'R' knows 'L' and cannot compete at this level. But 'R' could offer a median price 'PM' lower than 'H' that would improve the situation of customers. In spite of this, however, 'R' will not enter, conjecturing retaliation at 'L'. Customers will be deprived of an improvement. In the model, 'R' competes with a virtual price lower than that actually charged to customers.

One flaw in the Edlin and Farell model, that the authors concede, is that 'L' represents an *ex post* improving coalition if entry occurs. An even more fatal defect is the following: in real markets, there are two possible states of the world. In the first state of the world – that imagined by E & F – 'R' knows 'L'. There is perfect (or quasi-perfect) information. The reasons for this situation of informational perfection may be diverse: 'M' may have disclosed 'L' in the past during a previous anti-entry campaign; 'M' may be subject to a regulatory duty (to disclose cost information, to approximate prices to cost, etc.); the product manufactured by M is a commodity, technology is mature, etc.; 'M' has explicitly threatened 'R' from 'L' through press announcements, etc. The bottom line is that in all these cases, there is market

---

70. Giacomo Calzolari and Vincenzo Denicolò, *Price-Cost Tests and Loyalty Discounts*, CEPR Discussion Papers, 12924 (2018).
71. Giacomo Calzolari and Vincenzo Denicolò, *Exploring Rivals' Strengths*, CEPR Discussion Paper, DP15520 (2020).
72. Aaron Edlin and Joe Farrell, *Freedom to Trade and the Competitive Process*, NBER Working Paper, 16818 (2011).

transparency on 'L'. With this in mind, it should be equally, and safely, assumed that customers are also aware of L (especially if they are experienced industrial customers). This, in turn, has a critical implication: customers can and will first seek to form an improving coalition with M, and strike the best possible deal with it. And if they do not get it, customers will turn to 'R' who will give them L < PM < H. In both scenarios, there will be an improving coalition as to the real conditions of the market, and the competitive process will be kept intact.

In the second state of the world, 'R' does not know 'L'. There is imperfect information. In this variant, it is reasonable to assume that R must randomly under or overestimate 'L'. The unconfident R will overestimate L (L' < L). They will not enter the market. And the confident R will underestimate L (L' > L). They will thus not compete against the real 'L', but against a price they believe they can beat, and that is lower than 'H'. The confident 'R' will again enter the market and offer better coalitions to customers. The Edlin and Farell model of virtual limit pricing is thus not entirely in line with real-world observations.

[C] Legal Considerations: the Object/Effect Distinction as a Framework for Understanding Treatment of Rebates under Article 102 TFEU

Article 102 TFEU prohibits the abuse of a dominant position in general, and while it specifies certain conduct which could constitute such an abuse, it does not establish an exhaustive list of 'prohibited' conduct.

[1] Categories of Abuse in Context

Over time, numerous categories of abuse have developed under Article 102 TFEU, both in relation to non-pricing abuses (e.g., refusal to supply, tying, exclusivity) and pricing abuses (e.g., predation, margin squeeze), including various categories of abusive rebates (as set out above). For each of those categories, the EC and the EU courts have developed separate legal tests based on varying evidential standards. For some of those categories, it is sufficient to establish that the measure in question is capable of causing anticompetitive effects. In other words, that anticompetitive effects are a plausible outcome of carrying out such a measure. An example is predatory pricing, where the ECJ concluded in *AKZO v. Commission* that below-cost prices are capable of excluding equally efficient rivals.[73] Other categories of abuse impose a stricter standard on the authorities, requesting them to show actual or likely effects, as was the case in *MEO*,[74] where the ECJ held that discriminatory pricing can constitute an abuse only where the behaviour in question '*has an effect on the costs, profits and any other relevant interest*'

73. Case C-62/86, *AKZO v. Commission*, 3.7.1991, ECLI:EU:C:1991:286 (hereinafter '*AKZO v. Commission*'), para. 72.
74. Case C-525/16, *MEO v. Autoridade da Concorrencia*, 19.4.2018, ECLI:EU:C:2018:270 (hereinafter '*MEO*').

of one or more of the companies involved.[75] Finally, for the third category, even a likely anticompetitive effect is not sufficient to establish an abuse: the authorities need to demonstrate 'indispensability' (i.e., that the measure would eliminate all viable competition on the relevant market). This standard has been applied in certain refusal to supply cases.

The multitude of tests has led to much confusion, in particular in relation to the standard to which anticompetitive effects need to be established or observed (e.g., whether the putatively abusive conduct need only be *capable* of restricting competition, or if it must be *likely*).[76] This is partly due to the lack of a clear overarching framework which puts into context the various tests and standards which have been developed on an ad hoc basis. The situation has also not been helped by the fact that the underlying presumptions that form the basis of those tests have often not been made explicit, let alone rigorously tested.

As a working hypothesis, one can identify an inverse relationship between the presumption of harm for a particular type of abuse and the evidential standard which is applied to such an abuse: the less likely the presumed competitive harm of a particular type of unilateral behaviour, the stricter the evidentiary requirement for an authority to establish an abuse. The same is also true in reverse: the more likely the harm, the lower the evidentiary requirement. This is shown in *Figure 6.1*.

Figure 6.1 Categories of Abuse

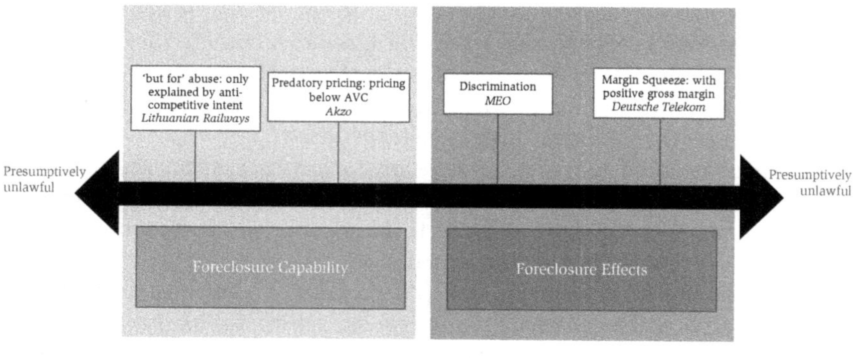

[2] *The Object and Effect Dichotomy under Article 101 TFEU*

The confusion which characterises the position under Article 102 TFEU is in stark contrast to the position under Article 101 TFEU, where the EU courts have done much

75. Case C-525/16, *MEO*, para. 37.
76. Pablo Ibanez Colomo, Capability and likelihood of anticompetitive effects: why the difference exists and why it matters, Chillin'Competition (29 January 2021), https://chillingcompetition.com/2021/01/29/capability-and-likelihood-of-anticompetitive-effects-why-the-difference-exists-and-why-it-matters/.

to develop an overarching framework, and which clarifies the relationship between the two main types of restrictions, namely object and effect restrictions.

AG Bobek in his Opinion in *Budapest Bank*[77] provides a clear synthesis of the legal position.

As a *starting point*, AG Bobek deals with the question of whether the same conduct can restrict competition under Article 101(1) TFEU both 'by object' and 'by effect'. According to AG Bobek, the answer to that question is clearly affirmative:

> The '*object/effect dichotomy is, by and large, a procedural device meant to guide the competition authority on the analysis to be carried out under Article 101(1) TFEU depending on the circumstances of the case. An authority is not required to carry out a fully-fledged analysis of the effects of an agreement – which is often lengthier and more resource intensive – when it maintains and establishes that the agreement is anti-competitive by object*'.[78]

Object restrictions are defined as a type of '*coordination between undertakings which reveal a sufficient degree of harm to competition and for which it is thus unnecessary to examine their effects*'. This is justified by the fact that certain types of arrangement can be regarded '*by their very nature as being harmful to the proper functioning of normal competition since they normally produce inefficient outcomes and reduce consumer welfare*'.[79]

To assess whether a restriction falls into the object category, the EU courts apply a two-stage analysis. At the *first stage*, the focus is mainly on the '*content of the provision of the agreement and its objectives*'; the key question is whether the '*agreement in question falls within a category of agreements whose harmful nature is in the light of experience commonly accepted and easily identifiable*'.[80] Two points to note here: (i) the analysis looks at the nature of the 'category of agreements' (e.g., horizontal price fixing agreement), not the individual agreement in question; and (ii) the emphasis at this stage of the analysis is on 'experience'.

What is required is '*robust and reliable experience about the nature of the agreement*'.[81] If there is no consensus about a practice (e.g., about its nature of effects on competition), then an object analysis is not appropriate. Furthermore, consensus can change over time in light of new economic theories or evidence.

At the *second stage* of the analysis, '*the authority is required to verify that the presumed anticompetitive nature of the agreement, determined on the basis of a merely formal assessment [at stage 1], is not called into question by considerations relating to the legal and economic context in which the agreement was implemented*'.[82]

77. Opinion of AG Bobek, Case C-228/18, *Gazdasági Versenyhivatal v. Budapest Bank Nyrt*, 5.9.2019, ECLI:EU:C:2019:678, (hereinafter '*AG Bobek Budapest Bank Opinion*').
78. Case C-228/18, *AG Bobek Budapest Bank Opinion*, para. 27.
79. Case C-228/18, *AG Bobek Budapest Bank Opinion*, para. 40.
80. Case C-228/18, *AG Bobek Budapest Bank Opinion*, para. 42.
81. Case C-228/18, *AG Bobek Budapest Bank Opinion*, para. 63; cited by the ECJ in C-228/18, *Gazdasági Versenyhivatal v. Budapest Bank Nyrt*, 2.4.2020, ECLI:EU:C:2020:265, para. 76.
82. Case C-228/18, *AG Bobek Budapest Bank Opinion*, para. 43.

AG Bobek makes clear that *'a purely formal assessment of an agreement'* (or one *'detached from reality'* as he puts it) is inappropriate, even in the context of an object restriction, as it *'could lead to condemning innocuous or procompetitive agreements'*.[83]

In order to demonstrate that an agreement is by its very nature harmful to the proper functioning of normal competition, the authorities have to show that the agreement has no plausible purpose other than the restriction of competition. This can be seen as a 'but for' screen: the restrictions make no sense but for their anticompetitive purpose.[84] AG Bobek applies a slightly stricter test: an agreement cannot be classified as restrictive of competition by object where it *'could reasonably have had some pro-competitive effects and those positive effects are not clearly outweighed by other, more profound, anti-competitive effects'*.[85] In other words, what seems to matter may be plausible *net* efficiencies.

Where an agreement has been established as a restriction by object, the authorities need to consider the actual or potential lawful competition which would have existed in the absence of the agreement, and it is open to the parties to argue that an agreement is *'not capable of restricting competition'*.

By contrast, where an examination of the object of the agreement *'does not reveal the effect on competition to be sufficiently deleterious, the consequences of the agreement should then be considered'*[86] (i.e., an effects analysis must be carried out).

[3] Applying the Object and Effect Dichotomy to Article 102 TFEU

[a] Validity of Read Across

The question to what extent it is appropriate to have a read across from the object/effect dichotomy of Article 101(1) TFEU to Article 102 TFEU arises. Indeed, there are arguments against the use of the concepts of 'object abuse' and 'effects abuse' in line with the developments under Article 101(1) TFEU.

First, on a purely formal basis, contrary to Article 101 TFEU, the wording of Article 102 TFEU does not explicitly refer to infringements by object or by effect. Secondly, while the tests under Article 101 TFEU have been binary and can be neatly classified into the two categories of restriction, the tests developed under Article 102 TFEU have shown far greater variance, and trying to categorise each of them as a by object or a by effect abuse may hide numerous shades of grey.

In the authors' view, the object-effect concept can be usefully applied to enforcement under Article 102 TFEU as a lens (and terminology) through which to view enforcement practice, not least in relation to rebates. None of the above objections is particularly persuasive.

While Article 102 TFEU does not explicitly identify an 'object abuse', pragmatism nevertheless suggests a harmonised approach between Articles 101 and 102 TFEU.

83. Case C-228/18, *AG Bobek Budapest Bank Opinion*, para. 45.
84. Case C-307/18, *Generics (UK) Ltd v. CMA*, 30.1.2020, ECLI:EU:C:2020:52.
85. Case C-228/18, *AG Bobek Budapest Bank Opinion*, para. 78.
86. Case C-228/18, *AG Bobek Budapest Bank Opinion*, para. 25.

Since both provisions regularly apply to the same practice (e.g., an exclusivity obligation), it would be hard to justify why one provision would trigger an object analysis while the other would assess the effects of such a practice.

Indeed, AG Bobek has specifically addressed the point that the economic and legal context needs to be considered not only in relation to Article 101 TFEU but also in relation to Article 102 TFEU, citing *Michelin I, Post Danmark I*[87] and *Intel* in support, the latter 'clarifying' the position under *Hoffmann-La Roche*:

> [T]he assessment of a practice under EU competition rules cannot be made in the abstract, but requires an examination of that practice in light of the legal and economic conditions prevailing on the markets concerned. The importance of this principle is confirmed by the fact that it has been found to be valid with regard to both Article 101(1) TFEU and Article 102 TFEU.[88]

The case law under Article 102 TFEU itself has slowly imported components of Article 101 TFEU. For example, in *Post Danmark I* and *Intel*, the EU courts reproduced *expressis verbis* the exoneration clause of Article 101(3) TFEU within Article 102 TFEU, suggesting a similar four-pronged test applied for the evaluation of justifications brought forward by a dominant firm.

More fundamentally, there are three obvious parallels between Article 101(1) TFEU and Article 102 TFEU which strongly support a translation from the object/effects restriction dichotomy under Article 101(1) TFEU into an objects/effects dichotomy for Article 102 TFEU: (i) the 'capability' standard developed by the courts under Article 102 TFEU has strong similarities with the test for object restrictions under Article 101 TFEU; (ii) the rationale for and presumptions underlying the different standards in both provisions are the same; and (iii) the 'but for' efficiency screen under Article 101(1) TFEU is reflected in a number of the Article 102 TFEU categories to which the capability standard is applicable. These three points are further explored in the remainder of this Section.

[b] Capability Standard and Object Abuses

The analytical framework developed by the ECJ for Article 102 TFEU abuses includes a 'capability' standard (i.e., the court considers whether the impugned conduct is capable of foreclosing competitors). As we will demonstrate in more detail in the next two Sections, this framework in many ways mirrors the test which AG Bobek set out in *Budapest Bank* for Article 101 TFEU.

The 'object abuse' framework is neatly encapsulated by the ECJ in *Michelin I*:

> In deciding whether Michelin NV abused its dominant position in applying its discount system, it is therefore necessary to *consider all the circumstances*, particularly the *criteria and rules for the grant of the discount*, and to investigate whether, in providing an *advantage not based on any economic service justifying it*,

87. Case C-209/10, *Post Danmark v. Konkurrenceradet*, 27.3.2012, ECLI:EU:C:2012:172 (hereinafter '*Post Danmark I*'), paras 28–35.
88. Case C-228/18, *AG Bobek Budapest Bank Opinion*, para. 46.

> the *discount tends to remove or restrict the buyer's freedom* to choose his sources of supply, to bar competition from access to the market, to apply dissimilar conditions to equivalent transactions with other trading parties or to strengthen the dominant position by distorting competition (emphasis added).[89]

Unpacking that framework reveals the key building blocks which we also *see*: first, the question is whether the type or category of unilateral conduct is harmful in nature (i.e., whether the discount '*tends to remove or restrict the buyer's freedom*'). In answering this question, the authorities are asked not only to assess the '*criteria and rules for the grant of the discount*' but also to consider all (other) circumstances. Finally, the framework also takes into account efficiency considerations ('*advantages based on any economic service justifying it*').

As we will show in more detail in *sections §6.04* and *§6.05*, there are however also noticeable differences between the object restriction, as set out in *Budapest Bank*, and the 'object abuses' as defined by the Focus Cases.

[c] Presumption of Object Abuses

In addition to the similarities of the analytical framework for object restrictions and abuses which are subject to the capability standard, there are also strong parallels regarding the underlying presumptions.

As the CFI put it in *Michelin II*: 'If it is shown that the object pursued by the conduct of an undertaking in a dominant position is to limit competition, that conduct will also be liable to have such an effect'.[90]

The CFI illustrates that point by referring to *AKZO v. Commission* where '*prices below average variable costs applied by an undertaking in a dominant position are regarded as abusive in themselves because the only interest which the undertaking may have in applying such prices is that of eliminating competitors*'.[91]

However, at the same time, if the dominant firm can demonstrate that, given the market circumstances the above presumption of harm is not valid, then the capability standard may not be appropriate. An example is zero pricing by multisided platforms, which may be driven by efficiency considerations (namely to solve the 'chicken and egg problem' of multisided platforms and to get all sides on board) rather than an anticompetitive object.[92]

The parallels to Article 101(1) TFEU and the considerations by the courts in relation to multisided platforms, such as those in *Cartes Bancaires*,[93] are glaringly obvious.

89. Case C-322/81, *Michelin I*, para. 73.
90. Case T-203/01, *Michelin II*, para. 241.
91. Case C-62/86, *AKZO v. Commission*, para. 72.
92. Case HC-2013-000090, *Streetmap.EU Ltd v. Google Inc. & Ors* [2016] EWHC 253 (Ch).
93. Case C-67/13 P, *Groupement des cartes bancaires*, 11.9.2014, ECLI:EU:C:2014:2204.

[d] *The 'But For' Logic of Object Infringements*

The underlying logic of the framework for object restrictions, as outlined by AG Bobek in *Budapest Bank,* is that an object approach is only suitable where the restriction imposed by the parties in question cannot be explained in any other way 'but for' the anticompetitive object of the arrangement; in other words, there can be no other (plausible) explanation. By contrast, if the parties to the arrangements can adduce a plausible efficiency justification, an effects analysis is required.

The same 'but for' logic has been applied in a number of cases in the context of Article 102 TFEU. The courts have considered conduct to be abusive (by object) on the basis that it could have no plausible purpose other than the elimination of competition. For example, in *Lithuanian Railways,* the incumbent railway operator dismantled 19 km of railway track connecting Lithuania and Latvia.[94] The General Court ('GC') found that the objective of this conduct was to prevent one of its major customers from using the services of a competitor. Rather than testing whether the conduct could be considered abusive under the essential facilities doctrine, the GC held that *'[i]t was sufficient, subject to any objective justification, to show that the conduct in question was such as to restrict competition, and in particular, to constitute an impediment to market entry'*.[95] A similar approach was taken in *Racal Decca* where the firm introduced changes in radio signals ('jamming') for the purpose of causing its rivals' products to malfunction.[96] After intervention by the EC, the firm agreed to abandon these practices.[97]

Finally, a third example which falls under the 'but for' logic is the *AstraZeneca*[98] case: as Colomo points out: *'Providing misleading information to a patent authority does not seem to serve any purpose other than the restriction of competition (via the extension of the protection)'*.[99] Colomo cites the *Hoffmann-La Roche* ruling of 2018[100] in support of this proposition:

> If providing misleading information by means of an agreement is deemed to have as its object of the case, I fail to see how it would be possible to reach a different

94. T-814/17, *Lithuanian Railways v. Commission,* 18.10.2020, ECLI:EU:T:2020:545, para. 99 (hereinafter '*Lithuanian Railways*').
95. T-814/17, *Lithuanian Railways,* para. 99.
96. Commission Decision 89/113/EEC of 21 December 1988 on IV/30.979 and 31.394 – Decca Navigator System, OJ L 43, 15.2.1989 (hereinafter '*Racal Decca*').
97. *Racal Decca Marine Navigation Limited,* Commission Press Release (22 December 1988), https://ec.europa.eu/commission/presscorner/detail/en/IP_88_866%3e.
98. Case C-457/10 P, *AstraZeneca AB v. European Commission,* 6.11.2012, ECLI:EU:C:2012:770 (hereinafter '*AstraZeneca*').
99. Pablo Ibanez Colomo, *Persistent Myths in Competition Law (V): 'There Is No Such Thing as an Abuse by Object (or by Effect) under Article 102 TFEU'*, Chillin'Competition (10 January 2020), https://chillingcompetition.com/2020/01/10/persistent-myths-in-competition-law-v-there-is-no-such-thing-as-an-abuse-by-object-or-by-effect-under-article-102-tfeu/.
100. Case C-179/16, *F. Hoffmann-La Roche Ltd and Others v. Autorità Garante della Concorrenza e del Mercato,* 23.1.18, ECLI:EU:C:2018:25.

conclusion under Article 102 TFEU (and the analysis in AstraZeneca by the EU courts only confirms this point).[101]

[D] Economic Building Blocks for an Effects-Based Analysis

This section considers what structural rules of reason may be developed based upon the economic literature covered in *section §6.03[B]* above in order to facilitate an effects-based analysis of conditional rebates. Our presentation of the theories of harm shows that three broad categories emerge:

(i) predation, which is a dynamic theory of harm where foreclosure is followed by a recoupment;
(ii) theories of harm where customers are directly compensated for their exclusivity and where recoupment takes place simultaneously (naked exclusion with offer targeted at strategic customers is the simplest conceptual version of this theory of harm); and
(iii) theories of harm where customers are not compensated (or where there is no profit sacrifice in the first place).

We have shown that the plausibility of these theories of harm, and in turn, of potential procompetitive justifications, will depend on specific market circumstances. For instance, it is more likely that schemes that significantly change customers' incentives to choose suppliers *ex post*, correspond to procompetitive rationales when the supplier sells non-standardised products that require significant specific investments and when renegotiation is unavoidable. Such conditions are not met in all markets and in all circumstances.

In the presence of established potential sources of pro and anti-competitive effects, it is perfectly understandable that different legal systems might choose slightly different legal standards depending on their aversion to type 1 or type 2 errors. It is, however, important that all legal systems rely on consistent principles, based on economic theory and experience. It is also important that the standards are fair and symmetrical. In particular, if presumptions of harm are wide and the legal standard is relatively easy to meet for enforcers, the efficiency of the legal system requires that the standard for rebuttals is equally open and transparent. In this sense, one could therefore consider that the legal standard of plausibility for procompetitive rationales presented in *section §6.03[C]* is a natural counterweight to the existence of wide presumptions of harm in EU law.

In this Section, we review the main building blocks for a structured rule of reason which might correspond to the theories of harm presented above and facilitate an effects analysis. We do not cover predation, as – being clearly an 'object' abuse – the

101. Pablo Ibanez Colomo, *Persistent Myths in Competition Law (V): 'There Is No Such Thing as an Abuse by Object (or by Effect) under Article 102 TFEU'*, Chillin'Competition (10 January 2020), https://chillingcompetition.com/2020/01/10/persistent-myths-in-competition-law-v-there-is-no-such-thing-as-an-abuse-by-object-or-by-effect-under-article-102-tfeu/.

legal and economic assessment of predation is conceptually simpler and clear principles are established and understood (i.e., that prices below short term (or marginal) costs are generally considered to be an abuse of dominance 'by object'[102]). Nonetheless, the established rules in relation to predation provide a helpful benchmark for our approach. While the test does not correspond exactly to the predation theories of harm delineated by economic theory (for economists, predation is not per se related to below-cost prices, but to short term profit sacrifice), it does correspond to the main mechanics and focuses on aspects at least positively *correlated* with most economic theories. It also focuses on the exclusion of at least as efficient competitors; as such exclusion is *more* likely to harm consumers. It is also a good rule because it is transparent and easy to administer. We therefore use this as a benchmark to assess how the two other classes of theories of harm could be translated into structural tests for evaluating the effects of conditional rebates, emphasising the relationship between the width of the presumption of harm and the fair standard for its rebuttal.

[1] Theories of Harm That Require a Significant Direct Profit Sacrifice (Naked Exclusion)

We turn first to the issue of foreclosure through various forms of individualised rebates. Whether based on exclusivity, growth targets or volumes, the important aspect for the purpose of this theory of harm is that the rebate is offered to some (if successfully executed, strategic) customers, but not all customers (i.e., the dominant supplier does not need to reduce its prices to all customers). What criteria that is equivalent to that used for predation could be used according to our framework to delineate, at least as a first pass, whether this theory of harm is particularly likely? The theory itself was actually developed with naked exclusivity in mind. Consequently, this theory of harm relies on the existence of some benefit to the customer which *induces* it to procure exclusively from the dominant supplier. The form of such inducement (incremental or with discontinuities, *ex ante* or *ex post*, individualised or standardised) is not directly relevant to the likelihood of the theory of harm being established (though it may become *indirectly* relevant if (i) they were at least *negatively correlated* with features that made procompetitive rationales more or less likely; or (ii) they were *positively correlated* with features that makes this theory of harm more likely).

The theory of harm (corresponding to the second, more plausible version of the naked exclusion theory outlined in *section §6.03[B]* above) is rather straightforward and rests on two main pillars:

(i) the rebates or discounts targets customers that are particularly strategic for competitors to enter or expand; and
(ii) the strategic customers need to receive a sufficiently large inducement to voluntarily participate in the scheme.

102. Case C-62/86, *AKZO v. Commission*, para. 71.

The question of individualisation identified in the case law is therefore indirectly relevant. However, it is not the fact that thresholds or nominal rebates/discounts are individualised that is important. Rather, what is significant is that some actors receive substantially larger inducements than others. Moreover, these customers need to be strategic for competition to develop in the market. Last, the inducements they receive need to be 'significant'. Typically, the dominant company needs to compensate the loss that this strategic consumer would gain from more open competition (i.e., the dominant company pays a foreclosure premium). This last factor is important to differentiate a situation where customers with more bargaining power simply get a 'better deal' from a situation where they are bribed to prevent entry or expansion.

For this reason, as for low prices, it is necessary to find a robust criterion to qualify whether an inducement is significant or not or, in other words, whether these strategic customers get too good a deal. This criterion would also ideally need to identify the types of non-linear prices that are unlikely to be associated with procompetitive rationales. As for predation, different legal systems might choose slightly different rules depending on agencies' priors and experience, as well as on their balancing of type 1 and 2 errors. However, the building blocks should be similar and when presumptions are wide, standards for rebuttals have to be equally clear, wide and fair.

The question in this context is whether one can trust the shape of the non-linear prices to design such a rule. As made clear earlier, what directly matters for the theory of harm is the magnitude of the inducement, not the shape. The case law in Europe seems to have considered that the existence of a discontinuity in the tariff meant that the inducement was more likely to be 'significant', at least locally (a discontinuity in the tariff necessarily means negative prices, at least formally and locally). However, this discontinuity could be relatively small and a point in customers' demand that does not lead to any real suction effects for competitors. Conversely, well-targeted and significant discounts can have real effects.

On balance, there exist small rebates and large discounts, and it seems difficult to argue that one type of linear price fits more squarely within this theory of harm (which was initially written with exclusive contracts in mind). By the same token, while some types of efficiencies require different types of non-linearities, all types of tariffs could correspond to some types of efficiencies.

In fact, likelihood of harm and plausibility of procompetitive rationales are multidimensional and sit on a sliding scale. For this reason, it is very difficult to find types of prices that are entirely safe (and this is the reason why the case law does not provide strong guidance on what is safe from a compliance perspective). It is also very difficult to find types of non-linear prices that cannot be justified by procompetitive rationales under certain circumstances.

Therefore, it is difficult to really trust the formal characteristics of the rebate. The alternative is to directly assess the magnitude of the inducements provided by the rebates. In the same way as it is difficult to determine whether prices are large or small in the abstract when assessing predation, it is difficult to assess whether a rebate or a discount is large or small without any reference to a relevant benchmark. The EC considered that such a relevant benchmark would be to compare the rebate or discount at risk with the margin that a competitor that is at least as efficient would make for a realistic order. Such an order could differ from the total demand of particular customers for various reasons (i.e., the demand is not entirely contestable).

This approach forms the basis of the structured rule of reason described in the Priorities Guidance (with the assessment of the strategic nature of the customers covered by the tariff).[103] As for predation, this approach does not perfectly match the theories of harm. It is however directly correlated with factors that matter for the theory of harm. For this reason, such an approach also seems relevant to assess any form of exclusion that requires a significant inducement (i.e.; whenever consumers need to be directly compensated for the exclusivity).

[2] All Other Theories of Harm That Do Not Require a Significant Direct Profit Sacrifice

The AEC based approach set out above might not, however, be the most effective test to assess any of the other types of theories of harm where strong direct inducements are not necessary. This can be the case, for instance, because foreclosure emerges due to a lack of coordination between buyers, or because any benefit of entry could be dissipated by downstream competition. These theories are more challenging to assess. They could, by definition, emerge in the presence of inducements, which could, purely on the basis of their magnitude, appear benign.

To put it differently: these theories of harm have sometimes been used by enforcers to justify very strict and wide prohibitions. Such an approach does not correspond to the economic framework set out in *section §6.03[B]*, because as we have shown, the likelihood of these theories of harm being established cannot be assumed in all circumstances.

In fact, all the theories of harm that can lead to anticompetitive foreclosure on the basis of 'small' inducements rely on assumptions that can be identified and tested. First, if one believes that customers do not need to be compensated for exclusivity because the benefits stemming from upstream competition would be dissipated by downstream competition, one should be able to find traces of such beliefs in customers' internal documents. Second, foreclosure is more likely to emerge with rebates that cover a large share of the total demand, whether they are set on an individual or standardised basis. These two assumptions provide two potentially useful screens: whether customers' internal documents evidence a view that upstream competition will not deliver benefits, and whether the rebates cover a large share of total contestable demand.

Most of these theories also rely on a very strong form of commitment to the tariff (i.e., they would not hold in cases where customers can easily renegotiate). Such commitment is more likely to be present in some market circumstances than in others, but it is difficult to identify a clear structural rule of reason to evaluate whether this is

103. Priorities Guidance, paras 20 et seq.

the case in a given market. An assessment of such theories of harm therefore necessarily requires an analysis of 'all the circumstances'.

§6.04 THE FOCUS CASES AND THE EVOLUTION OF THE LEGAL APPROACH TO REBATES

The EC and EU courts' approaches to assessment of conditional rebates can be considered to fall into three broad 'eras' (these eras are specific to conditional rebates under Article 102 TFEU and do not form part of a coherent approach across all enforcement under Article 102 TFEU[104]). In the first era, early cases, including *Michelin I*, established the principle that quantity rebates are generally permissible, while fidelity rebates (covering exclusivity rebates and target rebates) are generally not. In *Michelin I*, the Court took pains to point out that to assess whether a rebate was fidelity-inducing, all circumstances needed to be taken into account, including the relative market position of the dominant firm and its competitors. In the second era – where *BA/Virgin* and *Michelin II* fall – this approach was 'toughened', so that more kinds of rebates were considered to fall within the 'fidelity' category; the by object approach to the assessment of rebates was entrenched and more emphasis was put on the formal characteristics of the rebates. Finally, in the third era, in the period since *Michelin II* and *BA/Virgin*, the framework for conditional rebates has shifted from an object approach to an effects approach. This shift was set out in the Article 102 TFEU Priority Guidance, which acted as a catalyst for a greater emphasis on likely effects. It has since then also been reflected in the case law, most recently in the Court's decision in *Intel*.

Below, we summarise the evolution of approach to rebates in EU competition law through the lens of the Focus Cases. In all three Focus Cases, while the core anticompetitive harm identified related to the loyalty-inducing effects of the rebate scheme in question, the EC and EU courts also made findings that the rebate schemes were variously discriminatory, unfair and/or had a market-partitioning effect. These 'non-core' effects of the rebates were in all cases closely linked to the loyalty-inducing nature of the scheme. Indeed, in *Michelin II* the CFI found that a loyalty-inducing rebate system had foreclosure effects regardless of whether it was discriminatory.[105] The CFI also acknowledged that '*the alleged unfairness of the system was closely linked to its loyalty-inducing effect [and that] ... it must be held that a loyalty-inducing rebate system is, by its very nature, also partitioning, since it is designed to prevent the customer from obtaining supplies from other manufacturers*'.[106] This paper, therefore, focuses on the

---

104. For example, while Case C-95/04 P, *BA/Virgin* and Case T-203/01, *Michelin II* sit in the second, formalistic, era, other cases at the same time adopted an effects-based approach: e.g., Case T-65/98, *Van den Bergh Foods v. Commission*, 23.10.2003, ECLI:EU:T:2003:281, in which the CFI's judgment was delivered just a month after the CFI judgment (of a differently constituted chamber) in Case T-203/01, *Michelin II*, on 23 October 2003.
105. Case T-203/01, *Michelin II*, para. 65.
106. Case T-203/01, *Michelin II*, para. 66.

EC and EU courts' findings in relation to the loyalty-inducing nature of the rebate schemes.

[A] *Michelin I*: Early Consideration of the Fidelity/Quantity Rebate Distinction

[1] Background

In 1975, *Suiker Unie*[107] first established the principle that quantity rebates are generally considered not to give rise to foreclosure effects and are therefore presumptively *lawful*; and by contrast, fidelity (or fidelity-inducing) rebates typically lead to foreclosure and are presumptively *unlawful*. *Sukier Unie* considered numerous restrictions imposed by various sugar producers under Articles 101 and 102 TFEU. Most critically for current purposes, the case considered a rebate granted by SZV (a sugar producer), which was expressly tied to exclusivity. There was clear evidence of the rebate being removed when SZV became aware that a customer had purchased from an alternative supplier. The EC reasoned that because customers were dependent on SZV for at least a certain portion of their supplies, it would quickly become uneconomic for them to purchase from any alternative suppliers. Further, SZV had a good insight into this because it could estimate the average volumes purchased annually (which did not change significantly). The rebate was therefore found to further consolidate SZV's already dominant position.[108] Part of the EC's criticism of the rebate was that it '*does not depend on the amount bought*',[109] thus, the distinction between quantity-based and loyalty rebates was born – in the context of a rebate explicitly dependent on exclusivity. These findings were endorsed by the ECJ.[110]

The principle that rebates dependent on exclusivity infringe Article 102 TFEU was upheld and formalised in *Hoffmann-La Roche*. Like *Suiker Unie*, the case dealt with a system that was – for the most part – explicitly dependent upon customers obtaining all their supplies from Roche. The 'fidelity rebate' (as the EC referred to it) was one mechanism for ensuring exclusivity which existed in many of Roche's customer contracts. The ECJ's focus was very much on the link with exclusivity, finding that:

> obligations ... to obtain supplies exclusively from a particular undertaking, whether or not they are in consideration of rebates or of the granting of fidelity rebates intended to give the purchaser an incentive to obtain his supplies exclusively from the undertaking in a dominant position, are incompatible with the objective of undistorted competition within the Common Market ... The fidelity rebate, unlike quantity rebates exclusively linked with the volume of purchases from the producer concerned, is designed through the grant of a financial

107. Case C-40/73, *Cooperatieve Vereniging Suiker Unie UA v. Commission of the European Communities*, 16.12.1975, ECLI:EU:C:1975:174 (hereinafter '*Suiker Unie*').
108. Case C-40/73, *Suiker Unie*, page 1689.
109. Commission Decision 73/109/EEC of 2 January 1973 on IV/26 918 – European sugar industry, OJ L 140, 26.5.1973 (hereinafter '*Suiker Unie (EC)*'), page 39.
110. Case C-40/73, *Suiker Unie*, page 2005.

> advantage to prevent customers from obtaining their supplies from competing producers.[111]

However, in addition to the fixed rebates considered, which were explicitly dependent upon exclusivity, *Hoffmann-La Roche* also looked at rebates which were applicable at progressive rates (generally from 1% to 3%) based on the volume purchased. The ECJ found that although such rebates appeared prima facie to be based on quantities rather than fidelity:

> 'an examination of them however shows that they are in fact a specially worked out form of fidelity rebate'[112] as they were 'not dependent on quantities fixed objectively and applicable to all possible purchasers but on estimates made, from case to case, for each customer according to the latter's presumed capacity of absorption, the objective which it is sought to attain being not the maximum quantity but the maximum requirements'.[113]

These rebates were therefore also considered illegal, and this finding laid the groundwork for the assessment that followed in the Focus Cases.

Michelin I came just six years after *Suiker Unie*, in 1981,[114] and built directly on the law established in *Hoffmann-La Roche*. *Michelin I* therefore itself became key in this early development of the law on rebates, as summarised in depth below.

[2] Michelin I

[a] Conduct under Scrutiny

Michelin I considered a rebate system operated by Michelin NV for tyre dealers. The rebate system had various components, most (but not all) of which were target rebates.

First, the 'invoice discount' was granted to all dealers on each invoice. The invoice discount was at a fixed rate for all dealers, announced through a circular at the beginning of each calendar year.

In addition, various further 'bonuses' were available. The rebates were linked to the individual dealers increasing (or in a difficult economic situation, maintaining) purchases from Michelin NV, the estimated sales potential of the dealer, and the share of Michelin NV tyres in the dealers' sales (referred to as 'temperature Michelin'). In general, the targets (the number of which differed over time) were fixed in such a way that the target level was higher than the corresponding purchases in the previous year (though the discount did not increase). This meant that the rebate was tied to sales growth. The periods over which the bonuses were calculated varied over time from annual, to a monthly advance on the annual bonus and to a monthly and then four-monthly bonus. These 'bonuses' were generally informally negotiated with dealers without written confirmation. Michelin NV's internal documentation showed a

111. Case C-85/76, *Hoffmann-La Roche*, para. 90.
112. Case C-85/76, *Hoffmann-La Roche*, para. 98.
113. Case C-85/76, *Hoffmann-La Roche*, para. 100.
114. Commission Decision 81/969/EEC, *Michelin I (EC)*.

large degree of variation in the invoice discounts and bonuses paid to its dealers and that they were set in an ad hoc manner.

Separately, the case also considered an extra bonus of 0.5% granted in 1977, which was contingent on a certain target being achieved on the sale of light tyres. This was a one-off rebate offered at a time when Michelin NV was unable to meet demand for heavy tyres and wanted to stimulate demand for light tyres. There was also a 2% 'cash discount' available for payments made in accordance with the agreed terms.

[b] Market Definition and Assessment of Dominance

The EC considered the relevant market to be the market for new replacement tyres for trucks and buses in the Netherlands. Michelin NV's dominant position was considered apparent from its large market share compared to that of its competitors.

In its dominance assessment, the EC noted that Michelin NV had the highest market share in the European Economic Community and the second highest worldwide. Goodyear held the highest. Between 1975 and 1980, Michelin NV's share of the market for new truck and bus tyres in the Netherlands was between 57% and 65%, while competitors' market shares were between 4% and 8%. Goodyear was not considered to exercise any competitive pressure on the Dutch market (although the EC did not cite any evidence to support this, such as analysis of import-export flow or trade barriers). The EC found that consumers had a strong preference for Michelin NV's tyres and were loyal to its products because of perceived reliability and quality. This was considered an important determinant of Michelin NV's dominance. The ECJ similarly emphasised that Michelin NV was the only supplier on the market for certain tyres and that a dealer established in the Netherlands normally could not afford not to sell its tyres.

The EC also relied upon the rebate system to support its finding of dominance, stating that the '*system is of such a nature that it can only be practiced by an enterprise in a dominant position*'[115] and that dealers would never accept this system imposed by other manufacturers (who generally offered only an invoice discount, but at a much higher level than Michelin NV's, sometimes supplemented by an end of year bonus of a few per cent).[116]

[c] Legal Test to Establish Abuse

[i] Application of the Existing *Suiker Unie/Hoffmann-La Roche* Framework

In *Michelin I* the legal test applied was whether the rebate system represented a 'fidelity' or 'quantity-based' system. The ECJ drew a distinction between a quantity rebate '*which is linked solely to the volume of purchases from the manufacturer*

115. Commission Decision 81/969/EEC, *Michelin I (EC)*, para. 48.
116. Commission Decision 81/969/EEC, *Michelin I (EC)*, para. 22.

concerned'[117] and a fidelity rebate '*which by offering customers financial advantages tends to prevent them from obtaining their supplies from competing manufacturers*',[118] the latter of which was clearly illegal, referring to established law from *Suiker Unie* and *Hoffmann-La Roche*.

However, the ECJ was unable to neatly slot Michelin NV's rebate system into either the quantity or fidelity categories, noting that while it was not a '*mere quantity discount*',[119] it also '*did not require dealers to enter into any exclusive dealing arrangements or to obtain a specific proportion of their supplies from Michelin NV*'.[120]

Michelin I demonstrates the limited flexibility and direct applicability of the 'fidelity rebates' /'quantity rebates' framework. The EC argued that Michelin NV's target-based rebates were akin to exclusivity rebates as defined in *Hoffmann-LaRoche*, saying that '*a system based on annual targets puts strong pressure on the dealer to obtain his supplies from the same supplier because of the dealers' uncertainty as to the rates of discount and the risk of losing some of the discount if the sales target is not attained*'.[121] In response, Michelin NV denied that dealers are dependent upon it and that the purpose of the system is merely to '*reward the purchase of increasing quantities of goods*'.[122]

[ii] Development of a New Legal Framework for Assessment of 'Target Discounts'

The ECJ, therefore, found that it was '*necessary to consider all the circumstances, particularly the criteria and rules for the grant of the discount, and to investigate whether, in providing an advantage not based on any economic service justifying it, the discount tends to restrict the buyer's freedom to choose his sources of supply, to bar competitors from access to the market*'.[123] Unpacking this framework reveals the following building blocks for assessments of both harm and efficiencies.

With respect to assessment of harm, the test is outlined as to whether '*the discount tends to remove or restrict the buyer's freedom to choose his source of supply or to bar competitors from access to the market*'.[124] In other words, the question the ECJ posed is whether the rebate falls within a category of rebates that can be expected to (or 'tends to') have a harmful impact on competition (namely to remove or restrict the buyer's freedom to choose his sources). In answering this question, the ECJ makes clear that it is necessary, first, to assess the criteria and rules for the grant of the rebate; and subsequently to consider all other circumstances. With respect to assessment of

117. Case C-322/81, *Michelin I*, para. 71.
118. *Ibid.*
119. Case C-322/81, *Michelin I*, para. 72.
120. *Ibid.*
121. Case C-322/81, *Michelin I*, para. 78.
122. Case C-322/81, *Michelin I*, para. 79.
123. Case C-322/81, *Michelin I*, para. 73. The framework continued '*to apply dissimilar conditions to equivalent transactions ... or to strengthen the dominant position by distorting competition*', but these potential harms are not considered in depth in this paper.
124. Case C-322/81, *Michelin I*, para. 73.

efficiencies, the test is whether the rebate provides an advantage based on *'any economic service justifying it'*.[125]

[d] Assessment of Foreclosure Harm

[i] Rebates Tending to Harm Competition

Criteria and rules for the rebate system: The EC assessed the various criteria and rules for the rebate system. First, it considered the target nature of the rebate. The EC considered that the rebate system was clearly aimed at putting strong pressure on the dealer to sell more Michelin tyres each year than the previous year, noting, in particular, the fact that targets were set *'individually and selectively'* for each dealer.[126] The EC considered that the pressure was increased through regular visits made by Michelin NV representatives to dealers to check that targets were being reached (i.e., the 'temperature Michelin'), and the lack of transparency in relation to the rebate.[127]

The size of the rebate was also considered. Michelin NV raised the point that the size of the rebate was only limited. This was rejected by the EC, which found *'it is well known in the tyre trade that each percentage point more or less can play a critical role for the dealer's profitability'*.[128] It was similarly rejected by the ECJ on the basis of other existing factors discussed below (e.g., length of reference period and retroactive effect).

Both the EC and the ECJ considered the retroactive effect coupled with the length of the reference period (annual) to have important implications in terms of its effect on dealers. The ECJ makes the point that:

> any system under which discounts are granted according to the quantities sold during a relatively long reference period has the inherent effect, at the end of that period of increasing pressure on the buyer to reach the purchase figure needed to obtain the discount or to avoid suffering the expected loss for the entire period.[129]

All (other) circumstances: The EC and the ECJ were at pains to emphasise the relevance of wider market conditions for the analysis. Two factors were considered important when arriving at their ultimate conclusion that the rebate scheme had abusively bound dealers to Michelin NV.

First, the wide divergence between Michelin NV's market shares and those of its main competitors was considered important. The ECJ noted that other dealers would have to make up the largest absolute value of Michelin's annual target rebate over a much smaller volume of sales, in order to have an offer that could induce dealers *not* to meet their targets with Michelin NV.[130]

---

125. *Ibid.*
126. Commission Decision 81/969/EEC, *Michelin I (EC)*, para. 37.
127. Commission Decision 81/969/EEC, *Michelin I (EC)*, para. 38.
128. Commission Decision 81/969/EEC, *Michelin I (EC)*, para. 43.
129. Case C-322/81, *Michelin I*, para. 81.
130. Case C-322/81, *Michelin I*, para. 82.

Second, the lack of transparency of Michelin's entire rebate system, which also changed on several occasions, and the fact that neither the scale of the sales targets nor the rebates relating to them were communicated in writing. The ECJ (like the EC) found that this made it difficult for the dealers to predict with any confidence the effect of attaining their targets or failing to do so.[131]

Object assessment regarding foreclosure: In light of the above factors, the EC and the ECJ concluded that dealers were under considerable pressure, especially towards the end of the year, to attain Michelin NV's sales targets.[132] The ECJ found that the overall system was calculated to prevent dealers from being able to '*select freely at any time in light of the market situation the most favourable of the offers made by the various competitors and to change suppliers without suffering any appreciable economic disadvantage*'[133] and therefore constituted an abuse of dominance.[134]

[e] Assessment of Efficiencies

The assessment of efficiencies in *Michelin I* can fairly be described as minimalist. As mentioned in section §6.04[A][2][c][ii] above, the type of efficiencies to be taken into account is defined very narrowly (i.e., such that efficiencies are only relevant to the extent that the rebate provides an advantage based on any economic service justifying it).[135] The Court does not expand on this further. It distinguishes the rebate system in question from a mere volume discount, suggesting that a volume efficiency rationale may be accepted but provides no guidance on how such a discount or efficiency would be measured.

In any event, Michelin NV put forward two efficiency justifications. First, that the rebates were intended to lead to greater sales (though the classification of this argument as an efficiency justification is questionable). Second, and more clearly, that the rebates enabled Michelin NV to better plan its production. On the latter, Michelin NV also argued that the lack of official statistics in the Netherlands during 1975–1980 required the company to estimate sales through its customers, resulting in frequent meetings to measure dealers' 'temperature Michelin' and that such rebate schemes allowed them to plan their supply to the dealers.

Both efficiency defences got short shrift, with the ECJ finding that '*neither the wish to sell more nor the wish to spread production more evenly can justify such a restriction of the customer's freedom of choice and independence*'.[136]

131. Case C-322/81, *Michelin I*, para. 83.
132. Case C-322/81, *Michelin I*, para. 84.
133. Case C-322/81, *Michelin I*, para. 85.
134. Case C-322/81, *Michelin I*, para. 86.
135. Case C-322/81, *Michelin I*, para. 73.
136. Case C-322/81, *Michelin I*, para. 85.

[f] Conclusions

Michelin I saw the EC, and later the ECJ, take a relatively cautious approach to fidelity rebates. Although the test was articulated as one of capability, the ECJ did consider the practical effect of the rebate system on the dealers in some detail.[137] While *Michelin I* ultimately concluded that the rebate scheme sat within the prohibited 'fidelity rebate' category established in the earlier cases, it did so only after analysing the conduct as well as the market circumstances as set out above. Hence, the ECJ looked at not only the form of the arrangement (albeit there was minimal consideration of the plausible justifications for the conduct and the ECJ's assessment of the likely effect of the behaviour does not correspond to modern economic thinking).

As discussed further in *section §6.05[B]*, the legal framework set out for assessing harm has similarities with the one established by AG Bobek in *Budapest Bank* (i.e., identification of a category based on formal criteria which is vetted by considering all circumstances). By contrast, the assessment of efficiencies differs significantly: (i) the efficiencies are defined very narrowly (arguably so narrowly that they would never apply to target rebates); and (ii) the standard of proof is far higher than the plausibility standard articulated in *Budapest Bank*.

Neither the EC nor the ECJ articulated a specific economic theory of harm in this case (nor assess the impact on end consumers or plausible procompetitive rationale). Highlighting the divergent market shares between Michelin NV and its competitors, and the implications of this for competitors seeking to match Michelin NV's offer, could be equated with a crude and nascent form of the AEC test. However, no economic analysis of competitors' prices was conducted. Instead, the EC found: (i) the restriction of the tyre dealers' 'freedom of choice'; and (ii) the 'inequality of treatment' between tyre dealers as problematic in themselves.[138] The former had 'restricting effects on competition' and the latter 'discriminatory effects' (the ECJ's assessment of discriminatory effects is secondary and is not a focus of this paper).[139] Whilst the ECJ dismissed the EC's latter contention, it upheld the former on the basis that, by effectively '*binding dealers [...] to itself*', Michelin NV committed an abuse.[140]

[B] *BA/Virgin* and *Michelin II* Era: Entrenchment of the by Object Approach

[1] Background

In the cases that followed *Michelin I*, the EC and EU courts expressed a clear preference for concentrating on the form of rebate schemes, rather than engaging in any substantive inquiry into the specific effects that these schemes might have on the ability of competitors to compete or on the plausible procompetitive rationale for these

137. Case C-322/81, *Michelin I*, paras 82–84.
138. Commission Decision 81/969/EEC, *Michelin I (EC)*, para. 37.
139. Commission Decision 81/969/EEC, *Michelin I (EC)*, para. 56.
140. Case C-322/81, *Michelin I*, para. 86.

practices. Where rebate schemes could be identified as capable of inducing loyalty, they were regarded as effective by object infringements of Article 102 TFEU.

The view that many forms of rebates (and in particular, target rebates) were capable of restricting competition became entrenched. Unlike in *Michelin I*, the specific conduct and context were not analysed in the same level of detail. This was seen in various EC decisions made at the time. For instance, in *Deutsche Post*,[141] the EC considered a fidelity rebate policy for mail-order parcel services and noted that it was '*settled European case-law that rebate arrangements which are linked to meeting a percentage of customer requirement have … an anticompetitive tying effect*'[142] and rejected the need to demonstrate the anticompetitive effects of such rebate schemes.

A similar approach had been taken by the EC in *BA/Virgin* and *Michelin II*, and the CFI endorsed the principle in both cases:

- In *BA/Virgin*, the CFI held that '[…] *it is not necessary to demonstrate that the abuse in question had a concrete effect on the markets concerned. It is sufficient in that respect to demonstrate that the abusive conduct of the undertaking in a dominant position tends to restrict competition, or, in other words, that the conduct is capable of having, or likely to have, such an effect*'.[143]
- In *Michelin II*, the CFI held that '[…] *establishing the anti-competitive object and the anti-competitive effect are one and the same thing* […]. *If it is shown that the object pursued by the conduct of an undertaking in a dominant position is to limit competition, that conduct will also be liable to have such an effect*'.[144]

In many respects *BA/Virgin* and *Michelin II* can be viewed as the 'high water mark' for the object-based approach to assessment of conditional rebates. Each case is summarised in detail below.

[2] BA/Virgin

[a] Conduct under Scrutiny

In 1993, Virgin lodged a complaint against BA, alleging that certain commercial practices discount structures were incorporated in agreements between BA and its travel agents. Travel agents in the UK received a standard commission from BA which, between 1976 and 1997, was 9% for international sales and 7.5% for domestic sales. In 1998, Virgin lodged a supplementary complaint in relation to a performance reward scheme introduced in the previous year.

141. Commission Decision 2001/354/EC of 20 March 2001 on COMP/35.141—Deutsche Post AG (notified under document number C(2001) 728), OJ L 125, 5.5.2001 (hereinafter '*Deutsche Post (EC)*').
142. Commission Decision 2001/354/EC, *Deutsche Post (EC)*, para. 39.
143. Case T-219/99, *BA/Virgin (CFI)*, para. 293.
144. Case T-203/01, *Michelin II*, para. 241.

Virgin's complaint concerned the introduction of additional incentive schemes to supplement the standard commission for certain qualifying agents. Marketing agreements were offered to agents in the UK who received additional bonuses, calculated on the basis of a comparison between BA tickets purchased in the UK in the previous year, compared with the current year's sales. The reward was linked to the extent to which a travel agent increased the value of their sales for BA tickets, with different scales depending on the type of sector flown.

Similar global agreements were introduced for three travel agents with respect to their worldwide sales. These were in addition to local agreements in particular countries. If the agent achieved a minimum of 1.5% increase in their overall sales, BA rewarded the agent with 10% of the incremental revenue. The global agreements were based on a quarterly reference period.

Finally, the performance reward scheme, introduced in 1997, supplemented the standard commission, offering agents up to 3% for international tickets and 1% for domestic tickets for agents who sold more BA tickets in the UK in the current month than in the previous month.

The schemes were target rebates. In each case, meeting the target led to an increase in commission or cash reward paid on all tickets. Virgin alleged that these were 'requirement contracts' in breach of Article 102 TFEU and were just attempts by BA to foreclose the market for air travel to and from the UK from its competitors.

[b] Market Definition and Assessment of Dominance

The relevant markets considered were those for air travel agency services in the UK and passenger air transport to and from the UK.

The EC found that BA was the dominant purchaser on the UK market for travel agency services.[145] This arose from its dominance in the markets for air travel and, more specifically: (i) its structural position of offering the largest selection of flights in and out of the UK; (ii) its share of total sales of air travel in the UK (and hence its share of the purchases of air travel agency services); (iii) its share of the markets compared to its competitors; and (iv) the fact that this made BA the 'obligatory business partner' for travel agents.[146]

The EC noted that, while competing airlines did have alternatives to purchasing air travel agency services from travel agents (e.g., sales by telephone and the internet), these were effectively 'in-house' production of agency services. Travel agents at the time accounted for 85% of air travel sales and BA's abusive conduct had serious effects on competing airlines and potential new entrants, harming competition in general.

However, it must be noted that over the course of the infringement, the UK airline market became more competitive (in particular, with the entry of Virgin, which, on some routes, outsold BA), and, by the conclusion of the abuse, BA's market share was only 39%. This reflected BA's substantial losses due to the increased presence of

145. Commission Decision 2000/74/EC, *BA/Virgin (EC)*, para. 90.
146. Commission Decision 2000/74/EC, *BA/Virgin (EC)*, paras 91–92.

competitors. However, the CFI found that neither the decline in BA's ticket sales nor the advance in market share of certain rival competitors was sufficiently large to call into question BA's dominant position.[147] In particular, the CFI noted the substantial gap that existed between BA and its competitors' market shares and the fact that BA's position remained 'preponderant'.[148]

[c] *Legal Test to Establish Abuse*

The ECJ in *BA/Virgin* referred to the legal frameworks set out in *Hoffmann-La Roche* and *Michelin I.* In particular, it reiterated the analytical building blocks developed in the latter.[149] The ECJ also clarified and refined – and, in some respects, diverged from – the legal framework of the earlier cases.

First, the ECJ emphasised the fact that certain types of rebates granted by dominant firms, including exclusivity rebates (*Hoffmann-La Roche*) and target rebates, are to be assessed within the framework of an object abuse (i.e., that '*it cannot be inferred from* [*Hoffmann-La Roche* and *Michelin II*] *that bonuses and discounts granted by undertakings in a dominant position are abusive only in the circumstances there described*' but that '*the decisive factor is rather the underlying factors which have guided the previous case-law … and which can also be transposed to a case as the present*'.[150] The ECJ framed the question as being whether '*the bonus scheme at issue had a fidelity-building effect capable of producing an exclusionary effect*').[151]

Second, while the ECJ clearly stated that it is necessary to consider 'all the circumstances',[152] the factors considered were relatively few. Unlike in *Michelin I*, the CFI did not consider the duration of the reference period nor the size of the rebate, and in consideration of broader circumstances, focused only on BA's relative market share.[153] Thus, the range of circumstances considered was more limited than in *Michelin I.*

Third, and contrary to *Michelin I*, the ECJ in *BA/Virgin* set out, in far greater detail, the relevance and criteria for any efficiency defence. The ECJ started with the position that '*only discounts or bonuses which are not based on any economic counterpart to justify them must be regarded as an abuse*'.[154] It then established a balancing test between the (presumed) harm to competition and the (actual) efficiency benefits. The ECJ stated that it must be '*determined whether the exclusionary effect arising from such a system, which is disadvantageous for competition, may be counterbalanced, or outweighed, by advantages in terms of efficiency which also benefit the*

147. Case T-219/99, *BA/Virgin (CFI)*, para. 223. The question of BA's dominance was not considered by the ECJ.
148. Case T-219/99, *BA/Virgin (CFI)*, para. 224.
149. Case C-95/04 P, *BA/Virgin*, para. 67, referring to Case C-322/81, *Michelin I.*, para. 73.
150. Case C-95/04 P, *BA/Virgin*, para. 64.
151. Case C-95/04 P, *BA/Virgin*, para. 77.
152. Case C-95/04 P, *BA/Virgin*, para. 67.
153. Case T-219/99, *BA/Virgin (CFI)*, para. 277.
154. Case C-95/04 P, *BA/Virgin*, para. 84.

consumer'.[155] Finally, the ECJ made clear that efficiencies cannot be taken into account where the exclusionary effect of the rebate bears no relation to advantages for the market and consumers or where it goes beyond what is necessary in order to attain those advantages.[156]

Again this framework bears similarity to AG Bobek's object restriction analysis under Article 101(1) TFEU in *Budapest Bank*, particularly in relation to the assessment of competitive harm (i.e., identification of a category of rebates which 'tends to be harmful' on the basis of an assessment of the criteria of the rebates/bonuses and all (other) factors). As with abuse restrictions, it is open to the defendant to show that the conduct in question is not capable of restricting competition.

However, when it comes to the assessment of efficiencies, there is significant divergence between the framework in *BA/Virgin* and that set out by AG Bobek in *Budapest Bank*. This is most obvious in relation to the link between harm and efficiency and, by implication, the relationship between an object and an effects restriction/abuse. We will come back to this point in *section §6.05[A][2]* below.

[d] Assessment of Foreclosure Harm

In relation to the criteria and rules for applying the rebate, as in *Michelin I*, the ECJ highlighted that granting the rebate is '*linked to the attainment of sales objectives defined individually*'[157] and emphasised the retroactive nature of the rebates.[158]

In its analysis, the CFI focussed on the progressive nature of the performance reward scheme which it concluded had a very noticeable effect at the margin and that '*once the agent approached the benchmark for additional commission, the marginal commission which it earned on every additional BA sector sold increased exponentially*'.[159] Moreover, the commission rates themselves '*were capable of rising exponentially from one reference period to another, as the number of BA tickets sold by agents during successive reference periods progressed*'.[160]

When considering factors beyond the structure of the rebate scheme itself (i.e., 'other circumstances'), the CFI referred only to the fact that BA's sales invariably represented a multiple of those of its five main competitors,[161] meaning that BA's competitors were not in a position to grant similar advantages to travel agents.

The EC (and ultimately, the ECJ) found that the payments made by BA under the scheme were fidelity-building, and a means of rewarding loyalty by increasing marketing and ticket sales.

155. Case C-95/04 P, *BA/Virgin*, para. 86.
156. *Ibid.*
157. Case C-95/04 P, *BA/Virgin*, para. 71.
158. Case C-95/04 P, *BA/Virgin*, para. 73.
159. Case T-219/99, *BA/Virgin (CFI)*, para. 266.
160. Case T-219/99, *BA/Virgin (CFI)*, para. 272.
161. Case T-219/99, *BA/Virgin (CFI)*, para. 277.

[e] Efficiency Considerations

BA argued that it was economically justified in rewarding travel agents that allowed it to increase sales and help cover its high fixed costs by bringing additional passengers (due to the importance of high aircraft occupancy rates). BA also put forward evidence that there might be some cost savings for BA in selling its tickets through an agency that generates a large volume of business. BA further argued that operational costs (e.g., query processing, production and checking reports, distribution of fare information) could be reduced due to economies of scale and that cost savings could be realised on commercial costs.

However, as outlined above, the framework used for evaluating efficiencies required, as a first step, that the putative efficiencies would bear a close relationship to the purportedly restrictive conduct and would not go beyond what was necessary. The EC found that this was not the case: it noted instead that the commission schemes in question did not respond to the different volumes of sales, or levels of service, provided by travel agents to BA.[162] Rather, the commission was linked to the extent to which the agent met or exceeded its previous year's sales.

The CFI considered that because the increase in commission rates applied to the total number of tickets sold and not only the extra ones once the targets were met, the agents' additional remuneration was not related to the BA-claimed efficiency gains from the sale of the extra air tickets.[163] The ECJ upheld the conclusion that BA's scheme did not appear to be based on any economically justifiable consideration (albeit without considering the detail of the justifications put forward, which it considered to be a question of fact). Because BA's alleged efficiencies failed this first threshold test (namely that efficiencies put forward were not of a kind that can be taken into account), the EC did not conduct a detailed balancing exercise of the pro and anticompetitive effects of the commission scheme.

[f] Conclusions

As outlined above, the analysis in the original EC decision is rather cursory – it essentially reiterates the law stated in *Michelin I* and *Hoffmann-La Roche* before asserting that the '*commission schemes set out above are clearly related to loyalty rather than efficiencies*'.[164] The review of 'all circumstances' other than the characteristics of the rebate scheme (i.e., the review of market factors such as the supply structure) is perfunctory and falls short of the efforts undertaken in *Michelin I*. While more thought is given to efficiency considerations than was the case in *Michelin I*, the substantive engagement with the arguments is nevertheless limited, given the narrow scope of 'admissible' efficiencies.

162. Commission Decision 2000/74/EC, *BA/Virgin (EC)*, para. 110.
163. Case T-219/99, *BA/Virgin (CFI)*, paras 283–284.
164. Commission Decision 2000/74/EC, *BA/Virgin (EC)*, para. 102.

Neither the EC nor the EU courts articulated the specific economic harm in this case nor assessed the impact on end consumers. The EC and the EU courts explicitly stated that BA's rebate scheme had an exclusionary effect, but, as in *Michelin I*, neither assessed the contestable and non-contestable shares of demand as dictated by a modern economic approach.

This represents a significant hardening of the line taken in respect of target rebates. The EC and EU courts concentrated on outlining the form of the rebate scheme to effectively conclude that it is a by object restriction.

[3] Michelin II

[a] Conduct under Scrutiny

Michelin II considered a complex rebate system administered by Michelin France. The principal bonus was a retrospective retroactive quantity rebate, structured as an annual refund calculated as a percentage of turnover achieved at a gradually increasing rate, according to the quantities purchased, by each dealer (the 'Quantity Rebate'). The payment of the rebate was made on all sales achieved in the relevant reference period, not just on a tranche of incremental sales. In addition, rebates were provided for the '*quality of the dealer's service to users*'.[165] This rebate was based upon the market share which Michelin France represented of dealers' sales (the 'Service Bonus') – i.e., the basis of the reward was linked to winning business from competitors. A progress bonus was provided as a reward for increasing the level of purchases for Michelin France products compared to the previous year (the 'Progress Bonus'). Michelin France also entered into an agreement which applied to dealers purchasing new tyres and required them to present every truck tyre casing for retreading (the 'PRO Agreement').

Finally, certain larger tyre dealers were allowed into the 'Michelin Friends Club', after assuming the following commitments: carrying sufficient stock to respond immediately to customer requirements (the EC found that the stock would have to match Michelin France's share of a dealer's purchases); promoting the Michelin France brand, particularly its new products; disclosing certain information concerning their sales; and not diverting 'spontaneous demand' away from Michelin France tyres to other brands. Entry into the Michelin Friends Club came with a financial benefit.

[b] Market Definition and Assessment of Dominance

The relevant markets were the market for new replacement tyres and for re-treaded replacement tyres in France. Michelin France's dominant position on both was considered evident from its market shares, strong presence on adjacent markets, omnipresent commercial and technical service on the ground and leading position in the French distribution channels. Further, Michelin France's behaviour was considered to reflect the attitudes and practices typical of a company in a dominant position. The

165. Commission Decision 2002/405/EC, *Michelin II (EC)*, para. 56.

EC found its assessment confirmed the position of economic dependence that specialised dealers found themselves in, making Michelin an unavoidable trading partner.[166]

[c] Legal Test to Establish Abuse

Contrary to *BA/Virgin*, (which concerned target rebates and which could therefore be dealt with by the existing classification of object abuses set out by *Hoffmann-La Roche*, and, in particular, *Michelin I*) and *Michelin II*, addressed the issue of volume rebates.

By contrast, not only had volume rebates considered in *Michelin II* not been considered as abusive in the past, and hence did not exist as a category of loyalty enhancing rebates, but the ECJ had also previously held that *'quantity rebates systems linked solely to the volume of purchases made from the undertaking occupying a dominant position are generally considered not to have the foreclosure effect prohibited by Article [102 TFEU]'*.[167] In other words, there was an existing presumption (albeit rebuttable) that quantity rebates were lawful under the dominance provisions.

In *Michelin II*, the object abuse framework for loyalty enhancing rebates was effectively extended by the EC and the CFI from exclusivity rebates and target rebates to include certain retroactive volume rebates. This occurred through several steps.

First, the CFI effectively narrowed the scope of procompetitive 'quantity rebates' identified in previous case law to only those quantity rebates that *'reflect gains in efficiency and economies of scale made by the [dominant firm]'*.[168] It stated that quantity rebates were a proxy for passing on cost savings *'if increasing the quantity supplied results in lower costs for the supplier, the latter is entitled to pass on that reduction to customers in the form of a more favourable tariff. Quantity rebates are therefore deemed to reflect gains in efficiency and economies of scale made by the [dominant firm]'*.[169]

This had the effect of narrowing the presumption of legality so that it applied only to the extent that the underlying cost presumption could be shown to be valid:

> a rebate system in which the rate of the discount increases according to the volume purchased will not infringe Article [102 TFEU] unless the criteria and rules for granting the rebate reveal that the system is not based on an economically justified countervailing advantage but tends, following the example of a loyalty and target rebate, to prevent customers from obtaining their supplies from competitors.[170]

In addition, by linking the presumption of legality of quantity rebates to the narrow scope of efficiencies permitted in relation to loyalty enhancing rebates, the CFI, for the first time, created a uniform framework of analysis for all retroactive rebates. It can be seen to replace the binary 'quantity/fidelity' rebate distinction from

166. Commission Decision 2002/405/EC, *Michelin II (EC)*, para. 173.
167. Case T-203/01, *Michelin II*, para. 58 cross-referring to Case C-322/81, *Michelin I*, para. 71 and Case C-163/99, *Portugal v. Commission*, 29.3.2001, ECLI:EU:C:2001:189 (hereinafter '*Portugal v. Commission*'), para. 50.
168. Case T-203/01, *Michelin II*, para. 58.
169. *Ibid.*
170. Case T-203/01, *Michelin II*, para. 59.

Hoffmann-La Roche, with a new dichotomy between: (i) retroactive rebates which are deemed to reflect gains in efficiency and economies of scale made by the dominant firm and are presumed to be lawful; and (ii) those retroactive rebates that do not.

The second category included exclusivity rebates, target rebates and retroactive quantity rebates with a 'long' reference period and applied the object abuse framework, which the ECJ had developed for target rebates in *Michelin I*.[171] Specifically, in relation to quantity rebates, the CFI outlined that a familiar framework from *Michelin I* should apply '*it is necessary to consider all circumstances, particularly the criteria and rules governing the grant of the discounts and to investigate whether, in providing an advantage not based on any economic service justifying it, the quantity rebates tend to harm competition*'.[172]

While this broadly replicates *Michelin I*, there are nevertheless a few changes. First, while the two limbs under the object assessment still apply (i.e., criteria and rules of the rebates and 'all (other) circumstances'), there is a stronger emphasis on the former over the latter, which makes the analysis more formalistic. Second, the competitive harm of Michelin's quantity rebates was covered under three headings: (i) lack of fairness; (ii) loyalty inducing; and (iii) having a partitioning effect (which the CFI considered to flow directly from the loyalty-inducing effect). A discrimination claim was not pursued. The CFI held that any loyalty-inducing rebate system applied by a dominant firm that has foreclosure effects would contravene Article 102 TFEU irrespective of whether or not the rebate system was discriminatory.[173]

Michelin II concluded that certain retroactive quantity rebates, like exclusivity rebates and target rebates, should be assessed under an object framework and that (contrary to Article 101 TFEU) the category of an object abuse is a closed system where actual or likely effects do not have to be demonstrated.[174] No effects analysis was therefore required because, in the CFI's words, 'for the purposes of applying Article [102] EC, *establishing the anti-competitive object and the anti-competitive effect are one and the same thing*. If it is shown that the object pursued by the conduct of an undertaking in a dominant position is to limit competition, that conduct will also be liable to have such an effect' (emphasis added).[175]

To support this approach, the CFI relied upon the finding in *AKZO v. Commission* that '*prices below average variable costs applied by a dominant firm are regarded as abusive in themselves because the only interest which the undertaking may have in applying such prices is that of eliminating competitors*'.[176] The CFI considered that this can be extended to other conduct where the *purpose* (or the 'object') of the conduct is '*to strengthen a dominant position and thereby abuse it*',[177] as was the case in relation to Michelin France's rebate systems. The EC found that the purpose of the rebate systems was to tie dealers to Michelin France, and the practice restricted competition

171. Case T-203/01, *Michelin II*, para. 60, quoting Case C-322/81, *Michelin I*, para. 73.
172. Case T-203/01, *Michelin II*, para. 62.
173. Case T-203/01, *Michelin II*, para. 65.
174. Case T-203/01, *Michelin II*, para. 239.
175. Case T-203/01, *Michelin II*, paras 244, 258.
176. Case T-203/01, *Michelin II*, para. 242 citing Case C-62/86, *AKZO v. Commission*, para. 71.
177. Case T-203/01, *Michelin II*, para. 243.

because the dealers sought to make it more difficult for competitors to enter the market.[178] The CFI then found that, given this, the actual effect of the practice was irrelevant '*the fact that the result sought is not achieved is not enough to avoid the application of Art [102]*'.[179]

[d] Assessment of Foreclosure Harm

The EC considered whether the various schemes (quantity rebates, Service Bonus, Progress Bonus, PRO Agreement and Michelin Friends Club - described more fully above) were abusive. In particular, it assessed whether these schemes amounted to unfair practices, had loyalty-inducing effects and market-partitioning/foreclosing effects. As noted above, this paper focuses on loyalty-inducing effects.

[i] Quantity Rebates

Criteria and rules for the rebate system. In line with the framework established, the EC assessed the various criteria and rules for the rebate system.

While *Michelin I* and *BA/Virgin* had focused on the target nature of the rebates generating a loyalty-inducing effect (and *Hoffmann-La Roche* had dealt with the exclusivity rebates), *Michelin II* looked at retroactive quantity rebates. Thus, neither the target nature of a rebate nor an exclusivity obligation was considered to be required to establish foreclosure effects. Rather, the key features of Michelin's rebate system that raised concerns about loyalty-inducing effects were the combination of: (i) the retroactive nature of the rebates; (ii) combined with a one-year reference period; and (iii) the size of variation between the discount rates at various steps.[180]

In relation to the all-unit nature of the rebate, the CFI distinguished between 'forward looking' rebates, where the discount applies only to quantities exceeding a certain threshold, from 'retroactive discounts', where the discount applies to the total turnover achieved during the reference period.[181] The CFI pointed out that where a rebate is granted 'by tranche', it never exceeds the percentage for the tranche in question. By contrast, where the rebate applies to the total volume purchased, an increase in turnover close to the threshold may lead to a very significant discount at the margin. The CFI therefore concluded that '*the incentive to purchase created by a quantity rebate system is therefore much greater where the discounts are calculated on total turnover achieved during a certain period than where they are calculated only tranche by tranche*'.[182] Furthermore, '*[t]he longer the reference period, the more loyalty-inducing the quantity rebate system*'.[183]

---

178. Case T-203/01, *Michelin II*, para. 244.
179. Case T-203/01, *Michelin II*, para. 245.
180. Case T-203/01, *Michelin II*, paras 75–78, 95.
181. Case T-203/01, *Michelin II*, para. 85.
182. Case T-203/01, *Michelin II*, para. 88.
183. *Ibid.*

In relation to the 'long' reference period, which in *Michelin II* was one year, the CFI cited *Michelin I* according to which '*any system under which discounts are granted according to the quantities sold during a relatively long reference period has the inherent effect, at the end of that period, of increasing pressure on the buyer to reach the purchase figure needed to obtain the discount or to avoid suffering the expected loss for the entire period*'.[184] This was a key focus for the EC and the remedy ultimately negotiated between Michelin France and the EC replaced the annual scale of rebates with a quarterly scale, in order to reduce the pressure on dealers to reach the next level of the scale. The CFI distinguished *British Gypsum* where a one-year volume rebate had been held to be compatible with Article 102 TFEU on the basis that the rebates had been calculated from anticipated annual turnover *ex ante* rather than from actual turnover *ex post* (and that the quantity rebates in *British Gypsum* reflected actual costs savings for the dominant firm).

The CFI also considered the size of the variation between the discount rates between various steps. While the targets varied annually, they included a large number of target thresholds, varying from eighteen to fifty-four steps. The CFI found, in line with *Michelin I*, that even where '*the variation in the rate of discount is small it may nevertheless affect the dealer's margin of profits on the whole year's sales and hence even quite slight variations might put dealers under appreciable pressure*'.[185] The CFI found that where, as in this case, the variation of the rebates is significant, this should be regarded as an aggravating factor.

All (other) circumstances. Contrary to *Michelin I*, the EC and the CFI did not focus to the same extent as *Michelin I* (and even *BA/Virgin*) on circumstances other than the rebate system itself. In particular, the CFI held that the lack of transparency is not a necessary condition for an abusive rebate system: '*[a] loyalty-inducing rebate system is contrary to Article [102 TFEU], whether it is transparent or not*'.[186]

However, the CFI did highlight the uncertainty that dealers faced due to the complexity of the overall system as an important factor in establishing the loyalty-inducing effect '*the simultaneous application of various discount systems … made it impossible for the dealer to calculate the exact purchase price of Michelin tyres at the time of purchase. That situation inevitably put dealers in a position of uncertainty and dependence*'.[187]

Conclusions. The CFI concluded that '*a quantity rebate system in which there is a significant variation in the discount rates between the lower and higher steps which has a reference period of one year and in which the discount is fixed on the basis of total turnover achieved during the reference period has the characteristics of a loyalty-inducing discount system*'.[188] The CFI endorsed the EC's findings that the rebates prevented dealers from being able to select freely at any time, in the light of the market

184. Case T-203/01, *Michelin II*, para. 81.
185. Case T-203/01, *Michelin II*, para. 91.
186. Case T-203/01, *Michelin II*, para. 111.
187. *Ibid.*
188. Case T-203/01, *Michelin II*, para. 95.

situation, the most advantageous offers made by competitors and to change suppliers without suffering an appreciable economic disadvantage.

[ii] Other Rebates

Progress Bonus /PRO Agreement. The Progress Bonus and PRO Agreement were both essentially target bonuses: they were dependent on an increase in new tyre sales, or truck tyres, as the case may be. Such rebates were individually set and bore much more similarity to the rebates offered in *Michelin I* and *BA/Virgin*. In the case of the PRO Agreement, there were additional (standardised) amounts payable when tyres were presented for retreading. The EC considered both to be abusive and, on appeal, Michelin France did not raise any specific pleas against this finding (but only disputed it through its general argument that the EC had failed to carry out an effects analysis, which was rejected).[189]

Service Bonus. Michelin France argued that the Service Bonus was designed to encourage dealers to improve the quality of their services and the brand image of Michelin products. The CFI noted evidence that the bonus was fixed according to the quality of the service the dealer was able to provide, and therefore considered that there was evidence that the Service Bonus was remuneration for services rendered rather than a true rebate or discount.[190] However, the CFI found that the bonus nonetheless had a loyalty-inducing effect as, by offering a financial advantage, Michelin France sought to prevent the dealer from obtaining its supplies from rival manufacturers.[191]

Michelin Friends Club. The EC also maintained that the Michelin Friends Club was used as a tool to rigidify and improve Michelin France's position on the market in new replacement truck tyres. Dealers who were members of the club were obliged to promote the Michelin France brand and not divert spontaneous customer demand away from Michelin France tyres.[192] In addition, the Michelin Friends Club agreement allowed Michelin France an exceptionally far-reaching right to monitor the activities of the members, and which did not appear to be in any way justified other than by Michelin France's desire to supervise distribution in detail.[193] Any changes in the dealers' commercial or strategic policy would leave them open to reprisals on the part of Michelin France, so this was considered to have a loyalty-inducing effect.

[e] Assessment of Efficiencies

As part of the efficiencies assessment, the CFI raised the question of whether '*the quantity rebate system applied by the applicant is based on a countervailing advantage*

189. Case T-203/01, *Michelin II*, para. 45.
190. Case T-203/01, *Michelin II*, para. 139.
191. Case T-203/01, *Michelin II*, para. 160.
192. Commission Decision 2002/405/EC, *Michelin II (EC)*, para. 317.
193. Commission Decision 2002/405/EC, *Michelin II (EC)*, para. 322.

which may be economically justified'.[194] As in *Michelin I* and *BA/Virgin*, the efficiencies that were 'admissible' under this test were narrowly defined, such that '[a] quantity rebate system is [...] compatible with Article [102 TFEU] if the advantage conferred on dealers is 'justified by the volume of business *they* bring or by any economies of scale *they* allow the supplier to make'[195] (emphasis added) – i.e., the efficiencies must arise directly from the impugned rebate system. The CFI did not consider whether efficiencies can only be cost-based (i.e., because the extra volume allows certain savings) or whether it could also cover the part of any rebate which could be characterised as consideration paid to the customer to help achieve such higher volumes.

In addition, according to the CFI, it was not sufficient to show that efficiencies resulting from the rebate system were plausible; the dominant firm had to establish that the quantity rebate system, which presented the characteristics of a loyalty-inducing rebate system, was based on objective economic reasons.[196]

In this case, the CFI held that Michelin France '*merely states generally that the quantity rebates were justified by "economies of scale in the area of production costs and distribution"*'[197] and concluded that '*such a line of argument is too general and is insufficient to provide economic reasons to explain specifically the discount rates chosen for the various steps in the rebate system in question*'.[198] The CFI found that the EC was therefore entitled to conclude that the rebate system was not based on any economic justification.

[f] Conclusions

Michelin II extended the framework that had applied initially to exclusivity rebates (in *Hoffmann-La Roche*), and then to target rebates (in *Michelin I* and *BA/Virgin*), to quantity rebates. In so doing, it found, for the first time, that retroactive quantity rebates are an abuse of dominance capable of being assessed using the object framework.

Like *Michelin I* and *BA/Virgin*, neither the EC nor the CFI articulated the specific economic theory of harm in this case (nor assess the impact on end consumers) and the CFI explicitly found that an effects analysis was not needed.[199] Instead, the EC and the CFI inferred anticompetitive effects from the rebate system's '*unfairness*' (i.e., its exploitative nature vis-à-vis the tyre dealers),[200] its '*market-partitioning effect (and foreclosing effect)*'[201] and its '*tying of dealers to Michelin France*'.[202] Though not specifically framed as such, in a similar vein as both *Michelin I* and *BA/Virgin*, this latter proposition suggests an exclusion theory of harm but without assessment of

194. Case T-203/01, *Michelin II*, para. 98.
195. Case T-203/01, *Michelin II*, para. 100 referring to C-163/99, *Portugal v. Commission*, para. 58.
196. Case T-203/01, *Michelin II*, para. 107.
197. Case T-203/01, *Michelin II*, para. 108.
198. Case T-203/01, *Michelin II*, para. 109.
199. Case T-203/01, *Michelin II*, paras 235–246.
200. Commission Decision 2002/405/EC, *Michelin II* (EC), para. 219.
201. Commission Decision 2002/405/EC, *Michelin II* (EC), para. 240.
202. Commission Decision 2002/405/EC, *Michelin II* (EC), para. 227.

Michelin France's contestable and non-contestable demand (as would be demanded by a modern economic approach).

[C] Post-*Michelin I*, *Michelin II* and *BA/Virgin*: Towards an Effects-Based Approach

In a departure from the previous case law and in recognition of the potential procompetitive effects of discount and rebate practices, recent years have seen a shift in focus towards an effects-based approach, as reflected by the EC's 2008 Priorities Guidance and more recently the ECJ's landmark decision in *Intel.*

[1] EC's Review of Article 102 TFEU

Following *BA/Virgin* and *Michelin II*, the EC continued to apply the by object approach to assessing rebates, including in *Solvay*[203] and *Imperial Chemical Industries*[204] (both of which were endorsed by the EU courts). In 2003 however, the EC recognised the need to review law and policy under Article 102 TFEU, launching an internal review which resulted in the publication of a Discussion Paper in December 2005. While the initial aim was to produce Article 102 TFEU guidelines similar to those that exist for Article 101 TFEU and for merger control and state aid, diverging views at the EC between the Legal Service and DG Competition led to the publication of its Priorities Guidance in 2008.[205]

The Discussion Paper and Priorities Guidance both recognised that conditional rebates were not an uncommon practice and may be offered for non-exclusionary reasons such as stimulating demand and for the benefit of customers.[206] The Priorities Guidance sets out an economic and effects-based approach to examining exclusionary conduct such as discounts and rebates based on the AEC test. It also provides detail on the types of evidence that the EC would typically look at to assess anticompetitive foreclosure. While the type of assessment more directly corresponds to the economic theory of harm of naked exclusion (i.e., exclusion through rebates with targeted offers at strategic buyers, as outlined in *section §6.03[B]* above), it also provides a pragmatic manner for assessment of whether inducements are significant, which is of broader relevance. Although case law has confirmed the AEC test to be only '*one tool amongst others*' when determining whether a rebate is abusive under Article 102 TFEU,[207] the Priorities Guidance indicates that the EC should usually only intervene where the

203. Case T-57/01, *Solvay SA v. European Commission,* 17.12.2009, ECLI:EU:T:2009:519, para. 316.
204. Case T-66/01, *Chemical Industries Ltd v. European Commission,* 25.10.2010, ECLI: EU:T:2010:255, para. 296.
205. Nicholas Petit, *From Formalism to Effects? The Commission's Communication on Enforcement Priorities in Applying Article 82 EC,* 32 World Competition 487 (2009).
206. Priorities Guidance, para. 39.
207. Case C-23/14, *Post Danmark II,* para. 61.

conduct in question would hinder competition from competitors considered to be as (or more) efficient as the dominant undertaking.[208]

[2] Shifting Between 'Object' and 'Effects' Approaches

Around the time of these reforms, there was evidence of the EC and the EU courts beginning to analyse the effects of impugned rebates. For example, in *Tomra* the EC made an attempt to analyse likely effects but, as the ECJ noted on appeal, it '*merely complemented its findings of infringement with a brief examination of the likely effects*'[209] but did not base its findings on these. In *Tomra*, the EC relied on *Michelin II* and *BA/Virgin* for the principle that it is not necessary to show actual impact on the relevant markets.[210] While the ECJ did not directly apply the AEC test as outlined in the Priorities Guidance (which pre-dated the EC's decision in 2006 but was in force by the time of the ECJ appeal in 2012), AG Mazak did state in his opinion that '*reference to negative and anti-competitive effects should not be mechanical. The (likely) existence of such exclusionary effects in a particular case should not be merely presumed, it should be assessed and demonstrated*'.[211]

A further shift was seen in *Velux*,[212] *a* case concerning incremental rebates, which the EC found did not result in below-cost pricing and competitors were therefore not excluded from the market. This echoed the approach of the Priorities Guidance, which acknowledged that '*as long as the effective price remains consistently above the LRAIC of the dominant undertaking, this would normally allow an as efficient competitor to compete notwithstanding the rebate*'.[213] The EC went on to discuss a hypothetical situation where the same rebate scheme was retroactive and concluded that it could still have been lawful, provided the company used a large number of increments.[214]

At around the same time, the ECJ moved away from the object abuse approach for cases concerning pricing abuses – evident from the 2011 decision of *TeliaSonera*[215] and the 2012 *Post Danmark I* decision, where the EU courts applied the AEC test to consider whether pricing was predatory. However, the AEC test approach was not wholly extended to rebates, as seen in the ECJ's 2015 decision in *Post Danmark II*. In *Post Danmark II*, which considered target rebates, the ECJ found that there was no legal obligation to apply the AEC test to determine if a rebate scheme is abusive, but that it must be considered as merely one tool among others for examining the compatibility of

208. Priorities Guidance, para. 23.
209. Case T-155/06, *Tomra*, para. 288.
210. Case T-155/06, *Tomra*, paras 288–299.
211. Opinion of Advocate General Mazak in Case C-549/10 P, *Tomra Systems ASA and others v. Commission*, 2.2.2012, ECLI:EU:C:2012:55, paras 43–44.
212. Commission Decision on COMP/39.451 – *Velux* (2009) (not published); *see* Bill Batchelor and Kayvan Hazemi Jebelli, *Rebates in a State of Velux: Filling in the Gaps in the Article 102 Enforcement Priorities*, ECLR (2011).
213. Priorities Guidance, para. 43.
214. Svend Albaek and Adina Claici, *The Velux Case: An In-Depth Look at Rebates and More*, Competition Policy Newsletter (2009).
215. Case C-52/09, *TeliaSonera Sverige*, 17.2.2011, ECLI:EU:C:2011:83, paras 40–46.

rebates with Article 102 TFEU.[216] It did so, however, in a very specific context of a former state monopoly with extremely significant scale and scope externalities. The ECJ emphasised a more effects-based analysis, in particular the need to consider 'all circumstances' around granting of a rebate, including the extent of dominant position and competitive conditions prevailing in the market.

[3] The Intel Decision

The move towards an effects-based approach to assessment of rebates was confirmed in the ECJ's ruling in *Intel* in 2017, which focused primarily on exclusivity rebates but had clear application to target rebates also. The ECJ rejected the GC's view that, because fidelity rebates are always capable of restricting competition '*by their very nature*', it is unnecessary to consider whether the individual circumstances of the case involve a foreclosure effect.[217] In so doing however, rather than rejecting or replacing the object framework developed in *Hoffmann-La Roche* and the Focus Cases outright, *Intel* created two 'exit routes' from an object to an effects analysis: (i) establishing that the conduct is not capable of restricting competition; and (ii) showing that the anticompetitive harm is outweighed by efficiencies.

As a starting point, the ECJ clarified that the presumption that fidelity rebates infringe Article 102 TFEU developed in *Hoffmann-La Roche* and subsequent cases is rebuttable, the same as any other presumption under EU competition law.[218] While the evidential burden is initially on the dominant undertaking to show that its rebates are not capable of restricting competition if it submits plausible evidence to that effect, the burden then shifts to the EC to demonstrate that the rebates are capable of foreclosing as efficient competitors (i.e., to carry out an effects-based analysis).[219] In line with the framework of abuse restrictions under Article 101(1) object restrictions, the ECJ offered two ways of how to rebut the presumption of harm, namely: (i) showing lack of capability of harm; and (ii) establishing an efficiency defence.[220]

Lack of capability of harm. The first exit route out of the previously closed object abuse box established by *Hoffman La Roche* is '*evidence that [the dominant firm] was not capable of restricting competition and, in particular, of producing the alleged foreclosure effects*'.[221] This required a clear understanding of what amounts to anti-competitive foreclosure. In line with the *Post Danmark* cases, the Court seems to opt for the AEC standard, i.e., '*the intrinsic capability … to foreclose competitors that are at least as efficient as the dominant undertaking*'.[222] By contrast, the departure of less

216. Case C-23/14, *Post Danmark II*, paras 57–58.
217. Case T-286/09, *Intel v. Commission*, 12.6.2014, ECLI:EU:T:2014:547, paras 77, 81, 85 and 87; *Intel*, paras 141 and 144.
218. Case C-413/14 P, *Intel*, para. 137.
219. Case C-413/14 P, *Intel*, para. 139.
220. Case C-413/14 P, *Intel*, para. 140.
221. Case C-413/14 P, *Intel*, para. 138.
222. Case C-413/14 P, *Intel*, para. 140.

attractive rivals is an inherent feature of competitive process and is therefore unproblematic.[223]

The ECJ was not entirely clear about the type of evidence that the dominant firm has to put forward regarding lack of capability to move the case to an effects analysis. As is the case in relation to Article 101(1), plausibility seems to be an appropriate standard.

Efficiency defence. the ECJ also noted that a system of rebates may be objectively justified and that '*advantages in terms of efficiency which also benefit the consumer*' may counterbalance or outweigh anticompetitive foreclosure effects.[224] Such an analysis balancing the effects should be carried out only after considering the intrinsic capacity to foreclose as efficient competitors.[225] Thus, the ECJ provides a second exit door which could lead out of the object abuse box, namely the efficiency defence. Under Article 101 TFEU, the efficiency defence is explicit on the face of the statute and its requirements are clearly set out under Article 101(3) TFEU. In *Intel*, in a similar way, the ECJ states that exclusionary effects can be counterbalanced by efficiencies (i.e., a balancing exercise – only capable under an effects-based analysis which allows quantification of the relative harms and efficiencies, is required).[226] While the ECJ is silent as to what a dominant firm must establish to open the efficiency exit door out of the object abuse box, it would appear reasonable to apply a plausibility standard in line with *Budapest Bank* and the lack of capability defence above.

The ECJ did not address the novel threefold categorisation of rebates which had been proposed by the GC,[227] leaving the categorisation of rebates somewhat of a grey area under EU competition law. Neither did it consider the need to scrutinise 'all circumstances' of the rebates as argued by the appellant and *AG Wahl*. The switch to an effects-based analysis via a plausible 'lack of capability' provided an alternative solution.

The real impact of *Intel* was that it caused the debate to shift from considering whether an effects test is required to consider how anticompetitive effects may be demonstrated. It is clear that the level of analysis required to establish anticompetitive effect has increased substantially since the (fairly low) standard applied in the Focus Cases. Consequently, the ECJ imposed a procedural obligation on the EC to consider any evidence produced by the defendant tending to show a lack of anticompetitive

---

223. Pablo Ibáñez Colomo, *The Future of Article 102 after Intel*, 9(5) J. Eur. Competition L. & Prac. 298 (2018).
224. Case C-413/14 P, *Intel*, para. 140.
225. *Ibid.*
226. *Ibid.*
227. In Case T-286/09, *Intel v. Commission*, 12.6.2014, ECLI:EU:T:2014:547, paras 74–78, the GC identified three categories of rebates to which distinct legal rules apply: (i) quantity rebates, (ii) fidelity rebates and (iii) other types of rebates which do not fall neatly within either category. AG Wahl rejected this approach in his Opinion in the subsequent appeal to the ECJ, referring to quantity rebates and fidelity rebates as the only two types of rebates recognised by the case law (Opinion of AG Wahl in Case C-413/14 P, *Intel v. Commission*, 20.10.2016, ECLI: EU:C:2016:788 (hereinafter '*AG Wahl*'), para. 81). Whilst the ECJ set aside the GC's judgment, it did not comment on its threefold categorisation of rebates, leaving this somewhat of a grey area under EU law.

foreclosure effects. Although this applies as a rebuttable presumption for exclusivity rebates, it follows that the same is necessary for other forms of rebate. However, it is yet to be seen how complete or precise the EU courts will require the EC's assessment of foreclosure effects to be, and this will likely be a key question for future cases.

While the ECJ has formally confirmed the existence of a presumption (at least for exclusivity clauses), it has also clearly stated wide possibilities for its rebuttal. One can expect that prosecuted companies will systematically attempt to rebut this presumption, on the grounds that the non-linear prices correspond to plausible procompetitive rationales and/or that their conduct is not capable of restricting competition to the detriment of consumers. In this case, a debate on the likely effect of the behaviour will inevitably take place. In this context, one can question the relevance of the presumption in the first place.

§6.05 EVALUATION OF APPROACH TAKEN IN THE FOCUS CASES

In this Section, we seek to evaluate the approach taken by the EC and EU courts in the Focus Cases in light of modern legal and economic thinking. In so doing, we are conscious of the risk that reviewing these cases with the benefit of hindsight, a refined legal framework and an understanding of further progress in economic theory may lead to an unfair assessment (and to somewhat smug conclusions). We have tried not to fall into this trap and instead focused on how the frameworks used in the Focus Cases could inform the modern debate.

This *section §6.05* is divided into two parts. First, *section §6.05[A]* evaluates the analytical framework created by the Focus Cases for conditional rebates. In particular, we contrast this framework with the modern frameworks, under both Article 102 TFEU and in light of the development in the approach to the object/effects distinction in the context of Article 101 TFEU. Second, *section §6.05[B]* evaluates the results of the Focus Cases in light of the facts, applying a revised, up to date analytical framework. In this section, we look in particular at whether the facts as presented in the Focus Cases justify the conclusions reached at the time.

[A] Evaluation of the Analytical Framework Created by the Focus Cases

[1] Building an Object Abuse Framework for Conditional Rebates

As described in *section §6.04*, the Focus Cases built a comprehensive object abuse framework for conditional rebates. *Michelin I* established the two-stage framework, followed – at least nominally – in all three Focus Cases. At the first stage, the authority considers whether the discount is of a kind that can be expected to (or 'tends to') have a harmful impact on competition, taking into account: (i) the rules and criteria for grant of the rebate; and (ii) all other circumstances. The second stage of the analysis considers whether the rebate provides an advantage based on any economic service which would justify it.

[a] Definition of Categories of Object Abuses

The starting point for the Focus Cases was *Suiker Unie* and *Hoffmann-La Roche*, which had outlined a binary classification for rebates. On the one hand, 'exclusivity rebates', being rebates payable on the condition of obtaining '*supplies exclusively from a particular undertaking … [including] the granting of fidelity rebates intended to give the purchaser an incentive to obtain his supplies exclusively from the undertaking in a dominant position*'.[228] On the other hand, 'quantity rebates' are '*exclusively linked with the volume of purchases from the producer concerned*'.[229]

The classification created by *Suiker Unie* and *Hoffmann-La Roche* raised a number of conceptual problems which became increasingly visible through the Focus Cases. First, the two original categories of rebates defined in *Hoffmann-La Roche* (exclusivity rebates and quantity rebates) are not exhaustive: the Focus Cases saw the 'object' category expanded to include target rebates and, in *Michelin II*, rebates that were in the form of pure quantity rebates, but were nonetheless impugned as abusive as outlined above. The binary classification forced the EC and EU courts to continually expand the 'fidelity rebates' category as failure to classify a rebate, as such would result in a finding of no infringement. Second and closely related to this, the categories identified by *Hoffmann-La Roche* and the Focus Cases are not in reality strict or mutually exclusive: (i) standardised rebates linked to exclusive or near-exclusive dealing may be de facto exclusive (although that is unlikely, as they are standardised); (ii) target rebates may also be de facto exclusive; and (iii) retroactive quantity rebates may become de facto close to target rebates if you have multiple thresholds. Moreover, as explained in *section §6.03[B]*, economic theory does not suggest a distinction can be made on the basis of the form of a rebate alone.

Michelin I highlighted the first issue, namely that the categories of loyalty rebates are not exhaustive – despite the EC's best efforts to label target rebates as falling within the category of 'exclusivity rebates' within the meaning of *Hoffmann-La Roche*, and Michelin NV's attempts to characterise the rebates as 'quantity rebates' – it was clear, and indeed the ECJ concluded, that the rebates in *Michelin I* were neither exclusivity nor quantity rebates and belonged in a separate category (which the ECJ called 'target rebates').

As a result, the ECJ had to build an entirely new framework for this new category of rebates. It extended the object abuse framework to 'target rebates' defined as those '*characterised by the use of sales targets*', which differ from a '*mere quantity discount linked solely to the volume of goods purchased since the progressive scale of the previous year's turnover indicates only the limits within which the system applies*'.[230] Thus, the individualised nature of the targets was an important factor.

The categorisation issue arose again in *Michelin II*, where, this time, the potential abuse concerned quantity rebates which were not individualised but set on a 'standard' basis across dealers (albeit with many levels). Again, the CFI had to consider afresh

228. Case C-85/76, *Hoffmann-La Roche*, para. 90.
229. *Ibid.*
230. Case C-322/81, *Michelin I*, para. 72.

how to deal with yet another category, extending the object abuse consideration from target rebates and defining a new set of 'loyalty rebates' (retroactive rebates with a reference period of one year or more).

The second conceptual issue, namely that the categories are in reality neither strict nor mutually exclusive, was highlighted in *Michelin II.* Here, the binary distinction between exclusivity and target rebates (presumptively harmful) and quantity rebates (presumptively benign) were not found to reflect the versatile nature and impact of rebates. The CFI addressed that issue by further widening the concept of a by object abuse to also include certain quantity rebates. Indeed, *Michelin II* can be read to extend the object abuse framework to all rebates except rebates *'justified by "economies of scale in the area of production costs and distribution"'.*[231]

[2] The Consideration Regarding Competitive Harm

As outlined in *section §6.03[C][2]* above, the object/effect dichotomy under Article 101 TFEU is grounded in the consensus that certain types of arrangement can be regarded *'by their very nature as being harmful to the proper functioning of normal competition since they normally produce inefficient outcomes and reduce consumer welfare'.*[232] In other words, there are certain arrangements where an informed assumption can be made that it will harm competition.

This approach is perhaps most explicitly applied in an Article 102 TFEU context by the ECJ in *AKZO v. Commission*, which found that *'a dominant undertaking has no interest in applying such prices [below average variable costs] except that of eliminating competitors so as to enable it subsequently to raise its prices by taking advantage of its monopolistic position, since each sale generates a loss'.*[233] On this basis, the ECJ is confident in making the assumption that such pricing practices harm competition.

[a] Framework for Target Rebates

In *Michelin I,* the ECJ took the view that individualised rebates: (i) with a reference threshold relative to previous year's volume; (ii) which are retroactive; (iii) where the dominant player has a market share which is significantly larger than the shares of its competitors; and (iv) where there is a lack of transparency over the rebate system, inherently have a negative effect. The ECJ concluded that the combination of these factors put dealers under 'considerable pressure' to obtain the sales targets, and that competitors could not meet the offer because they would need to make up the absolute value of Michelin NV's rebate over a much smaller volume of sales.

231. Case T-203/01, *Michelin II*, para. 108.
232. Case C-228/18, *AG Bobek Budapest Bank Opinion.*
233. Case C-62/86, *AKZO v. Commission*, para. 72.

Lack of benchmark. Michelin I and indeed all Focus Cases suffer from the fact that, contrary to *AKZO*, or indeed *Intel*, they draw no clear division between procompetitive pricing (which happens to lead to the exit of certain competitors) and anticompetitive foreclosure pricing strategies:

- The Priorities Guidance outlines the AEC Test, which requires the EC to investigate whether the rebate system in question *'is capable of hindering expansion or entry even by competitors that are equally efficient'*.[234] In *Post Danmark II*, the ECJ did not consider the test binding but noted that it was one tool among others for examining the compatibility of rebates with Article 102 TFEU.[235] It took a similar view in *Intel* but appeared to effectively endorse the AEC test by noting that the EC is required to focus on *'the intrinsic capability … to foreclose competitors that are at least as efficient as the dominant undertaking'*.[236]
- While the ECJ's conclusion that it would be difficult for competing suppliers to meet Michelin NV's offer over a smaller volume of sales does bear some similarity to the AEC test, it is not clear whether the EC and the ECJ are concerned in this assessment with the protection of all competitors or only of equally efficient firms.
- As a result, there is (and indeed there can be) no evidence that the conditional rebates offered by Michelin and BA were harmful. This means the presumption that certain categories of rebates 'tend to be harmful' cannot be properly tested.

Questionable assumptions. In addition to the lack of a clear benchmark, the *Michelin I* analytical framework is based on a number of assumptions which may or may not be true. First, the impact of a growth-based target will depend to a large extent on whether the market is static, growing or declining. Nor does the framework take into account the possibility that the pricing system itself may expand demand (e.g., through efficient price discrimination leading to an overall increase in output, as explained in *section §6.03[B]* above).

Second, the retroactive mechanism coupled with Michelin NV's high market share would not necessarily foreclose access to most or even many customers, if customers buy predominantly or exclusively from one supplier (e.g., a 50% market share may be the result of the dominant firm satisfying the entire demand of customers whose volumes represent 50% of the market, which in turn could – and indeed is likely to – represent less than 50% of customers). Depending on those circumstances, the effect of a target rebate may be very different, but neither the EC nor the ECJ evaluate (or appear to consider the evidence that would be required to evaluate) whether the implicit assumptions hold true.

234. Priorities Guidance, para. 41.
235. Case C-23/14, *Post Danmark II*, paras 57–58.
236. Case C-413/14 P, *Intel*, para. 140.

In addition, the size of the rebate did not play any significant role, despite the fact that it is clearly a critical element in determining the foreclosure effect of any rebate. Without consideration of these factors, it is difficult to clearly identify a threshold level at which a procompetitive price reduction becomes an anticompetitive foreclosure strategy.

[b] Framework for Retroactive Quantity Rebates

Michelin II extends the presumption of harm from individualised retroactive growth rebates to all target rebates with a one-year reference period, where there is a significant variation in discount rates between the different steps of the rebate scheme. The deficiencies of the *Michelin I* framework (i.e., lack of clear benchmark of what constitutes anticompetitive foreclosure and assumptions which do not hold universally) are equally relevant here.

In addition, the presumptions of competitive harm appear even more tenuous. First, the key basis of presumed harm, for retroactive quantity rebates, seems to be that close to the trigger threshold, the effect of a retroactive rebate is likely to be 'predatory', and competitors will not be able to compete for those volumes. However, in most circumstances, competitors will not be restricted to compete for volumes at or near the target threshold. No thought seems to be given to what the competitive advantage of the dominant firm is, what volumes competitors are able to compete for (i.e., the share of demand that is contestable) or whether the rebate scheme in question makes it difficult or impossible for rivals to compete.

Second, the read across from individualised rebates in *Michelin I* and *BA/Virgin* to generalised rebates in *Michelin II* is questionable. A first principles approach would suggest that individualised rebates are more likely to harm competition, as outlined above. In principle, therefore, any anticompetitive effect of such a system is 'blunted' because of the inability to target individual purchasers' volume requirements.[237] Indeed, in both *Michelin I* and *BA/Virgin*, the individualised nature of the growth targets was considered a critical factor in generating the loyalty effect. Arguably, the number of 'standardised' rebate thresholds in *Michelin II* could be considered to have generated a similar effect to an individualised target, on the basis that, at any given point, a 'target' was available that would closely correspond to a buyer's total demand. However, such theory of harm is not made explicit by either the EC or the CFI.

In addition, the Court's claim in *Michelin II*, that even rebates of a small size are presumptively harmful while at the same time being very focused on the length of the reference period is surprising given that rebates of a smaller size with longer a reference period can be expected to have comparable effects on competition to rebates of a larger size with a smaller reference period. Along similar lines, it appears inconsistent that the large size of a rebate is an aggravating factor while the smaller size of a rebate is not a mitigating factor.

237. Robert O'Donoghue and Jorge Padilla, Law and Economics of Article 102 TFEU, 1228 (2020).

Finally, given that the presumption on competitive harm rests on relatively weak foundations, one would have expected the Court to put less emphasis on the characteristics of the rebate and more emphasis on all (other) circumstances, in particular the market characteristics. The opposite has occurred: in *Michelin II*, the focus of the analysis is clearly on characteristics of rebates rather than exploration of all (other) circumstances, and hence the analysis is even more form-driven. On such a form-driven approach, it can be observed that, taking the Focus Cases together, three of the four categories of rebates we outlined in *section §6.03[A]* are considered to give rise to presumptions of illegality, at least where certain conditions are met. The only categories of rebates which are not impugned are incremental rebates and retroactive quantity rebates with a short duration. This establishes a position that is not coherent with the prevailing economic view that rebates can be pro or anticompetitive, depending on the circumstances.

The use of a new presumption. Prior to *Michelin II*, the 'problematic', loyalty-inducing rebate systems had been defined by their contrast to quantity rebates[238] *Michelin II* effectively reversed this presumption that quantity rebates were permissible. The CFI instead noted the need to consider all circumstances, including whether the rebates were used '*to strengthen a dominant position and thereby abuse it*'.[239]

When identifying whether a category of conduct should fall into the object box under Article 101 TFEU, AG Bobek in his *Budapest Bank* opinion noted that the key question is whether its '*harmful nature is in light of experience commonly accepted*' and that there needs to be '*robust and reliable experience about the nature of the agreement*'.[240] It follows that novel categories of object abuses should not be created without consensus about the effect on competition (even if such consensus can change over time in light of new evidence).

The approach in *Michelin II* was vastly different. No evidence was adduced to show that retroactive quantity rebates tend to be harmful. Nor did the Court consider whether such rebates were used by non-dominant firms. The CFI noted the EC's approval of a quantity rebate scheme in *British Gypsum*, but highlighted specific differences in the form of the rebate schemes.[241] It appears to therefore reinterpret its presumption as applying to only a narrow subset of quantity rebates.

For completeness however, we note that the approach adopted in *Michelin II* has not been widely accepted as creating a presumption that retroactive quantity rebates are abusive. The Discussion Paper noted that when the '*threshold set in a standardised volume threshold, it is less likely that the rebate system will have a loyalty enhancing effect*'.[242] This position has been reiterated by the ECJ in *Post Danmark II*[243] and *Intel.*[244]

238. Case C-310/93 P, *British Gypsum*, para. 69.
239. Case T-203/01, *Michelin II*, para. 62.
240. Case C-228/18, *AG Bobek Budapest Bank Opinion*, para. 63; cited by the ECJ in C-228/18, *Gazdasági Versenyhivatal v. Budapest Bank Nyrt*, 2.4.2020, ECLI:EU:C:2020:265, para. 76.
241. Case T-203/01, *Michelin II*, para. 84.
242. Discussion Paper, para. 159.
243. Case C-23/14, *Post Danmark II*, para. 27: '*It is also settled case-law that, in contrast to a quantity discount linked solely to the volume of purchases from the manufacturer concerned, which is not, in principle, liable to infringe Article 82 EC, a loyalty rebate, which by offering customers*

[3] *The Considerations Regarding Efficiencies*

As discussed in *section §6.03[B][1]*, there is consensus among economists that rebates can have a number of procompetitive justifications.[245] The fact that a rebate is offered by a dominant entity does not preclude these procompetitive effects. The EC and the EU courts seem to acknowledge this, and state in all three Focus Cases that efficiencies are considered. In practice however, the analysis is very limited. The efficiency justifications put forward in *Michelin I* (largely disputing the characterisation of the rebate system) were not seriously considered. More detailed justifications were put forth in *Michelin II* and *BA/Virgin*, but the EC and EU courts dealt with the justifications put forward in a relatively perfunctory manner.

This is primarily because, in all three Focus Cases, the EC and EU courts narrowly defined the kinds of efficiencies that were 'admissible', such that efficiencies could only be considered to the extent that the rebate provided an advantage based on any economic service justifying it. In *Michelin II*, for example, the EC held that 'a rebate can only correspond to the *economies of scale* achieved by a firm as a result of the additional purchases which customers are induced to make' (emphasis added).[246] Similarly, in *BA/Virgin*, the EC argued that a dominant supplier can give discounts that relate to efficiencies (e.g., on a large order), but should not give discounts or incentives to encourage loyalty, suggesting that rebates could be either loyalty-based or efficiency-based, with no interaction between the two.[247]

The Focus Cases therefore seem to contemplate only efficiencies arising out of direct economies of scale in production and distribution. None of the Focus Cases justifies this narrow framing of permissible efficiencies nor explains why other kinds of efficiencies could not be relevant to the analysis.

This narrow definition of rebates means there is no real scope to explore the extent to which a rebate system could represent competition on the merits and when it crosses the line into being abusive. The ECJ in *Michelin I* opines that rebates are problematic when used by a dominant firm that has '*recourse to methods different from those governing normal competition*'.[248] However, neither the EC nor the ECJ explores whether target rebates are frequently used by non-dominant firms. While this would not necessarily provide a conclusive picture regarding abusiveness, it would be a relevant consideration as to whether efficiencies are prevalent. This issue is even more acute on the facts of *Michelin II*, given the standardised nature of the rebates, but it is not explored.

---

financial advantages tends to prevent them from obtaining all or most of their requirements from competing manufacturers, amounts to an abuse within the meaning of that provision'.

244. Case C-413/14 P, *Intel*, para. 75 accepted that quantity rebates '*are generally considered not to have the foreclosure effects prohibited by Article [102] TFEU*'.
245. These include enhancing efficiency through better covering fixed costs (i.e., economies of scale), alignment of incentives between the supplier and customer (particularly where the supplier has made a relationship-specific investment in the customer) and reducing double marginalisation.
246. Commission Decision 2002/405/EC, *Michelin II (EC)*, para. 216.
247. Commission Decision 2000/74/EC, *BA/Virgin (EC)*, para. 101.
248. Case C-322/81, *Michelin I*, para. 70.

Even if one were to accept the narrow interpretation taken in *Michelin II* and *BA/Virgin*, the requirements to meet this efficiency standard remain unclear in practice. It is well-established that quantity rebates may expand volumes and increase economic efficiency by allowing large customers to purchase goods closer to their marginal cost of production,[249] but the EC's insistence that each and every penny of price reduction needs to be causally linked to costs savings of each and every unit is impractical and disproportionate. No company does such accounting and there are a number of difficulties with forming a methodology to measure costs in an industry, deciding how cost savings can be attributed to each customer and laying down the appropriate time period for recovery of fixed costs.[250] The Focus Cases also fail to account for the fact that economies of scale are rarely linear.

More importantly, the framework established by the Focus Cases is ill-adapted to grapple with the complexities of the real world. Rather than a dichotomy between efficiency ties and loyalty ties, most commercial practices take place somewhere between the two extremes. The mere fact that a rebate is designed to acquire/retain clients does not necessarily imply an adverse effect on competition and can in fact have a procompetitive effect and vice versa.[251] Retroactive rebates are a common business practice and could make economic sense even in the absence of any exclusionary motive. In some cases, it may simply be cost efficient overall for firms in high fixed cost industries to make an extra effort to retain the marginal slice of a firm's demand.[252]

[4] Interaction Between Object and Effects Analysis

Open v. closed systems. Under Article 101 TFEU, there is a permeable border between object and effects restrictions: failure to meet the object standard means that authorities are required to apply an effects analysis. This has allowed the EU courts to set a relatively high threshold for object restrictions, namely that the restriction in question cannot be shown to have any plausible efficiencies (i.e., the application of a 'but for' standard or, on an alternative reading, an 'expected harm' standard).

By contrast, the Focus Cases have created a hermetically closed object abuse framework for conditional rebates. Failure to establish an object infringement leads to the conclusion that no abuse has been committed at all. There is no path between the object and effects frameworks. This way of thinking has its genesis in the early precedent from *Suiker Unie* and *Hoffmann-La Roche*, based on the binary distinction between illegal 'loyalty rebates' and permissible 'quantity rebates'. Despite each Focus Case considering a new kind of rebate, the approach remained focussed on placing the rebate scheme in the illegal or permissible 'box'.

249. Giuilio Federico, *When Are Rebates Exclusionary*, 26(9) ECLR, 477-480 (2005).
250. Denis Waelbroeck, *Michelin II: A Per Se Rule Against Rebates by Dominant Companies?*, 1(1) J. Competition L. & Econ., 158 (2005).
251. Denis Waelbroeck, *Michelin II: A Per Se Rule Against Rebates by Dominant Companies?*, 1(1) J. Competition L. & Econ., 156 (2005).
252. *See* Brian Sher, *Price Discounts and Michelin 2: What Goes Around, Comes Around*, Eur. Competition L. Rev. 486 (2002).

Risk of overinclusion. The closed nature of the abuse framework devised by the Focus Cases has a number of significant drawbacks. The binary outcome (finding of an object abuse or of no abuse) gives competition authorities a very stark choice between over-enforcement and under-enforcement, when, in many cases, the right answer would be to apply a detailed effects analysis. Furthermore, the stark consequence for failing to establish an object infringement creates a temptation to lower the bar for an object abuse and cast the net widely. This is precisely what we saw with the Focus Cases: rather than applying the strict 'but for' standard, the Focus Cases have defined efficiencies narrowly and required that the dominant firm show that efficiencies are not only plausible but that they can be established under the requisite standard of proof. While it is not possible to evaluate with hindsight whether a full evaluation of efficiencies would have changed the outcome of any of the Focus Cases, as we have shown above, such an approach makes over-enforcement inevitable.

Inconsistency between Article 101 and Article 102 TFEU. In addition, the approach in the Focus Cases creates a situation in which both the scope of the harm considered and the treatment of efficiencies is inconsistent between Articles 101 and 102 TFEU. The framework under Article 101 TFEU which allows an 'exit' from an object-based analysis at an early stage allows a much fuller assessment of both the scope of the harm and the range of efficiencies to be considered. This reinforces the closed nature of the object category under the Focus Cases framework.

Dynamic v. static. Finally, the open system under Article 101 TFEU has the advantage of being dynamic (i.e., it adapts to changing market conditions and is able to incorporate a better understanding of the underlying drivers of contested measures). This applies to both the assessment of harm and efficiencies. Only practices which are well understood and known to be harmful are suitable for the assessment under the object framework. AG Bobek in *Budapest Bank* emphasises that '*robust and reliable experience about the nature of the agreement*' is required to ground an object analysis.[253] At the same time, efficiency rationales for certain practices are better understood. It will be easier for defendants to meet the plausibility standard and to ensure that infringements are considered under the effects framework.

By contrast, the closed abuse framework of the Focus Cases has struggled to adapt to changing circumstances. The extension of the abuse framework to an ever wider range of conditional rebates has occurred without consideration of whether experience has demonstrated that those rebates are overwhelmingly harmful. This was particularly the case for retroactive quantity rebates in *Michelin II*. At the same time, given the rigid definition of 'acceptable efficiencies' and the high evidential bar for dominant firms to demonstrate such efficiencies, the system did not consider efficiencies in detail and was not able to 'learn' from the increased understanding of efficiency drivers of rebates.

253. Case C-228/18, *AG Bobek Budapest Bank Opinion*, para. 63.

[5] *Balancing of Harm and Efficiencies*

In its assessment, competition law foresees a balancing of competitive harm and efficiencies either explicitly (as is the case under Article 101 TFEU) or implicitly (e.g., EU Merger Regulation or Article 102 TFEU). In practice, these balancing exercises have turned out to be challenging, partly because it is difficult to quantify competitive harm and efficiencies in a comparable way and partly because litigation strategies will incentivise authorities to minimise harm or efficiencies depending on whether a case is heading towards an infringement finding or to no action.

Of the three Focus Cases, *BA/Virgin* is the only case that deals explicitly with this aspect of the competition analysis. It raises two potential problems. The case demonstrates that the object abuse framework is inherently incapable of balancing harm and efficiencies. This is because even if efficiencies can be proven and quantified, no balancing is possible when the competitive harm is analysed under an object framework (i.e., it is only established that a particular rebate *tends* to harm consumers, and such harm is not quantified). Indeed the abuse framework does not foresee a balancing at all: the moment an acceptable efficiency is identified, the presumption of harm is overturned and hence there is no finding of abuse. This is clearly unsatisfactory from a policy perspective, as even a very small acceptable efficiency would overturn a very large (presumed) harm. In response to this, the EC and EU courts have addressed this conundrum by drastically reducing the scope of 'admissible' efficiencies to such an extent that they are not relevant.

Flowing from this, the approach creates different standards of proof for harm and efficiencies, with harm effectively presumed, but the scope of efficiencies that can be considered severely curtailed to the extent that efficiencies would be taken into account under an effects-based approach are not even considered.

[6] *The Cases and Policy Developments Post Michelin II*

The policy developments (introduction of the Priorities Guidance) and more recent cases (*Post Danmark I, Post Danmark II* and *Intel*) have addressed some of the major deficiencies of the Focus Case framework.

The ECJ's clarification in *Intel* that, while the presumption that fidelity rebates infringe Article 102 TFEU stands, it is rebuttable, provides the previously missing bridge between an object and effects analysis of conditional rebates. As outlined above, *Intel* provides two possible 'exits' from an object-based analysis. First, if the dominant undertaking submits evidence that the rebate scheme is not capable of restricting competition, in which case the burden shifts to the EC to demonstrate that the rebates are capable of foreclosing competitors (i.e., to carry out an effects analysis).[254] Second, the submission of plausible evidence of efficiencies that outweigh the putative harm to competition can also lead to an effects-based analysis.

254. Case C-413/14 P, *Intel*, para. 139.

This also brings a greater level of harmony with the approach under Article 101 TFEU, as it lines up with the logic of the double test presented by AG Bobek in *Budapest Bank*.

In addition, the Priorities Guidance provides a detailed framework for an effects analysis of conditional rebates, as further explained below.

[B] Evaluation of the Analysis of the Focus Cases in Light of the Facts

[1] An Effects-Based Analysis Is Appropriate for the Focus Cases

Under the modern framework for assessment of fidelity rebates under Article 102 TFEU, as set out by the ECJ in *Intel*, even if the rebate schemes in question were appropriately classified as sitting within the 'object' box initially, the presumption of harm is rebuttable and evidence put forward by the investigated parties that its rebates are not capable of restricting competition would shift the burden to the EC to establish that the rebate scheme had an anticompetitive effect. As set out in *section §6.05[A]* above, the authors consider that there is insufficient evidence or experience to ground an assumption of harm in the first instance, especially in relation to *Michelin II*, and thus consider that an effects analysis should have been adopted from the outset. At a minimum however, and even if an object-based approach was appropriate in the first instance, we consider that there were potentially plausible efficiency justifications for the conduct in the Focus Cases, that would have justified a shift from an object-based to an effects-based approach.

While it is always difficult to assess *ex post* the quality of the procompetitive rationales brought forward by the parties, there are a number of plausible explanations in the Focus Cases that are not addressed at all.

In *Michelin I*, Michelin NV argued that the rebates would lead to increased sales. Michelin NV also argued that the rebates enabled it to better plan its production and that this was necessary due to a lack of official statistics in the relevant period. While the classification of both these arguments as efficiency justifications is questionable, the first at least conceivably corresponds with procompetitive price discrimination that increases overall output as described in *section §6.03[B]*. However, both justifications were dismissed by the EC and the ECJ and the decisions do not provide sufficient detail to allow the authors to form a view on their plausibility.

In *BA/Virgin*, BA argued that its rebate system represented competition on the merits. The EC and the EU courts ignored that rewarding the agents on the basis of absolute sales (as opposed to based on the targets set) would have only rewarded larger agents (even if their incremental sales were quite small). Under standard principal/agent theory, the BA scheme could very well be a reasonable way of providing incentives/rewards to their dealers. This justification, in the authors' view, at least, meets AG Bobek's standard of plausibility, such that it merits a fuller consideration.

Finally, in *Michelin II*, there is some evidence that manufacturers in the tyre sector were becoming more directly concerned with distribution of tyres and intended to solve these issues through the development of integrated networks and closer contacts with independent dealers. Arguably, Michelin France's rebate scheme was a means to align dealers' incentives with its sales expectations. Moreover, there was evidence that independent tyre dealers in France were operating on very thin profit margins due to strong downstream competition, and the direct invoice discounts were typically passed on to customers, meaning that the deferred discount paid through rebates was often a (if not the most) significant part of dealers' profits. These factors might, or might not, justify some of the precise features of Michelin's price system. Similarly to *BA/Virgin*, the authors consider this justification was at least sufficiently plausible to merit further consideration.

In each of the Focus Cases, only a full and thorough assessment of possible procompetitive justifications would have allowed an answer to the question of whether a procompetitive justification existed, and, in turn, whether the procompetitive effects of the rebate outweighed any anticompetitive effects.

[2] An Effects-Based Analysis Would Consider the Following Aspects

The Focus Cases were thin on evidence-based analysis of anticompetitive foreclosure effects, largely as a result of the view that establishing anticompetitive object and effect is the same.[255] An effects analysis would have required substantial additional information, which on the face of the decisions, did not appear to be in evidence in the Focus Cases.

First, and perhaps most critically, as recognised in the Priorities Guidance, the likelihood of foreclosure is greater when the dominant firm has an assured share of demand (i.e., there is a 'non-contestable' portion of demand), which provides the dominant company with the ability (if not the necessarily incentive) to leverage this share of the demand to increase its share of supply further. None of the Focus Cases involved an analysis of the contestable versus non-contestable demand in the market. Such information would have allowed the EC to assess the extent to which the rebate systems were capable of hindering expansion or entry by equally efficient competitors.

More generally, the Priorities Guidance lists a number of factors that are relevant to the assessment of anticompetitive foreclosure in Article 102 TFEU cases: (i) degree of dominance; (ii) market conditions (entry and expansion, economies of scale etc.); (iii) strength of competing undertakings; (iv) strength of customers and/or input suppliers; (v) extent of the anticompetitive conduct in question; (vi) possible evidence of actual foreclosure; and (vii) internal evidence of any exclusionary strategy.[256] The Focus Cases did not consider these types of evidence in detail and it is not apparent from the decisions that such evidence was even on file.

To take *Michelin I* as an example, while we cannot rule out that Michelin NV's rebate scheme generated harm, the facts provided in the decision do not allow us to independently assess the likelihood of harm or how the scheme would impede effective

255. *See* Case T-203/01, *Michelin II*, para. 241.
256. Priorities Guidance, para. 20.

competition. The case file (at least as evidenced in the decisions) leaves several open questions. For instance, what is preventing competitors from growing and making counter-offers; is there an issue of miscoordination of buyers? Such evidence would have allowed evaluation of whether foreclosure required 'large' price reductions that compensate dealers for anticompetitive loyalty (which could be assessed with the as efficient competitor principles presented in the Priorities Guidance), and if not, what mechanism would allow foreclosure. Finally, it would have been crucial to fully explore whether there was any reason to believe that restricting dealers' freedom corresponds to plausible procompetitive rationale.

An effects-based approach would seek and evaluate evidence on each of these questions in order to assess and balance pro and anticompetitive effects of the rebate scheme.

§6.06 CONCLUSION

The Focus Cases created an analytical framework for conditional rebates which can best be described as a 'hermetically closed object abuse' framework. As a result, exclusionary rebates, target rebates and ultimately certain retroactive quantity rebates were seen as categories of rebates which can be expected to (or 'tend to') have harmful impact on competition. While *Michelin I* imposed an obligation on the authority to take into consideration 'all circumstances', including the specific market conditions, this aspect of the framework subsequently lost importance which resulted in increasingly formalistic analysis. And although the framework of the Focus Cases contemplated an efficiency defence to reverse the presumption of abuse, the scope of acceptable efficiencies was defined so narrowly, that such defences were not adequately considered in practice.

The analytical framework of the Focus Cases proved to be a dead-end. Several of its deficiencies contributed to this outcome. First, the assumptions of harm underlying the various categories of conditional rebates were postulated. As the Focus Cases did not draw a dividing line between rebates leading to anti-competitive foreclosure and rebates which amounted to procompetitive low prices, there was no way to gather evidence from the cases whether the presumption of harm was actually justified.

A similar absence of evidence existed in relation to the efficiency consideration. While the authorities and courts in the Focus Cases referred to 'normal competition' and 'competition on the merits', they did not consider whether the presumptively harmful rebates were used by non-dominant firms which in turn would have supported an efficiency claim.

Furthermore, the framework did not build in any paths from an object to an effects analysis but resulted in a binary outcome, namely confirmation of the object abuse presumption or absence of abuse. The framework offered the unattractive choice between risk of significant over-enforcement or risk of significant under-enforcement (without an option of analytical fine-tuning).

The framework of the Focus Cases compares unfavourably with the object restriction framework developed under Article 101(1) TFEU, which includes important feedback mechanisms (such as adaptation of the object categories in light of 'experience') and is more open, in the sense that it allows switching to an effects analysis if the consideration of 'all circumstances' suggests plausible efficiencies. Adopting such a dynamic and open framework under Article 102 TFEU would have allowed the authorities to reflect on new 'experience' (including better economic insights) that showed conditional rebates will regularly involve both pro-and anti-competitive aspects and hence strongly points to the need for an effects analysis.

Two strands of cases have shown an alternative path towards the assessment of conditional rebates: *Post Danmark I* and *Post Danmark II* advocate the direct application of an effects analysis; and *Intel* preserves the object abuse framework of the Focus Cases but introduces a low threshold for switching to an effects analysis. What both strands have in common is the use of a benchmark, namely the AEC Test, which allows the identification of actual or likely competitive harm.

Finally, in our view, there is merit in developing further (and more clearly) the concepts of object and effects abuse under Article 102 TFEU along similar lines to those set out by AG Bobek in *Budapest Bank* for Article 101(1) TFEU. Not only would this lead to a more consistent application of the two provisions, but it would also help better understand and, where necessary, re-position the various categories of abuse.